EURIPIDES

II

LCL 484

EURIPIDES

CHILDREN OF HERACLES
HIPPOLYTUS
ANDROMACHE · HECUBA

EDITED AND TRANSLATED BY
DAVID KOVACS

HARVARD UNIVERSITY PRESS
CAMBRIDGE, MASSACHUSETTS
LONDON, ENGLAND
1995

Library of Congress Cataloging-in-Publication Data

Euripides.
Children of Heracles; Hippolytus; Andromache; Hecuba /
Euripides; edited and translated by David Kovacs.
p.   cm. — (Loeb classical library; L484)
Includes bibliographical references.
ISBN 0–674–99533–3
1. Euripides—Translations into English.
2. Greek drama (Tragedy)—Translations into English.
3. Mythology, Greek—Drama.
I. Kovacs, David.   II. Title.
III. Title: Children of Heracles; Hippolytus;
Andromache; Hecuba   IV. Series.
PA3979.A2   1995   95–7619
882'.01—dc20   CIP

Typeset by Chiron, Inc, Cambridge, Massachusetts.
Printed in Great Britain by St Edmundsbury Press Ltd,
Bury St Edmunds, Suffolk, on acid-free paper.
Bound by Hunter & Foulis Ltd, Edinburgh, Scotland.

CONTENTS

For Mark

PREFACE

This edition's editorial principles and its simplified system for reporting variants are explained in Volume One, pp. 36–39. I will discuss in my forthcoming *Euripidea Altera* some of the readings and conjectures I have adopted in this volume.

It is a pleasure to acknowledge generous assistance. A grant from the Division of Research of the National Endowment for the Humanities, an independent federal agency, enabled me to devote half of my time in the two academic years 1990–92 to this volume and its successor. At a later stage of revision, I was the beneficiary of a term as Visiting Fellow at All Souls College, Oxford. My thanks to the Warden and Fellows for their splendid hospitality and especially to Martin West, who was liberal of his time and counsel. I have also profited greatly from discussions with James Diggle, Charles Willink, Hugh Lloyd-Jones, and Justina Gregory. George Goold's criticisms and queries have been invaluable, and both he and Margaretta Fulton have improved the English translation.

This volume carries a dedication to a son by a proud father.

University of Virginia   David Kovacs

ABBREVIATIONS

AJP	*American Journal of Philology*
Anz. Akad. Wien	*Anzeiger der österreichischen Akademie der Wissenschaften zu Wien*
BICS	*Bulletin of the Institute of Classical Studies,* London
CP	*Classical Philology*
CQ	*Classical Quarterly*
CR	*Classical Review*
GRBS	*Greek, Roman, and Byzantine Studies*
HSCP	*Harvard Studies in Classical Philology*
JHS	*Journal of Hellenic Studies*
RFIC	*Rivista di Filologia ed Istruzione Classica*
TAPA	*Transactions of the American Philological Association*
YCS	*Yale Classical Studies*

CHILDREN OF HERACLES

INTRODUCTION

When Athenian orators of the fourth century wanted to extol the greatness of the city's past, one of the stories to which they repeatedly turned was Athens' defense of the helpless children of Heracles from the violence of Eurystheus. (See Lysias 2.11–16, Isocrates 4.54–60, 5.34, Demosthenes 60.8.) It is reasonable to suppose that fifth-century orators, whose work does not survive, did the same. The story appears or is alluded to in other fifth-century sources, including Herodotus 9.27.2, where the Athenians base their claim to a place of honor in the battle order at Plataea on their valorous defense of the Heraclids. Clearly this was a narrative that harmonized well with the Athenians' view of themselves as champions of the weak.

Euripides' *Children of Heracles* was put on, in all likelihood, in the first year of the Peloponnesian War (early spring of 430). The events of the day have had an effect on the telling of the story, particularly the end of the play, where allusion is made to the descendants of the Heraclids (i.e. the Spartans) and their invasion of Attica. But in its main outline the plot is the sequence of events known to patriotic oratory.

Iolaus, Heracles' aged kinsman, speaks the prologue, giving the antecedent history. After Heracles' death his children were persecuted by King Eurystheus of Argos, the same man who had sent Heracles himself on his perilous labors. Afraid that the sons might exact vengeance for what he had done to their father, Eurystheus determined to put them to death, and since they had been banished from Argos he pursued them all around the Greek world. Whenever they sought refuge with a city, he would threaten that city with war. Hitherto, all the cities they have fled to have succumbed to the threats of Eurystheus and have refused to take the Heraclids in. Now they have come to Marathon in Attica, ruled by the twin sons of Theseus. Iolaus with most of Heracles' sons sits as a suppliant at the altar; Alcmene, Heracles' mother, is inside with Heracles' daughters. The eldest of the sons have gone off to see where else they might settle if Athens fails them.

The action begins with the arrival of the abusive Herald of Eurystheus, who has come to assert Argos' right to kill the Heraclids and who actually begins to drag Iolaus forcibly from the altar. When a cry for help is raised, the Chorus, old men of Marathon, come on and express their outrage at the proceedings. They are followed by Theseus' son Demophon, King of Athens, who faces down the Herald's threats. This earns him the gratitude of Iolaus, who exhorts the Heraclids never to forget this kindness and, when they get their patrimony back, never to send a hostile force against Athens. Demophon accepts these expressions of gratitude and departs to prepare to defend the city against the Argive attack that will surely come.

The Heraclids themselves then get to show their bravery. Demophon returns with disturbing news: the oracles say that if Athens is to prevail in the coming war, a

maiden of noble family must be sacrificed to Demeter.
He is not willing to sacrifice a daughter of his own or to
force any of his citizens to sacrifice his. Unless Iolaus has
something to suggest, the war with Argos will be lost.
This perplexity is met by a daughter of Heracles, who
offers herself as a willing sacrifice. She is led away, and
Iolaus sinks down before the altar in grief. Good news
appears at once in the person of a servant of Hyllus, one
of the sons sent out to reconnoitre. He reports that Hyl-
lus has returned safe and with reinforcements. Iolaus, old
and infirm as he is, decides to go take part in the battle.
He cuts an almost comic figure as he leaves, hobbling
along on the arm of the servant.

After a choral ode a messenger appears to announce
to Alcmene the result of the battle. The Athenians and
their allies were victorious. What is more, Iolaus has
been miraculously rejuvenated and has performed a great
exploit, taking the defeated Eurystheus alive.

In the last scene, Eurystheus is brought in by the Ser-
vant. Alcmene denounces him for his crimes against Her-
acles and his family and then proclaims that he must die a
painful death. The Servant objects that this cannot be:
the Athenians do not kill prisoners. Alcmene insists that
she will kill him all the same. In his speech in his own
defense to Alcmene Eurystheus claims that he was forced
to take up the quarrel with Heracles, and that what he did
to him and his children was merely prudent self-defense.
The Chorus Leader recommends that Alcmene spare
him.

She, however, is determined to kill him and proposes a
sophistic interpretation of the Athenians' words: the
Athenians want me to let him go, she says, and I will fulfill

their words literally by releasing his body to his family when I have killed him. At this point, Eurystheus concedes his death to Alcmene. But in light of Athens' refusal to kill him, he makes them a present of an ancient prophecy of Apollo which said he was fated to be buried at Pallene in Attica and there to be a presence favorable to the Athenians and hostile to the descendants of Heracles' children: he will, that is, become a hero in the Greek sense, one of the mighty dead, and will bless the Athenians who worship at his grave and harm their enemies, the Spartans. Alcmene seizes on this prophecy to overcome the resistance of the Chorus, and Eurystheus is led away.

The play has a strong patriotic flavor, appropriately for a piece put on just after the invasion of Attica by the Spartans. Athens is portrayed throughout as a champion of the weak. She refuses to back down when threatened, just as she had in 431, even if it means enduring an invasion. At the start of the play, the objects of her protection demonstrate not only their innocence but also their bravery as the Maiden goes willingly to death to save her kin and the city that offered her protection. Iolaus too appears both decent and valorous. But by the end, Alcmene, who had earlier seemed timorous, now shows herself to be cruel and ready to violate established law. Like the Spartan Menelaus in *Andromache* she proposes to get her way by a quibbling interpretation of Athenian law (see 1020–4). Her descendants, it is now clear, are not going to carry out the behest Iolaus had laid on them never to raise a spear against the Athenians, their benefactors.

In the very act of taking unlawful vengeance against her enemy, Alcmene is sealing the fate of these descendants, who will get an evil homecoming from their invasion of Attica because Eurystheus lies buried in Attic soil. Thus Athens gets full credit for bravely defending the weak and at the same time is protected from the harm that sometimes comes from doing so. That is how matters appeared to Euripides in the first year of the war before it became apparent that the Spartans would be able to invade Attica with complete impunity. His praise of Athens is heartfelt, and although the play is in no way a masterpiece, it gives stirring and coherent expression to a view of Athens' character that continued, as the orators make plain, to waken an answering chord in the hearts of the Athenian people.

SELECT BIBLIOGRAPHY

Editions

A. C. Pearson (Cambridge, 1907).
A. Garzya (Leipzig, 1972).
J. Wilkins (Oxford, 1993).

Literary criticism

H. C. Avery, "Euripides' *Heraclidae*," *AJP* 92 (1971), 539–65.

P. Burian, "Euripides' *Heraclidae*: an Interpretation," *CP* 72 (1977), 1–21.

A. P. Burnett, "Tribe and City, Custom and Decree in *Children of Heracles*," *CP* 71 (1976), 4–26.

A. Lesky, "On the *Heraclidae* of Euripides," *YCS* 25 (1977), 227–38.

U. von Wilamowitz-Moellendorff, "De Euripidis Heracli-
   dis Commentatiuncula," Index schol. in Univ. Gryphis-
   waldensi 1982, rpt. in his *Kleine Schriften*, i.62–81.
——— "Exkurse zu Euripides Herakliden," *Hermes* 17
   (1882), 337–64, rpt. in his *Kleine Schriften*, i. 82–109.
G. Zuntz, "Is the *Heraclidae* Mutilated?" *CQ* 41 (1947),
   46–52.
——— *The Political Plays of Euripides* (Manchester,
   1955).

Dramatis Personae

ΙΟΛΑΟΣ   IOLAUS, kinsman of Heracles
ΚΗΡΥΞ   HERALD of Eurystheus
ΧΟΡΟΣ   CHORUS of men of Marathon
ΔΗΜΟΦΩΝ   DEMOPHON, King of Athens
ΠΑΡΘΕΝΟΣ   MAIDEN, daughter of Heracles
ΘΕΡΑΠΩΝ   SERVANT of Heracles' son, Hyllus
ΑΛΚΜΗΝΗ   ALCMENE, mother of Heracles
ΑΓΓΕΛΟΣ   MESSENGER
ΕΥΡΥΣΘΕΥΣ   EURYSTHEUS, King of Argos

A Note on Staging

The *skene* represents the temple of Zeus Agoraios in Marathon, not far from Athens. Eisodos A leads from abroad, Eisodos B from Athens.

ΗΡΑΚΛΕΙΔΑΙ

ΙΟΛΑΟΣ

Πάλαι ποτ' ἐστὶ τοῦτ' ἐμοὶ δεδογμένον·
ὁ μὲν δίκαιος τοῖς πέλας πέφυκ' ἀνήρ,
ὁ δ' ἐς τὸ κέρδος λῆμ' ἔχων ἀνειμένον
πόλει τ' ἄχρηστος καὶ συναλλάσσειν βαρύς,
5 αὑτῷ δ' ἄριστος· οἶδα δ' οὐ λόγῳ μαθών.
ἐγὼ γὰρ αἰδοῖ καὶ τὸ συγγενὲς σέβων,
ἐξὸν κατ' Ἄργος ἡσύχως ναίειν, πόνων
πλείστων μετέσχον εἷς ἀνὴρ Ἡρακλέει,
ὅτ' ἦν μεθ' ἡμῶν· νῦν δ', ἐπεὶ κατ' οὐρανὸν
10 ναίει, τὰ κείνου τέκν' ἔχων ὑπὸ πτεροῖς
σῴζω τάδ' αὐτὸς δεόμενος σωτηρίας.
ἐπεὶ γὰρ αὐτῶν γῆς ἀπηλλάχθη πατήρ,
πρῶτον μὲν ἡμᾶς ἤθελ' Εὐρυσθεὺς κτανεῖν·
ἀλλ' ἐξέδραμεν, καὶ πόλις μὲν οἴχεται,
15 ψυχὴ δ' ἐσώθη. φεύγομεν δ' ἀλώμενοι
ἄλλην ἀπ' ἄλλης ἐξοριζόντων πόλιν.
πρὸς τοῖς γὰρ ἄλλοις καὶ τόδ' Εὐρυσθεὺς κακοῖς
ὕβρισμ' ἐς ἡμᾶς ἠξίωσεν ὑβρίσαι·
πέμπων ὅπου γῆς πυνθάνοιθ' ἱδρυμένους

---

16 ἐξοριζόντων Diggle: ἐξορίζοντες L

CHILDREN OF HERACLES

The skene *represents the temple of Zeus Agoraios in Marathon, an outlying region of Attica. At an altar before the temple are* IOLAUS *and the young sons of Heracles, seated as suppliants.*

IOLAUS

I have long ago come to this conclusion: one man is by nature just to his neighbors, while the man whose heart runs unbridled toward gain is of no use to his city and hard to deal with, being good only to himself. This wisdom I know not at second hand but by experience. For out of a sense of honor and because I respected my kinship with him, I more than any other shared with Heracles in his many labors while he was in our midst, though I could have lived at peace in Argos. And now, since he has gone to dwell in heaven,[a] I protect these children of his beneath my wing, though I myself need someone to rescue *me*. When their father departed from the earth, first Eurystheus decided to kill us. But we escaped from him, and though we lost our city, we saved our lives. Yet we wandered in exile from one city to another as men banished us. For in addition to the other troubles Eurystheus plagued us with, he thought fit to commit this outrage against us: he would send heralds to whatever

[a] After his death Heracles became a god.

20 κήρυκας ἐξαιτεῖ τε κἀξείργει χθονός,
   πόλιν προτείνων Ἄργος οὐ σμικρὸν φίλην
   ἐχθράν τε θέσθαι, χαὐτὸν εὐτυχοῦνθ' ἅμα.
   οἱ δ' ἀσθενῆ μὲν τἀπ' ἐμοῦ δεδορκότες,
   σμικροὺς δὲ τούσδε καὶ πατρὸς τητωμένους,
25 τοὺς κρείσσονας σέβοντες ἐξείργουσι γῆς.
   ἐγὼ δὲ σὺν φεύγουσι συμφεύγω τέκνοις
   καὶ σὺν κακῶς πράσσουσι συμπράσσω κακῶς,
   ὀκνῶν προδοῦναι, μή τις ὧδ' εἴπῃ βροτῶν·
   Ἴδεσθ', ἐπειδὴ παισὶν οὐκ ἔστιν πατήρ,
30 Ἰόλαος οὐκ ἤμυνε συγγενὴς γεγώς.
      πάσης δὲ χώρας Ἑλλάδος τητώμενοι
   Μαραθῶνα καὶ σύγκληρον ἐλθόντες χθόνα
   ἱκέται καθεζόμεσθα βώμιοι θεῶν
   προσωφελῆσαι· πεδία γὰρ τῆσδε χθονὸς
35 δισσοὺς κατοικεῖν Θησέως παῖδας λόγος
   κλήρῳ λαχόντας ἐκ γένους Πανδίονος,
   τοῖσδ' ἐγγὺς ὄντας· ὧν ἕκατι τέρμονας
   κλεινῶν Ἀθηνῶν τήνδ' ἀφικόμεσθ' ὁδόν.
   δυοῖν γερόντοιν δὲ στρατηγεῖται φυγή·
40 ἐγὼ μὲν ἀμφὶ τοῖσδε καλχαίνων τέκνοις,
   ἡ δ' αὖ τὸ θῆλυ παιδὸς Ἀλκμήνη γένος
   ἔσωθε ναοῦ τοῦδ' ὑπηγκαλισμένη
   σῴζει· νέας γὰρ παρθένους αἰδούμεθα

   21 προτείνων Canter: προτιμῶν L   σμικρὸν
   Wilamowitz: -ὰν L
   21–22 φίλην / ἐχθράν Bothe: φίλων / ἔχθραν L
   22 τε Musgrave: γε L

12

part of the world he learned we were trying to settle in and would demand our surrender and keep us out of that land, alleging that the city of Argos was no slight power to make a friend or foe of and that he himself was a man enjoying heaven's favor. And these men, seeing that I was weak and that these children were small and had lost their father, bowed to might and kept us from their land. With these children who are exiled I too am in exile, and I join my own wretchedness to theirs. I shrink from abandoning them for fear someone may say, "Look, since the children lost their father, Iolaus has not come to their aid, though he is their kinsman!"

Because we have been banished from all the rest of Greece, we have come to Marathon and the land that borders it and are sitting at the altars of the gods supplicating for help. For it is said that Theseus' two sons rule this land, an honor they received when lots were cast among the descendants of Pandion.[a] Those two are kin to these boys. This is the reason we have made this journey to the borders of glorious Athens. Our flight is being marshaled by a pair of grayheads: I give anxious thought for these boys, while Alcmene guards the daughters of her son within the temple, clasping them in her embrace. Shame

---

[a] In this play Athens is governed, even in heroic times, on democratic lines: cf. 415–24. Choosing officials by lot from a pre-determined list of those eligible was a feature of fifth-century Athenian government.

---

38 τήνδ' . . . ὁδόν Stephanus: τόνδ' . . . ὅρον L

ὄχλῳ πελάζειν κἀπιβωμιοστατεῖν.
45 Ὕλλος δ' ἀδελφοί θ' οἷσι πρεσβεύει γένος
ζητοῦσ' ὅπου γῆς πύργον οἰκιούμεθα,
ἢν τῆσδ' ἀπωθώμεσθα πρὸς βίαν χθονός.
    ὦ τέκνα τέκνα, δεῦρο, λαμβάνεσθ' ἐμῶν
πέπλων· ὁρῶ κήρυκα τόνδ' Εὐρυσθέως
50 στείχοντ' ἐφ' ἡμᾶς, οὗ διωκόμεσθ' ὕπο
πάσης ἀλῆται γῆς ἀπεστερημένοι.
    ὦ μῖσος, εἴθ' ὄλοιο χὡ πέμψας σ' ἀνήρ,
ὡς πολλὰ δὴ καὶ τῶνδε γενναίῳ πατρὶ
ἐκ τοῦδε ταὐτοῦ στόματος ἤγγειλας κακά.

ΚΗΡΥΞ

55 ἦ που καθῆσθαι τήνδ' ἕδραν καλὴν δοκεῖς
πόλιν τ' ἀφῖχθαι σύμμαχον, κακῶς φρονῶν·
οὐ γάρ τις ἔστιν ὃς πάροιθ' αἱρήσεται
τὴν σὴν ἀχρεῖον δύναμιν ἀντ' Εὐρυσθέως.
χώρει· τί μοχθεῖς ταῦτ'; ἀνίστασθαί σε χρὴ
60 ἐς Ἄργος, οὗ σε λεύσιμος μένει δίκη.

ΙΟΛΑΟΣ

οὐ δῆτ', ἐπεί μοι βωμὸς ἀρκέσει θεοῦ,
ἐλευθέρα τε γαῖ' ἐν ᾗ βεβήκαμεν.

ΚΗΡΥΞ

βούλῃ πόνον μοι τῇδε προσθεῖναι χερί;

ΙΟΛΑΟΣ

οὔτοι βίᾳ γέ μ' οὐδὲ τούσδ' ἄξεις λαβών.

---

[a] In the *Iliad* and elsewhere, Eurystheus' herald is called

prevents us from exposing young girls to the crowd and standing them at the altar. Hyllus and the oldest of his brothers have gone to look for some place on earth where we might establish a stronghold if we are forcibly kept from this land.

Enter HERALD by Eisodos A.

O children, children, come here, take hold of my garments! I see Eurystheus' herald coming toward us, the man by whom we are pursued and banished as wanderers from the face of the earth! A curse on you, hateful creature, and on him who sent you! For on these children's noble father too your tongue laid many a woe!

HERALD[a]
No doubt you imagine this is a fine position you have taken up and that you have come to a city that is your ally. Fool! No one will choose to have your worthless strength in preference to Eurystheus! Move on! Why take all this trouble? You must get up from the altar and go on to Argos, where death by stoning awaits you.

IOLAUS
No: the god's altar will protect me, and the land on which we stand is free.

HERALD
Do you wish to make more work for this hand of mine?

IOLAUS
Surely you will not take me and these children away by force!

Copreus. Euripides does not name him in the text, and the speaker name "Copreus" given by our manuscripts is likely to be a later addition.

ΚΗΡΥΞ

65 γνώσῃ σύ· μάντις δ᾽ ἦσθ᾽ ἄρ᾽ οὐκ ἄκρος τάδε.

ΙΟΛΑΟΣ

οὐκ ἂν γένοιτο τοῦτ᾽ ἐμοῦ ζῶντός ποτε.

ΚΗΡΥΞ

ἄπερρ᾽· ἐγὼ δὲ τούσδε, κἂν σὺ μὴ θέλῃς,
ἄξω νομίζων οὗπέρ εἰσ᾽ Εὐρυσθέως.

ΙΟΛΑΟΣ

ὦ τὰς Ἀθήνας δαρὸν οἰκοῦντες χρόνον,
70 ἀμύνεθ᾽· ἱκέται δ᾽ ὄντες ἀγοραίου Διὸς
βιαζόμεσθα καὶ στέφη μιαίνεται,
πόλει τ᾽ ὄνειδος καὶ θεῶν ἀτιμίαν.

ΧΟΡΟΣ

ἔα ἔα· τίς ἡ βοὴ βωμοῦ πέλας
ἔστηκε; ποίαν συμφορὰν δείξει τάχα;
75 ἴδετε τὸν γέροντ᾽ ἀμαλὸν ἐπὶ πέδῳ χύμενον· ὦ τάλας,
πρὸς τοῦ ποτ᾽ ἐν γῇ πτῶμα δύστηνον πίτνεις;

στρ.

ΙΟΛΑΟΣ

ὅδ᾽ ὦ ξένοι με σοὺς ἀτιμάζων θεοὺς
ἕλκει βιαίως Ζηνὸς ἐκ προβωμίων.

---

65 οὐκ ἄκρος Herwerden: οὐ καλὸς L
67 ἄπερρ᾽ Cobet: ἄπαιρ᾽ L
72 ἀτιμίαν England: -ία L
75 γέροντ᾽ ἀμαλὸν Wesseling, Hemsterhuys: γέροντα
μᾶλλον L

16

HERALD

You'll see! You are not, it seems, a good prophet on this subject.

IOLAUS

It shall not happen while I am still alive!

HERALD

Off! Be gone!

He pulls Iolaus away from the altar and knocks him onto the ground.

And as for these, whether you like it or not I shall take them off, treating them as the property of Eurystheus, which they are.

IOLAUS

Dwellers in Athens from of old, help us! We, the suppliants of Zeus of the Marketplace, are being violently treated and our suppliant wreaths defiled, which disgraces the city and insults the gods!

Enter citizens of Marathon as CHORUS by Eisodos B.

CHORUS

Ah! What is this cry that has been raised near the altar? What disaster is it about to show us? See the feeble old man lying spread upon the ground! Unhappy man, who has thrown you for this terrible fall?

IOLAUS

This man, strangers, dishonors your gods and drags me by force from Zeus's altar steps.

ΧΟΡΟΣ

80 σὺ δ᾽ ἐκ τίνος γῆς, ὦ γέρον, τετράπτολιν
ξύνοικον ἦλθες λαόν; ἦ πέρα-
θεν ἁλίῳ πλάτᾳ κατέχετ᾽ ἐκλιπόντες Εὐβοῖδ᾽ ἀκτάν;

ΙΟΛΑΟΣ

οὐ νησιώτην, ὦ ξένοι, τρίβω βίον,
85 ἀλλ᾽ ἐκ Μυκηνῶν σὴν ἀφίγμεθα χθόνα.

ΧΟΡΟΣ

ὄνομα τί σε, γέρον, Μυκηναῖος ὠνόμαζεν λεώς;

ΙΟΛΑΟΣ

τὸν Ἡράκλειον ἴστε που παραστάτην
Ἰόλαον· οὐ γὰρ σῶμ᾽ ἀκήρυκτον τόδε.

μεσῳδ.

ΧΟΡΟΣ

90 οἶδ᾽ εἰσακούσας καὶ πρίν· ἀλλὰ τοῦ
ποτ᾽ ἐν χειρὶ σᾷ κομίζεις κόρους νεοτρεφεῖς; φράσον.

ΙΟΛΑΟΣ

Ἡρακλέους οἵδ᾽ εἰσὶ παῖδες, ὦ ξένοι,
ἱκέται σέθεν τε καὶ πόλεως ἀφιγμένοι.

ΧΟΡΟΣ

95 τί χρέος; ἦ λόγων πόλεος, ἔνεπέ μοι, μελόμενοι τυχεῖν;

80 σὺ δ᾽ Tyrwhitt: ὅδ᾽ L
83 κατέχετ᾽ Hermann: κατέσχετ᾽ L

18

CHORUS

From what land, old sir, have you come to this people of four cities?[a] Have you left the shore of Euboea and put in from beyond the water with seagoing oar?

IOLAUS

It is no islander's life that I live. I have come to your land from Mycenae.

CHORUS

What is the name the folk of Mycenae call you?

IOLAUS

You know, I am sure, of Iolaus, the man who stood at Heracles' side. I am not unknown to fame.

CHORUS

I have heard of you before. But whose are the young children you bring in your charge? Tell us.

IOLAUS

They are Heracles' sons, strangers, who have come as suppliants to you and your city.

CHORUS

What is your errand? Are you concerned to address the city? Tell us.

[a] The Marathonian tetrapolis (Marathon, Oenoe, Probalinthus, and Tricorythus) was an old confederacy of towns that existed before the unification of Attica under Theseus.

19

ΙΟΛΑΟΣ

μήτ' ἐκδοθῆναι μήτε πρὸς βίαν θεῶν
τῶν σῶν ἀποσπασθέντες εἰς Ἄργος μολεῖν.

ἀντ.

ΚΗΡΥΞ

ἀλλ' οὔτι τοῖς σοῖς δεσπόταις τάδ' ἀρκέσει,
100   οἳ σοῦ κρατοῦντες ἐνθάδ' εὑρίσκουσί σε.

ΧΟΡΟΣ

εἰκὸς θεῶν ἱκτῆρας αἰδεῖσθαι, ξένε,
καὶ μὴ βιαίῳ χειρὶ δαιμόνων
ἀπολιπεῖν σφ' ἕδη· πότνια γὰρ Δίκα τάδ' οὐ πείσεται.

ΚΗΡΥΞ

105   ἔκπεμπέ νυν γῆς τούσδε τοὺς Εὐρυσθέως,
κοὐδὲν βιαίῳ τῇδε χρήσομαι χερί.

ΧΟΡΟΣ

ἄθεον ἱκεσίαν μεθεῖναι πέλει ξένων προστροπάν.

ΚΗΡΥΞ

καλὸν δέ γ' ἔξω πραγμάτων ἔχειν πόδα,
110   εὐβουλίας τυχόντα τῆς ἀμείνονος.

ΧΟΡΟΣ

οὔκουν τυράννῳ τῆσδε γῆς φράσαντά σε
χρῆν ταῦτα τολμᾶν, ἀλλὰ μὴ βίᾳ ξένους
θεῶν ἀφέλκειν, γῆν σέβοντ' ἐλευθέραν;

ΚΗΡΥΞ

τίς δ' ἐστὶ χώρας τῆσδε καὶ πόλεως ἄναξ;

IOLAUS

We ask not to be surrendered, not to be forcibly dragged
off to Argos away from your gods.

HERALD

But this will not satisfy your masters. They are your
rulers and have found you here.

CHORUS

It is right to respect the gods' suppliants, stranger. They
should not be forced to leave their sanctuaries. Lady Jus-
tice will not be so treated.

HERALD

Then expel these chattels of Eurystheus from your land
and I shall not use force.

CHORUS

It is a godless act to yield up a suppliant band of strangers.

HERALD

Yes, but it is a fine thing to keep one's foot clear of trouble
and to practice a better sort of prudence.

CHORUS LEADER

Should you not have spoken to this land's ruler before tak-
ing this bold step rather than forcibly dragging these
strangers from the gods' sanctuary? That would have
shown respect for this land's sovereignty.

HERALD

Who is the ruler of this land and its city?

---

[103] ἀπολιπεῖν σφ' Musgrave (σφ') et Seidler: ἀπολείπειν σ'
L   [107] πέλει Elmsley: πόλει L
     [108] προστροπάν Canter: πρὸς τὸ πᾶν L

21

ΧΟΡΟΣ

115 ἐσθλοῦ πατρὸς παῖς Δημοφῶν ὁ Θησέως.

ΚΗΡΥΞ

πρὸς τοῦτον ἀγὼν ἆρα τοῦδε τοῦ λόγου
μάλιστ᾽ ἂν εἴη· τἄλλα δ᾽ εἴρηται μάτην.

ΧΟΡΟΣ

καὶ μὴν ὅδ᾽ αὐτὸς ἔρχεται σπουδὴν ἔχων
Ἀκάμας τ᾽ ἀδελφός, τῶνδ᾽ ἐπήκοοι λόγων.

ΔΗΜΟΦΩΝ

120 ἐπείπερ ἔφθης πρέσβυς ὢν νεωτέρους
βοηδρομήσας τήνδ᾽ ἐπ᾽ ἐσχάραν Διός,
λέξον, τίς ὄχλον τόνδ᾽ ἀθροίζεται τύχη;

ΧΟΡΟΣ

ἱκέται κάθηνται παῖδες οἵδ᾽ Ἡρακλέους
βωμὸν καταστέψαντες, ὡς ὁρᾷς, ἄναξ,
125 πατρός τε πιστὸς Ἰόλεως παραστάτης.

ΔΗΜΟΦΩΝ

τί δῆτ᾽ ἰυγμῶν ἥδ᾽ ἐδεῖτο συμφορά;

ΧΟΡΟΣ

βίᾳ νιν οὗτος τῆσδ᾽ ἀπ᾽ ἐσχάρας ἄγειν
ζητῶν βοὴν ἔστησε κἄσφηλεν γόνυ
γέροντος, ὥστε μ᾽ ἐκβαλεῖν οἴκτῳ δάκρυ.

ΔΗΜΟΦΩΝ

130 καὶ μὴν στολήν γ᾽ Ἕλληνα καὶ ῥυθμὸν πέπλων

---

129 μ᾽ ἐκβαλεῖν Reiske: μὴ βαλεῖν L

CHORUS LEADER

Demophon, son of noble Theseus.

HERALD

It is chiefly before him, then, that I must argue this plea of mine. Anything else I have said is a waste of words.

CHORUS LEADER

Look! Here he comes himself in haste, and his brother Acamas with him, to hear these words.

Enter DEMOPHON *and Acamas by Eisodos B.*

DEMOPHON

(to the Chorus Leader) Since you, old as you are, have outstripped younger men in anwering a call for help here at this altar of Zeus, tell me, what misfortune has brought this crowd together?

CHORUS LEADER

These are the sons of Heracles, and they sit as suppliants with their wreaths upon the altar, as you see, my lord, and with them is their father's trusty companion Iolaus.

DEMOPHON

But why did this circumstance call for cries of woe?

CHORUS LEADER

This man, trying to take them by force from this altar, caused them to cry out and has knocked the old man to the ground, which made me weep for pity.

DEMOPHON

The clothing he wears and the arrangement of his gar-

ἔχει, τὰ δ' ἔργα βαρβάρου χερὸς τάδε.
σὸν δὴ τὸ φράζειν ἐστί, μὴ μέλλειν δ', ἐμοὶ
ποίας ἀφῖξαι δεῦρο γῆς ὅρους λιπών.

ΚΗΡΤΞ

Ἀργεῖός εἰμι· τοῦτο γὰρ θέλεις μαθεῖν·
135 ἐφ' οἷσι δ' ἥκω καὶ παρ' οὗ λέγειν θέλω.
πέμπει Μυκηνῶν δεῦρό μ' Εὐρυσθεὺς ἄναξ
ἄξοντα τούσδε· πολλὰ δ' ἦλθον, ὦ ξένε,
δίκαι' ὁμαρτῇ δρᾶν τε καὶ λέγειν ἔχων.

Ἀργεῖος ὢν γὰρ αὐτὸς Ἀργείους ἄγω
140 ἐκ τῆς ἐμαυτοῦ τούσδε δραπέτας ἔχων,
νόμοισι τοῖς ἐκεῖθεν ἐψηφισμένους
θανεῖν· δίκαιοι δ' ἐσμὲν οἰκοῦντες πόλιν
αὐτοὶ καθ' αὑτῶν κυρίους κραίνειν δίκας.
πολλῶν δὲ κἄλλων ἑστίας ἀφιγμένοι
145 ἐν τοῖσιν αὐτοῖς τοισίδ' ἔσταμεν λόγοις,
κοὐδεὶς ἐτόλμησ' ἴδια προσθέσθαι κακά.
ἀλλ' ἤ τιν' ἐν σοὶ μωρίαν ἐσκεμμένοι
δεῦρ' ἦλθον ἢ κίνδυνον ἐξ ἀμηχάνων
ῥίπτοντες, εἴτ' οὖν εἴτε μὴ γενήσεται
<τὰ σ' ὧδ' ἀσύνετα καὶ φρενῶν τητώμενα>.
150 οὐ γὰρ φρενήρη γ' ὄντα σ' ἐλπίζουσί που
μόνον τοσαύτης ἣν ἐπῆλθον Ἑλλάδος
τὰς τῶνδ' ἀβούλως συμφορὰς κατοικτιεῖν.

135 καὶ παρ' οὗ . . . θέλω Stiblinus: καίπερ οὐ . . . θέλων L
140 ἔχων] ἑλών Kayser: κιχών Dobree
144 ἀφιγμένοι Firnhaber: -μένων L

ments are Greek, yet his deeds are those of a barbarian.
(to the Herald) But it is your task to tell me, and without
delay, from what land it is that you have come here.

HERALD

I am an Argive, since that is what you wish to know. But I
want to tell you why I have come and at whose behest.
Eurystheus, king of Mycenae, has sent me here to fetch
these children. I have come here, stranger, with many
rights at once to exercise and to plead.

I am an Argive myself, and those I am seeking to
remove are Argives who have run away from my own
country, persons sentenced to die in accordance with that
country's laws. We, who are the city's inhabitants, have
the right to pass binding sentences against our own num-
ber. To the homes of many another have we gone and
have taken our stand on these same principles, and no
one has dared to bring unnecessary trouble upon himself.
But these people have come here either because they
espy some folly in you or because out of desperation they
are risking their all to see whether <you> will or will not
prove to be <such a mad and brainless fool>. For they
surely do not expect that, while you are in your right
mind, you alone of all the Greeks they have approached
will take foolish pity on their misfortunes.

---

145 τοῖσιν . . . τοισίδ᾽ Canter: τοῖσι δ᾽ . . . τοῖσιν L

147 ἢ Jacobs: εἰ L   ἐν σοὶ Hartung: ἐς σὲ L

148 ἢ Jacobs: εἰς L

149 post h.v. lac. indic. et suppl. Diggle

152 ἀβούλως Kirchhoff: ἀβούλους L   κατοικτιεῖν Elms-
ley: -κτίσεις L

φέρ' ἀντίθες γάρ· τούσδε τ' ἐς γαῖαν παρεὶς
ἡμᾶς τ' ἐάσας ἐξάγειν, τί κερδανεῖς;
155 τὰ μὲν παρ' ἡμῶν τοιάδ' ἔστι σοι λαβεῖν,
Ἄργους τοσήνδε χεῖρα τήν τ' Εὐρυσθέως
ἰσχὺν ἅπασαν τῇδε προσθέσθαι πόλει.
ἢν δ' ἐς λόγους τε καὶ τὰ τῶνδ' οἰκτίσματα
βλέψας πεπανθῇς, ἐς πάλην καθίσταται
160 δορὸς τὸ πρᾶγμα· μὴ γὰρ ὡς μεθήσομεν
δόξῃς ἀγῶνος τοῦσδ' ἄτερ χαλυβδικοῦ.
τί δῆτα φήσεις, ποῖα πεδί' ἀφαιρεθείς,
τί ῥυσιασθείς, πόλεμον Ἀργείοις ἔχειν;
ποίοις δ' ἀμύνων συμμάχοις, τίνος δ' ὕπερ
165 θάψεις νεκροὺς πεσόντας; ἢ κακὸν λόγον
κτήσῃ πρὸς ἀστῶν, εἰ γέροντος οὕνεκα
τύμβου, τὸ μηδὲν ὄντος, ὡς εἰπεῖν ἔπος,
παίδων τε τῶνδ' ἐς ἄντλον ἐμβήσῃ πόδα.
†ἐρεῖς τὸ λῷστον ἐλπίδ' εὑρήσειν μόνον†·
170 καὶ τοῦτο πολλῷ τοῦ παρόντος ἐνδεές.
κακῶς γὰρ Ἀργείοισιν οἶδ' ὡπλισμένοις
μάχοιντ' ἂν ἡβήσαντες (εἴ τι τοῦτό σε
ψυχὴν ἐπαίρει), χοὖν μέσῳ πολὺς χρόνος
ἐν ᾧ διεργασθεῖτ' ἄν. ἀλλ' ἐμοὶ πιθοῦ·
175 δοὺς μηδὲν ἀλλὰ τἄμ' ἐὼν ἄγειν ἐμὲ
κτῆσαι Μυκήνας, μηδ' ὅπερ φιλεῖτε δρᾶν

153 τ' Reiske: γ' L
161 ἀγῶνος τοῦσδ' Dobree: ἀγῶνα τόνδ' L
163 τί ῥυσιασθείς Kirchhoff: τιρυνθίοις θῆς L

Come, make the comparison: what do you gain by let-
ting these persons into your country, or by letting us take
them away? From us this is what you stand to get: you
win for your city the great power of Argos and the whole
might of Eurystheus. But if you turn soft by heeding the
pleas and the lamentations of these persons, then the
matter becomes one for spears to settle: for you must not
suppose that we will let them go without a trial of steel.
What then will you say? What lands or booty will you
allege you have been robbed of that you go to war with
Argos? In defense of what allies, on whose behalf will you
bury the fallen? Your citizens will have nothing good to
say of you if you put your foot in the mire for an old man,
a nobody as good as dead, and for these children. You will
say, "There is hope that our city will find its true good and
the friendship of noble men only if these children's lives
are saved."[a] This too is a thing that falls far short of pre-
sent benefit. Against the Argives in their panoply these
boys, when grown to manhood, would be but poor fight-
ers—if it is this prospect that raises your spirits—and
there is a long stretch of time before then, when you
might well be destroyed. But take my advice: by giving
me nothing but merely allowing me to take what is mine,
win Mycenae for your ally. Do not make the mistake you

[a] The text is corrupt or lacunose or both. I translate my con-
jecture without any assurance that it gives even approximately
correct sense.

---

169 fort. ἐρεῖς· Τὸ λῷστον ἐλπὶς εὑρήσειν <πόλιν / ἐσθλῶν
τε φιλίαν τῶνδε σωθέντων> μόνον
171 ὡπλισμένοις Schenkl: -μένοι L

πάθῃς σὺ τοῦτο, τοὺς ἀμείνονας παρὸν
φίλους ἑλέσθαι τοὺς κακίονας λαβεῖν.

ΧΟΡΟΣ

τίς ἂν δίκην κρίνειεν ἢ γνοίη λόγον,
180 πρὶν ἂν παρ' ἀμφοῖν μῦθον ἐκμάθῃ σαφῶς;

ΙΟΛΑΟΣ

ἄναξ, ὑπάρχει γὰρ τόδ' ἐν τῇ σῇ χθονί,
εἰπεῖν ἀκοῦσαί τ' ἐν μέρει πάρεστί μοι,
κοὐδείς μ' ἀπώσει πρόσθεν, ὥσπερ ἄλλοθι.
    ἡμῖν δὲ καὶ τῷδ' οὐδέν ἐστιν ἐν μέσῳ·
185 ἐπεὶ γὰρ Ἄργους οὐ μέτεσθ' ἡμῖν ἔτι,
ψήφῳ δοκῆσαν, ἀλλὰ φεύγομεν πάτραν,
πῶς ἂν δικαίως ὡς Μυκηναίους ἄγοι
ὅδ' ὄντας ἡμᾶς, οὓς ἀπήλασαν χθονός;
ξένοι γάρ ἐσμεν. ἢ τὸν Ἑλλήνων ὅρον
190 φεύγειν δικαιοῦθ' ὅστις ἂν τἄργος φύγῃ;
οὔκουν Ἀθήνας γ'· οὐ γὰρ Ἀργείων φόβῳ
τοὺς Ἡρακλείους παῖδας ἐξελῶσι γῆς.
οὐ γάρ τι Τραχίς ἐστιν οὐδ' Ἀχαιικὸν
πόλισμ' ὅθεν σὺ τούσδε, τῇ δίκῃ μὲν οὔ,
195 τὸ δ' Ἄργος ὄγκων, οἷάπερ καὶ νῦν λέγεις,
ἤλαυνες ἱκέτας βωμίους καθημένους.
εἰ γὰρ τόδ' ἔσται καὶ λόγους κρινοῦσι σούς,

---

178 λαβεῖν Kirchhoff: λάβῃς L
179n Χο. Elmsley: Δη. L
181 γὰρ Wilamowitz: μὲν L
183 ἄλλοθι Elmsley: -θεν L
184 μέσῳ Valckenaer: μέρει L

Athenians so often make, taking the weak for your friends
when you might have chosen the strong.

CHORUS LEADER

Who can decide a plea or judge a speech until he has
heard a clear statement from both sides?

IOLAUS

(rising to his feet) My lord, since this is the law in your
land, I have the right to hear and be heard in turn, and no
one shall thrust me away before I am done, as they have
elsewhere.

We have nothing to do with this man. Since we no
longer have a share in Argos, and this has been ratified by
vote, but are in exile from our native land, how can this
man rightfully take us off as Mycenaeans, when they have
banished us from the country? We are now foreigners.
Or do you think it right that whoever is banished from
Argos should be banished from the whole Greek world?
Not from Athens, at any rate: they shall not drive Hera-
cles' children out of their land for fear of the Argives!
This is not Trachis or some Achaean town, places from
which you drove these children, suppliants though they
were and seated at the altar. This was not done by any
lawful plea but by prating of Argos' importance, just as
you are doing today. If that happens here and they judge

---

¹⁸⁵ οὐ μέτεσθ' Dobree: οὐδέν ἔσθ' L
¹⁸⁸ ὅδ' Tyrwhitt: ὧδ' L
¹⁹¹ οὐ γὰρ Stephanus: οὐκ ἄρ' L

29

οὔ φημ' Ἀθήνας τάσδ' ἐλευθέρας ἔτι.
ἀλλ' οἶδ' ἐγὼ τὸ τῶνδε λῆμα καὶ φύσιν·
200 θνῄσκειν θελήσουσ'· ἡ γὰρ αἰσχύνη <πάρος>
τοῦ ζῆν παρ' ἐσθλοῖς ἀνδράσιν νομίζεται.
    πόλει μὲν ἀρκεῖ· καὶ γὰρ οὖν ἐπίφθονον
λίαν ἐπαινεῖν ἐστι, πολλάκις δὲ δὴ
καὐτὸς βαρυνθεὶς οἶδ' ἄγαν αἰνούμενος.
205 σοὶ δ' ὡς ἀνάγκη τούσδε βούλομαι φράσαι
σῴζειν, ἐπείπερ τῆσδε προστατεῖς χθονός.
Πιτθεὺς μέν ἐστι Πέλοπος, ἐκ δὲ Πιτθέως
Αἴθρα, πατὴρ δ' ἐκ τῆσδε γεννᾶται σέθεν
Θησεύς. πάλιν δὲ τῶνδ' ἄνειμί σοι γένος.
210 Ἡρακλέης ἦν Ζηνὸς Ἀλκμήνης τε παῖς,
κείνη δὲ Πέλοπος θυγατρός. αὐτανεψίων
πατὴρ ἂν εἴη σός τε χὠ τούτων γεγώς.
    γένους μὲν ἥκεις ὧδε τοῖσδε, Δημοφῶν·
ἃ δ' ἐκτὸς ἤδη τοῦ προσήκοντός σε δεῖ
215 τεῖσαι λέγω σοι παισί· φημὶ γάρ ποτε
σύμπλους γενέσθαι τῶνδ' ὑπασπίζων πατρὶ
ζωστῆρα Θησεῖ τὸν πολυκτόνον μέτα.
<ἐπεὶ δὲ Θησεὺς Πειρίθῳ πρὸς ἡδονὴν
Κόρην ἀπάξων ἦλθε Ταρτάρου βάθη,
εἰρχθέντα δεσμοῖς ἐξέλυσεν Ἡρακλῆς>
Ἅιδου τ' ἐρεμνῶν ἐξανήγαγεν μυχῶν
πατέρα σόν· Ἑλλὰς πᾶσα τοῦτο μαρτυρεῖ.

198 οὔ φημ' Kirchhoff: οὐκ οἶδ' L
200 <πάρος> Reiske
202 πόλει Bothe: πόλιν L

your case the winner, Athens in my judgment is no longer free. But I know the nature and temper of these men: they will be willing to die. In the eyes of good men a sense of honor is more precious than life.

I have said enough to the city: for indeed to praise too much is hateful, and I myself know that I have felt disgust at being overpraised. But to you, sir, I want to say that it is your duty, since you rule this land, to save these children. Pittheus was the son of Pelops, and from him was begotten Aethra, and from her your father Theseus. Now I shall trace back for you these children's lineage. Heracles was the son of Zeus and Alcmene, and Alcmene was daughter of Pelops. And so your father and theirs are the sons of first cousins.

This is your standing in kinship with these children, Demophon. But I shall tell you what you are obligated to render these children, apart from the tie of blood. It is my claim that as right-hand man to their father I once sailed with Theseus to fetch the girdle that caused so many deaths.[a] <And when Theseus, to please Pirithöus, went to Hades to abduct Persephone, Heracles rescued him from his chains>[b] and brought your father out of the dark recesses of Hades. All Hellas bears witness to this.

---

[a] The girdle belonged to Hippolyta, queen of the Amazons.

[b] I give the minimum required to make sense of 218. Iolaus could have mentioned other benefits as well in the missing lines.

---

211 αὐτανεψίων Reisig: -ψίω L
212 χὠ Kirchhoff: καὶ L
217 post h.v. lac. indic. Dobree
218 ἐρεμνῶν Barnes: ἐρυμνῶν L

220 ὧν ἀντιδοῦναί σ' οἶδ' ἀπαιτοῦσιν χάριν
[μήτ' ἐκδοθῆναι μήτε πρὸς βίαν θεῶν
τῶν σῶν ἀποσπασθέντες ἐκπεσεῖν χθονός.
σοὶ γὰρ τόδ' αἰσχρὸν †χωρὶς ἔν τε πόλει κακόν†,
ἱκέτας ἀλήτας συγγενεῖς—οἴμοι κακῶν·
225 βλέψον πρὸς αὐτούς, βλέψον—ἕλκεσθαι βίᾳ].
    ἀλλ' ἄντομαί σε καὶ καταστέφων χεροῖν
καὶ πρὸς γενείου, μηδαμῶς ἀτιμάσῃς
τοὺς Ἡρακλείους παῖδας ἐς χέρας λαβεῖν·
γενοῦ δὲ τοῖσδε συγγενής, γενοῦ φίλος
230 πατὴρ ἀδελφὸς δεσπότης· ἅπαντα γὰρ
τἄλλ' ἐστὶ κρείσσω πλὴν ὑπ' Ἀργείοις πεσεῖν.

ΧΟΡΟΣ

ᾤκτιρ' ἀκούσας τούσδε συμφορᾶς, ἄναξ.
τὴν δ' εὐγένειαν τῆς τύχης νικωμένην
νῦν δὴ μάλιστ' ἐσεῖδον· οἵδε γὰρ πατρὸς
235 ἐσθλοῦ γεγῶτες δυστυχοῦσ' ἀναξίως.

ΔΗΜΟΦΩΝ

τρισσαί μ' ἀναγκάζουσι συννοίας ὁδοί,
Ἰόλαε, τοὺς σοὺς μὴ παρώσασθαι λόγους·
τὸ μὲν μέγιστον Ζεὺς ἐφ' οὗ σὺ βώμιος
θακεῖς νεοσσῶν τήνδ' ἔχων πανήγυριν,
240 τὸ συγγενές τε καὶ τὸ προυφείλειν καλῶς
πράσσειν παρ' ἡμῶν τούσδε πατρῴαν χάριν,

221-5 del. Paley (221–2 iam Pierson cl. 97–8, 223–5 Dindorf)
223 χωρὶς ἐν πόλει κακόν Erfurdt: χωρίς, ἅμα τε τῇ πόλει
[κακόν] Hartung   226 καταστέφων Diggle: -στέφω L

For these things his children here ask repayment [, not to be surrendered, not to be dragged off against the will of your gods and banished from the land. It is a calamity that brings disgrace on you especially in the eyes of the city if suppliants, wanderers, kinsmen—alas for the pain, look at them, look at them!—are dragged off by force].

(kneeling before Demophon as a suppliant) But I beg you both by my suppliant grasp and by your beard: do not refuse to take the children of Heracles into your embrace! Be to them kinsman, be friend, be father, brother, master: for all else is better than to fall under the power of the Argives!

CHORUS LEADER

My lord, I have listened and I pity these for what has befallen them. Nobility overwhelmed by mischance— this I now see in its full. For these children, born of a noble sire, are suffering undeserved misfortune.

DEMOPHON

(raising Iolaus to his feet) Three paths of conscience compel me, Iolaus, not to reject your words. Most important is Zeus, at whose altar you sit with this assembly of fledglings; second, kinship and the obligation long-standing that these children should for their father's sake

---

228 λαβεῖν Elmsley: λαβών L

231 τἄλλ' Häberlin: ταῦτ' L

236 συννοίας F. W. Schmidt: συμφορᾶς L

237 λόγους Kirchhoff: ξένους L

238 βώμιος Stephanus: βωμίους L

33

τό τ' αἰσχρόν, οὗπερ δεῖ μάλιστα φροντίσαι·
εἰ γὰρ παρήσω τόνδε συλᾶσθαι βίᾳ
ξένου πρὸς ἀνδρὸς βωμόν, οὐκ ἐλευθέραν
245　οἰκεῖν δοκήσω γαῖαν, Ἀργείων δ' ὄκνῳ
ἱκέτας προδοῦναι· καὶ τάδ' ἀγχόνης πέλας.
ἀλλ' ὤφελες μὲν εὐτυχέστερος μολεῖν,
ὅμως δὲ καὶ νῦν μὴ τρέσῃς ὅπως σέ τις
σὺν παισὶ βωμοῦ τοῦδ' ἀποσπάσει βίᾳ.
250　σὺ δ' Ἄργος ἐλθὼν ταῦτά τ' Εὐρυσθεῖ φράσον,
πρὸς τοῖσδέ τ', εἴ τι τοισίδ' ἐγκαλεῖ ξένοις,
δίκης κυρήσειν· τούσδε δ' οὐκ ἄξεις ποτέ.

ΚΗΡΤΞ

οὐδ' ἢν δίκαιον ᾖ τι καὶ νικῶ λόγῳ;

ΔΗΜΟΦΩΝ

καὶ πῶς δίκαιον τὸν ἱκέτην ἄγειν βίᾳ;

ΚΗΡΤΞ

255　οὔκουν ἐμοὶ τόδ' αἰσχρὸν ἀλλ' οὐ σοὶ βλάβος;

ΔΗΜΟΦΩΝ

ἐμοί γ', ἐάν σοι τούσδ' ἐφέλκεσθαι μεθῶ.

ΚΗΡΤΞ

σὺ δ' ἐξόριζε κᾆτ' ἐκεῖθεν ἄξομεν.

ΔΗΜΟΦΩΝ

σκαιὸς πέφυκας τοῦ θεοῦ πλείω φρονῶν.

245 Ἀργείων Dobree: -είοις L
253 οὐδ' Nauck: οὐκ L

34

be well treated at our hands; and last, fear of disgrace, the thing I must be most concerned about. For if I am to allow this altar to be forcibly plundered by a foreigner, it will be thought that it is no sovereign land I govern but that I have betrayed suppliants for fear of the Argives. That is almost cause to hang oneself. While I could wish that you had come in happier plight, still even so have no fear that anyone shall drag you and the children by force from the altar.

(to the Herald) As for you, go to Argos and report this to Eurystheus, and say in addition that if he makes any charge against these foreigners, he shall receive lawful treatment. But you shall never take these children away.

HERALD
Not even if I have a just cause and am victorious in my plea?

DEMOPHON
And how is it just to abduct a suppliant?

HERALD
Doesn't this injury disgrace me rather than you?

DEMOPHON
The disgrace is mine if I let you drag these children off.

HERALD
Put them beyond your border, and we will take them from there.

DEMOPHON
You are a fool to think you can outwit the god.

---

255 ἀλλ' οὐ Nauck: ἀλλὰ L

ΚΗΡΥΞ

δεῦρ᾽, ὡς ἔοικε, τοῖς κακοῖσι φευκτέον.

ΔΗΜΟΦΩΝ

260 ἅπασι κοινὸν ῥῦμα δαιμόνων ἕδρα.

ΚΗΡΥΞ

ταῦτ᾽ οὐ δοκήσει τοῖς Μυκηναίοις ἴσως.

ΔΗΜΟΦΩΝ

οὔκουν ἐγὼ τῶν ἐνθάδ᾽ εἰμὶ κύριος;

ΚΗΡΥΞ

βλάπτων <γ᾽> ἐκείνους μηδὲν ἢν σὺ σωφρονῇς.

ΔΗΜΟΦΩΝ

βλάπτεσθ᾽, ἐμοῦ γε μὴ μιαίνοντος θεούς.

ΚΗΡΥΞ

265 οὐ βούλομαί σε πόλεμον Ἀργείοις ἔχειν.

ΔΗΜΟΦΩΝ

κἀγὼ τοιοῦτος· τῶνδε δ᾽ οὐ μεθήσομαι.

ΚΗΡΥΞ

ἄξω γε μέντοι τοὺς ἐμοὺς ἐγὼ λαβών.

ΔΗΜΟΦΩΝ

οὐκ ἄρ᾽ ἐς Ἄργος ῥᾳδίως ἄπει πάλιν.

ΚΗΡΥΞ

πειρώμενος δὴ τοῦτό γ᾽ αὐτίκ᾽ εἴσομαι.

ΔΗΜΟΦΩΝ

270 κλαίων ἄρ᾽ ἅψῃ τῶνδε κοὐκ ἐς ἀμβολάς.

HERALD
This is the place, it seems, for criminals to take refuge.

DEMOPHON
The gods' sanctuaries are a common defense for all.

HERALD
Perhaps the Myceneans will not think so.

DEMOPHON
Am I not then the master of matters here?

HERALD
Yes, if you are wise enough not to injure *them*.

DEMOPHON
Be injured! I shall not defile the gods.

HERALD
I am not eager you should have war with Argos.

DEMOPHON
No more am I. But these I'll not let go.

HERALD
I'll take them all the same for they are mine.

DEMOPHON
Then you will find your return to Argos hard.

HERALD
I'll learn at once by trial if this is so.

DEMOPHON
You touch them to your cost—your present cost!

---

262 τῶν Reiske: τῶνδ' L
263 <γ'> Elmsley   ἢν Matthiae: ἂν L

ΧΟΡΟΣ

μὴ πρὸς θεῶν κήρυκα τολμήσῃς θενεῖν.

ΔΗΜΟΦΩΝ

εἰ μή γ' ὁ κῆρυξ σωφρονεῖν μαθήσεται.

ΧΟΡΟΣ

ἄπελθε· καὶ σὺ τοῦδε μὴ θίγῃς, ἄναξ.

ΚΗΡΤΞ

στείχω· μιᾶς γὰρ χειρὸς ἀσθενὴς μάχη.

275 ἥξω δὲ πολλὴν Ἄρεος Ἀργείου λαβὼν
πάγχαλκον αἰχμὴν δεῦρο. μυρίοι δέ με
μένουσιν ἀσπιστῆρες Εὐρυσθεύς τ' ἄναξ
αὐτὸς στρατηγῶν· Ἀλκάθου δ' ἐπ' ἐσχάτοις
καραδοκῶν τἀνθένδε τέρμασιν μένει.

280 λαμπρὸς δ' ἀκούσας σὴν ὕβριν φανήσεται
σοὶ καὶ πολίταις γῇ τε τῇδε καὶ φυτοῖς·
μάτην γὰρ ἥβην ὧδέ γ' ἂν κεκτήμεθα
πολλὴν ἐν Ἄργει, μή σε τιμωρούμενοι.

ΔΗΜΟΦΩΝ

φθείρου· τὸ σὸν γὰρ Ἄργος οὐ δέδοικ' ἐγώ.

285 ἐνθένδε δ' οὐκ ἔμελλες αἰσχύνας ἐμὲ
ἄξειν βίᾳ τούσδ'· οὐ γὰρ Ἀργείων πόλιν
ὑπήκοον τήνδ' ἀλλ' ἐλευθέραν ἔχω.

ΧΟΡΟΣ

ὥρα προνοεῖν, πρὶν ὅροις πελάσαι

282 κεκτήμεθα Brunck: -ώμεθα L
286 πόλιν Elmsley: πόλει L

38

He moves threateningly toward the Herald.

CHORUS LEADER
In the gods' name, don't dare to strike a herald!

DEMOPHON
I will, unless the herald learns some sense.

CHORUS LEADER
Be off! *(to Demophon)* And you, my lord, do not touch him.

HERALD
I am going: a single man can put up only a weak fight. But I shall return with a great force of Argive soldiers in full armor. Ten thousand warriors are waiting for me with Eurystheus their lord as general. He is standing by on the edge of Alcathöus' land,[a] awaiting the outcome of events here. When he hears of your insolence, he will appear in his fury to you, your citizens, your land, and its crops. There would be no point in Argos' possessing so great an army of young men if we did not punish you.

DEMOPHON
Clear off! I am not afraid of your Argos. You were not going to remove these suppliants from Athens and disgrace me. The city that I rule is not Argos' subject but sovereign.

Exit HERALD by Eisodos A.

CHORUS LEADER
Now is the time to show forethought, before the Argive

---

[a] Megara, on Attica's southern border.

στρατὸν Ἀργείων·
290 μάλα δ' ὀξὺς Ἄρης ὁ Μυκηναίων,
ἐπὶ τοισίδε δὴ μᾶλλον ἔτ' ἢ πρίν.
πᾶσι γὰρ οὗτος κήρυξι νόμος,
δὶς τόσα πυργοῦν τῶν γιγνομένων.
πόσα νιν λέξειν βασιλεῦσι δοκεῖς,
295 ὡς δείν' ἔπαθεν καὶ παρὰ μικρὸν
ψυχὴν ἦλθεν διακναῖσαι;

ΙΟΛΑΟΣ

οὐκ ἔστι τοῦδε παισὶ κάλλιον γέρας
ἢ πατρὸς ἐσθλοῦ κἀγαθοῦ πεφυκέναι
[γαμεῖν τ' ἀπ' ἐσθλῶν· ὃς δὲ νικηθεὶς πόθῳ
300 κακοῖς ἐκοινώνησεν οὐκ ἐπαινέσω,
τέκνοις ὄνειδος οὕνεχ' ἡδονῆς λιπεῖν]·
τὸ δυστυχὲς γὰρ ηὐγένει' ἀμύνεται
τῆς δυσγενείας μᾶλλον· ἡμεῖς γὰρ κακῶν
ἐς τοὔσχατον πεσόντες ηὕρομεν φίλους
305 καὶ ξυγγενεῖς τούσδ', οἳ τοσῆσδ' οἰκουμένης
Ἑλληνίδος γῆς τῶνδε προύστησαν μόνοι.
δότ', ὦ τέκν', αὐτοῖς χεῖρα δεξιάν, δότε,
ὑμεῖς τε παισί, καὶ πέλας προσέλθετε.
ὦ παῖδες, ἐς μὲν πεῖραν ἤλθομεν φίλων·
310 ἢν δ' οὖν ποθ' ὑμῖν νόστος ἐς πάτραν φανῇ
καὶ δώματ' οἰκήσητε καὶ τιμὰς πατρὸς
<πάλιν λάβητε, τῆσδε κοιράνους χθονὸς>
σωτῆρας αἰεὶ καὶ φίλους νομίζετε,
καὶ μήποτ' ἐς γῆν ἐχθρὸν αἴρεσθαι δόρυ
μέμνησθέ μοι τήνδ', ἀλλὰ φιλτάτην πόλιν

army approaches our borders. The fighting power of Mycenae is very fierce, but after what has happened it will be fiercer than ever. That is the way with all heralds: they exaggerate a tale to twice the size of truth. What grand story do you think he will tell his masters, how he suffered monstrous treatment and barely escaped with his life?

IOLAUS

There is no finer honor for children than this, to be born of a brave and noble father [and to marry into nobility. But I will not praise the man who is overcome by desire and makes a marriage alliance with the base, getting pleasure for himself but leaving his children disgrace]: noble birth repels misfortune better than ignoble birth. We ourselves, when we had fallen into the utmost disaster, found friends and kinsmen here, men who, alone in all the land of Greece, have been these children's champions. Children, draw near and give these men your right hands, and you, my friends, give the children yours!

The children and the Chorus clasp hands.

My children, we have put our friends to the test. And so if you ever return to your country and live in your ancestral home and <get> your patrimony <back again>, you must consider <the rulers of this land> for all time as your saviors and friends. Be sure never to raise a hostile force against this land, but consider it always your great-

---

299–301 del. Niejahr

311 post h.v. lac. indic. et suppl. Elmsley

314 μέμνησθέ μοι Kirchhoff: μεμνημένοι L   τήνδ' Murray: τῶνδ' L

41

EURIPIDES

315 πασῶν νομίζετ'. ἄξιοι δ' ὑμῖν σέβειν
οἳ γῆν τοσήνδε καὶ Πελασγικὸν λεὼν
ἡμῶν ἀπηλλάξαντο πολεμίους ἔχειν,
πτωχοὺς ἀλήτας εἰσορῶντες ἀλλ' ὅμως
[οὐκ ἐξέδωκαν οὐδ' ἀπήλασαν χθονός].
320 ἐγὼ δὲ καὶ ζῶν <εὐγενῆ σ' οὐ παύσομαι
320a πᾶσιν προφαίνων,> καὶ θανών, ὅταν θάνω,
πολλῷ σ' ἐπαίνῳ Θησέως ἑστὼς πέλας
ὑψηλὸν ἀρῶ καὶ λέγων τάδ' εὐφρανῶ,
ὡς εὖ τ' ἐδέξω καὶ τέκνοισιν ἤρκεσας
τοῖς Ἡρακλείοις, εὐκλεὴς δ' ἀν' Ἑλλάδα
325 σῴζεις πατρῴαν δόξαν, ἐξ ἐσθλῶν δὲ φὺς
οὐδὲν κακίων τυγχάνεις γεγὼς πατρός,
παύρων μετ' ἄλλων· ἕνα γὰρ ἐν πολλοῖς ἴσως
εὕροις ἂν ὅστις ἐστὶ μὴ χείρων πατρός.

ΧΟΡΟΣ
ἀεί ποθ' ἥδε γαῖα τοῖς ἀμηχάνοις
330 σὺν τῷ δικαίῳ βούλεται προσωφελεῖν.
τοιγὰρ πόνους δὴ μυρίους ὑπὲρ φίλων
ἤνεγκε, καὶ νῦν τόνδ' ἀγῶν' ὁρῶ πέλας.

ΔΗΜΟΦΩΝ
σοί τ' εὖ λέλεκται, καὶ τὰ τῶνδ' αὐχῶ, γέρον,
τοιαῦτ' ἔσεσθαι· μνημονεύσεται χάρις.
335 κἀγὼ μὲν ἀστῶν σύλλογον ποιήσομαι,
τάξω δ' ὅπως ἂν τὸν Μυκηναίων στρατὸν

315 ἄξιοι δ' Elmsley: ἄξιον L

42

est friend. The Athenians are worthy of your reverence
seeing that they rescued us from the great land of Argos
and its army, braving their enmity even though they saw
that we were wandering beggars [they did not give us up
or drive us from the land]. (*to Demophon*) In life <I shall
proclaim to everyone your nobility,> and in death, when I
die, I shall stand next to Theseus and extol you in praise
and cheer him with this story, how in kindness you took in
and defended the children of Heracles and how you now
enjoy good repute throughout all Hellas and keep your
father's reputation and, while born of noble stock, in no
way prove less noble than your father. Of few others can
this be said: only one man out of a great multitude can be
found who is not inferior to his father.

CHORUS LEADER

It is always the desire of this land to side with justice and
help the weak. Therefore she has borne countless toils on
behalf of friends, and now too I see another such struggle
coming upon us.

DEMOPHON

Your words are well spoken, old sir, and I am confident
that the deeds of these children will match them: our
favor to you will be remembered. I shall muster the citi-
zens and marshal them so that we may meet the army of

---

[317] ἐνηλλάξαντο Musgrave
[319] suspectum habuit Wecklein, del. Diggle
[320] θάνω Brodaeus: θάνῃς L
[320–20a] lac. indic. Kovacs
[321] ἑστὼς Broadhead: ὦ τᾶν L
[324] εὐκλεὴς Wecklein: εὐγενὴς L

πολλῇ δέχωμαι χειρί· πρῶτα μὲν σκοποὺς
πέμψω πρὸς αὐτόν, μὴ λάθῃ με προσπεσών·
ταχὺς γὰρ Ἄργει πᾶς ἀνὴρ βοηδρόμος·
340 μάντεις δ' ἀθροίσας θύσομαι. σὺ δ' ἐς δόμους
σὺν παισὶ χώρει, Ζηνὸς ἐσχάραν λιπών.
εἰσὶν γὰρ οἵ σου, κἂν ἐγὼ θυραῖος ὦ,
μέριμναν ἕξουσ'. ἀλλ' ἴθ' ἐς δόμους, γέρον.

ΙΟΛΑΟΣ

οὐκ ἂν λίποιμι βωμόν, εὐξόμεσθα δὲ
345 ἱκέται μένοντες ἐνθάδ' εὖ πρᾶξαι πόλιν.
ὅταν δ' ἀγῶνος τοῦδ' ἀπαλλαχθῇς καλῶς,
ἴμεν πρὸς οἴκους. θεοῖσι δ' οὐ κακίοσιν
χρώμεσθα συμμάχοισιν Ἀργείων, ἄναξ·
τῶν μὲν γὰρ Ἥρα προστατεῖ, Διὸς δάμαρ,
350 ἡμῶν δ' Ἀθάνα. φημὶ δ' εἰς εὐπραξίαν
καὶ τοῦθ' ὑπάρχειν, θεῶν ἀμεινόνων τυχεῖν·
νικωμένη γὰρ Παλλὰς οὐκ ἀνέξεται.

ΧΟΡΟΣ

στρ.

εἰ σὺ μέγ' αὐχεῖς, ἕτεροι
σοῦ πλέον οὐ μέλονται,
355 ξεῖν' <ἀπ'> Ἀργόθεν ἐλθών,
μεγαληγορίαισι δ' ἐμὰς φρένας οὐ φοβήσεις.
μήπω ταῖς μεγάλαισιν οὕ-
τω καὶ καλλιχόροις Ἀθά-
360 ναις εἴη· σὺ δ' ἄφρων ὅ τ' Ἄρ-
γει Σθενέλου τύραννος·

44

Mycenae with a large force: first I shall send scouts to spy
on it so that it may not attack without my knowledge (for
at Argos every man is a swift-footed warrior), and then I
shall gather the prophets and make sacrifice. But leave
Zeus's altar and go with the children to the palace. There
are men there who will take care of you, even if I am
away. Go to the palace, old sir.

IOLAUS

I will not leave the altar. We will stay here as suppliants
and pray for the city's good fortune. But when it has
escaped with honor from this struggle, then we will go to
the palace. The gods we have as allies are not worse than
those of the Argives, my lord. For Hera, Zeus's wife, is
their champion, but Athena is ours. This too, I maintain,
is a source of good fortune for us, that we have better
gods. For Pallas Athena will not brook defeat.

Exit DEMOPHON *by Eisodos B.*

CHORUS

Though you utter a great boast, others do not on that
account care the more for you, O stranger from Argos,
and with your high words you shall not daunt our hearts!
Long may it be before this happens to great Athens of the
fair dancing grounds! But you are a fool, and so is Argos'
king, the son of Sthenelus.[a]

---

[a] Eurystheus.

---

344 εὐξόμεσθα Cobet: ἐζόμεσθα L   δὲ Kirchhoff: δὴ L
355 <ἀπ'> Erfurdt

ἀντ.

ὃς πόλιν ἐλθὼν ἑτέραν
οὐδὲν ἐλάσσον᾽ Ἄργους
θεῶν ἱκτῆρας ἀλάτας
365 καὶ ἐμᾶς χθονὸς ἀντομένους ξένος ὢν βιαίως
ἕλκεις, οὐ βασιλεῦσιν εἴ-
ξας, οὐκ ἄλλο δίκαιον εἰ-
πών· ποῦ ταῦτα καλῶς ἂν εἴ-
370 η παρά γ᾽ εὖ φρονοῦσιν;
ἐπῳδ.

εἰρήνα μὲν ἐμοί γ᾽ ἀρέ-
σκει· σοὶ δ᾽, ὦ κακόφρων ἄναξ,
λέγω, εἰ πόλιν ἥξεις,
οὐχ οὕτως ἃ δοκεῖς κυρή-
375 σεις· οὐ σοὶ μόνῳ ἔγχος οὐδ᾽
ἰτέα κατάχαλκος.
ἀλλ᾽, ὦ πολέμων ἐρα-
στάς, μή μοι δορὶ συνταρά-
ξῃς τὰν εὖ χαρίτων ἔχου-
380 σαν πόλιν, ἀλλ᾽ ἀνάσχου.

ΙΟΛΑΟΣ

ὦ παῖ, τί μοι σύννοιαν ὄμμασιν φέρων
ἥκεις; νέον τι πολεμίων λέξεις πέρι;
μέλλουσιν ἢ πάρεισιν ἢ τί πυνθάνῃ;
οὐ γάρ τι μὴ ψεύσῃς γε κήρυκος λόγους·
385 ὁ γὰρ στρατηγὸς εὐτυχὴς τὰ πρόσθεν ὢν
εἶσιν, σάφ᾽ οἶδα, καὶ μάλ᾽ οὐ σμικρὸν φρονῶν

You came to another city, full equal of Argos, and foreigner that you are you tried to drag off by force wanderers, the god's suppliants and my country's petitioners, not yielding to our kings or urging any further plea of justice. How can such things be accounted honorable in the eyes of men of sense?

I for my part love peace. But I tell you, foolish king, if you come to this city, you will not win without further ado what you think to win. You are not alone in possessing a spear and a shield overlaid with bronze. No, my lover of wars, do not with your spear throw into turmoil the city rich in graces, but stay your hand!

Enter DEMOPHON *by Eisodos B.*

IOLAUS

My son, why have you come with worry in your glance? Are you going to tell me something new about the enemy? Are they tarrying, or have they arrived, or what news have you heard? For you will assuredly not prove false what the herald said. The general, who has been fortunate before now, will come to Athens, I am sure, and

---

365 ἀντομένους Nauck: ἀντεχομένους L

372 σοὶ Canter: σὺ L

376 κατάχαλκος Blomfield: κατάχαλκός ἐστιν L

377 ὦ Canter: οὐ L

379 εὖ χαρίτων Elmsley: εὐχαρίστως L

382 λέξεις Bothe: λέγεις L

384 ψεύσῃς Murray: ψεύσῃ vel -σου L

385 πρόσθεν ὢν Tyrwhitt: πρὸς θεῶν L

386 εἰσιν Elmsley: ἔστιν L

47

EURIPIDES

ἐς τὰς Ἀθήνας. ἀλλά τοι φρονημάτων
ὁ Ζεὺς κολαστὴς τῶν ἄγαν ὑπερφρόνων.

ΔΗΜΟΦΩΝ

ἥκει στράτευμ' Ἀργεῖον Εὐρυσθεύς τ' ἄναξ·
390 ἐγώ νιν αὐτὸς εἶδον. ἄνδρα γὰρ χρεών,
ὅστις στρατηγεῖν φησ' ἐπίστασθαι καλῶς,
οὐκ ἀγγέλοισι τοὺς ἐναντίους ὁρᾶν.
πεδία μὲν οὖν γῆς ἐς τάδ' οὐκ ἐφῆκέ πω
στρατόν, λεπαίαν δ' ὀφρύην καθήμενος
395 σκοπεῖ (δόκησιν δὴ τόδ' ἂν λέγοιμί σοι)
ποίᾳ προσάξει στρατόπεδον τοσόνδ' ὅροις
ἐν ἀσφαλεῖ τε τῆσδ' ἱδρύσεται χθονός.
καὶ τἀμὰ μέντοι πάντ' ἄραρ' ἤδη καλῶς·
πόλις τ' ἐν ὅπλοις, σφάγιά θ' ἡτοιμασμένα
400 ἕστηκεν οἷς χρὴ ταῦτα τέμνεσθαι θεῶν,
401 θυηπολεῖται δ' ἄστυ μάντεων ὕπο.
403 χρησμῶν δ' ἀοιδοὺς πάντας εἰς ἓν ἁλίσας
ἤλεγξα καὶ βέβηλα καὶ κεκρυμμένα
405 [λόγια παλαιά, τῇδε γῇ σωτήρια].
καὶ τῶν μὲν ἄλλων διάφορ' ἐστὶ θεσφάτοις
πόλλ'· ἓν δὲ πᾶσι γνῶμα ταὐτὸν ἐμπρέπει·
σφάξαι κελεύουσίν με παρθένον κόρῃ
409 Δήμητρος, ἥτις ἐστὶ πατρὸς εὐγενοῦς,
402 τροπαῖά τ' ἐχθρῶν καὶ πόλει σωτήριαν.

---

387 τοι Wecklein: τῶν L
393 τάδ' Stephanus: τόδ' L
394 λεπαίαν Stiblinus: λεπάραν L

48

in no humble mood. But Zeus, you may be sure, is the
punisher of thoughts that are too high and mighty.

DEMOPHON

The Argive army has arrived with Eurystheus its leader. I
have seen him myself: a man who claims to be a good
general should not observe the enemy by means of mes-
sengers. But he has not yet sent his army into the plain of
Attica. Rather, sitting upon a rocky brow, he is deliberat-
ing (I will tell you my impression) by what route he
should bring so great an army within the borders of our
land and safely encamp it. Furthermore, where my own
part is concerned, all is well prepared: the city is in arms,
the sacrificial victims stand in readiness for the gods to
whom they are to be sacrificed, and offerings are being
made throughout the city by diviners. But I gathered all
the chanters of oracles into one place and closely exam-
ined their prophecies, both public and secret [old oracles
making for the safety of the city]. On other points these
oracles showed many differences. But one thought shines
forth from them all: to rout the enemy and save the city,
they bid me sacrifice to Demeter's daughter a virgin born
of a noble father.

---

[396] τοσόνδ᾽ ὅροις Willink (ὅροις iam Reiske): τὰ νῦν δορὸς
L

[402] vide post 409

[405] del. Wilamowitz

[406] θεσφάτοις Kirchhoff: -των L

[408] κόρῃ Barnes: κόρην L

[402] post 409 praemonente Murray trai. Diggle   σωτηρίαν
Diggle: σωτηρία L

410 ἐγὼ δ' ἔχω μέν, ὡς ὁρᾷς, προθυμίαν
τοσήνδ' ἐς ὑμᾶς· παῖδα δ' οὔτ' ἐμὴν κτενῶ
οὔτ' ἄλλον ἀστῶν τῶν ἐμῶν ἀναγκάσω
ἄκονθ'· ἑκὼν δὲ τίς κακῶς οὕτω φρονεῖ,
ὅστις τὰ φίλτατ' ἐκ χερῶν δώσει τέκνα;
415 καὶ νῦν πυκνὰς ἂν συστάσεις ἂν εἰσίδοις,
τῶν μὲν λεγόντων ὡς δίκαιος ἢ ξένοις
ἱκέταις ἀρήγειν, τῶν δὲ μωρίαν ἐμοῦ
κατηγορούντων· εἰ δὲ δὴ δράσω τόδε,
οἰκεῖος ἤδη πόλεμος ἐξαρτύεται.
420 ταῦτ' οὖν ὅρα σὺ καὶ συνεξεύρισχ' ὅπως
αὐτοί τε σωθήσεσθε καὶ πέδον τόδε,
κἀγὼ πολίταις μὴ διαβληθήσομαι.
οὐ γὰρ τυραννίδ' ὥστε βαρβάρων ἔχω·
ἀλλ', ἢν δίκαια δρῶ, δίκαια πείσομαι.

ΧΟΡΟΣ

425 ἀλλ' ἦ πρόθυμον οὖσαν οὐκ ἐᾷ θεὸς
ξένοις ἀρήγειν τήνδε χρῄζουσιν πόλιν;

ΙΟΛΑΟΣ

ὦ τέκν', ἔοιγμεν ναυτίλοισιν οἵτινες
χειμῶνος ἐκφυγόντες ἄγριον μένος
ἐς χεῖρα γῇ συνῆψαν, εἶτα χερσόθεν
430 πνοαῖσιν ἠλάθησαν ἐς πόντον πάλιν.
οὕτω δὲ χἠμεῖς τῆσδ' ἀπωθούμεσθα γῆς
ἤδη πρὸς ἀκταῖς ὄντες ὡς σεσωμένοι.
οἴμοι· τί δῆτ' ἔτερψας ὦ τάλαινά με
ἐλπὶς τότ', οὐ μέλλουσα διατελεῖν χάριν;

As you see, I am very eager to help you, but I shall not kill my own daughter nor shall I force one of my citizens to do so against his will: and who would be so foolish as to give away of his own will the children he loves beyond all else? Now you will see crowded assemblies being held, with some maintaining that I was right to protect strangers who are suppliants, while others accuse me of folly. In fact if I do as I am bidden, civil war will break out.

Therefore, consider these facts and join with me in discovering how you yourselves may be saved and this land as well, and how I may not be discredited in the eyes of the citizens. I do not have a monarchy like that of the barbarians: only if I do what is fair will I be fairly treated.

CHORUS LEADER
Can it really be that a power divine forbids this city to protect the strangers, though it is eager to do so and they need its help?

IOLAUS
My children, we are like sailors who have escaped the wild blast of the storm and are a hand's breadth from dry land, but then are driven by winds into the deep again! That is how we are being thrust from this land when we are already at its shores and feeling safe. Ah me! Why did you give me pleasure before, cruel Hope, if you did not intend to carry out your favor to the end? For, of

---

415 πυκνὰς Bothe: πικρὰς L
416 δίκαιος Dobree: -ον L
417 ἐμοῦ Elmsley: ἐμὴν L
426 χρήζουσιν Herwerden: -ουσαν L

435 συγγνωστὰ γάρ τοι καὶ τὰ τοῦδ', εἰ μὴ θέλει
κτείνειν πολιτῶν παῖδας, αἰνέσαι δ' ἔχω
καὶ τἀνθάδ'· εἰ θεοῖσι δὴ δοκεῖ τάδε
πράσσειν ἔμ', οὔτοι σοί γ' ἀπόλλυται χάρις.
ὦ παῖδες, ὑμῖν δ' οὐκ ἔχω τί χρήσομαι.
440 ποῖ τρεψόμεσθα; τίς γὰρ ἄστεπτος θεῶν;
ποῖον δὲ γαίας ἔρκος οὐκ ἀφίγμεθα;
ὀλούμεθ', ὦ τέκν'· ἐκδοθησόμεσθα δή.
κἀμοῦ μὲν οὐδὲν εἴ με χρὴ θανεῖν μέλει,
πλὴν εἴ τι τέρψω τοὺς ἐμοὺς ἐχθροὺς θανών·
445 ὑμᾶς δὲ κλαίω καὶ κατοικτίρω, τέκνα,
καὶ τὴν γεραιὰν μητέρ' Ἀλκμήνην πατρός.
ὦ δυστάλαινα τοῦ μακροῦ βίου σέθεν,
τλήμων δὲ κἀγὼ πολλὰ μοχθήσας μάτην.
χρῆν χρῆν ἄρ' ἡμᾶς ἀνδρὸς εἰς ἐχθροῦ χέρας
450 πεσόντας αἰσχρῶς καὶ κακῶς λιπεῖν βίον.
    ἀλλ' οἶσθ' ὅ μοι σύμπραξον· οὐχ ἅπασα γὰρ
πέφευγεν ἐλπὶς τῶνδέ μοι σωτηρίας·
ἔμ' ἔκδος Ἀργείοισιν ἀντὶ τῶνδ', ἄναξ,
καὶ μήτε κινδύνευε, σωθήτω τέ μοι
455 τέκν'· οὐ φιλεῖν δεῖ τὴν ἐμὴν ψυχήν· ἴτω.
μάλιστα δ' Εὐρυσθεύς με βούλοιτ' ἂν λαβὼν
τὸν Ἡράκλειον σύμμαχον καθυβρίσαι·
σκαιὸς γὰρ ἀνήρ. τοῖς σοφοῖς δ' εὐκτὸν σοφῷ
ἔχθραν συνάπτειν, μὴ ἀμαθεῖ φρονήματι·
460 πολλῆς γὰρ αἰδοῦς καὶ δίκης τις ἂν τύχοι.

ΧΟΡΟΣ

ὦ πρέσβυ, μή νυν τῶνδ' ἐπαιτιῶ πόλιν·

course, Demophon's position is quite understandable,
that he is unwilling to kill the children of his citizens, and
I can find words of praise even for what has happened
here: if it is the gods' will that I should fare thus, you at
any rate have not lost the gratitude we owe you.

My children, I do not know what I am to do for you.
Where shall we turn? What god's altars have we not gar-
landed? To what land have we not come for refuge? We
are doomed, my children, now we shall be given up! I do
not care for myself if I must die, unless my death gives
pleasure to my enemies. It is you I weep for, you I pity,
my children, and Alcmene your aged grandmother! How
unlucky you are in your long life! I too am luckless for
having toiled so long in vain. It was fated, fated, I see it
now, that we must fall into the hands of our enemy and
lose our lives in disgrace and pain!

(to Demophon) But here is what you must help me to
do (for I have not completely lost hope for the safety of
the children): hand me over to the Argives, my lord, in
place of these children. Do not put yourself in danger,
but let these my children be saved. It is not right for me
to cling to my own life: let it pass. Eurystheus would
most like to get hold of me and outrage Heracles' old ally.
The man lacks all feeling. Wise men must pray that they
will have a wise man for a foe, not one of unfeeling pride:
for in that case a man gets pity and just treatment in full
measure.

CHORUS LEADER
Old sir, do not lay this charge against the city. For though

---

461 τῶνδ' Valckenaer: τήνδ' L

τάχ' ἂν γὰρ ἡμῖν ψευδὲς ἀλλ' ὅμως κακὸν
γένοιτ' ὄνειδος ὡς ξένους προυδώκαμεν.

ΔΗΜΟΦΩΝ

γενναῖα μὲν τάδ' εἶπας ἀλλ' ἀμήχανα.
465 οὐ σοῦ χατίζων δεῦρ' ἄναξ στρατηλατεῖ
(τί γὰρ γέροντος ἀνδρὸς Εὐρυσθεῖ πλέον
θανόντος;) ἀλλὰ τούσδε βούλεται κτανεῖν.
δεινὸν γὰρ ἐχθροῖς βλαστάνοντες εὐγενεῖς,
νεανίαι τε καὶ πατρὸς μεμνημένοι
470 λύμης· ἃ κεῖνον πάντα προσκοπεῖν χρεών.
ἀλλ' εἴ τιν' ἄλλην οἶσθα καιριωτέραν
βουλήν, ἑτοίμαζ', ὡς ἔγωγ' ἀμήχανος
χρησμῶν ἀκούσας εἰμὶ καὶ φόβου πλέως.

ΠΑΡΘΕΝΟΣ

ξένοι, θράσος μοι μηδὲν ἐξόδοις ἐμαῖς
475 προσθῆτε· πρῶτον γὰρ τόδ' ἐξαιτήσομαι·
γυναικὶ γὰρ σιγή τε καὶ τὸ σωφρονεῖν
κάλλιστον εἴσω θ' ἥσυχον μένειν δόμων.
τῶν σῶν δ' ἀκούσασ', Ἰόλεως, στεναγμάτων
ἐξῆλθον, οὐ ταχθεῖσα πρεσβεύειν γένους,
480 ἀλλ', εἰμὶ γάρ πως πρόσφορος, μέλει δέ μοι
μάλιστ' ἀδελφῶν τῶνδε κἀμαυτῆς πέρι,
θέλω πυθέσθαι μὴ 'πὶ τοῖς πάλαι κακοῖς
προσκείμενόν τι πῆμα σὴν δάκνει φρένα.

462 ψευδὲς Nauck: ψεῦδος L

[a] The speaker indication in the manuscripts calls her

54

it may be false, it would still be a shameful reproach, that we betrayed strangers.

DEMOPHON

The suggestion you make is noble but impossible. It is not from desire for you that the king has marched his army here (for what profit does Eurytheus have in the death of an old man?) but to kill these children. Noble offspring are a terror to enemies when they grow to manhood and remember the outrage committed against their father. Eurystheus must provide against all this. But if you know of any other more suitable plan, put it at our disposal, for I have heard the oracles and am helpless and full of fear.

Enter MAIDEN, *one of the daughters of Heracles, from the temple.*

MAIDEN[a]

Strangers, please do not consider my coming out to be overbold: this is the first indulgence I shall ask. I know that for a woman silence is best, and modest behavior, and staying quietly within doors. But since I heard your anguished words, Iolaus, I have come out. I have not, to be sure, been designated the family's most important member, but since I am in some way fit to hear this and since I care greatly about my brothers and myself, I wish to ask whether some new misfortune on top of our old troubles is vexing your mind.

Macaria, the name she bears in later tradition, but since the text of the play does not name her, editors suppose that Euripides would have called her simply "Maiden." See note on line 55 above.

ΙΟΛΑΟΣ

ὦ παῖ, μάλιστά σ᾽ οὐ νεωστὶ δὴ τέκνων
485 τῶν Ἡρακλείων ἐνδίκως αἰνεῖν ἔχω.
ἡμῖν δὲ δόξας εὖ προχωρῆσαι δρόμος
πάλιν μεθέστηκ᾽ αὖθις ἐς τἀμήχανον·
χρησμῶν γὰρ ᾠδοὺς φησι σημαίνειν ὅδε
οὐ ταῦρον οὐδὲ μόσχον ἀλλὰ παρθένον
490 σφάξαι κόρῃ Δήμητρος ἥτις εὐγενής,
εἰ χρὴ μὲν ἡμᾶς, χρὴ δὲ τήνδ᾽ εἶναι πόλιν.
ταῦτ᾽ οὖν ἀμηχανοῦμεν· οὔτε γὰρ τέκνα
σφάξειν ὅδ᾽ αὑτοῦ φησιν οὔτ᾽ ἄλλου τινός.
κἀμοὶ λέγει μὲν οὐ σαφῶς, λέγει δέ πως,
495 εἰ μή τι τούτων ἐξαμηχανήσομεν,
ἡμᾶς μὲν ἄλλην γαῖαν εὑρίσκειν τινά,
αὐτὸς δὲ σῶσαι τήνδε βούλεσθαι χθόνα.

ΠΑΡΘΕΝΟΣ

ἐν τῷδε κἀχόμεσθα σωθῆναι λόγῳ;

ΙΟΛΑΟΣ

ἐν τῷδε, τἆλλα γ᾽ εὐτυχῶς πεπραγότες.

ΠΑΡΘΕΝΟΣ

500 μή νυν τρέσῃς ἔτ᾽ ἐχθρὸν Ἀργείων δόρυ·
ἐγὼ γὰρ αὐτὴ πρὶν κελευσθῆναι, γέρον,
θνῄσκειν ἑτοίμη καὶ παρίστασθαι σφαγῇ.
τί φήσομεν γάρ, εἰ πόλις μὲν ἀξιοῖ
κίνδυνον ἡμῶν οὕνεκ᾽ αἴρεσθαι μέγαν,
505 αὐτοὶ δὲ προστιθέντες ἄλλοισιν πόνους,
παρόν σφε σῶσαι, φευξόμεσθα μὴ θανεῖν;

IOLAUS

My child, for a long time now I have been justified in praising you more than any other of the children of Heracles. We thought that our course had gone well, but now we find that it has changed once more into trouble past all help. This man says that the chanters of oracles tell us to sacrifice not a bull or a calf but a maiden of noble parentage to Demeter's daughter if we are to survive and this city likewise. This is our perplexity: the king says that he will not sacrifice either his own children or those of anyone else. And he tells me, not in plain words but all the same, that unless we find a way out of our difficulties, he wants us to find some other land, since he desires to save this country.

MAIDEN

Is it this prophecy that prevents us from reaching safety?

IOLAUS

Yes, this prophecy. In all else our fortune is good.

MAIDEN

Then fear no more the Argive enemy's spear! I am ready, old man, of my own accord and unbidden, to appear for sacrifice and be killed. For what shall we say if this city is willing to run great risks on our behalf, and yet we, who lay toil and struggle on others, run away from death when it lies in our power to rescue *them*? It must not be so, for

---

486 δρόμος Jacobs: δόμος L   490 κόρη Δήμητρος Pierson: κελεύειν μητρὸς L   497 βούλεσθαι Reiske: βούλεται L   498 κἀχόμεσθα Elmsley: κεύχ- L   500 Ἀργείων Elmsley: ἀργεῖον L   504 αἴρεσθαι Elmsley: αἱρεῖσθαι L   506 σφε σῶσαι Nauck: σεσῶσθαι L

57

οὐ δῆτ', ἐπεί τοι καὶ γέλωτος ἄξια,
στένειν μὲν ἱκέτας δαιμόνων καθημένους,
πατρὸς δ' ἐκείνου φύντας οὗ πεφύκαμεν
510 κακοὺς ὁρᾶσθαι· ποῦ τάδ' ἐν χρηστοῖς πρέπει;
κάλλιον, οἶμαι, τῆσδ'—ὃ μὴ τύχοι ποτέ—
πόλεως ἁλούσης χεῖρας εἰς ἐχθρῶν πεσεῖν
κἄπειτ' ἄτιμα πατρὸς οὖσαν εὐγενοῦς
παθοῦσαν Ἅιδην μηδὲν ἧσσον εἰσιδεῖν.
515 ἀλλ' ἐκπεσοῦσα τῆσδ' ἀλητεύσω χθονός;
κοὐκ αἰσχυνοῦμαι δῆτ', ἐὰν δή τις λέγῃ
Τί δεῦρ' ἀφίκεσθ' ἱκεσίοισι σὺν κλάδοις
αὐτοὶ φιλοψυχοῦντες; ἔξιτε χθονός·
κακοῖς γὰρ ἡμεῖς οὐ προσωφελήσομεν.
520 ἀλλ' οὐδὲ μέντοι, τῶνδε μὲν τεθνηκότων,
αὐτὴ δὲ σωθεῖσ', ἐλπίδ' εὖ πράξειν ἔχω·
πολλοὶ γὰρ ἤδη τῇδε προύδοσαν φίλους.
τίς γὰρ κόρην ἔρημον ἢ δάμαρτ' ἔχειν
ἢ παιδοποιεῖν ἐξ ἐμοῦ βουλήσεται;
525 οὔκουν θανεῖν ἄμεινον ἢ τούτων τυχεῖν
ἀναξίαν; ἄλλῃ δὲ κἂν πρέποι τινὶ
μᾶλλον τάδ', ἥτις μὴ 'πίσημος ὡς ἐγώ.
ἡγεῖσθ' ὅπου δὴ σῶμα κατθανεῖν τόδε
καὶ στεμματοῦσθαι καὶ κατάρχεσθαι δοκεῖ·
530 νικᾶτε δ' ἐχθρούς· ἥδε γὰρ ψυχὴ πάρα
ἑκοῦσα κοὐκ ἄκουσα, κἀξαγγέλλομαι
θνῄσκειν ἀδελφῶν τῶνδε κἀμαυτῆς ὕπερ.
εὕρημα γάρ τοι μὴ φιλοψυχοῦσ' ἐγὼ
κάλλιστον ηὕρηκ', εὐκλεῶς λιπεῖν βίον.

it deserves nothing but mockery if we sit and groan as
suppliants of the gods and yet, though we are descended
from that great man who is our father, show ourselves to
be cowards. How can this be fitting in the eyes of men of
nobility? Much finer, I suppose, if this city were to be
captured (God forbid!) and I were to fall into the hands of
the enemy! Then when I, daughter of a noble father, have
suffered dishonor, I shall go to my death all the same!
But shall I then accept exile from this land and be a wan-
derer? Shall I not feel shame if someone thereafter asks,
"Why do you come here with your suppliant branches
when you yourselves lack courage? Leave this land: for
we do not give help to the base"?

But not even if these boys perished and I lived on
would I have the hope of happiness (and many ere now
have betrayed friends in this hope): for who would wish
to take to wife a girl bereft of family or would desire to
beget children with me? Is it not better to die than to win
a fate I do not deserve? The other course might more
befit someone else who is not as illustrious as I.

Lead me to the place where it seems good that my
body should be killed and garlanded and consecrated to
the goddess! Defeat the enemy! For my life is at your
disposal, full willingly, and I offer to be put to death on
my brothers' behalf and on my own. For, mark it well, by
not clinging to my life I have made a most splendid dis-
covery, how to die with glory.

[511] ὅ Lenting: ἅ L   [513] κἄπειτ' ἄτιμα Kirchhoff: κἄπειτα
τινὰ L   [519] κακοῖς Blaydes: κακοὺς L   [526] κἄν Elmsley:
καὶ L   [528] δὴ Broadhead: δεῖ L   [529] στεμματοῦσθαι . . .
κατάρχεσθαι Broadhead: στεμματοῦτε . . . κατάρχεσθ' εἰ L

ΧΟΡΟΣ

535 φεῦ φεῦ, τί λέξω παρθένου μέγαν λόγον
κλυών, ἀδελφῶν ἢ πάρος θέλει θανεῖν;
τούτων τίς ἂν λέξειε γενναίους λόγους
μᾶλλον, τίς ἂν δράσειεν ἀνθρώπων ἔτι;

ΙΟΛΑΟΣ

ὦ τέκνον, οὐκ ἔστ' ἄλλοθεν τὸ σὸν κάρα
540 ἀλλ' ἐξ ἐκείνου· σπέρμα τῆς θείας φρενὸς
πέφυκας Ἡράκλειον· οὐδ' αἰσχύνομαι
τοῖς σοῖς λόγοισι, τῇ τύχῃ δ' ἀλγύνομαι.
ἀλλ' ᾗ γένοιτ' ἂν ἐνδικωτέρως φράσω·
πάσας ἀδελφὰς δεῦρο χρὴ τὰς σὰς καλεῖν,
545 κᾆθ' ἡ λαχοῦσα θνῃσκέτω γένους ὕπερ·
σὲ δ' οὐ δίκαιον κατθανεῖν ἄνευ πάλου.

ΠΑΡΘΕΝΟΣ

οὐκ ἂν θάνοιμι τῇ τύχῃ λαχοῦσ' ἐγώ·
χάρις γὰρ οὐ πρόσεστι· μὴ λέξῃς, γέρον.
ἀλλ', εἰ μὲν ἐνδέχεσθε καὶ βούλεσθέ μοι
550 χρῆσθαι προθύμῳ, τὴν ἐμὴν ψυχὴν ἐγὼ
δίδωμ' ἑκοῦσα τοῖσδ', ἀναγκασθεῖσα δ' οὔ.

ΙΟΛΑΟΣ

φεῦ·
ὅδ' αὖ λόγος σοι τοῦ πρὶν εὐγενέστερος,
κἀκεῖνος ἦν ἄριστος· ἀλλ' ὑπερφέρεις
555 τόλμῃ τε τόλμαν καὶ λόγῳ χρηστῷ λόγον.
οὐ μὴν κελεύω γ' οὐδ' ἀπεννέπω, τέκνον,
θνῄσκειν σ'· ἀδελφοὺς <δ'> ὠφελεῖς θανοῦσα σούς.

CHORUS LEADER

Ah me! What shall I say in response to the brave words of
this maiden, who is willing to die for her brothers? What
mortal will ever speak or carry out nobler sentiments than
these?

IOLAUS

My child, your spirit was born of none else than that hero:
you are the seed of that divine spirit of Heracles. And
your words bring me no disgrace, though your fate causes
me grief. Yet I shall tell you how things may be done with
greater justice: we must call all your sisters hither, and
the one that draws the lot must die for the family. It is not
right for you to die without drawing lots.

MAIDEN

I shall not die by the chance drawing of lots. For such a
death wins no thanks: do not suggest it, old man. Rather,
if you approve and desire to make use of my zeal, I give
my life willingly to these my brothers, but not under com-
pulsion.

IOLAUS

Ah! This speech is more noble than the last, and the last
was noble indeed! Each brave deed of yours and each
noble word surpasses its predecessor. I do not bid you to
die, nor yet do I forbid it. But if you die, you benefit your
brothers.

---

⁵⁴¹ Ἡράκλειον Hartung: -ῆος L
⁵⁴⁴ ἀδελφὰς δεῦρο χρὴ τὰς σὰς Nauck: ἀ. τῆσδε δ. χ. L
⁵⁵⁰ προθύμῳ Barnes: -μως L
⁵⁵⁷ σ' Reiske: γ' L   <δ'> Barnes

61

ΠΑΡΘΕΝΟΣ

σοφῶς ἔλεξας· μὴ τρέσῃς μιάσματος
τοὐμοῦ μετασχεῖν, ἀλλ' ἐλευθερῶ σ' ἐγώ.
560   ἔπου δέ, πρέσβυ (σῇ γὰρ ἐνθανεῖν χερὶ
θέλω) πέπλοις δὲ σῶμ' ἐμὸν κρύψον παρών,
ἐπεὶ σφαγῆς γε πρὸς τὸ δεινὸν εἶμ' ἐγώ,
εἴπερ πέφυκα πατρὸς οὗπερ εὔχομαι.

ΙΟΛΑΟΣ

οὐκ ἂν δυναίμην σῷ παρεστάναι μόρῳ.

ΠΑΡΘΕΝΟΣ

565   σὺ δ' ἀλλὰ τοῦδε χρῇζε, μή μ' ἐν ἀρσένων
ἀλλ' ἐν γυναικῶν χερσὶν ἐκπνεῦσαι βίον.

ΔΗΜΟΦΩΝ

ἔσται τάδ', ὦ τάλαινα παρθένων, ἐπεὶ
κἀμοὶ τόδ' αἰσχρόν, μή σε κοσμεῖσθαι καλῶς,
πολλῶν ἕκατι, τῆς τε σῆς εὐψυχίας
570   καὶ τοῦ δικαίου. τλημονεστάτην δέ σε
πασῶν γυναικῶν εἶδον ὀφθαλμοῖς ἐγώ.
ἀλλ', εἴ τι βούλῃ, τούσδε τὸν γέροντά τε
χώρει προσειποῦσ' ὕστατον προσφθεγμάτων.

ΠΑΡΘΕΝΟΣ

ὦ χαῖρε, πρέσβυ, χαῖρε καὶ δίδασκέ μοι
575   τοιούσδε τούσδε παῖδας, ἐς τὸ πᾶν σοφούς,
ὥσπερ σύ, μηδὲν μᾶλλον· ἀρκέσουσι γάρ.

558 ἔλεξας Nauck: κελεύεις L, ex 556 lapsum
559 ἐλευθερῶ σ' ἐγώ A. Palmer: ἐλευθέρως θάνω L

MAIDEN

Your words are wise. Do not be afraid that you will be partaker of the stain of my blood. Instead, I set you free from it.

But come with me, old man (for I wish to die in your arms) and stand by me and cover my dead body with my garments (for I am going to the terror of slaughter), if indeed I am sprung from the man I claim as father.

IOLAUS

I could not stand by as you are killed.

MAIDEN

Well at least ask this man's permission for me to breathe my last in the hands not of men but of women.

DEMOPHON

It shall be as you ask, luckless maiden, since it would be a disgrace to me also if you were not given due funeral rites. There are many reasons, your bravery and the justice of your request. You are the bravest of all women, the bravest I have ever seen. But, if it is your will, say your last words as a farewell to your brothers here and to the old man and go.

MAIDEN

Farewell, old man, farewell! Please train up these boys to be such men as yourself, wise for every occasion, not more wise than that: that will suffice. With all your zeal

---

[562] ἕπου (σφαγῆς γὰρ . . . ἐγώ) Willink

[567n] Δη. Heath: Ἰο. L   [573] προσφθεγμάτων Hermann: πρόσφθεγμά μοι L (μοι ex 574 oriundum)

[576] ἀρκέσουσι Stephanus: ἀρέσκουσι L

πειρῶ δὲ σῶσαι μὴ θανεῖν, πρόθυμος ὤν·
σοὶ παῖδές ἐσμεν, σαῖν χεροῖν τεθράμμεθα.
ὁρᾷς δὲ κἀμὲ τὴν ἐμὴν ὥραν γάμου
580   διδοῦσαν, ἀντὶ τῶνδε κατθανουμένην.
ὑμεῖς τ', ἀδελφῶν ἡ παροῦσ' ὁμιλία,
εὐδαιμονοῖτε, καὶ γένοιθ' ὑμῖν ὅσων
ἡμὴ πάροιθε καρδία σφαλήσεται.
καὶ τὸν γέροντα τήν τ' ἔσω γραῖαν δόμων
585   τιμᾶτε πατρὸς μητέρ' Ἀλκμήνην ἐμοῦ
ξένους τε τούσδε. κἂν ἀπαλλαγῇ πόνων
καὶ νόστος ὑμῖν εὑρεθῇ ποτ' ἐκ θεῶν,
μέμνησθε τὴν σώτειραν ὡς θάψαι χρεών·
κάλλιστά τοι δίκαιον· οὐ γὰρ ἐνδεὴς
590   ὑμῖν παρέστην ἀλλὰ προύθανον γένους.
τάδ' ἀντὶ παίδων ἐστί μοι κειμήλια
καὶ παρθενείας, εἴ τι δὴ κατὰ χθονός·
εἴη γε μέντοι μηδέν· εἰ γὰρ ἕξομεν
κἀκεῖ μερίμνας οἱ θανούμενοι βροτῶν,
595   οὐκ οἶδ' ὅποι τις τρέψεται· τὸ γὰρ θανεῖν
κακῶν μέγιστον φάρμακον νομίζεται.

ΙΟΛΑΟΣ

ἀλλ', ὦ μέγιστον ἐκπρέπουσ' εὐψυχίᾳ
πασῶν γυναικῶν, ἴσθι, τιμιωτάτη
καὶ ζῶσ' ὑφ' ἡμῶν καὶ θανοῦσ' ἔσῃ πολύ·
600   καὶ χαῖρε· δυσφημεῖν γὰρ ἅζομαι θεὰν
ᾗ σὸν κατῆρκται σῶμα, Δήμητρος κόρην.
ὦ παῖδες, οἰχόμεσθα· λύεται μέλη

try to save them from death. We are your children, we
have been raised by your hands. You see that I am sacri-
ficing my chance of marriage and am about to die in their
place. And you, my brothers who are with me, may you
have happiness, and may there fall to your lot all the
things my heart shall now not enjoy! Treat with honor the
old man and also the old woman within the house,
Alcmene, my grandmother, and also these your hosts.
And if the gods ever grant you a respite from your trou-
bles and a return to your home, remember what manner
of burial you ought to give to the woman who saved your
lives. A burial with all honors, you may be sure, would be
right. For I did not fail to help you but died on behalf of
the family. These deeds I have as treasures to replace
children and the days of my maidenhood—if indeed there
is any existence beneath the earth. But I pray that there
may not be. For if we mortals who are on the point of
death are to have cares even in that place, where can we
turn? For death, men think, is trouble's greatest cure.

IOLAUS

But know, O bravest of all women, that both in life and in
death we honor you above all others! Farewell! Rever-
ence keeps me from speaking ill of Demeter's daughter,
the goddess to whom your body is devoted.

Exit MAIDEN *and* DEMOPHON *by Eisodos B.*

My children, I am destroyed! My limbs melt with

---

[583] σφαλήσεται Badham: σφαγ- L
[597] εὐψυχίᾳ Scaliger: -ίας L
[602] λύεται Milton: δύεται L

λύπῃ· λάβεσθε κἀς ἕδραν μ' ἐρείσατε
αὐτοῦ πέπλοισι τοῖσδε κρύψαντες, τέκνα.
605 ὡς οὔτε τούτοις ἥδομαι πεπραγμένοις
χρησμοῦ τε μὴ κρανθέντος οὐ βιώσιμον·
μείζων γὰρ ἄτη· συμφορὰ δὲ καὶ τάδε.

ΧΟΡΟΣ

στρ.

οὔτινά φημι θεῶν ἄτερ ὄλβιον, οὐ βαρύποτμον,
ἄνδρα γενέσθαι·
610 οὐδὲ τὸν αὐτὸν ἀεὶ 'μβεβάναι δόμον
εὐτυχίᾳ· παρὰ δ' ἄλλαν ἄλλα
μοῖρα διώκει.
τὸν μὲν ἀφ' ὑψηλῶν βραχὺν ᾤκισε,
τὸν δ' †ἀλήταν† εὐδαίμονα τεύχει.
615 μόρσιμα δ' οὔτι φυγεῖν θέμις, οὐ σοφί-
ᾳ τις ἀπώσεται, ἀλλὰ μάταν
ὁ πρόθυμος ἀεὶ πόνον ἕξει.

ἀντ.

ἀλλὰ σὺ μὴ προπεσὼν τὰ θεῶν στένε μηδ' ὑπεράλγει
620 φροντίδα λύπᾳ·
εὐδόκιμον γὰρ ἔχει θανάτου μέρος
ἁ μελέα πρό τ' ἀδελφῶν καὶ γᾶς·
οὐδ' ἀκλεής νιν
δόξα πρὸς ἀνθρώπων ὑποδέξεται·
625 ἁ δ' ἀρετὰ βαίνει διὰ μόχθων.
ἄξια μὲν πατρός, ἄξια δ' εὐγενί-
ας τάδε γίγνεται· εἰ δὲ σέβεις
θανάτους ἀγαθῶν, μετέχω σοι.

66

grief! Take hold of me, children, and set me down on the altar, right here, covering me with my garments! For I take no pleasure in what has occurred, and if the oracle is not fulfilled, my life is no life at all. My ruin will be all the greater. What we have seen is already a calamity.

Some of the sons set Iolaus before the temple and cover his head.

CHORUS
No man, I say, is blessed or cursed with disaster without the will of the gods. The same house does not always tread the path of prosperity. One fortune after another pursues us. It takes one man from his loftiness and settles him in low estate, and moves another from misery to blessedness. It is not possible to flee from fate, no one by skill can ward it off, and the man who is eager to do so shall always toil in vain.

But do not fall prostrate and lament the gods' dispensation, do not grieve excessively in your heart. For the unhappy girl has a death that is glorious, a death on behalf of her brothers and the land, and high renown will await her on the lips of men. Heroic goodness treads a path of toil. Her deeds were worthy of her father, worthy of her noble lineage. If you show reverence to the death of the brave, in this I am your partner.

---

610 ’μβεβάναι Pearson: βεβάναι L
611 ἄλλαν Seidler: ἄλλον L
614 ἀτίταν Lobeck
619 στένε Lesky: ὕπερ L

ΘΕΡΑΠΩΝ

630 ὦ τέκνα, χαίρετ'· Ἰόλεως δὲ ποῦ γέρων
[μήτηρ τε πατρὸς τῆσδ' ἕδρας ἀποστατεῖ];

ΙΟΛΑΟΣ

πάρεσμεν, οἵα δή γ' ἐμοῦ παρουσία.

ΘΕΡΑΠΩΝ

τί χρῆμα κεῖσαι καὶ κατηφὲς ὄμμ' ἔχεις;

ΙΟΛΑΟΣ

φροντίς τις ἦλθ' οἰκεῖος, ᾗ συνειχόμην.

ΘΕΡΑΠΩΝ

635 ἔπαιρέ νυν σεαυτόν, ὄρθωσον κάρα.

ΙΟΛΑΟΣ

γέροντές ἐσμεν κοὐδαμῶς ἐρρώμεθα.

ΘΕΡΑΠΩΝ

ἥκω γε μέντοι χάρμα σοι φέρων μέγα.

ΙΟΛΑΟΣ

τίς δ' εἶ σύ; ποῦ σοι συντυχὼν ἀμνημονῶ;

ΘΕΡΑΠΩΝ

Ὕλλου πενέστης· οὔ με γιγνώσκεις ὁρῶν;

ΙΟΛΑΟΣ

640 ὦ φίλταθ', ἥκετ' ἆρα σῷ κᾆτερ βλάβης;

ΘΕΡΑΠΩΝ

μάλιστα· καὶ πρός γ' εὐτυχεῖς τὰ νῦν τάδε.

631 v. del. Klinkenberg
634 συνειχόμην Elmsley: -εσχόμην L

Enter SERVANT *by Eisodos A.*

SERVANT
Children, greeting. Where is the old man Iolaus [and where has your grandmother gone from this altar]?

IOLAUS
I am here, useless though my presence is.

SERVANT
Why are you lying down? Why is your face downcast?

IOLAUS
A family sorrow has come upon us. With that I was distressed.

SERVANT
Then rouse yourself up, raise up your head!

IOLAUS
I am an old man: I do not have the strength.

SERVANT
But I come bringing you great gladness.

IOLAUS
Who are you? Where is it I met you? I have forgotten.

SERVANT
I am Hyllus' vassal. Do you not recognize me?

IOLAUS
My dear man, so you have all arrived safe and unharmed?

SERVANT
Yes, and what is more we enjoy, at the moment, good fortune.

---

640 ἥκετ' . . . σῷ κᾶτερ Willink post Kovacs: ἥκεις ἆρα σωτὴρ νῷν

ΙΟΛΑΟΣ

ὦ μῆτερ ἐσθλοῦ παιδός, Ἀλκμήνην λέγω,
ἔξελθ', ἄκουσον τοῦδε φιλτάτους λόγους.
πάλαι γὰρ ὠδίνουσα τῶν ἀφιγμένων
645   ψυχὴν ἐτῆκου νόστος εἰ γενήσεται.

ΑΛΚΜΗΝΗ

τί χρῆμ' αὐτῆς πᾶν τόδ' ἐπλήσθη στέγος,
Ἰόλαε; μῶν τίς σ' αὖ βιάζεται παρὼν
κῆρυξ ἀπ' Ἄργους; ἀσθενὴς μὲν ἤ γ' ἐμὴ
ῥώμη, τοσόνδε δ' εἰδέναι σε χρή, ξένε·
650   οὐκ ἔστ' ἄγειν σε τούσδ' ἐμοῦ ζώσης ποτέ.
ἦ τἄρ' ἐκείνου μὴ νομιζοίμην ἐγὼ
μήτηρ ἔτ'· εἰ δὲ τῶνδε προσθίξῃ χερί,
δυοῖν γερόντοιν οὐ καλῶς ἀγωνιῇ.

ΙΟΛΑΟΣ

θάρσει, γεραιά, μὴ τρέσῃς· οὐκ Ἀργόθεν
655   κῆρυξ ἀφῖκται πολεμίους λόγους ἔχων.

ΑΛΚΜΗΝΗ

τί γὰρ βοὴν ἔστησας ἄγγελον φόβου;

ΙΟΛΑΟΣ

σὺ πρόσθε ναοῦ τοῦδ' ὅπως βαίης πέλας.

ΑΛΚΜΗΝΗ

οὐκ ἴσμεν ἡμεῖς ταῦτα· τίς γάρ ἐσθ' ὅδε;

---

643 τοῦδε Elmsley: τούσδε L
649 σε χρή Dobree: σ' ἐχρῆν L

IOLAUS

(*shouting*) Mother of a noble son, Alcmene, come out and hear the welcome words of this man! For you have long languished in doubt whether your grandsons would ever return, as now they have!

Enter ALCMENE *from the temple.*

ALCMENE

Why, Iolaus, has this whole temple been filled with shouting? Has a herald come a second time from Argos to do you violence? My strength may be weak, stranger, but you must realize this: you cannot remove these children while I still live. May I no longer be regarded as Heracles' mother! If you lay a hand on them, you will face a dishonorable struggle with a pair of grayheads.

IOLAUS

Courage, old woman, do not be afraid! No herald has come from Argos with hostile message.

ALCMENE

Then why did you raise the shout that signals fear?

IOLAUS

So that you would come out of the temple and meet this man.

ALCMENE

I do not understand. Who is he?

---

⁶⁵² προσθίξη Elmsley: -ξεις L
⁶⁵⁷ σὺ Brodaeus: σὲ L

71

ΙΟΛΑΟΣ

ἥκοντα παῖδα παιδὸς ἀγγέλλει σέθεν.

ΑΛΚΜΗΝΗ

660 ὦ χαῖρε καὶ σὺ τοῖσδε τοῖς ἀγγέλμασιν.
ἀτὰρ τί χώρᾳ τῇδε προσβαλὼν πόδα
<πατρὸς προσελθεῖν μητέρ' ὧδ' ἀναίνεται>;
ποῦ νῦν ἄπεστι; τίς νιν εἶργε συμφορὰ
σὺν σοὶ φανέντα δεῦρ' ἐμὴν τέρψαι φρένα;

ΘΕΡΑΠΩΝ

στρατὸν καθίζει τάσσεταί θ' ὃν ἦλθ' ἔχων.

ΑΛΚΜΗΝΗ

665 τοῦδ' οὐκέθ' ἡμῖν τοῦ λόγου μέτεστι δή.

ΙΟΛΑΟΣ

μέτεστιν· ἡμῶν δ' ἔργον ἱστορεῖν τάδε.

ΘΕΡΑΠΩΝ

τί δῆτα βούλῃ τῶν πεπραγμένων μαθεῖν;

ΙΟΛΑΟΣ

πόσον τι πλῆθος συμμάχων πάρεστ' ἔχων;

ΘΕΡΑΠΩΝ

πολλούς· ἀριθμὸν δ' ἄλλον οὐκ ἔχω φράσαι.

ΙΟΛΑΟΣ

670 ἴσασιν, οἶμαι, ταῦτ' Ἀθηναίων πρόμοι.

ΘΕΡΑΠΩΝ

ἴσασι, καὶ δὴ λαιὸν ἕστηκεν κέρας.

661 post h. v. lac. stat. Kovacs

72

IOLAUS

He brings word that your grandson has returned.

ALCMENE

I wish you joy as well, sir, for your news. But why, when he has arrived in this land, <does he refuse to come to see his grandmother?> Where is he? What misfortune prevents him from coming here with you and giving joy to my heart?

SERVANT

He is encamping and marshaling the army he brought with him.

ALCMENE

This last report is of no concern to us.

IOLAUS

But it is: it is my task to inquire into this.

SERVANT

Which events do you want to learn of?

IOLAUS

How large an allied force has he arrived with?

SERVANT

A large one. The number beyond this I cannot tell you.

IOLAUS

The Athenian leaders, I suppose, are aware of this.

SERVANT

Yes, and what is more, he is stationed on their left wing.

73

ΙΟΛΑΟΣ

ἤδη γὰρ ὡς ἐς ἔργον ὥπλισται στρατός;

ΘΕΡΑΠΩΝ

καὶ δὴ παρῆκται σφάγια τάξεων ἑκάς.

ΙΟΛΑΟΣ

πόσον τι δ' ἔστ' ἄπωθεν Ἀργεῖον δόρυ;

ΘΕΡΑΠΩΝ

675 ὥστ' ἐξορᾶσθαι τὸν στρατηγὸν ἐμφανῶς.

ΙΟΛΑΟΣ

τί δρῶντα; μῶν τάσσοντα πολεμίων στίχας;

ΘΕΡΑΠΩΝ

ἠκάζομεν ταῦτ'· οὐ γὰρ ἐξηκούομεν.
   ἀλλ' εἶμ'· ἐρήμους δεσπότας τοὐμὸν μέρος
οὐκ ἂν θέλοιμι πολεμίοισι συμβαλεῖν.

ΙΟΛΑΟΣ

680 κἄγωγε σὺν σοί· ταὐτὰ γὰρ φροντίζομεν,
φίλοις παρόντες, ὡς ἔοιγμεν, ὠφελεῖν.

ΘΕΡΑΠΩΝ

ἥκιστα πρὸς σοῦ μῶρον ἦν εἰπεῖν ἔπος.

ΙΟΛΑΟΣ

683 καὶ μὴ μετασχεῖν γ' ἀλκίμου μάχης φίλοις.

ΘΕΡΑΠΩΝ

688 οὐκ ἔστιν, ὦ τᾶν, ἥ ποτ' ἦν ῥώμη σέθεν.

ΙΟΛΑΟΣ

689 ἀλλ' οὖν μαχοῦμαί γ' ἀριθμὸν οὐκ ἐλάσσοσιν.

IOLAUS

What? Is the force already armed for battle?

SERVANT

Yes, and sacrificial victims have been brought in front of the lines.

IOLAUS

How far off is the Argive army?

SERVANT

Close enough to see their general clearly.

IOLAUS

What is he doing? Marshaling the enemy ranks?

SERVANT

That was our guess. We could not hear him clearly.
    But I shall go. I would not like my masters to close on the enemy deprived of my part in their defense.

IOLAUS

I shall go with you. For we have the same thought, to stand by our friends and help them, as is fitting.

SERVANT

It would be most unlike you to utter a foolish word.

IOLAUS

Unlike me, too, to fail to join my friends in battle.

SERVANT

The strength you once had, my good master, is no more.

IOLAUS

I shall, at all events, *fight* against as many foes as before.

683–90 hoc ordine Zuntz

ΘΕΡΑΠΩΝ

690   σμικρὸν τὸ σὸν σήκωμα προστίθης φίλοις.

ΙΟΛΑΟΣ

687   οὐδεὶς ἔμ' ἐχθρῶν προσβλέπων ἀνέξεται.

ΘΕΡΑΠΩΝ

684   οὐκ ἔστ' ἐν ὄψει τραῦμα μὴ δρώσης χερός.

ΙΟΛΑΟΣ

685   τί δ'; οὐ θένοιμι κἂν ἐγὼ δι' ἀσπίδος;

ΘΕΡΑΠΩΝ

686   θένοις ἄν, ἀλλὰ πρόσθεν αὐτὸς ἂν πέσοις.

ΙΟΛΑΟΣ

691   μή τοί μ' ἔρυκε δρᾶν παρεσκευασμένον.

ΘΕΡΑΠΩΝ

δρᾶν μὲν σύ γ' οὐχ οἷός τε, βούλεσθαι δ' ἴσως.

ΙΟΛΑΟΣ

ὡς μ' οὐ μενοῦντα τἄλλα σοι λέγειν πάρα.

ΘΕΡΑΠΩΝ

πῶς οὖν ὁπλίτης τευχέων ἄτερ φανῇ;

ΙΟΛΑΟΣ

695   ἔστ' ἐν δόμοισιν ἔνδον αἰχμάλωθ' ὅπλα
τοῖσδ', οἷσι χρησόμεσθα· κἀποδώσομεν
ζῶντες, θανόντας δ' οὐκ ἀπαιτήσει θεός.
ἀλλ' εἴσιθ' εἴσω κἀπὸ πασσάλων ἑλὼν

685–6 θένοιμι . . . θένοις Pierson: σθέν- . . . σθέν- L
693 μ' οὐ Kirchhoff: μὴ L
694 ὁπλίτης Elmsley: -ταις L

SERVANT
Slight is the weight you add to your friends' side.

IOLAUS
No enemy will be able to endure looking me in the eye.

SERVANT
The sight of you will not wound without the help of your hand.

IOLAUS
What? Will not even *my* blow pierce their shields?

SERVANT
You may strike a blow, but you might fall down first.

IOLAUS
Do not stand in my way when I am prepared to act.

SERVANT
To act is not in your power, though you may wish.

IOLAUS
Say on, if you like: I will not stay to hear your words.

SERVANT
How can you appear as a hoplite if you have no armor?

IOLAUS
There are captured weapons in this temple. I shall make use of them. If I live, I shall give them back, but if I die, the god will not ask me for their return. Go in, take down

ἔνεγχ' ὁπλίτην κόσμον ὡς τάχιστά μοι.
700 αἰσχρὸν γὰρ οἰκούρημα γίγνεται τόδε,
τοὺς μὲν μάχεσθαι, τοὺς δὲ δειλίᾳ μένειν.

ΧΟΡΟΣ

λῆμα μὲν οὔπω στόρνυσι χρόνος
τὸ σόν, ἀλλ' ἡβᾷ, σῶμα δὲ φροῦδον.
τί πονεῖς ἄλλως ἃ σὲ μὲν βλάψει,
705 σμικρὰ δ' ὀνήσει πόλιν ἡμετέραν;
χρῆν γνωσιμαχεῖν σὴν ἡλικίαν,
τὰ δ' ἀμήχαν' ἐᾶν· οὐκ ἔστιν ὅπως
ἥβην κτήσῃ πάλιν αὖθις.

ΑΛΚΜΗΝΗ

τί χρῆμα; μέλλεις σῶν φρενῶν οὐκ ἔνδον ὢν
710 λιπεῖν μ' ἔρημον σὺν <τέκνου> τέκνοις ἐμοῖς;

ΙΟΛΑΟΣ

ἀνδρῶν γὰρ ἀλκή· σοὶ δὲ χρὴ τούτων μέλειν.

ΑΛΚΜΗΝΗ

τί δ'; ἢν θάνῃς σύ, πῶς ἐγὼ σωθήσομαι;

ΙΟΛΑΟΣ

παιδὸς μελήσει παισὶ τοῖς λελειμμένοις.

ΑΛΚΜΗΝΗ

ἢν δ' οὖν, ὃ μὴ γένοιτο, χρήσωνται τύχῃ;

706 χρῆν Elmsley: χρὴ L   σὴν Porson: τὴν L
709 sic interpunxit Zuntz: cf. 711

a suit of armor from its peg and bring it to me with all speed. This home watch of mine is a disgraceful thing: some of the men are joining in battle while others in cowardice stay behind.

Exit the SERVANT *into the temple.*

CHORUS LEADER
Time has not yet laid low your proud spirit: it is in its youth, though your body is all spent. Why do you take on vain struggles that will do you harm and little good to our city? At your age you should be fighting down this impulse and leaving impossible things alone. There is no way you will get back your youth again.

ALCMENE
What? Are you out of your senses? Do you mean to leave me bereft with my grandchildren?

IOLAUS
Yes, for fighting is men's work, while you must care for these children.

ALCMENE
But if you die, how shall I survive?

IOLAUS
Your grandsons who are left will care for you.

ALCMENE
But what if, God forbid, something should happen to them?

---

710 <τέκνον> Vitelli
713 παισὶ Canter: πᾶσι L   τῶν λελειμμένων Kovacs

ΙΟΛΑΟΣ

715 οἵδ' οὐ προδώσουσίν σε, μὴ τρέσῃς, ξένοι.

ΑΛΚΜΗΝΗ

τοσόνδε γάρ τοι θάρσος, οὐδὲν ἄλλ', ἔχω.

ΙΟΛΑΟΣ

καὶ Ζηνὶ τῶν σῶν, οἶδ' ἐγώ, μέλει πόνων.

ΑΛΚΜΗΝΗ

φεῦ·
Ζεὺς ἐξ ἐμοῦ μὲν οὐκ ἀκούσεται κακῶς·
εἰ δ' ἐστὶν ὅσιος αὐτὸς οἶδεν εἰς ἐμέ.

ΘΕΡΑΠΩΝ

720 ὅπλων μὲν ἤδη τήνδ' ὁρᾷς παντευχίαν,
φθάνοις δ' ἂν οὐκ ἂν τοῖσδε σὸν κρύπτων δέμας·
ὡς ἐγγὺς ἀγὼν καὶ μάλιστ' Ἄρης στυγεῖ
μέλλοντας· εἰ δὲ τευχέων φοβῇ βάρος,
νῦν μὲν πορεύου γυμνός, ἐν δὲ τάξεσιν
725 κόσμῳ πυκάζου τῷδ'· ἐγὼ δ' οἴσω τέως.

ΙΟΛΑΟΣ

καλῶς ἔλεξας· ἀλλ' ἐμοὶ πρόχειρ' ἔχων
τεύχη κόμιζε, χειρὶ δ' ἔνθες ὀξύην,
λαιόν τ' ἔπαιρε πῆχυν, εὐθύνων πόδα.

ΘΕΡΑΠΩΝ

ἦ παιδαγωγεῖν γὰρ τὸν ὁπλίτην χρεών;

ΙΟΛΑΟΣ

730 ὄρνιθος οὕνεκ' ἀσφαλῶς πορευτέον.

---

⁷²¹ σὸν κρύπτων Dobree: συγκρύπτων L

IOLAUS

Fear not: our hosts here will not give you up.

ALCMENE

So much, and no more, are my grounds for hope!

IOLAUS

And Zeus, I am sure, is concerned for your troubles.

ALCMENE

Ah me! Zeus, to be sure, shall not hear words of reproach from me, but he knows best whether he has behaved in godly fashion toward me.

Enter SERVANT from the temple bearing armor.

SERVANT

Here, as you see, is a full suit of armor. It would not be premature to put it on. For the contest is near, and Ares hates the sluggard most of all. But if you are afraid of the weight of the weapons, walk without your armor and then, when you are in the ranks, cover yourself with this finery. I shall carry it in the meantime.

IOLAUS

Your suggestion is good. Carry my armor at the ready, and put the spear in my hand, then support my left fore-arm, directing my steps.

SERVANT

Must I lead a warrior as if he were a child?

IOLAUS

My foot must not slip. It is a bad omen.

Iolaus and the servant begin to move slowly to the eisodos.

ΘΕΡΑΠΩΝ

εἴθ' ἦσθα δυνατὸς δρᾶν ὅσον πρόθυμος εἶ.

ΙΟΛΑΟΣ

ἔπειγε· λειφθεὶς δεινὰ πείσομαι μάχης.

ΘΕΡΑΠΩΝ

σύ τοι βραδύνεις, οὐκ ἐγώ, δοκῶν τι δρᾶν.

ΙΟΛΑΟΣ

οὔκουν ὁρᾷς μου κῶλον ὡς ἐπείγεται;

ΘΕΡΑΠΩΝ

735   ὁρῶ δοκοῦντα μᾶλλον ἢ σπεύδοντά σε.

ΙΟΛΑΟΣ

οὐ ταῦτα λέξεις ἡνίκ' ἂν λεύσσῃς μ' ἐκεῖ . . .

ΘΕΡΑΠΩΝ

τί δρῶντα; βουλοίμην δ' ἂν εὐτυχοῦντά γε.

ΙΟΛΑΟΣ

. . . δι' ἀσπίδος θείνοντα πολεμίων τινά.

ΘΕΡΑΠΩΝ

εἰ δή ποθ' ἥξομέν γε· τοῦτο γὰρ φόβος.

ΙΟΛΑΟΣ

φεῦ·
740   εἴθ', ὦ βραχίων, οἷον ἡβήσαντά σε
μεμνήμεθ' ἡμεῖς, ἡνίκα ξὺν Ἡρακλεῖ
Σπάρτην ἐπόρθεις, σύμμαχος γένοιό μοι
τοιοῦτος· οἵαν ἂν τροπὴν Εὐρυσθέως
θείμην· ἐπεί τοι καὶ κακὸς μένειν δόρυ.

82

SERVANT

How I wish you were able to do all you long to do!

IOLAUS

Hurry! It will be terrible for me if I miss the battle!

SERVANT

But it is you who are slow, not I, thinking you are achieving something.

IOLAUS

Don't you see how my feet hasten?

SERVANT

I see more imagination than haste.

IOLAUS

This will not be your tune when you see me there . . .

SERVANT

Doing what? I could wish it were enjoying great success.

IOLAUS

. . . striking one of the enemy through his shield!

SERVANT

Yes, if we ever get there. That is a worry!

IOLAUS

Would that I could get you as an ally, O right arm of mine,
as I remember you when you were young, in the days
when in company with Heracles you sacked Sparta! How
I would put Eurystheus to flight! For, you know, he is too

---

^{733} δοκῶν Tyrwhitt: δοκῶ L: βραδύνειν, οὐκ ἐγώ, δοκεῖς
Kovacs ^{736} οὐ Reiske: σὺ L

^{738} θείνοντα Elmsley: θένοντα L

^{743} οἵαν Reiske: οἷος L ^{744} θείμην Cobet: θείην L

745 ἔστιν δ' ἐν ὄλβῳ καὶ τόδ' οὐκ ὀρθῶς ἔχον,
εὐψυχίας δόκησις· οἰόμεσθα γὰρ
τὸν εὐτυχοῦντα πάντ' ἐπίστασθαι καλῶς.

ΧΟΡΟΣ

στρ. α

Γᾶ καὶ παννύχιος σελά-
να καὶ λαμπρόταται θεοῦ
750 φαεσιμβρότου αὐγαί,
ἀγγελίαν μοι ἐνέγκαι,
ἰαχήσατε δ' οὐρανῷ
καὶ παρὰ θρόνον ἀρχέταν
γλαυκᾶς τ' ἐν Ἀθάνας·
755 μέλλω τᾶς πατριώτιδος
γᾶς, μέλλω καὶ ὑπὲρ δόμων
ἱκέτας ὑποδεχθεὶς
κίνδυνον πολιῷ τεμεῖν σιδάρῳ.

ἀντ. α

δεινὸν μὲν πόλιν ὡς Μυκή-
760 νας εὐδαίμονα καὶ δορὸς
πολυαίνετον ἀλκᾷ
μῆνιν ἐμᾷ χθονὶ κεύθειν·
κακὸν δ', ὦ πόλις, εἰ ξένους
ἱκτῆρας παραδώσομεν
765 κελεύσμασιν Ἄργους.
Ζεύς μοι σύμμαχος, οὐ φοβοῦ-
μαι, Ζεύς μοι χάριν ἐνδίκως
ἔχει· οὔποτε θνατῶν
ἥσσους <δαίμονες> ἔκ γ' ἐμοῦ φανοῦνται.

cowardly to stand up to the spear. There is this further injustice about prosperity: repute for courage. We suppose that the fortunate can do everything well.

Exit IOLAUS *and* SERVANT *by Eisodos A.*

CHORUS

O earth, O moon that stays aloft the night long, O gleaming rays of the god that brings light to mortals, be my messengers, I pray, and raise your shout to heaven, to the throne of Zeus and in the house of gray-eyed Athena! For we are about to cut a path through danger with the sword of gray iron on behalf of our fatherland, on behalf of our homes, since we have taken the suppliants in.

It is dreadful that a prosperous city like Mycenae, famed for its warrior might, should nurse a hatred against our land. But it is cowardly, O my city, if we hand over suppliant strangers at the behest of Argos. Zeus is my ally, I have no fear, Zeus is justly grateful to me: never shall I show the gods to be inferior to men.

---

750 φαεσιμβρότου Musgrave: φαεσίβροτοι L

751 ἐνέγκαι Wilamowitz: ἐνέγκατ' L

754 γλαυκᾶς . . . ’Αθάνας Schaefer: γλαυκᾶ . . . ἀθάνα L

756 ὑπὲρ Nauck: περὶ L

761 πολυαίνετον Scaliger: -αινέτου L

762 ἐμᾷ post Stephanum Canter: ἐμὲ L

765 κελεύσμασιν ῞Αργους Reiske: καὶ λεύσιμον ἄργος L

769 <δαίμονες> Kirchhoff   ἔκ γ' Reiske: εἴτ' L

στρ. β

770 ἀλλ', ὦ πότνια, σὸν γὰρ οὖ-
δας γᾶς καὶ πόλις, ἇς σὺ μά-
τηρ δέσποινά τε καὶ φύλαξ,
πόρευσον ἄλλᾳ τὸν οὐ δικαίως
τᾷδ' ἐπάγοντα δορυσσοῦν

775 στρατὸν Ἀργόθεν· οὐ γὰρ ἐμᾷ γ' ἀρετᾷ
δίκαιός εἰμ' ἐκπεσεῖν μελάθρων.

ἀντ. β

ἐπεί σοι πολύθυτος ἀεὶ
τιμὰ κραίνεται οὐδὲ λά-
θει μηνῶν φθινὰς ἁμέρα

780 νέων τ' ἀοιδαὶ χορῶν τε μολπαί.
ἀνεμόεντι δ' ἐπ' ὄχθῳ
ὀλολύγματα παννυχίοις ὑπὸ παρ-
θένων ἰαχεῖ ποδῶν κρότοισιν.

ΑΓΓΕΛΟΣ

δέσποινα, μύθους σοί τε καλλίστους φέρω

785 κλύειν λέγειν τε τῷδε συντομωτάτους·
νικῶμεν ἐχθρούς, καὶ τροπαῖ' ἱδρύεται
παντευχίαν ἔχοντα πολεμίων σέθεν.

ΑΛΚΜΗΝΗ

ὦ φίλταθ', ἥδε σ' ἡμέρα †διήλασεν†·

---

771 γᾶς Pearson: γᾶς σὸν L
773 ἄλλᾳ Canter: ἀλλὰ L
774 δορυσσοῦν Kirchhoff: δορύσσοντα L
784n Ἄγγελος Rassow: Θερ. L hic et infra passim

But, lady Athena, since yours is the soil of the land and yours the city, and you are its mother, its mistress, and its guardian, divert to some other land the man who is unjustly bringing the spear-hurling army here from Argos! By our goodness we do not deserve to be cast from our homes.

For the honor of rich sacrifice is always offered to you,[a] nor do the waning day of the month or the songs of young men or the tunes to accompany their dancing ever slip from our minds. On the wind-swept hill loud shouts of gladness resound to the beat of maiden dance steps the whole night long.

Enter MESSENGER *by Eisodos A.*

MESSENGER

My lady, I bring a report, one most lovely for you to hear and brief for me to tell: we are victorious over our enemies, and the trophies of victory are being raised with the armor of your enemies upon them!

ALCMENE

Dear friend, this day has brought you good fortune:

---

[a] This stanza describes aspects of the Panathenaea, a yearly festival in Athena's honor. The great sacrifice was offered on the last day of the month of Hecatombaion.

[784-5] καλλίστους φέρω / κλύειν λέγειν τε τῷδε συντομωτά-τους Wecklein: συν. / κλ. ἐμοί τε τῷδε κ. φ. L

[788] διώλβισεν dubitanter Diggle: post h. v. lac. stat. Wilkins, e.g. <ἐλευθέρων ἐς ἀριθμὸν ἐξ ὑπηρετῶν>

87

ἐλευθερῶ σε τοῖσδε τοῖς ἀγγέλμασιν.
790 μιᾶς δ' ἔμ' οὔπω συμφορᾶς ἐλευθεροῖς·
φόβος γὰρ εἴ μοι ζῶσιν οὓς ἐγὼ θέλω.

ΑΓΓΕΛΟΣ
ζῶσιν, μέγιστόν γ' εὐκλεεῖς κατὰ στρατόν.

ΑΛΚΜΗΝΗ
ὁ μὲν γέρων οὖν ἔστιν Ἰόλεως ἔτι;

ΑΓΓΕΛΟΣ
μάλιστα, πράξας γ' ἐκ θεῶν κάλλιστα δή.

ΑΛΚΜΗΝΗ
795 τί δ' ἔστι; μῶν τι κεδνὸν ἠγωνίζετο;

ΑΓΓΕΛΟΣ
νέος μεθέστηκ' ἐκ γέροντος αὖθις αὖ.

ΑΛΚΜΗΝΗ
θαυμάστ' ἔλεξας· ἀλλά σ' εὐτυχῆ φίλων
μάχης ἀγῶνα πρῶτον ἀγγεῖλαι θέλω.

ΑΓΓΕΛΟΣ
εἷς μου λόγος σοι πάντα σημανεῖ τάδε.
800 ἐπεὶ γὰρ ἀλλήλοισιν ὁπλίτην στρατὸν
κατὰ στόμ' ἐκτείνοντες ἀντετάξαμεν,
ἐκβὰς τεθρίππων Ὕλλος ἁρμάτων πόδα
ἔστη μέσοισιν ἐν μεταιχμίοις δορός.
κἄπειτ' ἔλεξεν· Ὦ στρατήγ' ὃς Ἀργόθεν
805 ἥκεις, τί τήνδε γαῖαν οὐκ εἰάσαμεν
805a <καὶ τὰς Μυκήνας αὖθις εἰρήνην ἄγειν;

because of your message I set you free! But there is one
stroke of misfortune from which you have not freed me: I
am worried whether those I wish to live are still alive.

MESSENGER

They are alive and enjoy great glory in the army.

ALCMENE

Is aged Iolaus then still among the living?

MESSENGER

Yes, and his fortune from the gods is good.

ALCMENE

What? Did he perform some noble deed of valor?

MESSENGER

He has changed from old back to young.

ALCMENE

A remarkable story! But first I want you to tell me that
our friends have been successful in battle.

MESSENGER

A single account by me will tell you all. When we had
drawn up our hoplite lines, deploying them face to face
with each other, Hyllus, stepping from his four-horse
chariot, took his stand in the middle of the space between
the armies. Then he said, "Argive general, why can we
not let this land <and Mycenae be once more at peace? If

---

789 ἐλευθερῶ σε Diggle: ἐλευθερῶσαι L

793 οὖν . . . ἔτι Elmsley: οὐκ . . . ὅδε L

794 γ' Elmsley: δ' L

805 τί Heath: ἐπὶ L   post h.v. lac. indic. Heath: 805a
suppl. Elmsley, ceteros Kovacs

805b ἦν γὰρ πίθῃ μοι, τήνδ' Ἀθηναίαν πόλιν,
805c λεών γε δεινόν, πολεμίαν οὐχ ἕξετε,>
      καὶ τὰς Μυκήνας οὐδὲν ἐργάσῃ κακὸν
      ἀνδρῶν στερήσας· ἀλλ' ἐμοὶ μόνος μόνῳ
      μάχην συνάψας, ἢ κτανὼν ἄγου λαβὼν
      τοὺς Ἡρακλείους παῖδας ἢ θανὼν ἐμοὶ
810   τιμὰς πατρῴους καὶ δόμους ἔχειν ἄφες.
      στρατὸς δ' ἐπήνεσ' ἔς τ' ἀπαλλαγὰς πόνων
      καλῶς λελέχθαι μῦθον ἔς τ' εὐψυχίαν.
      ὁ δ' οὔτε τοὺς κλύοντας αἰδεσθεὶς λόγων
      οὔτ' αὐτὸς αὑτοῦ δειλίαν στρατηγὸς ὢν
815   ἐλθεῖν ἐτόλμησ' ἐγγὺς ἀλκίμου δορός,
      ἀλλ' ἦν κάκιστος· εἶτα τοιοῦτος γεγὼς
      τοὺς Ἡρακλείους ἦλθε δουλώσων γόνους;
          Ὕλλος μὲν οὖν ἀπῴχετ' ἐς τάξιν πάλιν·
      μάντεις δ', ἐπειδὴ μονομάχου δι' ἀσπίδος
820   διαλλαγὰς ἔγνωσαν οὐ τελουμένας,
      ἔσφαζον, οὐκ ἔμελλον, ἀλλ' ἀφίεσαν
      λαιμῶν βοτείων εὐθὺς οὔριον φόνον.
      οἱ δ' ἅρματ' εἰσέβαινον, οἱ δ' ὑπ' ἀσπίδων
      πλευροῖς ἔχριμπτον πλεύρ'· Ἀθηναίων δ' ἄναξ
825   στρατῷ παρήγγελλ' οἷα χρὴ τὸν εὐγενῆ·
      Ὦ ξυμπολῖται, τῇ τε βοσκούσῃ χθονὶ
      καὶ τῇ τεκούσῃ νῦν τιν' ἀρκέσαι χρεών.
      ὁ δ' αὖ τό τ' Ἄργος μὴ καταισχῦναι θέλειν
      καὶ τὰς Μυκήνας συμμάχους ἐλίσσετο.

      [807] ἀνδρῶν Hartung: ἀνδρὸς L

90

you take my advice, you will not have the city of Athens, a
formidable host, as your enemy,> and you will not harm
Mycenae by depriving it of its soldiery. Rather, join in
single combat with me, and either, if you kill me, take
away the children of Heracles, or, if you are killed, cede to
me the honors and the house that are mine from my
father." The army murmured its approval of this speech
both for the escape from toil it promised and for its
courage. But Eurystheus, who neither respected the lis-
tening army nor felt shame at his own cowardice as gen-
eral, could not bring himself to enter battle, but showed
himself a coward. Has a man like this, then, come to
enslave the children of Heracles?

So Hyllus went back into the ranks. The diviners,
when they realized that peace by single combat was not
going to be brought about, proceeded to slaughter with-
out delay, and they released at once the propitious stream
of blood from the necks of the sheep. Others mounted
their chariots, while the foot soldiers put flank against
flank under the protection of their shields. The leader of
the Athenians gave his men such exhortation as a brave
man ought to give: "Fellow citizens, now must a man pro-
tect the land that gave him birth and nurtured him." The
enemy general for his part fervently urged his allies to
refuse to bring disgrace on Argos and Mycenae.

---

808 μάχην Reiske: μάχη L
819–23 del. Wilamowitz
822 βοτείων Paley: βροτείων L
824 πλευροῖς Elmsley: -αῖς L   ἔχριμπτον Diggle:
ἔκρυπτον L
828 θέλειν Reiske: θέλων L

830   ἐπεὶ δ' ἐσήμην' ὄρθιον Τυρσηνικῇ
        σάλπιγγι καὶ συνῆψαν ἀλλήλοις μάχην,
        πόσον τιν' αὐχεῖς πάταγον ἀσπίδων βρέμειν,
        πόσον τινὰ στεναγμὸν οἰμωγήν θ' ὁμοῦ;
        τὰ πρῶτα μέν νυν πίτυλος Ἀργείου δορὸς
835   ἐρρήξαθ' ἡμᾶς, εἶτ' ἐχώρησαν πάλιν.
        τὸ δεύτερον δὲ ποὺς ἐπαλλαχθεὶς ποδί,
        ἀνὴρ δ' ἐπ' ἀνδρὶ στάς, ἐκαρτέρει μάχῃ·
        πολλοὶ δ' ἔπιπτον. ἦν δὲ δύο κελεύσματα
        Ὦ τὰς Ἀθήνας—Ὦ τὸν Ἀργείων γύην
840   σπείροντες—οὐκ ἀρήξετ' αἰσχύνην πόλει;
        μόλις δὲ πάντα δρῶντες οὐκ ἄτερ πόνων
        ἐτρεψάμεσθ' Ἀργεῖον ἐς φυγὴν δόρυ.
            κἀνταῦθ' ὁ πρέσβυς Ὕλλον ἐξορμώμενον
        ἰδών, ὀρέξας ἱκέτευσε δεξιὰν
845   Ἰόλαος ἐμβῆσαί νιν ἵππειον δίφρον.
        λαβὼν δὲ χερσὶν ἡνίας Εὐρυσθέως
        πώλοις ἐπεῖχε. τἀπὸ τοῦδ' ἤδη κλυὼν
        λέγοιμ' ἂν ἄλλων, δεῦρο γ' αὐτὸς εἰσιδών.
        Παλληνίδος γὰρ σεμνὸν ἐκπερῶν πάγον
850   δίας Ἀθάνας, ἅρμ' ἰδὼν Εὐρυσθέως,
        ἠράσαθ' Ἥβῃ Ζηνί θ' ἡμέραν μίαν
        νέος γενέσθαι κἀποτείσασθαι δίκην
        ἐχθρούς. κλυεῖν δὴ θαύματος πάρεστί σοι.
        δισσὼ γὰρ ἀστέρ' ἱππικοῖς ἐπὶ ζυγοῖς
855   σταθέντ' ἔκρυψαν ἅρμα λυγαίῳ νέφει·
        σὸν δὴ λέγουσι παῖδά γ' οἱ σοφώτεροι
        Ἥβην θ'· ὁ δ' ὄρφνης ἐκ δυσαιθρίου νέων
        βραχιόνων ἔδειξεν ἡβητὴν τύπον.

92

But when the Tuscan trumpet gave its high-pitched signal and the two armies clashed in battle, what a great roar of shields was there, do you think, what mingled sound of groans and cries of pain? At first the rhythmic clash of the Argive infantry broke our ranks, but then they retreated. Thereafter foot was locked with foot and man stood against man and the battle continued fierce. Many soldiers fell. All about were heard two cries, "Dwellers in Athens—or You who sow the Argive field—keep disgrace from our city!" By bending all our strength, with great toil, we at length put the Argive army to flight.

Then old Iolaus, seeing Hyllus rushing off, stretched out his right hand and begged him to take him onto his chariot. He took the reins and followed hard upon the chariot of Eurystheus. What I have said to this point I saw myself, but from here on I will give you what I heard from the lips of others. As he was passing through the sacred district of Athene Pallenis,[a] looking toward Eurystheus' chariot he prayed to Hebe[b] and to Zeus that he might be young again for a single day and exact retribution from his enemies. Now you may hear a marvel. A pair of stars stood above the chariot yoke and covered the chariot in dark cloud. Those who are wise say that it was your son Heracles and Hebe: out of this murky darkness he showed forth the youthful form of his young arms.

[a] Cult name of Athena as worshiped in the deme of Pallene.

[b] Goddess of youthfulness. She became Heracles' bride after his death.

---

838 δύο κελεύσματα L. Dindorf: τοῦ κελεύσματος

848 λέγοιμ' ἂν Valckenaer: λέγοι μὲν L   ἄλλων Elmsley: ἄλλος L   γ' Fix: δ' L

854 ἐπὶ Reiske: ὑπὸ L

αἱρεῖ δ' ὁ κλεινὸς Ἰόλεως Εὐρυσθέως
860 τέτρωρον ἅρμα πρὸς πέτραις Σκιρωνίσιν,
δεσμοῖς τε δήσας χεῖρας ἀκροθίνιον
κάλλιστον ἥκει τὸν στρατηλάτην ἄγων
τὸν ὄλβιον πάροιθε. τῇ δὲ νῦν τύχῃ
βροτοῖς ἅπασι λαμπρὰ κηρύσσει μαθεῖν,
865 τὸν εὐτυχεῖν δοκοῦντα μὴ ζηλοῦν πρὶν ἂν
θανόντ' ἴδῃ τις· ὡς ἐφήμεροι τύχαι.

ΧΟΡΟΣ

ὦ Ζεῦ τροπαῖε, νῦν ἐμοὶ δεινοῦ φόβου
ἐλεύθερον πάρεστιν ἦμαρ εἰσιδεῖν.

ΑΛΚΜΗΝΗ

ὦ Ζεῦ, χρόνῳ μὲν τἄμ' ἐπεσκέψω κακά,
870 χάριν δ' ὅμως σοι τῶν πεπραγμένων ἔχω·
καὶ παῖδα τὸν ἐμὸν πρόσθεν οὐ δοκοῦσ' ἐγὼ
θεοῖς ὁμιλεῖν νῦν ἐπίσταμαι σαφῶς.
  ὦ τέκνα, νῦν δὴ νῦν ἐλεύθεροι πόνων,
ἐλεύθεροι δὲ τοῦ κακῶς ὀλουμένου
875 Εὐρυσθέως ἔσεσθε καὶ πόλιν πατρὸς
ὄψεσθε, κλήρους δ' ἐμβατεύσετε χθονὸς
καὶ θεοῖς πατρῴοις θύσεθ', ὧν ἀπειργμένοι
ξένοι πλανήτην εἴχετ' ἄθλιον βίον.
  ἀτὰρ τί κεύθων Ἰόλεως σοφόν ποτε
880 Εὐρυσθέως ἐφείσαθ' ὥστε μὴ κτανεῖν;
λέξον· παρ' ἡμῖν μὲν γὰρ οὐ σοφὸν τόδε,
ἐχθροὺς λαβόντα μὴ ἀποτείσασθαι δίκην.

ΑΓΓΕΛΟΣ

τὸ σὸν προτιμῶν, ὥς νιν ὀφθαλμοῖς ἴδοις

Glorious Iolaus captured the four-horse chariot of Eurys-
theus near the Skironian cliffs. He has bound his hands
and returned with the general who once was so fortunate,
the glorious first fruits of battle. By this present blow of
fortune he gives all men a lesson plain to learn, that none
should envy him who seems fortunate until they see he
has died. For our fortunes may change with the day.

CHORUS LEADER
O Zeus, lord of victory, now I may look upon a day that
has been set free from dreadful fear!

ALCMENE
O Zeus, though it was late in the day that you looked upon
my afflictions, yet I feel gratitude for what you have done.
And although before I did not believe that my son lived in
the company of the gods, now I know it beyond any
doubt.

Children, now at last you will be free from trouble,
free from the accursed Eurystheus! You will see your
father's city and take possession of your estates and sacri-
fice to the gods of your ancestors, from whom you have
been cut off as you lived the life of wandering strangers.

But with what clever idea in mind did Iolaus spare
Eurystheus' life? Tell me, for in our judgment it is no
wise thing, when you have captured your enemies, not to
exact vengeance from them.

MESSENGER
He acted in deference to you so that you might see Eurys-

---

859 Ἰόλεως Victorius: πόλεως L
868 ἐλευθέρῳ Dobree

†κρατοῦντα† καὶ σῇ δεσποτούμενον χερί.
885 οὐ μὴν ἑκόντα γ' αὐτὸν ἀλλὰ πρὸς βίαν
ἔζευξ' ἀνάγκη· καὶ γὰρ οὐκ ἐβούλετο
ζῶν ἐς σὸν ἐλθεῖν ὄμμα καὶ δοῦναι δίκην.

  ἀλλ', ὦ γεραιά, χαῖρε καὶ μέμνησό μοι
  ὃ πρῶτον εἶπας ἡνίκ' ἠρχόμην λόγου,
890 ἐλευθερώσειν μ'· ἐν δὲ τοῖς τοιοῖσδε χρὴ
  ἀψευδὲς εἶναι τοῖσι γενναίοις στόμα.

ΧΟΡΟΣ

στρ. α

  ἐμοὶ χορὸς μὲν ἡδὺ καὶ
  λίγεια λωτοῦ χάρις ἀμφὶ δαῖτα·
  ἡδεῖα δ' εὔχαρις Ἀφροδί-
895 τα· τερπνὸν δέ τι καὶ φίλων
  ἆρ' εὐτυχίαν ἰδέ-
  σθαι τῶν πάρος οὐ δοκούντων.
  πολλὰ γὰρ τίκτει Μοῖρα τελεσσιδώ-
900 τειρ' Αἰών τε Χρόνου παῖς.

ἀντ. α

  ἔχεις ὁδόν τιν', ὦ πόλις,
  δίκαιον· οὐ χρή ποτε τοῦδ' ἀφέσθαι,
  τιμᾶν θεούς· ὁ δὲ μή σε φά-
  σκων ἐγγὺς μανιῶν ἐλαύ-
905 νει, δεικνυμένων ἐλέγ-
  χων τῶνδ'· ἐπίσημα γάρ τοι
  θεὸς παραγγέλλει, τῶν ἀδίκων παραι-
  ρῶν φρονήματος αἰεί.

theus with your own eyes suffering misfortune and in your power. But it was not willingly but against his will that Iolaus yoked him to necessity. For Eurystheus did not wish to come before you alive and pay the penalty.

But farewell, old woman, and remember what you said at first when I began my tale, that you would set me free. For in matters like this the tongues of the noble ought to be truthful.

Exit MESSENGER *by Eisodos A.*

CHORUS

Sweet in my eyes is dancing and the high-pitched beauty of the flute at a feast. Sweet is Aphrodite the gracious. But, it now appears, it is also a pleasure to see the prosperity of friends who formerly were as nought. Fate that gives completion and Life, Time's child, bring many things to pass.

You, my city, are holding steadfast to a course of justice. Never should you let go of this, your worship of the gods. The man who denies that you are just skirts close to madness, with these clear proofs in evidence. For the message god gives is manifest, ever stripping the unjust of their pride.

---

884 fort. κάμνοντα: κρατοῦσα Reiske, tum τῇ Paley

888 μοι Reiske: μου L

890 ἐλευθερώσειν Porson: ἐλευθέρωσόν L

892 ἡδὺ καὶ Bothe: ἡδὺς εἰ L

893 ἀμφὶ δαῖτα Willink: ἐνὶ δαΐ L

894 ἡδεῖα Madvig: εἴη L

902 ἀφέσθαι Herwerden: ἀφελέσθαι L

στρ. β
910 ἔστιν ἐν οὐρανῷ βεβα-
κὼς ὁ σὸς γόνος, ὦ γεραιά·
φεύγω λόγον ὡς τὸν Ἅι-
δα δόμον κατέβα, πυρὸς
δεινᾷ φλογὶ σῶμα δαισθείς·
915 Ἥβας τ' ἐρατὸν χροΐ-
ζει λέχος χρυσέαν κατ' αὐλάν.
ὦ Ὑμέναιε, δισ-
σοὺς παῖδας Διὸς ἠξίωσας.

ἀντ. β
συμφέρεται δὲ πολλὰ πολ-
920 λοῖς· καὶ γὰρ πατρὶ τῶνδ' Ἀθάναν
λέγουσ' ἐπίκουρον εἶ-
ναι, καὶ τούσδε θεᾶς πόλις
καὶ λαὸς ἔσωσε κείνας·
ἔσχεν δ' ὕβριν ἀνδρὸς ᾧ
925 θυμὸς ἦν πρὸ δίκας βίαιος.
μήποτ' ἐμοὶ φρόνη-
μα ψυχά τ' ἀκόρεστος εἴη.

ΘΕΡΑΠΩΝ
δέσποιν', ὁρᾷς μέν, ἀλλ' ὅμως εἰρήσεται·
Εὐρυσθέα σοι τόνδ' ἄγοντες ἥκομεν,
930 ἄελπτον ὄψιν τῷδέ τ' οὐχ ἧσσον τύχην·
οὐ γάρ ποτ' ηὔχει χεῖρας ἵξεσθαι σέθεν,
ὅτ' ἐκ Μυκηνῶν πολυπόνῳ σὺν ἀσπίδι
ἔστειχε μείζω τῆς δίκης φρονῶν, πόλιν

Your son has taken his place in heaven, old woman. I will not accept the story that he went down to the house of Hades, his body consumed by the dread flame. It is fair Hebe whose bed he enjoys in that hall of gold. You have honored, O Hymen, two of Zeus's children.[a]

Many things correspond with one another: just as they say that their father was aided by Athena, so too these children were saved by that goddess' city and folk. She has checked the insolence of the man whose nature preferred violence to justice. Never may my spirit, my soul, be so hard to sate!

Enter SERVANT *by Eisodos A with* EURYSTHEUS *under guard.*

SERVANT

My lady, though you see it yourself, still I will tell you: we have come bringing Eurystheus to you, a sight you had not expected to see and a stroke of fortune he had not looked to feel. For he never supposed that he would fall into your hands when he set off from Mycenae with his throng of toiling soldiers, with more pride than is right, to

[a] Hebe, like Heracles, was a child of Zeus.

---

911 ὁ σὸς Wecklein: θεὸς L   912 φεύγω Elmsley: -γει L
919 δὲ Paley: τὰ L   924 ὕβριν Heath: ὕβρεις L
925 βίαιος Musgrave: βιαίως L
928n Θε. Rassow: Ἀγγ. L hic et ubique
930 τῷδέ Canter: τῶνδέ L   τύχην Wecklein: τυχεῖν L
932 πολυπόνῳ σὺν ἀσπίδι Hermann: πολυπόνων σὺν ἀσπίσιν L
933 πόλιν Jacobs: πολὺ L

πέρσων Ἀθάνας. ἀλλὰ τὴν ἐναντίαν
935 δαίμων ἔθηκε καὶ μετέστησεν τύχην.
    Ὕλλος μὲν οὖν ὅ τ' ἐσθλὸς Ἰόλεως βρέτας
Διὸς τροπαίου καλλίνικον ἵστασαν·
ἐμοὶ δὲ πρὸς σὲ τόνδ' ἐπιστέλλουσ' ἄγειν,
τέρψαι θέλοντες σὴν φρέν'· ἐκ γὰρ εὐτυχοῦς
940 ἥδιστον ἐχθρὸν ἄνδρα δυστυχοῦνθ' ὁρᾶν.

ΑΛΚΜΗΝΗ

ὦ μῖσος, ἥκεις; εἷλέ σ' ἡ Δίκη χρόνῳ;
πρῶτον μὲν οὖν μοι δεῦρ' ἐπίστρεψον κάρα
καὶ τλῆθι τοὺς σοὺς προσβλέπειν ἐναντίον
ἐχθρούς· κρατῇ γὰρ νῦν γε κοὐ κρατεῖς ἔτι.
945 ἐκεῖνος εἶ σύ, βούλομαι γὰρ εἰδέναι,
ὃς πολλὰ μὲν τὸν ὄνθ' ὅπου 'στὶ νῦν ἐμὸν
947 παῖδ' ἀξιώσας, ὦ πανοῦργ', ἐφυβρίσαι
950 ὕδρας λέοντάς τ' ἐξαπολλύναι λέγων
951 ἔπεμπες; ἄλλα δ' οἷ' ἐμηχανῶ κακὰ
952 σιγῶ· μακρὸς γὰρ μῦθος ἂν γένοιτό μοι.
948 τί γὰρ σὺ κεῖνον οὐκ ἔτλης καθυβρίσαι
949 ὃς καὶ παρ' Ἅιδην ζῶντά νιν κατήγαγες;
953 κοὐκ ἤρκεσέν σοι ταῦτα τολμῆσαι μόνον,
ἀλλ' ἐξ ἁπάσης κἀμὲ καὶ τέκν' Ἑλλάδος
955 ἤλαυνες ἱκέτας δαιμόνων καθημένους,
τοὺς μὲν γέροντας, τοὺς δὲ νηπίους ἔτι.
ἀλλ' ηὗρες ἄνδρας καὶ πόλισμ' ἐλεύθερον,
οἵ σ' οὐκ ἔδεισαν. δεῖ σε κατθανεῖν κακῶς,
καὶ κερδανεῖς ἅπαντα· χρῆν γὰρ οὐχ ἅπαξ
960 θνήσκειν σε πολλὰ πήματ' ἐξειργασμένον.

sack Athena's city. But fate has cast its vote against him
and altered his fortunes.

Hyllus and brave Iolaus were erecting a victory statue
in honor of Zeus, God of the Rout. But they instructed
me to bring this man to you, intending to delight your
heart. For there is no pleasanter sight than to see one's
enemy fallen from prosperity into misfortune.

ALCMENE

Have you come, hateful creature? Has Justice caught you
at long last? Come, first turn your head toward me and
steel yourself to look your enemy in the face: you are the
ruled now, no longer the ruler. Are you, villainous crea-
ture, the man (for I wish to know) who thought it right to
commit so many outrages against my son, wherever he
now is, and sent him off with orders to kill hydras and
lions? I say nothing of all the other troubles you con-
trived for him, for my tale would become too long. What
outrages against him exceeded your daring? You even
took him down alive to the house of Hades! You were not
content with these acts of brazenness but drove me and
these children, who sat as suppliants of the gods, from
every corner of Greece, though some of us were old and
others still babes! But you found men and a city who
were free, who did not fear you. You must die a villain's
death, and that will be all gain to you. For you should die
not once but many times over for causing us so many
griefs.

---

⁹³⁷ ἵστασαν Elmsley: ἔστασαν L
⁹⁴³ ἐναντίον Elmsley: -ίους L   ⁹⁴⁷ ἀξιώσας Jackson:
ἠξίωσας L   ^{950–2} post 947 trai. Wilamowitz   ⁹⁵⁹ χρῆν
Reiske: χρὴ L

ΘΕΡΑΠΩΝ

οὐκ ἔστ' ἀνυστὸν τόνδε σοι κατακτανεῖν.

ΑΛΚΜΗΝΗ

ἄλλως ἄρ' αὐτὸν αἰχμάλωτον εἵλομεν.

<ΘΕΡΑΠΩΝ

ἄλλως· ἀφεῖναι τοῖς Μυκηναίοις χρεών.>

<ΑΛΚΜΗΝΗ>

εἴργει δὲ δὴ τίς τόνδε μὴ θνήσκειν νόμος;

ΘΕΡΑΠΩΝ

τοῖς τῆσδε χώρας προστάταισιν οὐ δοκεῖ.

ΑΛΚΜΗΝΗ

965   τί δὴ τόδ'; ἐχθροὺς τοισίδ' οὐ καλὸν κτανεῖν;

ΘΕΡΑΠΩΝ

οὐχ ὅντιν' ἄν γε ζῶνθ' ἕλωσιν ἐν μάχῃ.

ΑΛΚΜΗΝΗ

καὶ ταῦτα δόξανθ' Ὕλλος ἐξηνέσχετο;

ΘΕΡΑΠΩΝ

χρῆν αὐτόν, οἶμαι, τῇδ' ἀπιστῆσαι χθονί.

ΑΛΚΜΗΝΗ

χρῆν τόνδε μὴ ζῆν μηδ' ἔτ' εἰσορᾶν φάος.

961, 964, 966, 968, 970, 972, 974 famulo (immo nuntio) trib. Tyr-
whitt, choro L
962–3, 965, 967, 969, 971 Alcmenae trib. Barnes, nuntio L
962 post h.v. responsum excidisse coni. Kirchhoff
968 χρῆν Bothe: χρῆν δ' L
969 ἔτ' εἰσορᾶν φάος Erfurdt: ὁρᾶν φάος ἔτι L

SERVANT

You may not kill this man.

ALCMENE

It is for nothing then that we have taken him prisoner.

<SERVANT

For nothing: we must release him to the Argives.>

<ALCMENE>

But what law is it that prevents his being killed?

SERVANT

Those who rule this land do not deem it right.

ALCMENE

What is the meaning of this? Do men here not approve of killing their enemies?

SERVANT

Not an enemy they have taken alive in battle.

ALCMENE

And did Hyllus put up with this decision?

SERVANT

He ought, no doubt, to have disobeyed this land's orders.

ALCMENE

Eurytheus ought not to live and look any more on the light of the sun.

<ΘΕΡΑΠΩΝ

ἀλλ' οὐ δίκαιον τόνδε μὴ λῦσαι φίλοις.>

ΑΛΚΜΗΝΗ

970 τότ' ἠδικήθη πρῶτον οὐ θανὼν ὅδε.

<ΘΕΡΑΠΩΝ

τότ' ἦν δίκαιον, οἶδα, τόνδ' ἀποκτανεῖν.>

ΑΛΚΜΗΝΗ

οὔκουν ἔτ' ἐστὶν ἐν καλῷ δοῦναι δίκην;

ΘΕΡΑΠΩΝ

οὐκ ἔστι τοῦτον ὅστις ἂν κατακτάνοι.

ΑΛΚΜΗΝΗ

ἔγωγε· καίτοι φημὶ κἄμ' εἶναί τινα.

ΘΕΡΑΠΩΝ

πολλὴν ἄρ' ἕξεις μέμψιν, εἰ δράσεις τόδε.

ΑΛΚΜΗΝΗ

975 φιλῶ πόλιν τήνδ'· οὐδὲν ἀντιλεκτέον·
τοῦτον δ', ἐπείπερ χεῖρας ἦλθεν εἰς ἐμάς,
οὐκ ἔστι θνητῶν ὅστις ἐξαιρήσεται.
πρὸς ταῦτα τὴν θρασεῖαν ὅστις ἂν θέλῃ
καὶ τὴν φρονοῦσαν μεῖζον ἢ γυναῖκα χρὴ
980 λέξει· τὸ δ' ἔργον τοῦτ' ἐμοὶ πεπράξεται.

ΧΟΡΟΣ

δεινόν τι καὶ συγγνωστὸν ὦ γύναι σ' ἔχει
νεῖκος πρὸς ἄνδρα τόνδε, γιγνώσκω καλῶς.

---

970 Alcmenae trib., lac. utrimque stat. Zuntz: choro trib. L

<SERVANT
But it would be unjust not to release him for ransom.>

ALCMENE
The first injustice he suffered was not being killed *then*.

<SERVANT
It would, I admit, have been right to kill him then.>

ALCMENE
Well, is it not still a fine thing for him to pay the penalty?

SERVANT
There is no one to put him to death.

ALCMENE
I shall. I claim to be someone.

SERVANT
You will be much censured if you do so.

ALCMENE
I love this city—no one shall say I do not—yet as for this
man, since he has fallen into my hands there is no mortal
who shall rescue him. In view of this, anyone who likes
may call me rash or too proud for woman's estate: this
deed is one I shall accomplish!

CHORUS LEADER
The wrath you feel toward this man, lady, is dreadful and
yet, I know well, understandable.

---

973 καίτοι φημὶ κἄμ' εἶναί Tyrwhitt: καὶ τί φημι κἂν μεῖναι
L

ΕΥΡΥΣΘΕΥΣ

γύναι, σάφ' ἴσθι μή με θωπεύσοντά σε
μηδ' ἄλλο μηδὲν τῆς ἐμῆς ψυχῆς πέρι
985 λέξονθ' ὅθεν χρὴ δειλίαν ὀφλεῖν τινα.
ἐγὼ δὲ νεῖκος οὐχ ἑκὼν τόδ' ἠράμην·
ἤδη γε σοὶ μὲν αὐτανέψιος γεγώς,
τῷ σῷ δὲ παιδὶ συγγενὴς Ἡρακλέει.
ἀλλ' εἴτ' ἔχρῃζον εἴτε μή—θεὸς γὰρ ἦν—
990 Ἥρα με κάμνειν τήνδ' ἔθηκε τὴν νόσον.
ἐπεὶ δ' ἐκείνῳ δυσμένειαν ἠράμην
κἄγνων ἀγῶνα τόνδ' ἀγωνιούμενος,
πολλῶν σοφιστὴς πημάτων ἐγιγνόμην
καὶ πόλλ' ἔτικτον νυκτὶ συνθακῶν ἀεί,
995 ὅπως διώσας καὶ κατακτείνας ἐμοὺς
ἐχθροὺς τὸ λοιπὸν μὴ συνοικοίην φόβῳ,
εἰδὼς μὲν οὐκ ἀριθμὸν ἀλλ' ἐτητύμως
ἄνδρ' ὄντα τὸν σὸν παῖδα· καὶ γὰρ ἐχθρὸς ὢν
ἀκούσεται γοῦν ἐσθλὰ χρηστὸς ὢν ἀνήρ.
1000 κείνου δ' ἀπαλλαχθέντος οὐκ ἐχρῆν μ' ἄρα,
μισούμενον πρὸς τῶνδε καὶ ξυνειδότα
ἔχθραν πατρῴαν, πάντα κινῆσαι πέτρον
κτείνοντα κἀκβάλλοντα καὶ τεχνώμενον;
τοιαῦτα δρῶντι τἄμ' ἐγίγνετ' ἀσφαλῆ.
1005 οὔκουν σύ γ' ἀναλαβοῦσα τὰς ἐμὰς τύχας
ἐχθροῦ λέοντος δυσμενῆ βλαστήματα
ἤλαυνες ἂν κακοῖσιν, ἀλλὰ σωφρόνως
εἴασας οἰκεῖν Ἄργος· οὔτιν' ἂν πίθοις.
   νῦν οὖν ἐπειδή μ' οὐ διώλεσαν τότε

106

EURYSTHEUS

You should know, madam, that I shall not truckle to you
or say any word on behalf of my life by which a man might
win the name of coward. I did not take up this quarrel of
my own will. I knew that I was first cousin to you and kin
to your son Heracles. But whether I wished to or not—
for a divinity was at work—Hera caused me to suffer this
disease. When I had taken up a quarrel with Heracles
and realized that this was the struggle I would be engaged
in, I became the inventor of much trouble, and staying
awake constantly in the night I thought up many ways to
thrust off and kill my enemies so as not to live the rest of
my life a companion to fear. I knew that your son was no
cipher but a true man—for though he is my enemy, he
shall at all events hear good things spoken of him as befits
a noble man. But now that he is out of the way, seeing
that I am hated by these children and aware of their
inherited hatred of me, should I have left any stone
unturned to plot their murder or exile? If I acted thus,
my interests were likely to be safe. You, no doubt, claim
that if you had taken up my fortunes you would not have
hounded the hostile offspring of the lion your enemy but
would have modestly allowed them to live in Argos. You
will convince no one of this.

Now, accordingly, since they did not kill me on the

---

987 ἤδη Schaefer: ἤδη L
999 γοῦν Headlam: γ᾽ L
1004 τἄμ᾽ ἐγίγνετ᾽ Musgrave: τἀμὰ γίγνετ᾽ L
1006 δυσμενῆ Stephanus: -γενῆ L

1010 πρόθυμον ὄντα, τοῖσιν Ἑλλήνων νόμοις
οὐχ ἁγνός εἰμι τῷ κτανόντι κατθανών·
πόλις τ' ἀφῆκε σωφρονοῦσα, τὸν θεὸν
μεῖζον τίουσα τῆς ἐμῆς ἔχθρας πολύ.
προσεῖπας, ἀντήκουσας· ἐντεῦθεν δὲ χρὴ
1015 τὸν προστρόπαιον τόνδε <δυσσεβῶς θανεῖν
1015a ἤ σ' ἐκ φόνου σωθέντα> γενναῖον καλεῖν.
οὕτω γε μέντοι τἄμ' ἔχει· θανεῖν μὲν οὐ
χρῄζω, λιπὼν δ' ἂν οὐδὲν ἀχθοίμην βίον.

ΧΟΡΟΣ
παραινέσαι σοι σμικρόν, Ἀλκμήνη, θέλω,
τὸν ἄνδρ' ἀφεῖναι τόνδ', ἐπεὶ δοκεῖ πόλει.

ΑΛΚΜΗΝΗ
1020 τί δ', ἢν θάνῃ τε καὶ πόλει πιθώμεθα;

ΧΟΡΟΣ
τὰ λῷστ' ἂν εἴη· πῶς τάδ' οὖν γενήσεται;

ΑΛΚΜΗΝΗ
ἐγὼ διδάξω ῥᾳδίως· κτανοῦσα γὰρ
τόνδ' εἶτα νεκρὸν τοῖς μετελθοῦσιν φίλων
δώσω· τὸ γὰρ σῶμ' οὐκ ἀπιστήσω χθονί,

1014 προσεῖπας Elmsley: πρὸς ἅ γ' εἶπας L
1015 τόνδε F. W. Schmidt: τόν τε L
1015-5a lac. indic. Kovacs
1015a γενναίαν possis, sed cf. Hec. 592
1020 ἢν . . . πιθώμεθα Elmsley: ἂν . . . πειθ- L

battlefield when I was eager to die, by the usages of the Greeks my death, for the man who kills me, is an unholy act; and it was sober good judgment on the city's part that they spared my life, setting a much higher value on the god than on their hatred of me. You have spoken, you have heard my reply: henceforth I, who am under a god's protection, must either <be impiously put to death, or if I am delivered from slaughter,> must call <you> noble.[a] Yet this is how things stand with me: while I do not wish to die, I would not be at all loath to leave life.

CHORUS LEADER
Alcmene, I want to give you a little advice: release this man since that is what the city has decided.

ALCMENE
What if he were to be killed and we also were to comply with the city's wish?

CHORUS LEADER
That would be best. How can it be done?

ALCMENE
It will be easy to tell you. I shall kill him and then give the corpse to those of his kin who come to fetch it. As regards his body I shall not be disobeying the city, and by his

---

[a] Editors translate the transmitted text "Henceforth you must call me at once the murdered man who calls for vengeance and the noble-hearted hero." But these words, like the rest of the speech, are addressed to Alcmene, and it is not easy to see why she should call him "noble-hearted." Eurystheus' coming hero-ization (1030–6) has not been mentioned yet, and a reference to addressing him as hero would be unintelligible, as well as inappropriate for Alcmene, who will not be among his worshipers.

1025 οὗτος δὲ δώσει τὴν δίκην θανὼν ἐμοί.

ΕΥΡΥΣΘΕΥΣ

κτεῖν᾽, οὐ παραιτοῦμαί σε· τήνδε δὲ πτόλιν,
ἐπεί μ᾽ ἀφῆκε καὶ κατῃδέσθη κτανεῖν,
χρησμῷ παλαιῷ Λοξίου δωρήσομαι,
ὃς ὠφελήσει μεῖζον᾽ ἢ δοκεῖ χρόνῳ.
1030 θανόντα γάρ με θάψεθ᾽ οὗ τὸ μόρσιμον,
δίας πάροιθε παρθένου Παλληνίδος·
καὶ σοὶ μὲν εὔνους καὶ πόλει σωτήριος
μέτοικος αἰεὶ κείσομαι κατὰ χθονός,
τοῖς τῶνδε δ᾽ ἐκγόνοισι πολεμιώτατος,
1035 ὅταν μόλωσι δεῦρο σὺν πολλῇ χερὶ
χάριν προδόντες τήνδε. τοιούτων ξένων
προύστητε. πῶς οὖν ταῦτ᾽ ἐγὼ πεπυσμένος
δεῦρ᾽ ἦλθον ἀλλ᾽ οὐ χρησμὸν ἡζόμην θεοῦ;
Ἥραν νομίζων θεσφάτων κρείσσω πολὺ
1040 κοὐκ ἂν προδοῦναί μ᾽. ἀλλὰ μήτε μοι χοὰς
μήθ᾽ αἷμ᾽ ἐάσῃτ᾽ εἰς ἐμὸν στάξαι τάφον.
κακὸν γὰρ αὐτοῖς νόστον ἀντὶ τῶνδ᾽ ἐγὼ
δώσω· διπλοῦν δὲ κέρδος ἕξετ᾽ ἐξ ἐμοῦ·
ὑμᾶς τ᾽ ὀνήσω τούσδε τε βλάψω θανών.

ΑΛΚΜΗΝΗ

1045 τί δῆτα μέλλετ᾽, εἰ πόλει σωτηρίαν
κατεργάσασθαι τοῖσί τ᾽ ἐξ ὑμῶν χρεών

1026 τήνδε δὲ πτόλιν Elmsley: τὴν δὲ δὴ πόλιν L
1029 δοκεῖ Wecklein: δοκεῖν L
1038 ἡζόμην Cobet: ἡρόμην L
1039 νομίζων Barnes: -ζω L

death he will pay the penalty to me.

EURYSTHEUS

Kill on, I do not ask for mercy! But as for this city, since it released me and shrank from killing me, I shall make a present to it of an ancient oracle of Loxias, an oracle which will do greater good in time to come than you can now imagine. For you Athenians will bury me in the place I was fated to lie, in front of the shrine of the divine maiden, Athena Pallenis. I shall lie for all time beneath the earth, a foreign visitor who is kindly to you and a protector of the city, but most hostile to the descendants of Heracles' children[a] when they come here with a great army, betraying the kindness you showed them. That is the kind of guest-friends you have defended. How then, you will ask, when I knew these things, did I come here instead of respecting the oracle of the god? It was because I thought that Hera was far greater than any oracles and would not abandon me. But do not omit to pour either libations or the blood of victims onto my tomb. In return for this I will give them a disastrous home coming. You shall have a double profit from me: by dying I shall bring benefit to you and harm to the Heraclids.

ALCMENE

(to the Chorus) Why then do you hesitate if you can secure safety for the city and for your descendants [to kill

---

[a] The Spartans, who claimed descent from Heracles, had invaded Attica a short time before this play was put on.

1041 ἐάσητ' Reiske: ἐάσῃς L: fort. ὀκνήσητ' vel ἀπό-
στητ'   τάφον Heath: τόπον L

111

[κτείνειν τὸν ἄνδρα τόνδ', ἀκούοντες τάδε];
δείκνυσι γὰρ κέλευθον ἀσφαλεστάτην·
ἐχθρὸς μὲν ἀνήρ, ὠφελεῖ δὲ κατθανών.
1050 κομίζετ' αὐτόν, δμῶες, ἔνθα χρὴ †κυσὶν†
δοῦναι κτανόντας· μὴ γὰρ ἐλπίσῃς ὅπως
αὖθις πατρῴας ζῶν ἔμ' ἐκβαλεῖς χθονός.

ΧΟΡΟΣ

ταῦτα δοκεῖ μοι. στείχετ', ὀπαδοί.
τὰ γὰρ ἐξ ἡμῶν
καθαρῶς ἔσται βασιλεῦσιν.

[1047] del. Wecklein
[1050] ἔνθα Madvig: εἶτα L   κυσὶν] πυρὶ Elmsley: τάφῳ
M. Haupt: κόνει Housman: fort. χύσιν: cf. 1040–1 et Aesch.
Cho. 97: quo recepto 1051 θανόντι Willink

this man, hearing these things]? He shows us the safest course. For the man is an enemy, and by dying he does us good. Take him away, servants, to the place where we must kill and bury him.[a] *(to Eurystheus)* For you must not hope that you will live to exile me yet again from my native land.

CHORUS LEADER

This course seems best to me. Be off, servants. For as far as our part is concerned, no taint attaches to our royal house.

Exit by Eisodos A EURYSTHEUS *under guard, then* ALC-MENE, SERVANT, *and* CHORUS.

[a] The transmitted texts says "kill and give him to the dogs." This cannot be correct, for it violates both the proposal Alcmene made in 1022–4 and the hero's tomb for Eurystheus on which his benefactions to Athens depend. Moreover, Alcmene's next words are a justification for *killing*, not for leaving to the dogs. Some editors put a lacuna after 1052. Had Alcmene suggested leaving Eurystheus unburied, of course, someone would have had to reply to her, if only to prevent the loss of the benefits to Athens of the hero's tomb. But 1053 joins so perfectly with 1052 that a lacuna becomes an unlikely hypothesis.

HIPPOLYTUS

INTRODUCTION

Hippolytus was produced in 428, the third year of the Peloponnesian War, on one of four occasions during Euripides' lifetime when his entries won first prize. (An earlier treatment by Euripides of the same story had apparently been a failure: for a reconstruction of that play see Barrett's edition, pp. 10–45.) Subsequent ages, despite changes of critical fashion in the assessment of Euripides' work, have agreed in regarding *Hippolytus* as one of his masterpieces. But in spite of this consensus, there are sharp disagreements between critics about how the play is to be interpreted. How are we to judge the character and actions of the play's two chief figures, Hippolytus and Phaedra? What are we to make of the two divinities that appear at its beginning and end?

Hippolytus, illegitimate son of Theseus and the queen of the Amazons, is the special favorite of Artemis. He lives a life of chastity in the goddess' company and calls Aphrodite the basest of deities. To avenge this slight to her honor, Aphrodite uses her power as goddess of love to bring about his death by indirect means, a complicated but clearly foreseen chain of causality. She causes Theseus' wife Phaedra to fall in love with him. The passion is doubly discreditable, being both adulterous and quasi-incestuous, Hippolytus being her stepson. Rather than give in to it Phaedra means to starve herself in silence, but her secret is wormed from her by her old nurse, who determines to save Phaedra's life by gratifying her passion. Though she is under strict instructions not to tell Hippolytus, she goes to him and, after putting him under oath to reveal to no one what she is about to say, tells him of Phaedra's love for him and urges him to become her lover. Hippolytus, under the impression that Phaedra has sent her, excoriates his stepmother and the whole female sex but promises to keep his oath. Phaedra, afraid that her secret will be revealed to the world at large, decides to hang herself and to leave a note accusing Hippolytus of raping her. When Theseus finds his wife dead and reads her note, he calls upon his father Poseidon (who had promised him three curses) to kill Hippolytus. Poseidon keeps his promise and causes a monstrous bull to come out of the sea and frighten Hippolytus' horses, driving his chariot onto the rocks and mangling his body. Before he dies, however, Artemis comes to tell Theseus the truth about both his wife and his son. Their good name is restored to them both, and father and son are reconciled. Artemis promises revenge on Aphrodite and lasting honors for Hippolytus.

As regards the two humans, there seem to be essentially two critical approaches. One group of critics finds Hippolytus deeply flawed: he is foolish in his attempt to suppress sexual love in himself, arrogantly convinced of his superiority to the mass of mankind, intolerant of weakness in others, and warped by fanatical misogyny. This first group of critics find Phaedra a sympathetic character, since she resists the passion Aphrodite has inspired in her and causes Hippolytus' death only when stung by the injustice of his condemnation of her.

A second group reverses the judgments. For them Phaedra is weak and vacillating, she thinks too much about her good name and too little about the reality of virtue, and her failure to make the distinction between being and seeming virtuous betrays her into the unjust act of slandering Hippolytus. These critics regard Hippolytus in a sympathetic light: he is seen as single-minded in his devotion to Artemis and a man of integrity.

The gods, too, have provoked the most divergent judgments. For some critics Aphrodite is the force of the sexual instinct and is given personal and bodily form only, as it were, for dramatic convenience. The goddesses are ideas or abstractions, representations of important powers in the world and as such worthy of respect. Others have seen theological satire (the goddesses are clearly vindictive and callous), a covert invitation to disbelieve in the anthropomorphic divinities of traditional Greek religion. Both the abstraction view and the satire view receive support from the biographical tradition, parts of which regard Euripides as the nursling of the philosophers and a disbeliever in the gods of tradition.

It would be rash to place much reliance in what the biographical tradition tells us about Euripides given its general level of unreliability. We are obliged to form our own judgment by comparing his gods with those of Sophocles and Aeschylus and seeing whether Euripides' treatment is sufficiently different to invite a Greek audience to suspect satire. There are clear instances in the extant plays where Sophocles' gods are as cruel or uncaring as those of Euripides (Athena, for example, at the beginning of *Ajax* or the end of *Women of Trachis*, where the final comment on all the carnage is "There is nothing here that is not Zeus"). Aeschylus likewise often portrays the gods as putting men in impossible situations where there is no good choice, and Plato criticized him sharply for attributing malice to the gods. All three tragic poets portray essentially the Homeric pantheon, and their gods often act on motives other than pure and disinterested justice, rewarding favorites and punishing enemies. It is hard to make out that Euripides' gods are a different kind of thing, so discreditable that the audience is driven to disbelief.

As for their being mere abstractions, the story requires not abstractions, such as the sexual instinct, but anthropomorphic divinities. There is no naturalistic reason why, just because Hippolytus rejects love, Phaedra should fall in love with him. It takes a personal Aphrodite, avenging an affront, to explain the connection. Likewise, unless Poseidon is a person who has made a promise to his son Theseus, Hippolytus' destruction by a bull rising from the sea is unconnected with his rejection of Aphrodite.

As regards the human figures, there is no reason to sympathize with one of them to the exclusion of the other. Both are victims of Aphrodite, as is Theseus. It is also a mistake to see the outcome of the play as the result of human shortcomings and to ignore the cardinal element of divine malice. Aphrodite's revenge makes use of the tragic mutual misunderstanding of Phaedra and Hippolytus and of Theseus' pardonable misjudgment of the evidence. Hippolytus berates Phaedra to the Nurse for a proposal she did not authorize, Phaedra slanders Hippolytus in order to discredit an accusation he does not intend to make. In reply to his father's accusation

Hippolytus, bound by his oath, can say only things that make the suspicion against him all the deeper. Artemis at the end of the play remarks, "When the gods so ordain, it is to be expected that men will make disastrous mistakes." This accurately describes what has happened. Artemis' final judgment on the nobility of the two mortals is surely meant to be accepted.

If we put to one side Hippolytus' initial fault in calling Aphrodite the basest of divinities, the play portrays undeserved suffering inflicted on three mortals by a goddess. The extreme situation brought about by the malice of Aphrodite shows the reverses to which human life is subject. Mortals can be fatally ignorant of some important fact, and their confident reasoning utterly mistaken. Yet in spite of their overwhelming inferiority to the gods in power and knowledge, men and women can still be upright in disaster and win as consolation the admiring song of later ages. Mortals, perhaps because they are subject to loss and death, exhibit a sympathy with misfortune and a loyalty to each other of which the gods are incapable. The reconciliation of father and son at the play's end is a demonstration of such sympathy and loyalty in the face of disaster.

SELECT BIBLIOGRAPHY

Editions

U. von Wilamowitz-Moellendorff (Berlin, 1891).
W. S. Barrett (Oxford, 1964).

Literary criticism

H. Avery, "'My Tongue Swore, But My Mind Is Unsworn,'" *TAPA* 99 (1968), 19–35.

D. Claus, "Phaedra and the Socratic Paradox," *YCS* 22 (1972), 223–38.

B. M. W. Knox, "The *Hippolytus* of Euripides," *YCS* 13 (1952), 3–31.

D. Kovacs, "Euripides *Hippolytus* 100 and the Meaning of the Prologue," *CP* 75 (1980), 130–7.

––––––– "Shame, Pleasure, and Honor in Phaedra's Great Speech (Euripides, *Hippolytus* 375–87)," *AJP* 101 (1980), 287–303.

––––––– *The Heroic Muse: Studies in the* Hippolytus *and* Hecuba *of Euripides* (Baltimore, 1987).

R. Lattimore, "Euripides' Phaedra and Hippolytus," *Arion* 1 (1962), 5–18.

S. Østerud, "Who Sings the Monody 669–79 in Euripides' *Hippolytus*?" *GRBS* 11 (1970), 307–20.

C. P. Segal, "The Tragedy of the *Hippolytus*: The Waters of Ocean and the Untouched Meadow," *HSCP* 70 (1965), 117–69.

––––––– "Shame and Purity in Euripides' *Hippolytus*," *Hermes* 98 (1970), 278–99.

W. D. Smith, "Staging in the Central Scene of the *Hippolytus*," *TAPA* 91 (1960), 162–77.

F. Solmsen, "'Bad Shame' and Related Problems in Phaedra's Speech (Eur. *Hipp*. 380–388)," *Hermes* 101 (1973), 420–5.

Dramatis Personae

ΑΦΡΟΔΙΤΗ	APHRODITE
ΙΠΠΟΛΥΤΟΣ	HIPPOLYTUS, son of Theseus
ΘΕΡΑΠΟΝΤΕΣ	SERVANTS of Hippolytus as secondary chorus
ΧΟΡΟΣ	CHORUS of women of Trozen
ΤΡΟΦΟΣ	NURSE to Phaedra
ΦΑΙΔΡΑ	PHAEDRA, wife of Theseus
ΘΗΣΕΥΣ	THESEUS, King of Athens
ΑΓΓΕΛΟΣ	MESSENGER, a servant of Hippolytus
ΑΡΤΕΜΙΣ	ARTEMIS

A Note on Staging

The *skene* represents the palace in Trozen in the northern Peloponnesus where Theseus, Phaedra, and Hippolytus live. Eisodos A leads to the countryside and abroad, Eisodos B to other parts of the city of Trozen.

ΙΠΠΟΛΥΤΟΣ

ΑΦΡΟΔΙΤΗ

Πολλὴ μὲν ἐν βροτοῖσι κοὐκ ἀνώνυμος
θεὰ κέκλημαι Κύπρις οὐρανοῦ τ' ἔσω·
ὅσοι τε Πόντου τερμόνων τ' Ἀτλαντικῶν
ναίουσιν εἴσω, φῶς ὁρῶντες ἡλίου,
5 τοὺς μὲν σέβοντας τἀμὰ πρεσβεύω κράτη,
σφάλλω δ' ὅσοι φρονοῦσιν εἰς ἡμᾶς μέγα.
ἔνεστι γὰρ δὴ κἀν θεῶν γένει τόδε·
τιμώμενοι χαίρουσιν ἀνθρώπων ὕπο.
δείξω δὲ μύθων τῶνδ' ἀλήθειαν τάχα.
10 ὁ γάρ με Θησέως παῖς, Ἀμαζόνος τόκος,
Ἱππόλυτος, ἁγνοῦ Πιτθέως παιδεύματα,
μόνος πολιτῶν τῆσδε γῆς Τροζηνίας
λέγει κακίστην δαιμόνων πεφυκέναι·
ἀναίνεται δὲ λέκτρα κοὐ ψαύει γάμων,
15 Φοίβου δ' ἀδελφὴν Ἄρτεμιν, Διὸς κόρην,
τιμᾷ, μεγίστην δαιμόνων ἡγούμενος,
χλωρὰν δ' ἀν' ὕλην παρθένῳ ξυνὼν ἀεὶ
κυσὶν ταχείαις θῆρας ἐξαιρεῖ χθονός,
μείζω βροτείας προσπεσὼν ὁμιλίας.
20 τούτοισι μέν νυν οὐ φθονῶ· τί γάρ με δεῖ;

124

HIPPOLYTUS

Enter APHRODITE *on the* theologeion *above the* skene.

APHRODITE

Mighty and of high renown, among mortals and in heaven alike, I am called the goddess Cypris.[a] Of all who dwell between the Euxine Sea and the Pillars of Atlas and look on the light of the sun, I honor those who reverence my power, but I lay low all those whose thoughts toward me are proud. For in the gods as well one finds this trait: they enjoy receiving honor from mortals.

The truth of these words I shall shortly demonstrate. Theseus' son Hippolytus, offspring of the Amazon woman and ward of holy Pittheus, alone among the citizens of this land of Trozen, says that I am the worst of deities. He shuns the bed of love and will have nothing to do with marriage. Instead, he honors Apollo's sister Artemis, Zeus's daughter, thinking her the greatest of deities. In the green wood, ever consort to the maiden goddess, he clears the land of wild beasts with his swift dogs and has gained a companionship greater than mortal. To this pair I feel no ill will: why should I? Yet for his sins against me

---

[a] Another name for Aphrodite, probably derived from her worship on Cyprus.

ἃ δ' εἰς ἔμ' ἡμάρτηκε τιμωρήσομαι
Ἱππόλυτον ἐν τῇδ' ἡμέρᾳ· τὰ πολλὰ δὲ
πάλαι προκόψασ', οὐ πόνου πολλοῦ με δεῖ.
ἐλθόντα γάρ νιν Πιτθέως ποτ' ἐκ δόμων
25 σεμνῶν ἐς ὄψιν καὶ τέλη μυστηρίων
Πανδίονος γῆν πατρὸς εὐγενὴς δάμαρ
ἰδοῦσα Φαίδρα καρδίαν κατέσχετο
ἔρωτι δεινῷ τοῖς ἐμοῖς βουλεύμασιν.

    καὶ πρὶν μὲν ἐλθεῖν τήνδε γῆν Τροζηνίαν,
30 πέτραν παρ' αὐτὴν Παλλάδος, κατόψιον
γῆς τῆσδε, ναὸν Κύπριδος ἐγκαθείσατο,
ἐρῶσ' ἔρωτ' ἔκδημον, Ἱππολύτῳ δ' ἔπι
τὸ λοιπὸν ὀνομάσουσιν ἱδρῦσθαι θεάν.
ἐπεὶ δὲ Θησεὺς Κεκροπίαν λείπει χθόνα
35 μίασμα φεύγων αἵματος Παλλαντιδῶν
καὶ τήνδε σὺν δάμαρτι ναυστολεῖ χθόνα,
ἐνιαυσίαν ἔκδημον αἰνέσας φυγήν,
ἐνταῦθα δὴ στένουσα κἀκπεπληγμένη
κέντροις ἔρωτος ἡ τάλαιν' ἀπόλλυται
40 σιγῇ, ξύνοιδε δ' οὔτις οἰκετῶν νόσον.
ἀλλ' οὔτι ταύτῃ τόνδ' ἔρωτα χρὴ πεσεῖν,
δείξω δὲ Θησεῖ πρᾶγμα κἀκφανήσεται.

33 ὀνομάσουσιν Jortin: ὠνόμαζεν C

---

[a] The mysteries of Demeter and Kore were celebrated at Eleusis in Attica.
[b] The rock of Athena is the Athenian Acropolis.

I shall this day punish Hippolytus. I have long since come far with my plans, and I need little further effort. One day when he came from Pittheus' house to the land of Pandion to witness and perform the august Mysteries,[a] his father's high-born wife Phaedra saw him, and her heart was seized with a dreadful longing: this was my devising.

Before she came to this land of Trozen, she built, next to the rock of Pallas,[b] a temple to Cypris overlooking this land since she loved a foreign love. After ages shall name the goddess' shrine for Hippolytus.[c] But Theseus left the land of Cecrops,[d] fleeing the blood guilt he incurred for the murder of the Pallantidae,[e] and sailed with his wife to this land, consenting to a year-long exile from his home. Ever since then the poor woman, groaning and made distraught by the goad of love, means to die in silence, and none of her household knows of her malady. But that is not the way this passion of hers is fated to end. I shall reveal the matter to Theseus and it will come to light,[f]

[c] There was a shrine of Aphrodite on the Acropolis near a hero sanctuary dedicated to Hippolytus. The shrine was called "Aphrodite near Hippolytus" from its proximity to the hero's sanctuary, though here Euripides makes a closer connection between them.

[d] Athens.

[e] Theseus' cousins, the sons of Pallas, disputed the throne with him. He is said to have killed them treacherously.

[f] The fact of Phaedra's love is actually first revealed to the Nurse, then to Hippolytus. What is "revealed" to Theseus is Phaedra's false accusation of rape. If the text is correct, Aphrodite's forecast is misleadingly abbreviated, perhaps to leave room for some surprise in how the plot will develop.

127

καὶ τὸν μὲν ἡμῖν πολέμιον νεανίαν
κτενεῖ πατὴρ ἀραῖσιν ἃς ὁ πόντιος
45 ἄναξ Ποσειδῶν ὤπασεν Θησεῖ γέρας,
μηδὲν μάταιον ἐς τρὶς εὔξασθαι θεῷ.
ἡ δ' εὐκλεὴς μὲν ἀλλ' ὅμως ἀπόλλυται
Φαίδρα· τὸ γὰρ τῆσδ' οὐ προτιμήσω κακὸν
τὸ μὴ οὐ παρασχεῖν τοὺς ἐμοὺς ἐχθροὺς ἐμοὶ
50 δίκην τοσαύτην ὥστε μοι καλῶς ἔχειν.
    ἀλλ' εἰσορῶ γὰρ τόνδε παῖδα Θησέως
στείχοντα, θήρας μόχθον ἐκλελοιπότα,
Ἱππόλυτον, ἔξω τῶνδε βήσομαι τόπων.
πολὺς δ' ἅμ' αὐτῷ προσπόλων ὀπισθόπους
55 κῶμος λέλακεν, Ἄρτεμιν τιμῶν θεὰν
ὕμνοισιν· οὐ γὰρ οἶδ' ἀνεῳγμένας πύλας
Ἅιδου, φάος δὲ λοίσθιον βλέπων τόδε.

ΙΠΠΟΛΥΤΟΣ

ἔπεσθ' ᾄδοντες ἔπεσθε
τὰν Διὸς οὐρανίαν
60 Ἄρτεμιν, ᾇ μελόμεσθα.

ΙΠΠΟΛΥΤΟΣ ΚΑΙ ΘΕΡΑΠΟΝΤΕΣ

πότνια πότνια σεμνοτάτα,
Ζηνὸς γένεθλον,
χαῖρε, χαῖρέ μοι, ὦ κόρα
65 Λατοῦς Ἄρτεμι καὶ Διός,
καλλίστα πολὺ παρθένων,
ἃ μέγαν κατ' οὐρανὸν
ναίεις εὐπατέρειαν αὐ-

and the young man who wars against me shall be killed by
his father with curses the sea lord Poseidon granted him
as a gift: three times Theseus can pray to the god and
have his prayer fulfilled. But Phaedra, though she dies
with her honor intact, shall nonetheless die. I do not set
such store by *her* misfortune as not to inflict on my ene-
mies such penalty as will satisfy me.

But now I see Hippolytus coming, finished with the
toil of the hunt, and so I shall leave this place. A great
throng of his servants treads close at his heels and shouts,
joining him in singing the praises of the goddess Artemis.
Clearly he does not know that the gates of the Under-
world stand open for him and that today's light is the last
he shall ever look upon.

*Exit APHRODITE. Enter HIPPOLYTUS by Eisodos A, car-
rying a garland, with CHORUS OF SERVANTS.*[a]

HIPPOLYTUS
(*sung*) Come follow me and sing of Zeus's heavenly
daughter Artemis, who cares for us!

HIPPOLYTUS AND CHORUS OF SERVANTS
(*sung*) Lady, lady most revered, daughter of Zeus, my
greeting, daughter of Leto and of Zeus, of maidens the
fairest by far, who dwell in great heaven in the court of

---

[a] *Hippolytus* is unusual in having two choruses, the main
chorus being the women of Trozen.

61n ῾Ιπ. καὶ Θεράποντες Barrett: Χο. C
67 μεγάλαν Weil

λάν, Ζηνὸς πολύχρυσον οἶκον.
70 χαῖρέ μοι, ὦ καλλίστα
καλλίστα τῶν κατ᾽ Ὄλυμπον
[παρθένων Ἄρτεμι].

ΙΠΠΟΛΥΤΟΣ

σοὶ τόνδε πλεκτὸν στέφανον ἐξ ἀκηράτου
λειμῶνος, ὦ δέσποινα, κοσμήσας φέρω,
75 ἔνθ᾽ οὔτε ποιμὴν ἀξιοῖ φέρβειν βοτὰ
οὔτ᾽ ἦλθέ πω σίδηρος, ἀλλ᾽ ἀκήρατον
μέλισσα λειμῶν᾽ ἠρινὴ διέρχεται,
Αἰδὼς δὲ ποταμίαισι κηπεύει δρόσοις,
ὅσοις διδακτὸν μηδὲν ἀλλ᾽ ἐν τῇ φύσει
80 τὸ σωφρονεῖν εἴληχεν ἐς τὰ πάνθ᾽ ὁμῶς,
τούτοις δρέπεσθαι, τοῖς κακοῖσι δ᾽ οὐ θέμις.
ἀλλ᾽, ὦ φίλη δέσποινα, χρυσέας κόμης
ἀνάδημα δέξαι χειρὸς εὐσεβοῦς ἄπο.
μόνῳ γάρ ἐστι τοῦτ᾽ ἐμοὶ γέρας βροτῶν·
85 σοὶ καὶ ξύνειμι καὶ λόγοις ἀμείβομαι,
κλύων μὲν αὐδῆς, ὄμμα δ᾽ οὐχ ὁρῶν τὸ σόν.
τέλος δὲ κάμψαιμ᾽ ὥσπερ ἠρξάμην βίου.

ΘΕΡΑΠΩΝ

ἄναξ—θεοὺς γὰρ δεσπότας καλεῖν χρεών—
ἆρ᾽ ἄν τί μου δέξαιο βουλεύσαντος εὖ;

ΙΠΠΟΛΥΤΟΣ

90 καὶ κάρτα γ᾽· ἦ γὰρ οὐ σοφοὶ φαινοίμεθ᾽ ἄν.

ΘΕΡΑΠΩΝ

οἶσθ᾽ οὖν βροτοῖσιν ὃς καθέστηκεν νόμος;

your good father, the gilded house of Zeus! My greeting
to you, fairest of all who dwell in Olympus!

HIPPOLYTUS

For you, lady, I bring this plaited garland I have made,
gathered from a virgin meadow, a place where the shep-
herd does not dare to pasture his flocks, where the iron
scythe has never come: no, virgin it is, and the bee makes
its way through it in the springtime. Reverence tends it
with streams of river water, for those to pluck who owe
nothing to teaching but in whose very nature chastity in
all things alike has won its place: the base may not gather.
So, dear lady, take this coronal for your golden hair from a
worshipful hand. I alone of mortals have this privilege: I
spend my days with you and speak with you, I hear your
voice but never see your face. May I end life's race even
as I began it!

SERVANT

Lord—for it is as gods that one should address one's
masters[a]—would you accept a word of good advice from
me?

HIPPOLYTUS

Most certainly. Else I should not seem wise.

SERVANT

The rule observed by mortals—do you know it?

[a] Or "Lord—for it is the gods one should call masters." For a
defense of the translation given above, see M. L. West, *CR* 15
(1965), 156 and 16 (1966), 17 and D. Kovacs, *CP* 75 (1980),
136–7.

70–1 fort. ὦ μάλιστα καλ- / λίστα cl. 485, 1421, *Hec.* 337
72 om. a: praebet b: del. Nauck

ΙΠΠΟΛΥΤΟΣ

οὐκ οἶδα· τοῦ δὲ καί μ' ἀνιστορεῖς πέρι;

ΘΕΡΑΠΩΝ

μισεῖν τὸ σεμνὸν καὶ τὸ μὴ πᾶσιν φίλον.

ΙΠΠΟΛΥΤΟΣ

ὀρθῶς γε· τίς δ' οὐ σεμνὸς ἀχθεινὸς βροτῶν;

ΘΕΡΑΠΩΝ

95 ἐν δ' εὐπροσηγόροισίν ἐστί τις χάρις;

ΙΠΠΟΛΥΤΟΣ

πλείστη γε, καὶ κέρδος γε σὺν μόχθῳ βραχεῖ.

ΘΕΡΑΠΩΝ

ἦ κἀν θεοῖσι ταὐτὸν ἐλπίζεις τόδε;

ΙΠΠΟΛΥΤΟΣ

εἴπερ γε θνητοὶ θεῶν νόμοισι χρώμεθα.

ΘΕΡΑΠΩΝ

πῶς οὖν σὺ σεμνὴν δαίμον' οὐ προσεννέπεις;

ΙΠΠΟΛΥΤΟΣ

100 τίν'; εὐλαβοῦ δὲ μή τί σου σφαλῇ στόμα.

ΘΕΡΑΠΩΝ

τήνδ', ἣ πύλαισι σαῖς ἐφέστηκεν πέλας.

¹⁰¹ πέλας Π: Κύπρις C

HIPPOLYTUS

No. What is the law you question me about?

SERVANT

To hate what's haughty and not friend to all.

HIPPOLYTUS

Quite right. What haughty person gives no pain?

SERVANT

And is there charm in being affable?

HIPPOLYTUS

Yes, much, and profit too with little toil.

SERVANT

Do you think this holds among the gods as well?

HIPPOLYTUS

Yes, if we mortals follow heavenly usage.

SERVANT

How then no word for a high and mighty[a] goddess?

HIPPOLYTUS

Who? Careful lest your tongue commit some slip.[b]

SERVANT

(pointing to the statue of Aphrodite) The goddess here,
who stands beside your gate.

---

[a] Six lines earlier the servant had used σεμνός in its unfavorable sense. Here he uses it to mean "august, revered," with, however, an unintentional overtone of "haughty" my translation tries to suggest.

[b] Several gods, among them Demeter's daughter Persephone, were called "august" and were considered unsafe to call by their proper names.

ΙΠΠΟΛΥΤΟΣ

πρόσωθεν αὐτὴν ἁγνὸς ὢν ἀσπάζομαι.

ΘΕΡΑΠΩΝ

103 σεμνή γε μέντοι κἀπίσημος ἐν βροτοῖς.

ΙΠΠΟΛΥΤΟΣ

106 οὐδείς μ᾽ ἀρέσκει νυκτὶ θαυμαστὸς θεῶν.

ΘΕΡΑΠΩΝ

107 τιμαῖσιν, ὦ παῖ, δαιμόνων χρῆσθαι χρεών.

ΙΠΠΟΛΥΤΟΣ

104 ἄλλοισιν ἄλλος θεῶν τε κἀνθρώπων μέλει.

ΘΕΡΑΠΩΝ

105 εὐδαιμονοίης, νοῦν ἔχων ὅσον σε δεῖ.

ΙΠΠΟΛΥΤΟΣ

108 χωρεῖτ᾽, ὀπαδοί, καὶ παρελθόντες δόμους
σίτων μέλεσθε· τερπνὸν ἐκ κυναγίας
110 τράπεζα πλήρης· καὶ καταψήχειν χρεὼν
ἵππους, ὅπως ἂν ἅρμασι ζεύξας ὕπο
βορᾶς κορεσθεὶς γυμνάσω τὰ πρόσφορα.
τὴν σὴν δὲ Κύπριν πόλλ᾽ ἐγὼ χαίρειν λέγω.

ΘΕΡΑΠΩΝ

ἡμεῖς δέ—τοὺς νέους γὰρ οὐ μιμητέον
115 φρονοῦντας οὕτως—ὡς πρέπει δούλοις λέγειν
προσευξόμεσθα τοῖσι σοῖς ἀγάλμασιν,
δέσποινα Κύπρι. χρὴ δὲ συγγνώμην ἔχειν·

104–5 post 107 trai. Gomperz

HIPPOLYTUS

I greet her from afar, for I am pure.

SERVANT

Yet she's revered and famous among mortals.

HIPPOLYTUS

I like no god whose worship is at night.

SERVANT

My son, to honor the gods is only just.

HIPPOLYTUS

Each has his likes, in gods and men alike.

SERVANT

I wish you fortune—and the good sense you need!

HIPPOLYTUS

Go, servants, enter the house and prepare the meal. After the hunt a full table is a pleasure. And you must rub down my horses so that when I have eaten my fill I can yoke them to my chariot and give them proper exercise.

Exit CHORUS OF SERVANTS into the palace.

As for your Cypris, I bid her good day!

Exit HIPPOLYTUS into the palace.

SERVANT

Yet since we should not imitate the young when their thoughts are like these, I shall pray, in words befitting a slave, to your statue, my lady Cypris. One should be for-

εἴ τίς σ' ὑφ' ἥβης σπλάγχνον ἔντονον φέρων
μάταια βάζει, μὴ δόκει τούτου κλυεῖν.
120 σοφωτέρους γὰρ χρὴ βροτῶν εἶναι θεούς.

ΧΟΡΟΣ

στρ. α
Ὠκεανοῦ τις ὕδωρ στάζουσα πέτρα λέγεται,
βαπτὰν κάλπισι πα-
γὰν ῥυτὰν προιεῖσα κρημνῶν·
125 τόθι μοί τις ἦν φίλα
πορφύρεα φάρη ποταμίᾳ δρόσῳ
τέγγουσα, θερμᾶς δ' ἐπὶ νῶτα πέτρας
εὐαλίου κατέβαλλ'· ὅθεν
130 μοι πρῶτα φάτις ἦλθε δεσποίνας,

ἀντ. α
τειρομέναν νοσερᾷ κοίτᾳ δέμας ἐντὸς ἔχειν
οἴκων, λεπτὰ δὲ φά-
ρη ξανθὰν κεφαλὰν σκιάζειν·
135 τριτάταν δέ νιν κλύω
τάνδ' ἑκὰς ἀβρώτου στόματος ἁμέραν
Δάματρος ἀκτᾶς δέμας ἁγνὸν ἴσχειν,
κρυπτῷ πένθει θανάτου θέλου-
140 σαν κέλσαι ποτὶ τέρμα δύστανον.

στρ. β
ἦ γὰρ ἔνθεος, ὦ κούρα,
εἴτ' ἐκ Πανὸς εἴθ' Ἑκάτας
ἢ σεμνῶν Κορυβάντων

123–4 παγὰν ῥυτὰν Willink: ῥ- π- C

giving: if youth makes someone's heart stiff with pride and he utters folly, pretend not to hear him. For gods should be wiser than mortals.

Exit SERVANT *into the palace. Enter women of Trozen as* CHORUS *by Eisodos B.*

CHORUS

There is a cliff dripping water whose source, men say, is the river Oceanus:[a] it pours forth over its beetling edge a flowing stream into which pitchers are dipped. It was there that I found a friend soaking her brightly colored clothes in the river water and laying them out on the warm rock's broad back in the sun. From there it was that I first had news of my queen.

She lies afflicted, they say, on a bed of sickness and keeps indoors, with fine-spun cloths shading her blond head. I hear that for three days now, her mouth taking no food, she has kept far off the holy substance of Demeter's grain, wishing because of some secret grief to ground her life's craft in the unhappy journey's-end of death.

Has some god, Pan or Hecate, possessed you, dear girl? Do your wits wander under the spell of the august

[a] In Greek mythic geography Oceanus is a river that goes around the entire known world.

---

126 φάρη Hartung: φάρεα C

136 τάνδ' ἑκὰς Reiske: τάνδε κατ' C   ἀβρώτου Verrall: ἀμβροσίου C

141 ἦ γὰρ Nauck: σὺ γὰρ C

φοιτᾷς ἢ ματρὸς ὀρείας;
145 ἆρ᾽ ἀμφὶ τὰν πολύθη-
ρον Δίκτυνναν ἀμπλακίαις
ἀνίερος ἀθύτων πελάνων τρύχῃ;
φοιτᾷ γὰρ καὶ διὰ Λί-
μνας χέρσον θ᾽ ὑπὲρ πελάγους
150 δίναις ἐν νοτίαις ἅλμας.

ἀντ. β

ἢ πόσιν, τὸν Ἐρεχθειδᾶν
ἀρχαγόν, τὸν εὐπατρίδαν,
ποιμαίνει τις ἐν οἴκοις
κρυπτᾷ κοίτᾳ λεχέων σῶν;
155 ἢ ναυβάτας τις ἔπλευ-
σεν Κρήτας ἔξορμος ἀνὴρ
λιμένα τὸν εὐξεινότατον ναύταις
φήμαν πέμπων βασιλεί-
ᾳ, λύπᾳ δ᾽ ὑπὲρ παθέων
160 εὐναία δέδεται ψυχά;

ἐπῳδ.

φιλεῖ δὲ τᾷ δυστρόπῳ γυναικῶν
ἁρμονίᾳ κακὰ
δύστανος ἀμηχανία συνοικεῖν
ὠδίνων τε καὶ ἀφροσύνας.
165 δι᾽ ἐμᾶς ᾖξέν ποτε νηδύος ἅδ᾽
αὔρα· τὰν δ᾽ εὔλοχον οὐρανίαν
τόξων μεδέουσαν ἀύτευν
Ἄρτεμιν, καί μοι πολυζήλωτος αἰεὶ
σὺν θεοῖσι φοιτᾷ.

Corybantes or the mountain mother?[a] Are you being worn down for some fault against Dictynna of the wild beasts,[b] having failed to offer her the holy batter? For she also haunts the Lake and passes over the dry land in the sea, that stands in the eddies of the surf.

Or is it your husband, the nobly born king of Erechtheus' folk?[c] Does some other woman rule his passion, someone in the palace, making secret love to him apart from your bed? Or has some mariner from Crete put in at that harbor most hospitable to sailors bearing news to the queen, so that her soul is bound bedfast in grief over her misfortunes?

Women's nature is an uneasy harmony, and with it is wont to dwell the painful unhappy helplessness of birth pangs and their delirium. Through my womb also has this breath darted. But I called on the heavenly easer of travail, Artemis, mistress of arrows, and she is always—the gods be praised—my much-envied visitor.

Enter NURSE *from the palace, then* PHAEDRA *supported by servants. Other servants bring a couch onto the stage on which Phaedra lies down.*

---

[a] The mountain mother, Cybele, and her divine ministers the Corybantes were thought to afflict people with madness.

[b] A Cretan goddess identified with Artemis.

[c] Erechtheus was an earlier king of Athens.

---

144 φοιτᾷς ἢ ματρὸς ὀρείας Bothe: ἢ μ- ὀ- φ- C
145 ἆρ' Barrett: σὺ δ' C

170— ἀλλ' ἥδε τροφὸς γεραιὰ πρὸ θυρῶν
τήνδε κομίζουσ' ἔξω μελάθρων.
στυγνὸν δ' ὀφρύων νέφος αὐξάνεται.
τί ποτ' ἐστὶ μαθεῖν ἔραται ψυχή,
τί δεδήληται
175 δέμας ἀλλόχροον βασιλείας.

TΡΟΦΟΣ

ὦ κακὰ θνητῶν στυγεραί τε νόσοι·
τί σ' ἐγὼ δράσω; τί δὲ μὴ δράσω;
τόδε σοι φέγγος, λαμπρὸς ὅδ' αἰθήρ,
ἔξω δὲ δόμων ἤδη νοσερᾶς
180 δέμνια κοίτης.
δεῦρο γὰρ ἐλθεῖν πᾶν ἔπος ἦν σοι,
τάχα δ' ἐς θαλάμους σπεύσεις τὸ πάλιν.
ταχὺ γὰρ σφάλλῃ κοὐδενὶ χαίρεις,
οὐδέ σ' ἀρέσκει τὸ παρόν, τὸ δ' ἀπὸν
185 φίλτερον ἡγῇ.
κρεῖσσον δὲ νοσεῖν ἢ θεραπεύειν·
τὸ μέν ἐστιν ἁπλοῦν, τῷ δὲ συνάπτει
λύπη τε φρενῶν χερσίν τε πόνος.
πᾶς δ' ὀδυνηρὸς βίος ἀνθρώπων
190 κοὐκ ἔστι πόνων ἀνάπαυσις.
ἀλλ' ὅ τι τοῦ ζῆν φίλτερον ἄλλο
σκότος ἀμπίσχων κρύπτει νεφέλαις.
δυσέρωτες δὴ φαινόμεθ' ὄντες
τοῦδ' ὅ τι τοῦτο στίλβει κατὰ γῆν
195 δι' ἀπειροσύνην ἄλλου βιότου

CHORUS LEADER

But here is her aged nurse before the door, bringing her
out of the palace. The cloud of unhappiness on her brow
is growing. My heart longs to know what it is, why the
Queen's body is so ravaged, her color so changed.

NURSE

Oh, the troubles mortals have, the hateful illnesses! What
shall I do for you? What shall I not? Here is daylight and
here the bright sky, and your sickbed stands now outside
the house. For to come out here was all you talked of.
But soon you will hurry back into your chamber, for you
soon slip from contentment and find joy in nothing, tak-
ing no pleasure in what is at hand but loving instead what
you do not have. Better it is to be sick than to tend the
sick. The first is a single thing, while the second joins
grief of heart to toil of hand. But the life of mortals is
wholly trouble, and there is no rest from toil. Anything
we might love more than life is hid in a surrounding cloud
of darkness, and we show ourselves unhappy lovers of
whatever light there is that shines on earth because we

191–7 in suspicionem voc. Barrett

κοὐκ ἀπόδειξιν τῶν ὑπὸ γαίας,
μύθοις δ' ἄλλως φερόμεσθα.

ΦΑΙΔΡΑ

αἴρετέ μου δέμας, ὀρθοῦτε κάρα·
λέλυμαι μελέων σύνδεσμα φίλων.
200 λάβετ' εὐπήχεις χεῖρας, πρόπολοι.
βαρύ μοι κεφαλῆς ἐπίκρανον ἔχειν·
ἄφελ', ἀμπέτασον βόστρυχον ὤμοις.

ΤΡΟΦΟΣ

θάρσει, τέκνον, καὶ μὴ χαλεπῶς
μετάβαλλε δέμας·
205 ῥᾷον δὲ νόσον μετά θ' ἡσυχίας
καὶ γενναίου λήματος οἴσεις.
μοχθεῖν δὲ βροτοῖσιν ἀνάγκη.

ΦΑΙΔΡΑ

αἰαῖ·
πῶς ἂν δροσερᾶς ἀπὸ κρηνῖδος
καθαρῶν ὑδάτων πῶμ' ἀρυσαίμαν,
210 ὑπό τ' αἰγείροις ἔν τε κομήτῃ
λειμῶνι κλιθεῖσ' ἀναπαυσαίμαν;

ΤΡΟΦΟΣ

ὦ παῖ, τί θροεῖς;
οὐ μὴ παρ' ὄχλῳ τάδε γηρύσῃ,
μανίας ἔποχον ῥίπτουσα λόγον;

ΦΑΙΔΡΑ

215 πέμπετέ μ' εἰς ὄρος· εἶμι πρὸς ὕλαν

are ignorant of another life, and the world below is not revealed to us. We are aimlessly borne along by mere tales.

PHAEDRA

Raise up my body, hold my head erect! My limbs are unstrung! Take my fair arms, servants! It is a burden to have this headdress on my head. Take it off, spread my tresses on my shoulders!

NURSE

Courage, my child! Do not shift your body so violently. You will endure your sickness more easily with calm and nobility of heart. Mortals must endure trouble.

PHAEDRA[a]

Oh, oh! How I long to draw a drink of pure water from a dewy spring and to take my rest lying under the poplar trees and in the uncut meadow!

NURSE

My child, what are these words of yours? Stop saying such things before the crowd, hurling wild words that are borne on madness!

PHAEDRA

Take me to the mountain: I mean to go to the wood, to

---

[a] Between here and 239, Phaedra's anapests exhibit the Doric alpha associated with lyric delivery, though metrically they are no different from the Nurse's non-lyric anapests. Lyric delivery is often associated with delirium (Alcestis at *Alc.* 244–72, Cassandra at Aesch. *Ag.* 1085ff, etc.), and although Phaedra's lines are spoken, the Doric vocalism may help to suggest an abnormal state of mind.

καὶ παρὰ πεύκας, ἵνα θηροφόνοι
στείβουσι κύνες
βαλιαῖς ἐλάφοις ἐγχριμπτόμεναι.
πρὸς θεῶν, ἔραμαι κυσὶ θωῦξαι
220 καὶ παρὰ χαίταν ξανθὰν ῥῖψαι
Θεσσαλὸν ὅρπακ', ἐπίλογχον ἔχουσ'
ἐν χειρὶ βέλος.

ΤΡΟΦΟΣ

τί ποτ', ὦ τέκνον, τάδε κηραίνεις;
τί κυνηγεσίων καί σοι μελέτη;
225 τί δὲ κρηναίων νασμῶν ἔρασαι;
πάρα γὰρ δροσερὰ πύργοις συνεχὴς
κλειτύς, ὅθεν σοι πῶμα γένοιτ' ἄν.

ΦΑΙΔΡΑ

δέσποιν' ἁλίας Ἄρτεμι Λίμνας
καὶ γυμνασίων τῶν ἱπποκρότων,
230 εἴθε γενοίμαν ἐν σοῖς δαπέδοις
πώλους Ἐνετὰς δαμαλιζομένα.

ΤΡΟΦΟΣ

τί τόδ' αὖ παράφρων ἔρριψας ἔπος;
νῦν δὴ μὲν ὄρος βᾶσ' ἐπὶ θήρας
πόθον ἐστέλλου, νῦν δ' αὖ ψαμάθοις
235 ἐπ' ἀκυμάντοις πώλων ἔρασαι.
τάδε μαντείας ἄξια πολλῆς,
ὅστις σε θεῶν ἀνασειράζει
καὶ παρακόπτει φρένας, ὦ παῖ.

144

the pine wood, where hounds that kill wild beasts tread, running close after the dappled deer! In heaven's name, how I want to shout to the hounds and to let fly past my golden hair a javelin of Thessaly, holding in my hand the sharp-tipped lance!

NURSE

Why, my child, these fevered thoughts? Why concern yourself with hunting? Why are you yearning for fountain springs? Hard by the city wall is a dewy slope where you may drink.

PHAEDRA

Mistress of the Salt Lake, Artemis, mistress of the coursing ground for horses, O that I might find myself on your plains taming Venetian colts!

NURSE

What whirling words are these you utter again in your frenzy? One time you are off going to the mountains to the hunt you long for, another time on the sands not reached by the waves you yearn for horses! All this calls for a skillful diviner to say which of the gods is making you swerve from the course, my child, and striking your wits awry.[a]

[a] The audience, thanks to the prologue, know the answer to the Nurse's question: Aphrodite is bringing Phaedra's secret to light.

EURIPIDES

δύστηνος ἐγώ, τί ποτ᾽ εἰργασάμην;
240 ποῖ παρεπλάγχθην γνώμης ἀγαθῆς;
ἐμάνην, ἔπεσον δαίμονος αἴσῃ.
φεῦ φεῦ τλήμων.
μαῖα, πάλιν μου κρύψον κεφαλήν,
αἰδούμεθα γὰρ τὰ λελεγμένα μοι.
245 κρύπτε· κατ᾽ ὄσσων δάκρυ μοι βαίνει,
καὶ ἐπ᾽ αἰσχύνην ὄμμα τέτραπται.
τὸ γὰρ ὀρθοῦσθαι γνώμην ὀδυνᾷ,
τὸ δὲ μαινόμενον κακόν· ἀλλὰ κρατεῖ
μὴ γιγνώσκοντ᾽ ἀπολέσθαι.

250 κρύπτω· τὸ δ᾽ ἐμὸν πότε δὴ θάνατος
σῶμα καλύψει;
πολλὰ διδάσκει μ᾽ ὁ πολὺς βίοτος·
χρῆν γὰρ μετρίας εἰς ἀλλήλους
φιλίας θνητοὺς ἀνακίρνασθαι
255 καὶ μὴ πρὸς ἄκρον μυελὸν ψυχῆς,
εὔλυτα δ᾽ εἶναι στέργηθρα φρενῶν
ἀπό τ᾽ ὤσασθαι καὶ ξυντεῖναι.
τὸ δ᾽ ὑπὲρ δισσῶν μίαν ὠδίνειν
ψυχὴν χαλεπὸν βάρος, ὡς κἀγὼ
260 τῆσδ᾽ ὑπεραλγῶ.
βιότου δ᾽ ἀτρεκεῖς ἐπιτηδεύσεις
φασὶ σφάλλειν πλέον ἢ τέρπειν
τῇ θ᾽ ὑγιείᾳ μᾶλλον πολεμεῖν·

PHAEDRA

Luckless me, what have I done? Where have I wandered from the path of good sense? I was mad, I fell, and it was the doing of some divinity. Oh, how unhappy I am! Nurse, cover my head up again! For I am ashamed of my words. Go on, cover it: the tears stream down from my eyes and my gaze is turned to shame. For to be right in my mind is grievous pain, while this madness is an ill thing. Best to perish in unconsciousness!

The Nurse veils Phaedra's head.

NURSE

I cover your head. But when will my body be covered in death? My long life has taught me many lessons: mortals should mix the cup of their affection to one another in moderation. It should not sink to their very marrow, but the affection that binds their hearts should be easy to loosen, easy either to cast aside or draw tightly to them. It is a grievous burden that one soul should so travail over two as I grieve for her. Men say that an unswerving way of life leads more to a fall than to satisfaction and is more

---

²⁴¹ αἴσῃ Π: ἄτη C

οὕτω τὸ λίαν ἧσσον ἐπαινῶ
265 τοῦ μηδὲν ἄγαν·
καὶ ξυμφήσουσι σοφοί μοι.

ΧΟΡΟΣ

γύναι γεραιά, βασιλίδος πιστὴ τροφέ,
Φαίδρας ὁρῶμεν τάσδε δυστήνους τύχας.
ἄσημα δ' ἡμῖν ἥτις ἐστὶν ἡ νόσος·
270 σοῦ δ' ἂν πυθέσθαι καὶ κλυεῖν βουλοίμεθ' ἄν.

ΤΡΟΦΟΣ

†οὐκ οἶδ' ἐλέγχουσ'†· οὐ γὰρ ἐννέπειν θέλει.

ΧΟΡΟΣ

οὐδ' ἥτις ἀρχὴ τῶνδε πημάτων ἔφυ;

ΤΡΟΦΟΣ

ἐς ταὐτὸν ἥκεις· πάντα γὰρ σιγᾷ τάδε.

ΧΟΡΟΣ

ὡς ἀσθενεῖ τε καὶ κατέξανται δέμας.

ΤΡΟΦΟΣ

275 πῶς δ' οὔ, τριταίαν γ' οὖσ' ἄσιτος ἡμέραν;

ΧΟΡΟΣ

πότερον ὑπ' ἄτης ἢ θανεῖν πειρωμένη;

ΤΡΟΦΟΣ

οὐκ οἶδ', ἀσιτεῖ δ' εἰς ἀπόστασιν βίου.

ΧΟΡΟΣ

θαυμαστὸν εἶπας, εἰ τάδ' ἐξαρκεῖ πόσει.

271 fort. ἀπεῖπ' (vel ἔληξ' vel κέκμηκ') ἐλέγχουσ'

hurtful to health. That is why I have much less praise for
excess than for moderation. The wise will bear me out.

CHORUS LEADER
Old woman, faithful nurse to the Queen, we see Phaedra's
unhappy plight, yet it is unclear to us what is wrong with
her. We want to ask you and hear your answer.

NURSE
I cannot tell: she will not say.

CHORUS LEADER
Not even how the trouble first began?

NURSE
'Tis all one: on all these questions she is mute.

CHORUS LEADER
How weak and wasted her body is!

NURSE
No wonder: she's been three days without food.

CHORUS LEADER
Is she deranged, or does she mean to die?

NURSE
I know not. But her fast will end her there.

CHORUS LEADER
'Tis very strange if this contents her husband.

---

[276] κατθανεῖν Willink
[277] οὐκ οἶδ' Wilamowitz: θανεῖν C

ΤΡΟΦΟΣ

κρύπτει γὰρ ἥδε πῆμα κοὔ φησιν νοσεῖν.

ΧΟΡΟΣ

280 ὁ δ᾽ ἐς πρόσωπον οὐ τεκμαίρεται βλέπων;

ΤΡΟΦΟΣ

ἔκδημος ὢν γὰρ τῆσδε τυγχάνει χθονός.

ΧΟΡΟΣ

σὺ δ᾽ οὐκ ἀνάγκην προσφέρεις, πειρωμένη
νόσον πυθέσθαι τῆσδε καὶ πλάνον φρενῶν;

ΤΡΟΦΟΣ

ἐς πάντ᾽ ἀφῖγμαι κοὐδὲν εἴργασμαι πλέον.
285 οὐ μὴν ἀνήσω γ᾽ οὐδὲ νῦν προθυμίας,
ὡς ἂν παροῦσα καὶ σύ μοι ξυμμαρτυρῇς
οἷα πέφυκα δυστυχοῦσι δεσπόταις.
    ἄγ᾽, ὦ φίλη παῖ, τῶν πάροιθε μὲν λόγων
λαθώμεθ᾽ ἄμφω, καὶ σύ θ᾽ ἡδίων γενοῦ
290 στυγνὴν ὀφρῦν λύσασα καὶ γνώμης ὁδόν,
ἐγώ θ᾽ ὅπῃ σοι μὴ καλῶς τόθ᾽ εἱπόμην
μεθεῖσ᾽ ἐπ᾽ ἄλλον εἶμι βελτίω λόγον.
κεἰ μὲν νοσεῖς τι τῶν ἀπορρήτων κακῶν,
γυναῖκες αἵδε συγκαθιστάναι νόσον·
295 εἰ δ᾽ ἔκφορός σοι συμφορὰ πρὸς ἄρσενας,
λέγ᾽, ὡς ἰατροῖς πρᾶγμα μηνυθῇ τόδε.
εἶέν, τί σιγᾷς; οὐκ ἐχρῆν σιγᾶν, τέκνον,
ἀλλ᾽ ἤ μ᾽ ἐλέγχειν, εἴ τι μὴ καλῶς λέγω,
ἢ τοῖσιν εὖ λεχθεῖσι συγχωρεῖν λόγοις.
300 φθέγξαι τι, δεῦρ᾽ ἄθρησον. ὦ τάλαιν᾽ ἐγώ,

NURSE

No, for she hides it and denies she's ill.

CHORUS LEADER

Can he not guess by looking at her face?

NURSE

No, for it happens that he is abroad.

CHORUS LEADER

Aren't you then applying force, trying to discover the malady that is causing her wits to wander?

NURSE

I have tried everything and made no progress. Yet I shall not even now relax my efforts, so that you standing by may also bear witness on my behalf what kind of servant I have been to my mistress in distress.

Come, dear child, let us both forget the words that are past: *you* be more gracious, smoothing your morose brow and the path your thoughts take, while *I*, where in the past I was not able to follow you sympathetically, shall let that be and take another and better tack. If your malady is one of those that are unmentionable, here are women to help set it to rights. If your misfortune may be spoken of to men, speak so that the thing may be revealed to doctors. *(Phaedra is silent.)* Well, why are you silent? You ought not to be silent, child, but should either refute me if I have said something amiss or agree with what has been said aright. *(She remains silent.)* Say something!

γυναῖκες, ἄλλως τούσδε μοχθοῦμεν πόνους,
ἴσον δ᾽ ἄπεσμεν τῷ πρίν· οὔτε γὰρ τότε
λόγοις ἐτέγγεθ᾽ ἥδε νῦν τ᾽ οὐ πείθεται.
    ἀλλ᾽ ἴσθι μέντοι—πρὸς τάδ᾽ αὐθαδεστέρα
305 γίγνου θαλάσσης—εἰ θανῇ, προδοῦσα σοὺς
παῖδας, πατρῴων μὴ μεθέξοντας δόμων,
μὰ τὴν ἄνασσαν ἱππίαν Ἀμαζόνα,
ἣ σοῖς τέκνοισι δεσπότην ἐγείνατο,
νόθον φρονοῦντα γνησί᾽, οἶσθά νιν καλῶς,
Ἱππόλυτον . . .

ΦΑΙΔΡΑ

οἴμοι.

ΤΡΟΦΟΣ

310   θιγγάνει σέθεν τόδε;

ΦΑΙΔΡΑ

ἀπώλεσάς με, μαῖα, καί σε πρὸς θεῶν
τοῦδ᾽ ἀνδρὸς αὖθις λίσσομαι σιγᾶν πέρι.

ΤΡΟΦΟΣ

ὁρᾷς; φρονεῖς μὲν εὖ, φρονοῦσα δ᾽ οὐ θέλεις
παῖδάς τ᾽ ὀνῆσαι καὶ σὸν ἐκσῶσαι βίον.

ΦΑΙΔΡΑ

315 φιλῶ τέκν᾽· ἄλλῃ δ᾽ ἐν τύχῃ χειμάζομαι.

ΤΡΟΦΟΣ

ἁγνὰς μέν, ὦ παῖ, χεῖρας αἵματος φορεῖς;

302 τῷ Scaliger: τῶν C

Look at me! Oh unlucky me, women, my efforts are a
waste of time: I am just as far off as before! Words failed
to soften her before, and now too she is not won over.

But you may be sure of this—and then go on being
more stubborn than the sea—that if you die you have
betrayed your sons, who shall have no share in their
father's house, none! I tell you in the name of that horse-
riding queen of the Amazons who bore a master to rule
over your sons, a bastard with thoughts of legitimacy, you
know him well, Hippolytus . . .

PHAEDRA

Oh misery!

NURSE

So this touches you?

PHAEDRA

You are killing me, Nurse, and I beg you by the gods
never to say anything of this man again!

NURSE

You see? You *are* in your right mind, but though you are,
you are not willing to benefit your sons and to save your
own life.

PHAEDRA

I love my children. It is another fate that buffets me.

NURSE

Your hands, I presume, are clean of blood, my child?

ΦΑΙΔΡΑ

χεῖρες μὲν ἁγναί, φρὴν δ' ἔχει μίασμά τι.

ΤΡΟΦΟΣ

μῶν ἐξ ἐπακτοῦ πημονῆς ἐχθρῶν τινος;

ΦΑΙΔΡΑ

φίλος μ' ἀπόλλυσ' οὐχ ἑκοῦσαν οὐχ ἑκών.

ΤΡΟΦΟΣ

320   Θησεύς τιν' ἡμάρτηκεν ἔς σ' ἁμαρτίαν;

ΦΑΙΔΡΑ

μὴ δρῶσ' ἔγωγ' ἐκεῖνον ὀφθείην κακῶς.

ΤΡΟΦΟΣ

τί γὰρ τὸ δεινὸν τοῦθ' ὅ σ' ἐξαίρει θανεῖν;

ΦΑΙΔΡΑ

ἔα μ' ἁμαρτεῖν· οὐ γὰρ ἔς σ' ἁμαρτάνω.

ΤΡΟΦΟΣ

οὐ δῆθ' ἑκοῦσά γ', ἐν δὲ σοὶ λελείψομαι.

ΦΑΙΔΡΑ

325   τί δρᾷς; βιάζῃ, χειρὸς ἐξαρτωμένη;

ΤΡΟΦΟΣ

καὶ σῶν γε γονάτων, κοὐ μεθήσομαί ποτε.

ΦΑΙΔΡΑ

κάκ' ὦ τάλαινά σοι τάδ', εἰ πεύσῃ, κακά.

ΤΡΟΦΟΣ

μεῖζον γὰρ ἤ σου μὴ τυχεῖν τί μοι κακόν;

328 σε μὴ εὐτυχεῖν Nauck

PHAEDRA

My hands are clean. It is my heart that's stained.

NURSE

Could it be spells launched by some enemy?

PHAEDRA

A friend destroys me. Neither of us wills it.

NURSE

Has Theseus done some wrong against you then?

PHAEDRA

Never may I be found out wronging him!

NURSE

What *is* this dread that makes you wish to die?

PHAEDRA

Oh, let me sin! My sin is not against you!

NURSE

Not willingly! If I fail, the fault is yours.

The Nurse assumes the posture of a suppliant, grasping Phaedra's hand and knees.

PHAEDRA

What's this? Are you using force, seizing my hand?

NURSE

Yes, and your knees, too! Never shall I let go!

PHAEDRA

To learn the truth, poor woman, will be your doom!

NURSE

Why, what could be worse for me than not to win you?

ΦΑΙΔΡΑ

ὀλῇ. τὸ μέντοι πρᾶγμ' ἐμοὶ τιμὴν φέρει.

ΤΡΟΦΟΣ

330 κἄπειτα κρύπτεις, χρήσθ' ἱκνουμένης ἐμοῦ;

ΦΑΙΔΡΑ

ἐκ τῶν γὰρ αἰσχρῶν ἐσθλὰ μηχανώμεθα.

ΤΡΟΦΟΣ

οὔκουν λέγουσα τιμιωτέρα φανῇ;

ΦΑΙΔΡΑ

ἄπελθε πρὸς θεῶν δεξιάν τ' ἐμὴν μέθες.

ΤΡΟΦΟΣ

οὐ δῆτ', ἐπεί μοι δῶρον οὐ δίδως ὃ χρῆν.

ΦΑΙΔΡΑ

335 δώσω· σέβας γὰρ χειρὸς αἰδοῦμαι τὸ σόν.

ΤΡΟΦΟΣ

σιγῷμ' ἂν ἤδη· σὸς γὰρ οὑντεῦθεν λόγος.

ΦΑΙΔΡΑ

ὦ τλῆμον, οἷον, μῆτερ, ἠράσθης ἔρον.

ΤΡΟΦΟΣ

ὃν ἔσχε ταύρου, τέκνον; ἢ τί φὴς τόδε;

ΦΑΙΔΡΑ

σύ τ', ὦ τάλαιν' ὅμαιμε, Διονύσου δάμαρ.

ᵃ Phaedra's mother was Pasiphaë, wife of Minos. She was cursed by Aphrodite with an unnatural passion for a bull and gave birth to the Minotaur.

PHAEDRA

It will be your death. To me the affair brings honor.

NURSE

Why hide it, then, when my request is noble?

PHAEDRA

Since out of shame I'm plotting to win credit.

NURSE

If you reveal it, won't you be more honored?

PHAEDRA

I ask you by the gods, leave me, let go!

NURSE

No, for you do not give the gift you ought.

PHAEDRA

I shall: your suppliant hand commands respect.

NURSE

I'll be silent. Henceforth it is your turn to speak.

The Nurse releases her grasp.

PHAEDRA

Unhappy mother,[a] what a love was yours!

NURSE

For the Cretan bull, my child? Or what do you mean?

PHAEDRA

And you, poor sister, Dionysus' bride![b]

[b] In the best known version of this story, Ariadne, who helped Theseus escape from the Labyrinth, was abandoned by him on Naxos and taken up by Dionysus. The version alluded to here makes her the unfaithful bride of Dionysus.

ΤΡΟΦΟΣ

340 τέκνον, τί πάσχεις; συγγόνους κακορροθεῖς;

ΦΑΙΔΡΑ

τρίτη δ' ἐγὼ δύστηνος ὡς ἀπόλλυμαι.

ΤΡΟΦΟΣ

ἔκ τοι πέπληγμαι· ποῖ προβήσεται λόγος;

ΦΑΙΔΡΑ

ἐκεῖθεν ἡμεῖς, οὐ νεωστί, δυστυχεῖς.

ΤΡΟΦΟΣ

οὐδέν τι μᾶλλον οἶδ' ἃ βούλομαι κλυεῖν.

ΦΑΙΔΡΑ

φεῦ·

345 πῶς ἂν σύ μοι λέξειας ἁμὲ χρὴ λέγειν;

ΤΡΟΦΟΣ

οὐ μάντις εἰμὶ τἀφανῆ γνῶναι σαφῶς.

ΦΑΙΔΡΑ

τί τοῦθ' ὃ δὴ λέγουσιν ἀνθρώπους ἐρᾶν;

ΤΡΟΦΟΣ

ἥδιστον, ὦ παῖ, ταὐτὸν ἀλγεινόν θ' ἅμα.

ΦΑΙΔΡΑ

ἡμεῖς ἂν εἶμεν θατέρῳ κεχρημένοι.

ΤΡΟΦΟΣ

350 τί φής; ἐρᾷς, ὦ τέκνον; ἀνθρώπων τίνος;

NURSE

What ails you, child? Are you slandering your kin?

PHAEDRA

And I the third, how wretchedly I perish!

NURSE

I am utterly stunned. Where will these words lead?

PHAEDRA

From far back came my woe, not from recent times!

NURSE

Of what I wish to hear I'm no whit wiser.

PHAEDRA

Oh! Could you but speak the words that I must say!

NURSE

I am no seer, to know for certain what's hidden.

PHAEDRA

What is it when we say "people are in love"?

NURSE

At once, my child, great pleasure and great pain.

PHAEDRA

It will be the second that I have experienced.

NURSE

What, are you in love, my child? Who's the man?

ΦΑΙΔΡΑ

ὅστις ποθ᾽ οὗτός ἐσθ᾽, ὁ τῆς Ἀμαζόνος . . .

ΤΡΟΦΟΣ

Ἱππόλυτον αὐδᾷς;

ΦΑΙΔΡΑ

σοῦ τάδ᾽, οὐκ ἐμοῦ κλύεις.

ΤΡΟΦΟΣ

οἴμοι, τί λέξεις, τέκνον; ὥς μ᾽ ἀπώλεσας.
γυναῖκες, οὐκ ἀνασχέτ᾽, οὐκ ἀνέψομαι
355 ζῶσ᾽· ἐχθρὸν ἦμαρ, ἐχθρὸν εἰσορῶ φάος.
[ῥίψω μεθήσω σῶμ᾽, ἀπαλλαχθήσομαι
βίου θανοῦσα· χαίρετ᾽, οὐκέτ᾽ εἴμ᾽ ἐγώ.]
οἱ σώφρονες γάρ, οὐχ ἑκόντες ἀλλ᾽ ὅμως,
κακῶν ἐρῶσι. Κύπρις οὐκ ἄρ᾽ ἦν θεός,
360 ἀλλ᾽ εἴ τι μεῖζον ἄλλο γίγνεται θεοῦ,
ἣ τήνδε κἀμὲ καὶ δόμους ἀπώλεσεν.

ΧΟΡΟΣ

στρ.

ἄιες ὤ, ἔκλυες ὤ,
ἀνήκουστα τᾶς
τυράννου πάθεα μέλεα θρεομένας;
ὀλοίμαν ἔγωγε πρὶν σᾶν, φίλα,
365 κατανύσαι φρενῶν. ἰώ μοι, φεῦ φεῦ·
ὦ τάλαινα τῶνδ᾽ ἀλγέων·
ὦ πόνοι τρέφοντες βροτούς.
ὄλωλας, ἐξέφηνας ἐς φάος κακά.
τίς σε παναμέριος ὅδε χρόνος μένει;

PHAEDRA

Whatever his name is, son of the Amazon . . .

NURSE

You mean Hippolytus?

PHAEDRA

Yours are the words, not mine.

NURSE

Ah, what can you mean, my child? You have killed me!
Women, this is unbearable, I cannot bear to live! Hateful
to me is the day, the light I see! [I shall throw myself
down, die and be quit of life! Farewell, I live no more!]
For someone virtuous—she does not will it but yet 'tis
so—is in love with baseness! Cypris is not after all a deity
but something even mightier. She has destroyed Phae-
dra, me, and the royal house!

CHORUS

Oh, did you catch, oh, did you hear the queen uttering
woes past hearing? Death take me, my friend, before I
come to share your thoughts! Ah me! Alas! Oh, how
wretched you are because of this woe! Oh, the troubles
that have mortals in their keeping! You are undone, you
have brought calamity into the daylight! The hours of this
long day—what awaits you in them? Some unlucky

356–7 del. West
364 φίλα Elmsley: φίλαν C

370   τελευτάσεταί τι καινὸν δόμοις·
   ἄσημα δ' οὐκέτ' ἐστὶν οἷ φθίνει τύχα
   Κύπριδος, ὦ τάλαινα παῖ Κρησία.

ΦΑΙΔΡΑ

   Τροζήνιαι γυναῖκες, αἳ τόδ' ἔσχατον
   οἰκεῖτε χώρας Πελοπίας προνώπιον,
375   ἤδη ποτ' ἄλλως νυκτὸς ἐν μακρῷ χρόνῳ
   θνητῶν ἐφρόντισ' ᾗ διέφθαρται βίος.
   καί μοι δοκοῦσιν οὐ κατὰ γνώμης φύσιν
   πράσσειν κάκιον· ἔστι γὰρ τό γ' εὖ φρονεῖν
   πολλοῖσιν· ἀλλὰ τῇδ' ἀθρητέον τόδε·
380   ἃ χρήστ' ἐπιστάμεσθα καὶ γιγνώσκομεν
   οὐκ ἐκπονοῦμεν, οἱ μὲν ἀργίας ὕπο,
   οἱ δ' ἡδονὴν προθέντες ἀντὶ τοῦ καλοῦ
   ἄλλην τιν'. εἰσὶ δ' ἡδοναὶ πολλαὶ βίου,
   μακραί τε λέσχαι καὶ σχολή, τερπνὸν κακόν,
385   αἰδώς τε. δισσαὶ δ' εἰσίν, ἡ μὲν οὐ κακή,
   ἡ δ' ἄχθος οἴκων. εἰ δ' ὁ καιρὸς ἦν σαφής,
   οὐκ ἂν δύ' ἤστην ταῦτ' ἔχοντε γράμματα.
   ταῦτ' οὖν ἐπειδὴ τυγχάνω φρονοῦσ' ἐγώ,
   οὐκ ἔσθ' ὁποίῳ φαρμάκῳ διαφθερεῖν
390   ἔμελλον, ὥστε τοὔμπαλιν πεσεῖν φρενῶν.
   λέξω δὲ καί σοι τῆς ἐμῆς γνώμης ὁδόν.
   ἐπεί μ' ἔρως ἔτρωσεν, ἐσκόπουν ὅπως
   κάλλιστ' ἐνέγκαιμ' αὐτόν. ἠρξάμην μὲν οὖν
   ἐκ τοῦδε, σιγᾶν τήνδε καὶ κρύπτειν νόσον.
395   γλώσσῃ γὰρ οὐδὲν πιστόν, ἣ θυραῖα μὲν
   φρονήματ' ἀνδρῶν νουθετεῖν ἐπίσταται,

change for the house will be brought to pass. It is no longer uncertain how the fortune sent by Cypris will end, O unhappy Cretan girl!

PHAEDRA

Women of Trozen, dwellers in this outermost forecourt to the land of Pelops, I have pondered before now in other circumstances in the night's long watches how it is that the lives of mortals have been ruined. I think that it is not owing to the nature of their wits that they fare badly, since many people possess good sense. Rather, one must look at it this way: what we know and understand to be noble we fail to carry out, some from laziness, others because they give precedence to some other pleasure than honor. Life's pleasures are many, long talks and leisure, a pleasant bane, and modest restraint. Yet they are of two sorts,[a] one pleasure being no bad thing, another a burden upon houses. If propriety were clear, there would not be two things designated by the same letters. Since these are the views I happen to hold, there is no drug could make me pervert them and reverse my opinion.

I shall also tell you the way my thoughts went. When love wounded me, I considered how I might best bear it. My starting point was this, to conceal my malady in silence. For the tongue is not to be trusted: it knows well how to admonish the thoughts of others but gets from

[a] Some take the subject here to be two kinds of "awe" or "shame." For a summary of other views and a defense of the translation above, see *AJP* 101 (1980), 287–303.

αὐτὴ δ᾽ ὑφ᾽ αὑτῆς πλεῖστα κέκτηται κακά.
τὸ δεύτερον δὲ τὴν ἄνοιαν εὖ φέρειν
τῷ σωφρονεῖν νικῶσα προυνοησάμην.
400 τρίτον δ᾽, ἐπειδὴ τοισίδ᾽ οὐκ ἐξήνυτον
Κύπριν κρατῆσαι, κατθανεῖν ἔδοξέ μοι,
κράτιστον—οὐδεὶς ἀντερεῖ—βουλευμάτων.
ἐμοὶ γὰρ εἴη μήτε λανθάνειν καλὰ
μήτ᾽ αἰσχρὰ δρώσῃ μάρτυρας πολλοὺς ἔχειν.
405 τὸ δ᾽ ἔργον ἤδη τὴν νόσον τε δυσκλεᾶ,
γυνή τε πρὸς τοῖσδ᾽ οὖσ᾽ ἐγίγνωσκον καλῶς,
μίσημα πᾶσιν. ὡς ὄλοιτο παγκάκως
ἥτις πρὸς ἄνδρας ἤρξατ᾽ αἰσχύνειν λέχη
πρώτη θυραίους. ἐκ δὲ γενναίων δόμων
410 τόδ᾽ ἦρξε θηλείαισι γίγνεσθαι κακόν·
ὅταν γὰρ αἰσχρὰ τοῖσιν ἐσθλοῖσιν δοκῇ,
ἦ κάρτα δόξει τοῖς κακοῖς γ᾽ εἶναι καλά.
μισῶ δὲ καὶ τὰς σώφρονας μὲν ἐν λόγοις,
λάθρᾳ δὲ τόλμας οὐ καλὰς κεκτημένας·
415 αἳ πῶς ποτ᾽, ὦ δέσποινα ποντία Κύπρι,
βλέπουσιν ἐς πρόσωπα τῶν ξυνευνετῶν
οὐδὲ σκότον φρίσσουσι τὸν ξυνεργάτην
τέραμνά τ᾽ οἴκων μή ποτε φθογγὴν ἀφῇ;
ἡμᾶς γὰρ αὐτὸ τοῦτ᾽ ἀποκτείνει, φίλαι,
420 ὡς μήποτ᾽ ἄνδρα τὸν ἐμὸν αἰσχύνασ᾽ ἁλῶ,
μὴ παῖδας οὓς ἔτικτον· ἀλλ᾽ ἐλεύθεροι
παρρησίᾳ θάλλοντες οἰκοῖεν πόλιν
κλεινῶν Ἀθηνῶν, μητρὸς οὕνεκ᾽ εὐκλεεῖς.
δουλοῖ γὰρ ἄνδρα, κἂν θρασύσπλαγχνός τις ᾖ,

itself a great deal of trouble. My second intention was to
bear this madness nobly, overcoming it by means of self-
control. But third, when with these means I was unable
to master Cypris, I resolved on death, the best of plans, as
no one shall deny. For just as I would not have my good
deeds unknown, so may I not have a throng of witnesses
to my shameful ones! I knew that both the deed and the
longing for it brought disgrace, knew besides that I was a
woman, a thing all men hate. Damnation take the woman
who first began to besmirch her marriage bed with other
men! This contagion began for the female sex with the
nobility. For when those of noble station resolve on base
acts, surely the base-born will regard such acts as good.
But I also hate women who are chaste in word but in
secret possess an ignoble daring. How, O Cypris, Lady of
the Sea, how can these women look into the faces of their
husbands? How can they not be afraid that the darkness,
their accomplice, and the timbers of the house will break
into speech?

My friends, it is this very purpose that is bringing
about my death, that I may not be convicted of bringing
shame to my husband or to the children I gave birth to
but rather that they may live in glorious Athens as free
men, free of speech and flourishing, enjoying good repute
where their mother is concerned. For it enslaves even a

---

[400] τοισίδ' Valckenaer: τοῖσιν C

425 ὅταν ξυνειδῇ μητρὸς ἢ πατρὸς κακά.
μόνον δὲ τοῦτό φασ' ἁμιλλᾶσθαι βίῳ,
γνώμην δικαίαν κἀγαθὴν ὅτῳ παρῇ.
κακοὺς δὲ θνητῶν ἐξέφην' ὅταν τύχῃ,
προθεὶς κάτοπτρον ὥστε παρθένῳ νέᾳ,
430 χρόνος· παρ' οἷσι μήποτ' ὀφθείην ἐγώ.

ΧΟΡΟΣ

φεῦ φεῦ, τὸ σῶφρον ὡς ἁπανταχοῦ καλὸν
καὶ δόξαν ἐσθλὴν ἐν βροτοῖς καρπίζεται.

ΤΡΟΦΟΣ

δέσποιν', ἐμοί τοι συμφορὰ μὲν ἀρτίως
ἡ σὴ παρέσχε δεινὸν ἐξαίφνης φόβον·
435 νῦν δ' ἐννοοῦμαι φαῦλος οὖσα, κἀν βροτοῖς
αἱ δεύτεραί πως φροντίδες σοφώτεραι.
οὐ γὰρ περισσὸν οὐδὲν οὐδ' ἔξω λόγου
πέπονθας, ὀργαὶ δ' ἐς σ' ἀπέσκηψαν θεᾶς.
ἐρᾷς; τί τοῦτο θαῦμα; σὺν πολλοῖς βροτῶν.
440 κἄπειτ' ἔρωτος οὕνεκα ψυχὴν ὀλεῖς;
οὔ τἄρα λύει τοῖς ἐρῶσι τῶν πέλας,
ὅσοι τε μέλλουσ', εἰ θανεῖν αὐτοὺς χρεών.
Κύπρις γὰρ οὐ φορητὸν ἢν πολλὴ ῥυῇ,
ἣ τὸν μὲν εἴκονθ' ἡσυχῇ μετέρχεται,
445 ὃν δ' ἂν περισσὸν καὶ φρονοῦνθ' εὕρῃ μέγα,
τοῦτον λαβοῦσα πῶς δοκεῖς καθύβρισεν.
    φοιτᾷ δ' ἀν' αἰθέρ', ἔστι δ' ἐν θαλασσίῳ
κλύδωνι Κύπρις, πάντα δ' ἐκ ταύτης ἔφυ·
ἥδ' ἐστὶν ἡ σπείρουσα καὶ διδοῦσ' ἔρον,

bold-hearted man when he is conscious of sins committed
by his mother or father. One thing only, they say, com-
petes in value with life,[a] the possession of a heart blame-
less and good. But as for the base among mortals, they
are exposed, late or soon, by Time, who holds up to them,
as to a young girl, a mirror. In their number may I never
be found!

CHORUS LEADER

Oh, what a fine thing is chastity everywhere, and how
splendid is the repute it gains among mortals!

NURSE

Mistress, though the misfortune you just told me of gave
me a sudden fright, yet now I realize that I was being
simple-minded—and among mortals second thoughts
are, perhaps, wiser. It is not anything extraordinary, any-
thing beyond all reckoning, that has befallen you, but it is
the wrath of the goddess that has descended on you. Are
you in love? Why is that so strange? It is a condition you
share with many. Will you, because of love, take your own
life? Those who are in love with their neighbors or shall
be tomorrow get little profit, then, if they must die for it.
Cypris, if she streams upon us in full flood, cannot be
withstood. Against those who yield to her demands she
comes in mildness, but the one whom she finds to be
superior and proud, such a one she takes and mistreats
ever so badly.

Cypris moves through the air, she dwells in the sea
wave, and all things come from her. She it is that gives

---

[a] Or "competes in life."

441 λύει Valckenaer: γ᾽ οὐ δεῖ C

167

EURIPIDES

450　οὗ πάντες ἐσμὲν οἱ κατὰ χθόν' ἔκγονοι.
　　ὅσοι μὲν οὖν γραφάς τε τῶν παλαιτέρων
　　ἔχουσιν αὐτοί τ' εἰσὶν ἐν μούσαις ἀεὶ
　　ἴσασι μὲν Ζεὺς ὥς ποτ' ἠράσθη γάμων
　　Σεμέλης, ἴσασι δ' ὡς ἀνήρπασέν ποτε
455　ἡ καλλιφεγγὴς Κέφαλον ἐς θεοὺς Ἔως
　　ἔρωτος οὕνεκ'· ἀλλ' ὅμως ἐν οὐρανῷ
　　ναίουσι κοὐ φεύγουσιν ἐκποδὼν θεούς,
　　στέργουσι δ', οἶμαι, ξυμφορᾷ νικώμενοι.
　　σὺ δ' οὐκ ἀνέξῃ; χρῆν σ' ἐπὶ ῥητοῖς ἄρα
460　πατέρα φυτεύειν ἢ 'πὶ δεσπόταις θεοῖς
　　ἄλλοισιν, εἰ μὴ τούσδε γε στέρξεις νόμους.
　　πόσους δοκεῖς δὴ κάρτ' ἔχοντας εὖ φρενῶν
　　νοσοῦνθ' ὁρῶντας λέκτρα μὴ δοκεῖν ὁρᾶν;
　　πόσους δὲ παισὶ πατέρας ἡμαρτηκόσιν
465　συνεκκομίζειν Κύπριν; ἐν σοφοῖσι γὰρ
　　τόδ' ἐστὶ θνητῶν, λανθάνειν τὰ μὴ καλά.
　　οὐδ' ἐκπονεῖν τοι χρὴ βίον λίαν βροτούς·
　　οὐδὲ στέγην γὰρ ἢ κατηρεφεῖς δόμοι
　　καλῶς ἀκριβώσαις ἄν· ἐς δὲ τὴν τύχην
470　πεσοῦσ' ὅσην σύ, πῶς ἂν ἐκνεῦσαι δοκεῖς;
　　ἀλλ' εἰ τὰ πλείω χρηστὰ τῶν κακῶν ἔχεις,
　　ἄνθρωπος οὖσα κάρτα γ' εὖ πράξειας ἄν.
　　ἀλλ', ὦ φίλη παῖ, λῆγε μὲν κακῶν φρενῶν,
　　λῆξον δ' ὑβρίζουσ'· οὐ γὰρ ἄλλο πλὴν ὕβρις
475　τάδ' ἐστί, κρείσσω δαιμόνων εἶναι θέλειν,

---

466 τόδ' Wilamowitz: τάδ' C　　　468 ἢ Valckenaer: ἧς C

168

and implants love, that love of which all we of earth are begotten. Those who know the writings of the ancients and are themselves concerned with the Muses know that Zeus once lusted for Semele's bed, know too that Dawn, goddess of lovely light, once abducted Cephalus to heaven for love's sake. But these deities still continue to live in heaven and do not exile themselves from the sight of the gods.[a] They are content that mischance has bested them.

But you won't stand for this? Your father, then, should have begotten you on fixed terms or with a different set of gods as masters if you are not going to put up with these rules. How many men do you think, men well endowed with sense, see their wives unfaithful and pretend to see nothing? How many fathers do you think help to supply their wayward sons with the pleasures of Cypris? This is one of the wise principles mortals follow—dishonorable deeds should remain hidden from view. Mortals, you know, should not try to bring to their lives too high a perfection: no more would you make fine and exact the roof over a house. But when you have plunged into misfortunes as great as yours, how can you think you will swim out of them? No, if the good you have done outweighs the bad, then on the human scale you would be fortunate indeed.

So, dear child, leave off these wicked thoughts, leave off this pride! It is pride, nothing else, to try to best the

[a] This would be the equivalent, among the immortals, of suicide among human beings.

---

469 ἀκριβώσαις ἄν Hadley: ἀκριβώσειαν fere C

τόλμα δ' ἐρῶσα· θεὸς ἐβουλήθη τάδε.
νοσοῦσα δ' εὖ πως τὴν νόσον καταστρέφου.
εἰσὶν δ' ἐπῳδαὶ καὶ λόγοι θελκτήριοι·
φανήσεταί τι τῆσδε φάρμακον νόσου.
480 ἦ τἄρ' ἂν ὀψέ γ' ἄνδρες ἐξεύροιεν ἄν,
εἰ μὴ γυναῖκες μηχανὰς εὑρήσομεν.

ΧΟΡΟΣ

Φαίδρα, λέγει μὲν ἥδε χρησιμώτερα
πρὸς τὴν παροῦσαν ξυμφοράν, αἰνῶ δὲ σέ.
ὁ δ' αἶνος οὗτος δυσχερέστερος λόγων
485 τῶν τῆσδε καί σοι μᾶλλον ἀλγίων κλυεῖν.

ΦΑΙΔΡΑ

τοῦτ' ἔσθ' ὃ θνητῶν εὖ πόλεις οἰκουμένας
δόμους τ' ἀπόλλυσ', οἱ καλοὶ λίαν λόγοι.
οὐ γάρ τι τοῖσιν ὠσὶ τερπνὰ χρὴ λέγειν
ἀλλ' ἐξ ὅτου τις εὐκλεὴς γενήσεται.

ΤΡΟΦΟΣ

490 τί σεμνομυθεῖς; οὐ λόγων εὐσχημόνων
δεῖ σ' ἀλλὰ τἀνδρός. ὡς τάχος διιστέον,
τὸν εὐθὺν ἐξειπόντας ἀμφὶ σοῦ λόγον.
εἰ μὲν γὰρ ἦν σοι μὴ 'πὶ συμφοραῖς βίος
τοιαῖσδε, σώφρων δ' οὖσ' ἐτύγχανες γυνή,
495 οὐκ ἄν ποτ' εὐνῆς οὕνεχ' ἡδονῆς τε σῆς
προῆγον ἄν σε δεῦρο· νῦν δ' ἀγὼν μέγας
σῶσαι βίον σόν, κοὐκ ἐπίφθονον τόδε.

496 προῆγον Scaliger: προσῆγον C

gods. Bear up under your love: it was a god that willed it. And if you are ill with it, use some *good* measures to subdue your illness. There are incantations, and words that charm: something will turn up to cure this love. Men will be slow to invent such contrivances if we women do not find them.

CHORUS LEADER

Phaedra, the advice she gives is more expedient in view of the disaster that is upon you, but it is you that I praise. Yet this praise is harder and more painful for you to hear than her words are.[a]

PHAEDRA

This is the thing that destroys the well-ordered cities and homes of mankind: speeches that are too enticing! Words to delight the ear—that is not at all what you must speak, but rather such advice as brings a good name!

NURSE

Why this high and haughty tone? Noble-sounding words are not what you need but the man! We must get things clear this instant and speak the forthright truth about you. If your life were not in the grip of misfortunes like these and you were in fact a woman of self-control, I would not be leading you to this point for the sake of sexual pleasure. But as things stand, the struggle is a great one—to save your life—and no one can begrudge us this course.

[a] The Chorus Leader praises Phaedra's sentiments but feels delicacy about implicitly seconding her resolve to kill herself.

ΦΑΙΔΡΑ

ὦ δεινὰ λέξασ’, οὐχὶ συγκλήσεις στόμα
καὶ μὴ μεθήσεις αὖθις αἰσχίστους λόγους;

ΤΡΟΦΟΣ

500 αἴσχρ’, ἀλλ’ ἀμείνω τῶν καλῶν τάδ’ ἐστί σοι·
κρεῖσσον δὲ τοὔργον, εἴπερ ἐκσώσει γέ σε,
ἢ τοὔνομ’, ᾧ σὺ κατθανῇ γαυρουμένη.

ΦΑΙΔΡΑ

ἃ μή σε πρὸς θεῶν—εὖ λέγεις γάρ, αἰσχρὰ δέ—
πέρα προβῇς τῶνδ’· ὡς ὑπείργασμαι μὲν εὖ
505 ψυχὴν ἔρωτι, τἀσχρὰ δ’ ἢν λέγῃς καλῶς,
ἐς τοῦθ’ ὃ φεύγω νῦν ἀναλωθήσομαι.

ΤΡΟΦΟΣ

εἴ τοι δοκεῖ σοι, χρῆν μὲν οὔ σ’ ἁμαρτάνειν,
εἰ δ’ οὖν, πιθοῦ μοι· δευτέρα γὰρ ἡ χάρις.
ἔστιν κατ’ οἴκους φίλτρα μοι θελκτήρια
510 ἔρωτος, ἦλθε δ’ ἄρτι μοι γνώμης ἔσω,
ἅ σ’ οὔτ’ ἐπ’ αἰσχροῖς οὔτ’ ἐπὶ βλάβῃ φρενῶν
παύσει νόσου τῆσδ’, ἢν σὺ μὴ γένῃ κακή.
δεῖ δ’ ἐξ ἐκείνου δή τι τοῦ ποθουμένου
σημεῖον, ἢ πλόκον τιν’ ἢ πέπλων ἄπο,
515 λαβεῖν, συνάψαι τ’ ἐκ δυοῖν μίαν χάριν.

ΦΑΙΔΡΑ

πότερα δὲ χριστὸν ἢ ποτὸν τὸ φάρμακον;

503 ἃ μή σε Weil: καὶ μή γε fere C
514 πλόκον Reiske: λόγον vel λόγων C

PHAEDRA

O monstrous! Hold your tongue and never again utter such vile words!

NURSE

Vile, yes, but better for you than your fine sentiments! Better the deed, if it will save your life, than the word you will plume yourself on and die!

PHAEDRA

Do not, by the gods (for your words are fair but their meaning base) do not, I beg of you, go any further! My soul is all made ready by desire, and if you continue to champion dishonor eloquently, I shall give way completely to what I now flee!

NURSE

If that is what you wish, then although you were better not to err, yet if you do, be ruled by me: for that is the favor that is next best.[a] I have love medicine within the house—I just thought of it this very moment—that will free you from this malady without disgrace to you or harm to your mind, if only you do not flinch. We must get some token from the man you love, a lock of hair or a piece of clothing, then compound from the twain a single blessing.

PHAEDRA

This drug, is it an ointment or a potion?

[a] There may be an allusion here to the well-known words of Hesiod, *Works and Days* 293–97, advising those who do not themselves know what is good to take good advice as a second-best course.

ΤΡΟΦΟΣ

οὐκ οἶδ᾽· ὄνασθαι, μὴ μαθεῖν, βούλου, τέκνον.

ΦΑΙΔΡΑ

δέδοιχ᾽ ὅπως μοι μὴ λίαν φανῇς σοφή.

ΤΡΟΦΟΣ

πάντ᾽ ἂν φοβηθεῖσ᾽ ἴσθι· δειμαίνεις δὲ τί;

ΦΑΙΔΡΑ

520   μή μοί τι Θησέως τῶνδε μηνύσῃς τόκῳ.

ΤΡΟΦΟΣ

ἔασον, ὦ παῖ· ταῦτ᾽ ἐγὼ θήσω καλῶς.
μόνον σύ μοι, δέσποινα ποντία Κύπρι,
συνεργὸς εἴης. τἄλλα δ᾽ οἷ᾽ ἐγὼ φρονῶ
τοῖς ἔνδον ἡμῖν ἀρκέσει λέξαι φίλοις.

ΧΟΡΟΣ

στρ. α

525   Ἔρως Ἔρως, ὁ κατ᾽ ὀμμάτων
στάζων πόθον, εἰσάγων γλυκεῖ-
αν ψυχᾷ χάριν οὓς ἐπιστρατεύσῃ,
μή μοί ποτε σὺν κακῷ φανεί-
ης μηδ᾽ ἄρρυθμος ἔλθοις.

530   οὔτε γὰρ πυρὸς οὔτ᾽ ἄστρων ὑπέρτερον βέλος
οἷον τὸ τᾶς Ἀφροδίτας ἵησιν ἐκ χερῶν
Ἔρως ὁ Διὸς παῖς.

ἀντ. α

535   ἄλλως ἄλλως παρά τ᾽ Ἀλφεῷ
Φοίβου τ᾽ ἐπὶ Πυθίοις τεράμ-
νοις βούταν φόνον Ἑλλὰς <αἶ᾽> ἀέξει,

NURSE

I know not: strive for benefit, child, not lore.

PHAEDRA

I fear you'll prove too clever for my good.

NURSE

Then know you'd quake at shadows. What's your fear?

PHAEDRA

Your telling some word of this to Theseus' son.

NURSE

Dismiss the thought, my child! I shall arrange this business well. My only prayer is that you, Cypris, Lady of the Sea, may be my helper! As for what else I have in mind, it will be enough for me to speak to friends within.

Exit NURSE into the palace.

CHORUS

Eros, Eros, distilling liquid desire upon the eyes, bringing sweet pleasure to the souls of those you make war against, never may you show yourself to me for my hurt nor ever come but in harmony. For neither the shafts of fire nor of stars are more powerful than that of Aphrodite, which Eros, Zeus's son,[a] hurls from his hand.

'Tis folly, folly, for the land of Greece to multiply the slaughter of cattle by the banks of the Alpheus and in the Pythian shrine of Apollo[b] if we pay no honor to Eros,

---

[a] In Hesiod the god of love has no parents at all.

[b] Olympia and Delphi, holy places of Zeus and Apollo.

---

526 στάζων Bothe: στάζεις C
537 ⟨αἲ'⟩ Hermann

Ἔρωτα δέ, τὸν τύραννον ἀν-
δρῶν, τὸν τᾶς Ἀφροδίτας
540 φιλτάτων θαλάμων κληδοῦχον, οὐ σεβίζομεν,
πέρθοντα καὶ διὰ πάσας ἱέντα συμφορᾶς
θνατοὺς ὅταν ἔλθῃ.

στρ. β

545 τὰν μὲν Οἰχαλίᾳ
πῶλον ἄζυγα λέκτρων,
ἄνανδρον τὸ πρὶν καὶ ἄνυμφον, οἴκων
ζεύξασ' ἀπ' Εὐρυτίων
550 δρομάδα ναΐδ' ὅπως τε βάκ-
χαν σὺν αἵματι, σὺν καπνῷ,
φονίοισι νυμφείοις
Ἀλκμήνας τόκῳ Κύπρις ἐξέδωκεν· ὦ
τλάμων ὑμεναίων.

ἀντ. β

555 ὦ Θήβας ἱερὸν
τεῖχος, ὦ στόμα Δίρκας,
συνείποιτ' ἂν ἁ Κύπρις οἷον ἔρπει·
βροντᾷ γὰρ ἀμφιπύρῳ
560 τοκάδα τὰν διγόνοιο Βάκ-
χου νυμφευσαμένα πότμῳ
φονίῳ κατηύνασεν.
δεινὰ γὰρ τὰ πάντ' ἐπιπνεῖ, μέλισσα δ' οἷ-
α τις πεπόταται.

549 ἀπ' Εὐρυτίων Buttmann: ἀπειρεσίαν C
552 φονίοισι νυμφείοις Barrett: φονίοις θ' ὑμεναίοις fere C

mankind's despot, who holds the keys to the sweet chambers of Aphrodite! He ruins mortals and launches them among every kind of disaster when he visits them.

That filly in Oechalia,[a] unjoined as yet to marriage bed, unhusbanded, unwed, Cypris took from the house of her father Eurytus and yoked her like a footloose Naiad or a Bacchant and gave her—with bloodshed, with burning, a murderous bridal—to Alcmene's son. O unhappy in her marriage!

O holy fortress of Thebes, O source of Dirce's fountain, you can second my account of how Cypris comes. For she gave as bride to the blazing thunder the mother of twice-born Bacchus[b] and with deadly fate brought her to bed. She is terrible, her breath blows over all and she flits and hovers like a bee.

A shout is heard from within. Phaedra rises from her couch and stands with her ear to the palace door.

[a] Iole, daughter of the king of Oechalia, was beloved by Heracles, who sacked her city, killed her family, and took her away by force.

[b] Semele, daughter of Cadmus, king of Thebes, was loved by Zeus, who visited her in his full Olympian glory and thus caused her death. The child of this union was Dionysus, whom Zeus rescued from his dead mother's womb and sewed up in his own thigh, so that he was "twice-born."

---

558 ἁ Κύπρις οἷον Bothe: οἷον ἁ K- C
561 νυμφευσαμένα Kirchhoff: -μέναν C

ΦΑΙΔΡΑ

565   σιγήσατ᾽, ὦ γυναῖκες· ἐξειργάσμεθα.

ΧΟΡΟΣ

τί δ᾽ ἐστί, Φαίδρα, δεινὸν ἐν δόμοισί σοι;

ΦΑΙΔΡΑ

ἐπίσχετ᾽, αὐδὴν τῶν ἔσωθεν ἐκμάθω.

ΧΟΡΟΣ

σιγῶ· τὸ μέντοι φροίμιον κακὸν τόδε.

ΦΑΙΔΡΑ

ἰώ μοι, αἰαῖ·
570   ὦ δυστάλαινα τῶν ἐμῶν παθημάτων.

ΧΟΡΟΣ

τίνα θροεῖς αὐδάν; τίνα βοᾷς λόγον;
ἔνεπε, τίς φοβεῖ σε φήμα, γύναι,
φρένας ἐπίσσυτος;

ΦΑΙΔΡΑ

575   ἀπωλόμεσθα· ταῖσδ᾽ ἐπιστᾶσαι πύλαις
ἀκούσαθ᾽ οἷος κέλαδος ἐν δόμοις πίτνει.

ΧΟΡΟΣ

σὺ παρὰ κλῇθρα, σοὶ μέλει πομπίμα
φάτις δωμάτων·
580   ἔνεπε δ᾽ ἔνεπέ μοι, τί ποτ᾽ ἔβα κακόν;

ΦΑΙΔΡΑ

ὁ τῆς φιλίππου παῖς Ἀμαζόνος βοᾷ
Ἱππόλυτος, αὐδῶν δεινὰ πρόσπολον κακά.

PHAEDRA

Silence, women! I am done for!

CHORUS LEADER

What is there in the house to cause you fright?

PHAEDRA

Wait! Let me hear the voice of those within!

CHORUS LEADER

I hold my peace. But what you say bodes ill.

PHAEDRA

Oh, alas, alas! Oh, what suffering is mine!

CHORUS

What is the word you utter, the message you cry out? Tell us, lady: what report is it that affrights you, rushing upon your heart?

PHAEDRA

I am destroyed! Stand next to this door and hear what kind of turmoil is falling on the house.

CHORUS

You are by the door. Tidings transmitted from the house are for you to tell. Tell me, tell me, what disaster has come upon you?

PHAEDRA

It is Hippolytus, son of the horse-loving Amazon, who shouts, calling my servant dreadful names!

---

566 σοι Elmsley: σοῖς C

ΧΟΡΟΣ

585 ἰὰν μὲν κλύω, σαφὲς δ' οὐκ ἔχω·
γεγώνει δ' οἷα
διὰ πύλας ἔμολεν ἔμολέ σοι βοά.

ΦΑΙΔΡΑ

καὶ μὴν σαφῶς γε τὴν κακῶν προμνήστριαν,
590 τὴν δεσπότου προδοῦσαν ἐξαυδᾷ λέχος.

ΧΟΡΟΣ

ὤμοι ἐγὼ κακῶν· προδέδοσαι, φίλα.
τί σοι μήσομαι;
τὰ κρύπτ' ἀμπέφηνε, διὰ δ' ὄλλυσαι,
595 αἰαῖ, ἓ ἔ, πρόδοτος ἐκ φίλων.

ΦΑΙΔΡΑ

ἀπώλεσέν μ' εἰποῦσα συμφορὰς ἐμάς,
φίλως, καλῶς δ' οὔ, τήνδ' ἰωμένη νόσον.

ΧΟΡΟΣ

πῶς οὖν; τί δράσεις, ὦ παθοῦσ' ἀμήχανα;

ΦΑΙΔΡΑ

οὐκ οἶδα πλὴν ἕν, κατθανεῖν ὅσον τάχος,
600 τῶν νῦν παρόντων πημάτων ἄκος μόνον.

---

586 γεγώνει δ' Schroeder: γεγωνεῖν C   οἷα nescioquis
ap. Valckenaer: ὅπᾳ fere C
594 κρύπτ' ἀμπέφηνε Weil: κρυπτὰ γὰρ πέφηνε C

CHORUS

I hear a voice, but I do not hear its message clearly. Utter aloud to me what kind of cry it is that comes to you through the door.

PHAEDRA

It's clear enough. He calls her pander for the wicked, one who has betrayed her master's marriage bed!

CHORUS

Oh, disaster! You are betrayed, my friend! What can I do for you? What was hidden is now revealed and you are ruined—oh! ah!—betrayed by one close to you!

PHAEDRA

She has destroyed me by speaking of my troubles, try-ing—in kindness but dishonorably—to heal this malady of mine.

CHORUS LEADER

What then? What will you do, you that have suffered things no one can deal with?

PHAEDRA

I know but one thing, to die with all speed, the sole remedy for my present troubles.

EURIPIDES

ΙΠΠΟΛΥΤΟΣ

ὦ γαῖα μῆτερ ἡλίου τ' ἀναπτυχαί,
οἵων λόγων ἄρρητον εἰσήκουσ' ὄπα.

ΤΡΟΦΟΣ

σίγησον, ὦ παῖ, πρίν τιν' αἰσθέσθαι βοῆς.

ΙΠΠΟΛΥΤΟΣ

οὐκ ἔστ' ἀκούσας δείν' ὅπως σιγήσομαι.

ΤΡΟΦΟΣ

605   ναί, πρός σε τῆσδε δεξιᾶς εὐωλένου.

ΙΠΠΟΛΥΤΟΣ

οὐ μὴ προσοίσεις χεῖρα μηδ' ἅψῃ πέπλων;

ΤΡΟΦΟΣ

ὦ πρός σε γονάτων, μηδαμῶς μ' ἐξεργάσῃ.

ΙΠΠΟΛΥΤΟΣ

τί δ', εἴπερ, ὡς φῄς, μηδὲν εἴρηκας κακόν;

ΤΡΟΦΟΣ

ὁ μῦθος, ὦ παῖ, κοινὸς οὐδαμῶς ὅδε.

ΙΠΠΟΛΥΤΟΣ

610   τά τοι κάλ' ἐν πολλοῖσι κάλλιον λέγειν.

---

[a] This stage direction is not clearly marked in the text:
though "to die with all speed" seems to preclude any delay and is
a good exit line, this by itself is not conclusive. But the assump-
tion of Phaedra's departure here explains two things, why Hip-
polytus refers to her only in the third person and why Phaedra
thinks, in spite of his assurances at 657–62, that he will tell The-
seus about her. If Phaedra is off-stage during this interview, she
will be unaware that the Nurse has placed Hippolytus under

Exit PHAEDRA *into the palace.*[a] *Enter from the palace*
HIPPOLYTUS, *followed by the* NURSE.

HIPPOLYTUS

O mother earth, O open sunlight, what unspeakable
words I have heard uttered!

NURSE

Silence, my son, before someone hears your shout!

HIPPOLYTUS

I have heard dread things: I cannot now be silent.

NURSE

*She kneels as a suppliant before Hippolytus and tries to
grasp his hand.*

Do so, I beg you by your fair right hand!

HIPPOLYTUS

Keep your hands from me! Do not touch my cloak!

NURSE

I beg you by your knees, do not destroy me!

HIPPOLYTUS

What? Didn't you say your tale was not so bad?

NURSE

The story, my son, was not for the ears of all!

HIPPOLYTUS

Fine tales make finer telling to many hearers!

oath and that he has promised to keep it. The result is parallel
misunderstanding: Hippolytus excoriates Phaedra for a proposal
she did not authorize (the Nurse does not disabuse him). Phae-
dra in turn denounces Hippolytus to prevent an accusation he
has no intention of making.

183

ΤΡΟΦΟΣ

ὦ τέκνον, ὅρκους μηδαμῶς ἀτιμάσῃς.

ΙΠΠΟΛΥΤΟΣ

ἡ γλῶσσ' ὀμώμοχ', ἡ δὲ φρὴν ἀνώμοτος.

ΤΡΟΦΟΣ

ὦ παῖ, τί δράσεις; σοὺς φίλους διεργάσῃ;

ΙΠΠΟΛΥΤΟΣ

ἀπέπτυσ'· οὐδεὶς ἄδικός ἐστί μοι φίλος.

ΤΡΟΦΟΣ

615   σύγγνωθ'· ἁμαρτεῖν εἰκὸς ἀνθρώπους, τέκνον.

ΙΠΠΟΛΥΤΟΣ

ὦ Ζεῦ, τί δὴ κίβδηλον ἀνθρώποις κακὸν
γυναῖκας ἐς φῶς ἡλίου κατῴκισας;
εἰ γὰρ βρότειον ἤθελες σπεῖραι γένος,
οὐκ ἐκ γυναικῶν χρῆν παρασχέσθαι τόδε,
620   ἀλλ' ἀντιθέντας σοῖσιν ἐν ναοῖς βροτοὺς
ἢ χαλκὸν ἢ σίδηρον ἢ χρυσοῦ βάρος
παίδων πρίασθαι σπέρμα τοῦ τιμήματος
τῆς ἀξίας ἕκαστον, ἐν δὲ δώμασιν
ναίειν ἐλευθέροισι θηλειῶν ἄτερ.
625   [νῦν δ' ἐς δόμους μὲν πρῶτον ἄξεσθαι κακὸν
μέλλοντες ὄλβον δωμάτων ἐκτίνομεν.]
τούτῳ δὲ δῆλον ὡς γυνὴ κακὸν μέγα·
προσθεὶς γὰρ ὁ σπείρας τε καὶ θρέψας πατὴρ

625–6 del. Bothe

HIPPOLYTUS

NURSE
My child, I beg you, do not break your oath!

HIPPOLYTUS
My tongue swore, but my mind is not on oath.

NURSE
Son, what will you do? Destroy your near and dear?

HIPPOLYTUS
(*spitting*) Pah! No criminal shall be near and dear to me!

NURSE
Forgive! To err is mankind's lot, my son!

HIPPOLYTUS
O Zeus, why have you settled women, this bane to cheat
mankind, in the light of the sun?[a] If you wished to propa-
gate the human race, it was not from women that you
should have provided this. Rather, men should put down
in the temples either bronze or iron or a mass of gold and
buy offspring, each for a price appropriate to his means,
and then dwell in houses free from the female sex. [But
as matters stand, when we are about to take unto our-
selves a bane, we pay out the wealth of our homes.] The
clear proof that woman is a great bane is this: her father,

---

[a] According to Hesiod, *Theogony* 570–612, women are a pun-
ishment sent by Zeus to afflict the male sex. They make a man
poor by their spend-thrift ways and drone-like unproductivity.
Men are faced with a choice: marry and face economic ruin or
die childless and have no one to whom they may bequeath their
property.

φερνὰς ἀπῴκισ', ὡς ἀπαλλαχθῇ κακοῦ.
630 ὁ δ' αὖ λαβὼν ἀτηρὸν ἐς δόμους φυτὸν
γέγηθε κόσμον προστιθεὶς ἀγάλματι
καλὸν κακίστῳ καὶ πέπλοισιν ἐκπονεῖ
δύστηνος, ὄλβον δωμάτων ὑπεξελών.
[ἔχει δ' ἀνάγκην· ὥστε κηδεύσας καλῶς
635 γαμβροῖσι χαίρων σῴζεται πικρὸν λέχος,
ἢ χρηστὰ λέκτρα πενθεροὺς δ' ἀνωφελεῖς
λαβὼν πιέζει τἀγαθῷ τὸ δυστυχές.]
    ῥᾷστον δ' ὅτῳ τὸ μηδέν—ἀλλ' ἀνωφελὴς
εὐηθίᾳ κατ' οἶκον ἵδρυται γυνή.
640 σοφὴν δὲ μισῶ· μὴ γὰρ ἔν γ' ἐμοῖς δόμοις
εἴη φρονοῦσα πλείον' ἢ γυναῖκα χρή.
τὸ γὰρ κακοῦργον μᾶλλον ἐντίκτει Κύπρις
ἐν ταῖς σοφαῖσιν· ἡ δ' ἀμήχανος γυνὴ
γνώμῃ βραχείᾳ μωρίαν ἀφῃρέθη.
645   χρῆν δ' ἐς γυναῖκα πρόσπολον μὲν οὐ περᾶν,
ἄφθογγα δ' αὐταῖς συγκατοικίζειν δάκη
θηρῶν, ἵν' εἶχον μήτε προσφωνεῖν τινα
μήτ' ἐξ ἐκείνων φθέγμα δέξασθαι πάλιν.
νῦν δ' ἔνδον ἐννοοῦσιν αἱ κακαὶ κακὰ
650 βουλεύματ', ἔξω δ' ἐκφέρουσι πρόσπολοι.
    ὡς καὶ σύ γ' ἡμῖν πατρός, ὦ κακὸν κάρα,
λέκτρων ἀθίκτων ἦλθες ἐς συναλλαγάς·
ἁγὼ ῥυτοῖς νασμοῖσιν ἐξομόρξομαι
ἐς ὦτα κλύζων. πῶς ἂν οὖν εἴην κακός,

634-7 del. Barthold   634 καλῶς Kirchhoff: καλοῖς C

who begot and raised her, sends her off by settling a dowry on her in order to rid himself of trouble. But her husband, who has taken this creature of ruin into his house, takes pleasure in adding finery to the statue, lovely finery to worthless statue, and tricks her out with clothing, wretch that he is, destroying by degrees the wealth of his house. [There is a fatal necessity: either a man marries into a good family, and his joy in his in-laws makes him preserve a marriage that gives him pain, or he gets a good wife and pernicious in-laws and uses his blessing to counteract his misery.]

That man has it easiest whose wife is a nothing— although a woman who sits in the house in her folly causes harm. But a clever woman—that I loathe! May there never be in my house a woman with more intelligence than befits a woman! For Cypris engenders more mischief in the clever ones. The woman without ability is kept from indiscretion by the slenderness of her wit.

One ought to let no slave have access to a wife. Rather one should give them as companions wild and brute beasts so that they would be unable either to speak to anyone or to be spoken to in return. But as things are, the wicked ones hatch their wicked plans indoors, and their servants carry them abroad.

It is in this fashion, despicable creature, that you have come to traffic with me in the sacred bed of my father. I shall pour running water into my ears to wash away your proposals! How could I be such a traitor? The very

---

649 δ᾽ ἔνδον ἐννοοῦσιν Heiland: δ᾽ αἱ μὲν ἔνδον δρῶσιν C

655 ὃς οὐδ' ἀκούσας τοιάδ' ἁγνεύειν δοκῶ;
εὖ δ' ἴσθι, τοὐμόν σ' εὐσεβὲς σῴζει, γύναι·
εἰ μὴ γὰρ ὅρκοις θεῶν ἄφαρκτος ᾑρέθην,
οὐκ ἄν ποτ' ἔσχον μὴ οὐ τάδ' ἐξειπεῖν πατρί.
νῦν δ' ἐκ δόμων μέν, ἔστ' ἂν ἐκδημῇ χθονὸς
660 Θησεύς, ἄπειμι, σῖγα δ' ἕξομεν στόμα.
θεάσομαι δὲ σὺν πατρὸς μολὼν ποδὶ
πῶς νιν προσόψῃ, καὶ σὺ καὶ δέσποινα σή.
[τῆς σῆς δὲ τόλμης εἴσομαι γεγευμένος.]
ὄλοισθε. μισῶν δ' οὔποτ' ἐμπλησθήσομαι
665 γυναῖκας, οὐδ' εἴ φησί τίς μ' ἀεὶ λέγειν·
ἀεὶ γὰρ οὖν πώς εἰσι κἀκεῖναι κακαί.
ἤ νύν τις αὐτὰς σωφρονεῖν διδαξάτω
ἢ κἄμ' ἐάτω ταῖσδ' ἐπεμβαίνειν ἀεί.

ΤΡΟΦΟΣ

ἀντ.

τάλανες ὦ κακοτυχεῖς
γυναικῶν πότμοι.
670 τίν' ἢ νῦν τέχναν ἔχομεν ἢ τίνας
σφαλεῖσαι κάθαμμα λύειν λόγους;
ἐτύχομεν δίκας. ἰὼ γᾶ καὶ φῶς·

657 ᾑρέθην Pierson: εὑρέθην C
663 del. Barrett
664–8 in suspicionem voc. Valckenaer
669n Τρ. W. Smith, *TAPA* 91 (1960), 169: Χο. vel Φα. C
670 τίν' ἢ νῦν Page, Conomis: τίνα νῦν ἢ vel τίνα νῦν vel
τίνας νῦν C   τίνας Barthold: λόγους vel λόγον C
671 λύειν Musgrave: λύσιν vel λύσειν C

sound of such things makes me feel unclean! I tell you
plainly, it is my piety that saves you, woman. For if I had
not been off my guard and trapped through my oath by
the gods, I would never have kept myself from telling this
whole story to my father. But as things are, while Theseus
is out of the country, I shall leave the house and hold my
tongue. But I shall return in company with my father and
then see how you look upon him, you and your mistress.
[I shall know this, having had experience of your bold-
ness.] A curse on you all! I shall never take my fill of hat-
ing women, not even if someone says that I am always
talking of it. For they too are always in some way evil.
Let a man accordingly either teach them to be chaste or
allow me to tread upon them forever!

Exit HIPPOLYTUS *by Eisodos B.*

NURSE[a]
(sung) How luckless, how ill-starred, is the fate of
women! What craft do we have, what words, once we
have faltered, that can undo the noose? I have received
my just deserts! O earth, O sunlight! How shall I escape

---

[a] Two manuscripts give this song to Phaedra (the rest, impos-
sibly, to the Chorus), and editors have followed. But much in the
lines is contrary to Phaedra's character: she has not been a pro-
ponent of craftiness, she does not believe she has gotten her
deserts (cf. 682–7, 690), and she is not the one to wish for a god
to help her unjust deeds. These same things are in character for
the Nurse (cf. 480–1, 522–3). If it is argued that the speaker acts
as if she were the principal person affected ("How shall I escape
what has befallen?"), so does the Nurse at 607.

πᾷ ποτ' ἐξαλύξω τύχας;
πῶς δὲ πῆμα κρύψω, φίλαι;
675 τίς ἂν θεῶν ἀρωγὸς ἢ τίς ἂν βροτῶν
πάρεδρος ἢ ξυνεργὸς ἀδίκων ἔργων
φανείη; τὸ γὰρ παρ' ἡμῖν πάθος
πέραν δυσεκπέρατον ἔρχεται βίου.
κακοτυχεστάτα γυναικῶν ἐγώ.

ΧΟΡΟΣ

680 φεῦ φεῦ, πέπρακται, κοὐ κατώρθωνται τέχναι,
δέσποινα, τῆς σῆς προσπόλου, κακῶς δ' ἔχει.

ΦΑΙΔΡΑ

ὦ παγκακίστη καὶ φίλων διαφθορεῦ,
οἷ' εἰργάσω με. Ζεύς σε γεννήτωρ ἐμὸς
πρόρριζον ἐκτρίψειεν οὐτάσας πυρί.
685 οὐκ εἶπον, οὐ σῆς προυνοησάμην φρενός,
σιγᾶν ἐφ' οἷσι νῦν ἐγὼ κακύνομαι;
σὺ δ' οὐκ ἀνέσχου· τοιγὰρ οὐκέτ' εὐκλεεῖς
θανούμεθ'. ἀλλὰ δεῖ με δὴ καινῶν λόγων.
οὗτος γὰρ ὀργῇ συντεθηγμένος φρένας
690 ἐρεῖ καθ' ἡμῶν πατρὶ σὰς ἁμαρτίας,
[ἐρεῖ δὲ Πιτθεῖ τῷ γέροντι συμφοράς,]
πλήσει τε πᾶσαν γαῖαν αἰσχίστων λόγων.
ὄλοιο καὶ σὺ χὥστις ἄκοντας φίλους
πρόθυμός ἐστι μὴ καλῶς εὐεργετεῖν.

ΤΡΟΦΟΣ

695 δέσποιν', ἔχεις μὲν τἀμὰ μέμψασθαι κακά,
τὸ γὰρ δάκνον σου τὴν διάγνωσιν κρατεῖ·

what has befallen, how hide the painful fact, my friends?
What god, what mortal will appear to help me, sit at my
side, and lend a hand to my unjust deeds? For my pre-
sent misfortune crosses now—unhappy the crossing—to
the farther bourn of life. Unluckiest am I of women!

Enter PHAEDRA *from the palace.*

CHORUS LEADER
Oh dear, all is over, mistress, and the designs of your ser-
vant have not succeeded: all is lost.

PHAEDRA
Vile destroyer of your friends, see what you have done to
me! May Zeus the father of my race destroy you root and
branch with his thunderbolt! Did I not warn you—did I
not guess your purpose—to say nothing of the things now
causing me disgrace? But you could not bear to do so:
and so I shall no longer die with an honorable name. I
need some new plan. For *he*, with his mind whetted to a
fine edge with anger, will utter to his father against my
name the wrongs *you* have committed [, he will tell the
aged Pittheus of my misfortune,] and will fill the whole
land with ugly tales. My curse on you, and on whoever
itches to benefit friends dishonorably against their will!

NURSE
Mistress, you can, to be sure, find fault with the troubles I
have caused you, for the sting of them controls your

---

678 πέραν Wilamowitz: παρὸν C
683 Ζεύς σε Wolff: Ζεύς σ' ὁ fere C
691 om. a: praebet b: del. Brunk

ἔχω δὲ κἀγὼ πρὸς τάδ', εἰ δέξῃ, λέγειν.
ἔθρεψά σ' εὔνους τ' εἰμί· τῆς νόσου δέ σοι
ζητοῦσα φάρμαχ' ηὗρον οὐχ ἀβουλόμην.
700   εἰ δ' εὖ γ' ἔπραξα, κάρτ' ἂν ἐν σοφοῖσιν ἦ·
πρὸς τὰς τύχας γὰρ τὰς φρένας κεκτήμεθα.

ΦΑΙΔΡΑ

ἦ γὰρ δίκαια ταῦτα κἀξαρκοῦντά μοι,
τρώσασαν ἡμᾶς εἶτα συγχωρεῖν λόγοις;

ΤΡΟΦΟΣ

μακρηγοροῦμεν· οὐκ ἐσωφρόνουν ἐγώ.
705   ἀλλ' ἔστι κἀκ τῶνδ' ὥστε σωθῆναι, τέκνον.

ΦΑΙΔΡΑ

παῦσαι λέγουσα· καὶ τὸ πρὶν γὰρ οὐ καλῶς
παρήνεσάς μοι κἀπεχείρησας κακά.
ἀλλ' ἐκποδὼν ἄπελθε καὶ σαυτῆς πέρι
φρόντιζ'· ἐγὼ γὰρ τἀμὰ θήσομαι καλῶς.
710   ὑμεῖς δέ, παῖδες εὐγενεῖς Τροζήνιαι,
τοσόνδε μοι παράσχετ' ἐξαιτουμένῃ,
σιγῇ καλύπτειν ἀνθάδ' εἰσηκούσατε.

ΧΟΡΟΣ

ὄμνυμι σεμνὴν Ἄρτεμιν, Διὸς κόρην,
μηδὲν κακῶν σῶν ἐς φάος δείξειν ποτέ.

706 τὸ Kovacs: τὰ C

192

reason. But if you will listen, I too have something to say in reply. I brought you up and wish your good. When I looked to find a remedy for your malady, what I found was not what I hoped for. But if I had had success, I would have been numbered among the very wise. For our wisdom varies with the outcome.

PHAEDRA

What? Is this justice and satisfaction for me, to run me through and then to admit you have done so?

NURSE

We are wasting words. I admit I went too far. But even after what has happened, my child, you can escape with your life.[a]

PHAEDRA

No more from you! The advice you gave me before was dishonorable, and what you attempted to do was wrong. Get out of my way and worry about yourself! My own business I shall myself arrange well.

Exit NURSE into the palace.

Noble women of Trozen, grant me this one request: keep what you have heard here a secret.

CHORUS LEADER

I swear by Artemis the holy, Zeus's daughter, that I shall never reveal to the daylight any of your troubles!

---

[a] The Nurse may be alluding to the oath Hippolytus is under and which he has promised to keep (656–60), circumstances Phaedra is unaware of if she is off-stage during the scene between Hippolytus and the Nurse.

ΦΑΙΔΡΑ

715 καλῶς ἐλέξαθ'· ἓν δὲ πρὸς τούτοις ἐρῶ·
εὕρημα δή τι τῆσδε συμφορᾶς ἔχω,
ὥστ' εὐκλεᾶ μὲν παισὶ προσθεῖναι βίον
αὐτή τ' ὄνασθαι πρὸς τὰ νῦν πεπτωκότα.
οὐ γάρ ποτ' αἰσχυνῶ γε Κρησίους δόμους
720 οὐδ' ἐς πρόσωπον Θησέως ἀφίξομαι
αἰσχροῖς ἐπ' ἔργοις οὕνεκα ψυχῆς μιᾶς.

ΧΟΡΟΣ

μέλλεις δὲ δὴ τί δρᾶν ἀνήκεστον κακόν;

ΦΑΙΔΡΑ

θανεῖν· ὅπως δέ, τοῦτ' ἐγὼ βουλεύσομαι.

ΧΟΡΟΣ

εὔφημος ἴσθι.

ΦΑΙΔΡΑ

καὶ σύ γ' εὖ με νουθέτει.

725 ἐγὼ δὲ Κύπριν, ἥπερ ἐξόλλυσί με,
ψυχῆς ἀπαλλαχθεῖσα τῇδ' ἐν ἡμέρᾳ
τέρψω, πικροῦ δ' ἔρωτος ἡσσηθήσομαι.
ἀτὰρ κακόν γε χἀτέρῳ γενήσομαι
θανοῦσ', ἵν' εἰδῇ μὴ 'πὶ τοῖς ἐμοῖς κακοῖς
730 ὑψηλὸς εἶναι· τῆς νόσου δὲ τῆσδέ μοι
κοινῇ μετασχὼν σωφρονεῖν μαθήσεται.

---

[715] πρὸς τούτοις Barrett: προτρέπουσ' fere C   ἐρῶ
Hadley: ἐγὼ C

PHAEDRA

Thank you for your words. I have one further thing to add: I have discovered a remedy for this trouble of mine so that I may bequeath to my sons a life of good repute and gain myself some advantage in my present plight. For I shall never disgrace my Cretan home nor shall I go to face Theseus with shameful deeds against my name, all to save a single life.

CHORUS LEADER

What harm past cure do you mean to do?

PHAEDRA

To die. But the manner of it—that shall be *my* devising.

CHORUS LEADER

Say no more shocking words!

PHAEDRA

And you, give me advice that is good! This day, when I have taken leave of my life, I shall gladden the heart of Cypris, who is bent on destroying me, and I shall fall as victim to a hateful passion. But my death will prove a bane to someone else so that he may learn not to exult over my misfortune; by sharing with me in this malady he will learn moderation.[a]

Exit PHAEDRA *into the palace.*

[a] In Greek, *sôphronein*: the same word is used throughout the play to mean "chastity."

ΧΟΡΟΣ

στρ. α

ἠλιβάτοις ὑπὸ κευθμῶσι γενοίμαν,
ἵνα με πτερουσσαν ὄρ-
νιν θεὸς ἀμφὶ ποταναῖς ἀγέλαις θείη·
735 ἀρθείην δ' ἐπὶ πόντιον
κῦμ' <ἐς> τὰς Ἀδριηνὰς
ἀκτὰς Ἠριδανοῦ θ' ὕδωρ,
ἔνθα πορφύρεον σταλάσ-
σουσ' ἐς οἶδμα τάλαι-
740 ναι κόραι Φαέθοντος οἴκτῳ δακρύων
τὰς ἠλεκτροφαεῖς αὐγάς.

ἀντ. α

Ἑσπερίδων δ' ἐπὶ μηλόσπορον ἀκτὰν
ἀνύσαιμι τᾶν ἀοι-
δῶν, ἵν' ὁ ποντομέδων πορφυρέας λίμνας
745 ναύταις οὐκέθ' ὁδὸν νέμει,
σεμνὸν τέρμονα κυρῶν
οὐρανοῦ, τὸν Ἄτλας ἔχει·
κρῆναί τ' ἀμβρόσιαι χέον-
ται Ζηνὸς παρὰ κοί-
750 ταις, ἵν' ὀλβιόδωρος αὔξει ζαθέα
χθὼν εὐδαιμονίαν θεοῖς.

στρ. β

ὦ λευκόπτερε Κρησία
πορθμίς, ἃ διὰ πόντιον
κῦμ' ἁλικτύπον ἅλμας
755 ἐπόρευσας ἐμὰν ἄνασσαν ὀλβίων ἀπ' οἴκων

CHORUS

O that I could live in the secret clefts of the mountains,
and that there a god might make me a winged bird amid
the flying flocks! O that I could soar aloft over the sea
swell to the shore of the Adriatic and the waters of Eri-
danus, where into the deep-blue wave the luckless girls,
in grief for Phaëthon, drop the amber radiance of their
tears![a]

To the apple-bearing shore of the melodious Hes-
perides would I go my way, there where the lord of the
sea[b] forbids sailors further passage in the deep-blue
mere, fixing the sacred boundary of the skies, the pillar
held up by Atlas. There divine springs flow by the place
where Zeus lay, and holy Earth with her rich gifts makes
the gods' prosperity wax great.

O Cretan vessel with wing of white canvas, that ferried
my lady over the loud-sounding sea wave from her house
of blessedness, a boon that was no boon to make an

---

[a] Phaëthon, son of Helios, the sun god, attempted to drive his
father's sun chariot but could not control the horses. His sisters,
in grief for his fall, were changed into amber-dropping trees.

[b] Perhaps an allusion to the Old Man of the Sea, called Pro-
teus in the *Odyssey*.

---

734 ἀμφὶ Willink: ἐν C
736 κῦμ' ἐς τὰς Ἀδριηνὰς ἀκτὰς Willink: κῦμα τᾶς -ᾶς -ᾶς
C
739 οἶδμα Barthold: οἶδμα πατρὸς C
749 Ζηνὸς Barthold: Ζηνὸς μελάθρων C

κακονυμφοτάταν ὄνασιν·
ἢ γὰρ ἀπ' ἀμφοτέρων οἱ
Κρησίας <τ'> ἐκ γᾶς δύσορνις
760 ἔπτατ' <ἐς> κλεινὰς Ἀθήνας Μουνίχου τ' ἀ-
κταῖσιν ἐκδήσαντο πλεκτὰς πεισμάτων ἀρ-
χὰς ἐπ' ἀπείρου τε γᾶς ἔβασαν.

ἀντ. β

ἀνθ' ὧν οὐχ ὁσίων ἐρώ-
765 των δεινᾷ φρένας Ἀφροδί-
τας νόσῳ κατεκλάσθη·
χαλεπᾷ δ' ὑπέραντλος οὖσα συμφορᾷ τεράμνων
ἀπὸ νυμφιδίων κρεμαστὸν
ἅψεται ἀμφὶ βρόχον λευ-
770 κᾷ καθαρμόζουσα δείρᾳ,
δαίμονα στυγνὸν καταιδεσθεῖσα, τὰν τ' εὔ-
δοξον ἀνθαιρουμένα φήμαν ἀπαλλάσ-
775 σουσά τ' ἀλγεινὸν φρενῶν ἔρωτα.

ΤΡΟΦΟΣ

(ἔσωθεν)
ἰοὺ ἰού·
βοηδρομεῖτε πάντες οἱ πέλας δόμων·
ἐν ἀγχόναις δέσποινα, Θησέως δάμαρ.

ΧΟΡΟΣ

φεῦ φεῦ, πέπρακται· βασιλὶς οὐκέτ' ἔστι δὴ
γυνή, κρεμαστοῖς ἐν βρόχοις ἠρτημένη.

ΤΡΟΦΟΣ

780 οὐ σπεύσετ'; οὐκ οἴσει τις ἀμφιδέξιον
σίδηρον, ᾧ τόδ' ἅμμα λύσομεν δέρης;

unhappy bride: it was with evil omen, at the start of her journey and its end, that she sped from the land of Crete to glorious Athens, where they tied the plaited ends of the mooring cable on Munichus' shore[a] and trod the main-land.

Therefore her mind is wrenched by a terrible malady of unholy passion sent from Aphrodite; and sinking under her cruel misfortune she will put about her as it hangs from the beams of her bridal chamber a noose, fitting it to her white neck, feeling shame at her bitter fate, choosing in its stead the glory of a good name, and putting from her heart her painful desire.

NURSE

(within) Help, help! Come, help, anyone near the palace! My lady, Theseus' wife, has hanged herself!

CHORUS LEADER

Alas! It is all over! The Queen is no more, caught in a suspended noose!

NURSE

(within) Hurry! Someone fetch a double-edged sword to cut this noose about her neck!

---

[a] Munichus was the eponymous hero of the Athenian port of Munichion.

759 οἱ Willink: ἢ vel ἤ C   <τ’> Weil
760 <ἐς> Seidler
761 Μουνίχου τ’ Weil: Μουνιχίου δ’ fere C

EURIPIDES

ΧΟΡΟΣ

φίλαι, τί δρῶμεν; ἢ δοκεῖ περᾶν δόμους
λῦσαί τ' ἄνασσαν ἐξ ἐπισπαστῶν βρόχων;
— τί δ'; οὐ πάρεισι πρόσπολοι νεανίαι;
785 τὸ πολλὰ πράσσειν οὐκ ἐν ἀσφαλεῖ βίου.

ΤΡΟΦΟΣ

ὀρθώσατ' ἐκτείνοντες ἄθλιον νέκυν·
πικρὸν τόδ' οἰκούρημα δεσπόταις ἐμοῖς.

ΧΟΡΟΣ

ὄλωλεν ἡ δύστηνος, ὡς κλύω, γυνή·
ἤδη γὰρ ὡς νεκρόν νιν ἐκτείνουσι δή.

ΘΗΣΕΥΣ

790 γυναῖκες, ἴστε τίς ποτ' ἐν δόμοις βοὴ
ἠχοῖ βαρείᾳ προσπόλων <μ'> ἀφίκετο;
οὐ γάρ τί μ' ὡς θεωρὸν ἀξιοῖ δόμος
πύλας ἀνοίξας εὐφρόνως προσεννέπειν.
μῶν Πιτθέως τι γῆρας εἴργασται νέον;
795 πρόσω μὲν ἤδη βίοτος, ἀλλ' ὅμως ἔτ' ἂν
λυπηρὸς ἡμῖν τούσδ' ἂν ἐκλίποι δόμους.

ΧΟΡΟΣ

οὐκ ἐς γέροντας ἤδε σοι τείνει τύχη,
Θησεῦ· νέοι θανόντες ἀλγύνουσί σε.

ΘΗΣΕΥΣ

οἴμοι, τέκνων μοι μή τι συλᾶται βίος;

---

791 ἠχοῖ βαρείᾳ Musgrave: ἠχὼ βαρεῖα C   <μ'> Markland

200

CHORUS LEADER

Friends, what should we do? Shall we go into the house
and free our lady from the tight-drawn noose?

CHORUS MEMBER

Are there not young slaves nearby? To meddle is not a
safe course in life.

NURSE

Lay her straight and stretch out her wretched corpse!
Bitter is this house-tendance for my lord!

CHORUS LEADER

The poor woman is dead, to judge from this report. For
they are already laying out her corpse.

Enter THESEUS *by Eisodos A wearing the garlands of a
sacred ambassador.*

THESEUS

Women, do you know what shout of servants came with
leaden sound to my ears? For the house has not seen fit
to open its gates and greet me in friendly fashion as befits
a sacred ambassador.[a] I trust nothing untoward has hap-
pened to old Pittheus. He is far on in years, and yet his
going from this house would be a grief to me.

CHORUS LEADER

It is not the old this stroke of fortune affects, Theseus:
the death of the young is your grief.

THESEUS

Oh no! Surely it not my sons whose lives I am robbed of?

---

[a] A *theôros* is one who visits an oracle or a festival as a repre-
sentative of his city.

ΧΟΡΟΣ

800 ζῶσιν, θανούσης μητρὸς ὡς ἄλγιστά σοι.

ΘΗΣΕΤΣ

τί φῄς; ὄλωλεν ἄλοχος; ἐκ τίνος τύχης;

ΧΟΡΟΣ

βρόχον κρεμαστὸν ἀγχόνης ἀνήψατο.

ΘΗΣΕΤΣ

λύπῃ παχνωθεῖσ᾽ ἢ ἀπὸ συμφορᾶς τίνος;

ΧΟΡΟΣ

τοσοῦτον ἴσμεν· ἄρτι γὰρ κἀγὼ δόμους,
805 Θησεῦ, πάρειμι σῶν κακῶν πενθήτρια.

ΘΗΣΕΤΣ

αἰαῖ· τί δῆτα τοῖσδ᾽ ἀνέστεμμαι κάρα
πλεκτοῖσι φύλλοις, δυστυχὴς θεωρὸς ὤν;
χαλᾶτε κλῇθρα, πρόσπολοι, πυλωμάτων,
ἐκλύεθ᾽ ἁρμούς, ὡς ἴδω πικρὰν θέαν
810 γυναικός, ἥ με κατθανοῦσ᾽ ἀπώλεσεν.

ΧΟΡΟΣ

ἰὼ ἰὼ τάλαινα μελέων κακῶν·
ἔπαθες, εἰργάσω
τοσοῦτον ὥστε τούσδε συγχέαι δόμους,
αἰαῖ <αἰαῖ> τόλμας,
βιαίῳ θανοῦσ᾽ ἀνοσίῳ τε συμ-

---

809 h.v. et post 824 (πικρὰν θέαν praebentes) et hic (δυσδαί-
μονα vel τὸν δαίμονα) codd.
813 <αἰαῖ> Willink

CHORUS LEADER

They live. Their mother—great grief to you—is dead.

THESEUS

What do you mean? My wife is dead? But how?

CHORUS LEADER

She tied aloft a noose to hang herself.

THESEUS

Chilled in her heart by grief? Or for what reason?

CHORUS LEADER

That is as much as I know. For I too have but lately arrived at your house, Theseus, to mourn your misfortune.

THESEUS

Oh! Oh! Why then is my head crowned with these plaited leaves since my mission to the oracle has ended in disaster? *(He throws his garland to the ground.)* Unlock the doors that bar the portal, servants, loose their fastenings, so that I may see the bitter sight of my wife, who by her death has destroyed me!

The central doors open and the eccyclema *is wheeled out revealing the body of Phaedra.*

CHORUS

Alas, poor woman, how luckless you are! You have endured, you have done such things as to destroy this house! What hardihood was yours: you have died by a

815 φορᾷ, σᾶς πάλαισμα μελέας χερός.
τίς ἄρα σάν, τάλαιν᾽, ἀμαυροῖ ζόαν;

ΘΗΣΕΥΣ

στρ.

ὤμοι ἐγὼ πόνων· ἔπαθον, ὦ τάλας,
τὰ μάκιστ᾽ ἐμῶν κακῶν. ὦ τύχα,
ὥς μοι βαρεῖα καὶ δόμοις ἐπεστάθης,
820 κηλὶς ἄφραστος ἐξ ἀλαστόρων τινός·
κατακονὰ μὲν οὖν ἀβίοτος βίου.
κακῶν δ᾽, ὦ τάλας, πέλαγος εἰσορῶ
τοσοῦτον ὥστε μήποτ᾽ ἐκνεῦσαι πάλιν
824 μηδ᾽ ἐκπερᾶσαι κῦμα τῆσδε συμφορᾶς.
826 τίνι λόγῳ, τάλας, τίνι τύχαν σέθεν
βαρύποτμον, γύναι, προσαυδῶν τύχω;
ὄρνις γὰρ ὥς τις ἐκ χερῶν ἄφαντος εἶ,
πήδημ᾽ ἐς Ἅιδου κραιπνὸν ὁρμήσασά μοι.
830 αἰαῖ αἰαῖ, μέλεα μέλεα τάδε πάθη·
πρόσωθεν δέ ποθεν ἀνακομίζομαι
τύχαν δαιμόνων ἀμπλακίαισι τῶν
πάροιθέν τινος.

ΧΟΡΟΣ

οὐ σοὶ τάδ᾽, ὦναξ, ἦλθε δὴ μόνῳ κακά,
835 πολλῶν μετ᾽ ἄλλων δ᾽ ὤλεσας κεδνὸν λέχος.

ΘΗΣΕΥΣ

ἀντ.

τὸ κατὰ γᾶς θέλω, τὸ κατὰ γᾶς κνέφας
μετοικεῖν σκότῳ θανών, ὦ τλάμων,

violent and unhallowed deed, given a wrestler's throw by
your own unhappy hand. Who was it, poor woman, that
brought your life down to darkness?

THESEUS

(sung) What misery is mine! I have suffered, luckless
man that I am, the greatest of my woes! O fate, how heav-
ily you have fallen upon me and upon my house, an
unperceived blight sent upon me by some avenging
power! Nay more, it is the very destruction of my life!
Unhappy woman, I look upon a sea of troubles so great, I
cannot swim out of them or cross the flood of this sorrow.
With what name, poor woman, with what name, can I call
your grievous fate and hit the mark? For you are gone
from my hands like a bird, and have sped your swift leap
into the house of Hades. Alas! Alas! Terrible, terrible
are my sufferings! I am reaping the stroke of the gods
because of the sin of someone before me, someone in
time now gone!

CHORUS LEADER

My lord, it is not upon you alone that these ills have come:
you have lost a trusty wife, but so have many others.

THESEUS

(sung) To the gloom under earth, under earth, I would
change my dwelling and die in darkness, luckless man

---

815 πάλαισμα μελέας χερός Enger: χ- π- μ- C
821 οὖν· ἀβίοτος βίος Triclinius
825 vide ad 809
826 τίνι λόγῳ . . . τίνι Diggle: τίνα λόγον . . . τίνα C

τῆς σῆς στερηθεὶς φιλτάτης ὁμιλίας·
ἀπώλεσας γὰρ μᾶλλον ἢ κατέφθισο.
840 τοῦ δὲ κλύω πόθεν θανάσιμος τύχα,
γύναι, σάν, τάλαιν᾽, ἔβα καρδίαν;
εἴποι τις ἂν τὸ πραχθέν, ἢ μάτην ὄχλον
στέγει τύραννον δῶμα προσπόλων ἐμῶν;
ὤμοι μοι <τάλας, ἰώ μοι> σέθεν,
845 μέλεος, οἷον εἶδον ἄλγος δόμων,
οὐ τλητὸν οὐδὲ ῥητόν. ἀλλ᾽ ἀπωλόμην·
ἔρημος οἶκος, καὶ τέκν᾽ ὀρφανεύεται.
<αἰαῖ αἰαῖ,> ἔλιπες ἔλιπες, ὦ φίλα
γυναικῶν ἀρίστα θ᾽ ὁπόσας ὁρᾷ
850 φέγγος θ᾽ ἁλίοιο καὶ νυκτὸς ἀ-
στερωπὸν σέλας.

ΧΟΡΟΣ
ὦ τάλας, ὅσον κακὸν ἔχει δόμος.
δάκρυσί μου βλέφαρα καταχυθέντα τέγ-
γεται σᾷ τύχᾳ·
855 τὸ δ᾽ ἐπὶ τῷδε πῆμα φρίσσω πάλαι.

ΘΗΣΕΥΣ
ἔα ἔα·
τί δή ποθ᾽ ἥδε δέλτος ἐκ φίλης χερὸς
ἠρτημένη; θέλει τι σημῆναι νέον;
ἀλλ᾽ ἦ λέχους μοι καὶ τέκνων ἐπιστολὰς
ἔγραψεν ἡ δύστηνος, ἐξαιτουμένη;
860 θάρσει, τάλαινα· λέκτρα γὰρ τὰ Θησέως
οὐκ ἔστι δῶμά θ᾽ ἥτις εἴσεισιν γυνή.

that I am, bereft of your sweet converse! You have
destroyed me more utterly than you perished yourself!
From whom can I hear whence came against your heart,
poor wife, the deadly stroke of fortune? Will someone
tell what has happened, or does the royal house shelter
my host of slaves for nothing? Ah me, <how wretched am
I at your death>, luckless man that I am, what a grief to
my house I have seen, grief that cannot be endured or
uttered! I am undone: my house is bereft, my children
are orphaned. <Alas, alas,> you have left them, dear wife,
best of women looked on by the brightness of the sun and
the starry gleam of night!

CHORUS

Unhappy man, great is the grief your house has received.
My eyes are drenched with tears and melt at your misfor-
tune. But I have long been shuddering at the calamity
that is to follow.

THESEUS

What's this? What can it be, this tablet hanging from her
dear hand? Does it want to tell me of something I do not
know? Has the poor woman written me a message of
entreaty about our marriage and children? Fear not, poor
creature: there is no woman who shall take possession of
the bed and house of Theseus. *(He takes up the tablet.)*

---

840 τοῦ δὲ Enger: τίνος C
841 τάλαιν᾽, ἔβα Elmsley: ἔ- τ- C
844 lac. indic. et suppl. Seidler
848 <αἰαῖ αἰαῖ> Kirchhoff
849 ὁρᾷ Hartung: ἐφορᾷ C
850 θ᾽ ἁλίοιο Kirchhoff: ἀελίου τε C
850–1 ἀστερωπὸν σέλας Jacobs: ἀστερωπὸς σελάνα fere C

καὶ μὴν τύποι γε σφενδόνης χρυσηλάτου
τῆς οὐκέτ' οὔσης οἵδε προσσαίνουσί με.
φέρ' ἐξελίξας περιβολὰς σφραγισμάτων
865   ἴδω τί λέξαι δέλτος ἥδε μοι θέλει.

ΧΟΡΟΣ

φεῦ φεῦ, τόδ' αὖ νεοχμὸν ἐκδοχαῖς
ἐπεισφρεῖ θεὸς κακόν. †ἐμοὶ [μὲν οὖν ἀβίοτος βίου]
τύχα πρὸς τὸ κρανθὲν εἴη τυχεῖν†
ὀλομένους γάρ, οὐκέτ' ὄντας, λέγω,
870   φεῦ φεῦ, τῶν ἐμῶν τυράννων δόμους.
[ὦ δαῖμον, εἴ πως ἔστι, μὴ σφήλῃς δόμους,
αἰτουμένης δὲ κλῦθί μου· πρὸς γάρ τινος
οἰωνὸν ὥστε μάντις εἰσορῶ κακόν.]

ΘΗΣΕΥΣ

οἴμοι, τόδ' οἷον ἄλλο πρὸς κακῷ κακόν,
875   οὐ τλητὸν οὐδὲ λεκτόν· ὦ τάλας ἐγώ.

ΧΟΡΟΣ

τί χρῆμα; λέξον, εἴ τί μοι λόγου μέτα.

ΘΗΣΕΥΣ

βοᾷ βοᾷ δέλτος ἄλαστα. πᾷ φύγω
βάρος κακῶν; ἀπὸ γὰρ ὀλόμενος οἴχομαι,
οἷον οἷον εἶδον μέλος ἐν γραφαῖς
880   φθεγγόμενον τλάμων.

ΧΟΡΟΣ

αἰαῖ, κακῶν ἀρχηγὸν ἐκφαίνεις λόγον.

See, the impress of the dead woman's gold-chased seal
charms my eyes! Come, let me open its sealed wrappings
and see what this tablet wishes to tell me!

He opens the tablet and reads it silently.

CHORUS

Oh! Oh! This is some fresh disaster the god is sending as
successor to the other! < . . . . > For I say that the
house of my king has perished, ah me, is no more. [O
fate, if it is at all possible, do not overthrow this house but
hear my prayer. For from some quarter I see, prophet-
like, an evil omen.]

THESEUS

O woe! What second pain on top of pain is this, pain
unendurable, unspeakable! What misery is mine!

CHORUS LEADER

What is it? Speak, if I may hear it.

THESEUS

(*sung*) The tablet cries aloud, it cries aloud of horror!
How shall I escape from the weight of my misfortunes? I
am utterly undone, such is the song I in my wretchedness
have seen whose tune sounds in the writing!

CHORUS LEADER

Ah me! The word you utter is one that foretells woe!

---

863 οἵδε Wilamowitz: τῆσδε C

867 μὲν οὖν ἀβίοτος βίου del. Burges cl. 821

867–8 fort. ἐμοὶ βίος / τίς ἂν πρὸς τὸ κρανθὲν εἴη τυχεῖν;

871–3 del. Nauck

879 μέλος ἐν γραφαῖς Willink: ἐ- γ- μ- C

ΘΗΣΕΥΣ

τόδε μὲν οὐκέτι στόματος ἐν πύλαις
καθέξω δυσεκπέρατον <λόγοι-
σιν> ὀλοὸν κακόν·
ἰὼ πόλις.
885 Ἱππόλυτος εὐνῆς τῆς ἐμῆς ἔτλη θιγεῖν
βίᾳ, τὸ σεμνὸν Ζηνὸς ὄμμ' ἀτιμάσας.
    ἀλλ', ὦ πάτερ Πόσειδον, ἃς ἐμοί ποτε
ἀρὰς ὑπέσχου τρεῖς, μιᾷ κατέργασαι
τούτων ἐμὸν παῖδ', ἡμέραν δὲ μὴ φύγοι
890 τήνδ', εἴπερ ἡμῖν ὤπασας σαφεῖς ἀράς.

ΧΟΡΟΣ

ἄναξ, ἀπεύχου ταῦτα πρὸς θεῶν πάλιν,
γνώσῃ γὰρ αὖθις ἀμπλακών· ἐμοὶ πιθοῦ.

ΘΗΣΕΥΣ

οὐκ ἔστι. καὶ πρός γ' ἐξελῶ σφε τῆσδε γῆς,
δυοῖν δὲ μοίραιν θατέρᾳ πεπλήξεται·
895 ἢ γὰρ Ποσειδῶν αὐτὸν εἰς Ἅιδου δόμους
θανόντα πέμψει τὰς ἐμὰς ἀρὰς σέβων,
ἢ τῆσδε χώρας ἐκπεσὼν ἀλώμενος
ξένην ἐπ' αἶαν λυπρὸν ἀντλήσει βίον.

ΧΟΡΟΣ

καὶ μὴν ὅδ' αὐτὸς παῖς σὸς ἐς καιρὸν πάρα

884 <λόγοισιν> Willink

210

THESEUS

(sung) No more shall I hold this ruinous bane, hard <for words> to utter though it is, within the gates of my mouth!

(spoken in a loud voice, calling everyone in earshot to witness)

City of Athens! Hear me!

Bystanders enter quickly by Eisodos B and gather around.

Hippolytus has dared to put his hand by force to my marriage bed, dishonoring the holy eye of Zeus!

But, father Poseidon, those three curses you once promised me—with one of them kill my son, and may he not live out this day, if indeed you have granted me curses I may rely on!

CHORUS LEADER

My lord, I beg you by the gods, take back your prayer! For you will learn in time that you have made a mistake. Take my advice!

THESEUS

It cannot be. And what is more, I shall banish him from this land, and of two fates one shall strike him: either Poseidon, honoring my curses, will send him dead to the house of Hades or being banished from here he will wander over foreign soil and drain to the dregs a life of misery.

Enter HIPPOLYTUS by Eisodos B.

CHORUS LEADER

Look! Your son Hippolytus is here himself, a timely

900 Ἱππόλυτος· ὀργῆς δ' ἐξανεὶς κακῆς, ἄναξ
Θησεῦ, τὸ λῷστον σοῖσι βούλευσαι δόμοις.

ΙΠΠΟΛΥΤΟΣ

κραυγῆς ἀκούσας σῆς ἀφικόμην, πάτερ,
σπουδῇ· τὸ μέντοι πρᾶγμ' ὅτῳ στένεις ἔπι
οὐκ οἶδα, βουλοίμην δ' ἂν ἐκ σέθεν κλυεῖν.
905   ἔα, τί χρῆμα; σὴν δάμαρθ' ὁρῶ, πάτερ,
νεκρόν· μεγίστου θαύματος τόδ' ἄξιον·
ἣν ἀρτίως ἔλειπον, ἣ φάος τόδε
οὔπω χρόνος παλαιὸς εἰσεδέρκετο.
τί χρῆμα πάσχει; τῷ τρόπῳ διόλλυται;
910 πάτερ, πυθέσθαι βούλομαι σέθεν πάρα.
σιγᾷς; σιωπῆς δ' οὐδὲν ἔργον ἐν κακοῖς·
[ἡ γὰρ ποθοῦσα πάντα καρδία κλύειν
κἂν τοῖς κακοῖσι λίχνος οὖσ' ἁλίσκεται.]
οὐ μὴν φίλους γε, κἄτι μᾶλλον ἢ φίλους,
915 κρύπτειν δίκαιον σάς, πάτερ, δυσπραξίας.

ΘΗΣΕΥΣ

ὦ πόλλ' ἁμαρτάνοντες ἄνθρωποι μάτην,
τί δὴ τέχνας μὲν μυρίας διδάσκετε
καὶ πάντα μηχανᾶσθε κἀξευρίσκετε,
ἐν δ' οὐκ ἐπίστασθ' οὐδ' ἐθηράσασθέ πω,
920 φρονεῖν διδάσκειν οἷσιν οὐκ ἔνεστι νοῦς;

ΙΠΠΟΛΥΤΟΣ

δεινὸν σοφιστὴν εἶπας, ὅστις εὖ φρονεῖν
τοὺς μὴ φρονοῦντας δυνατός ἐστ' ἀναγκάσαι.
ἀλλ' οὐ γὰρ ἐν δέοντι λεπτουργεῖς, πάτερ,

arrival! Abate your harsh anger, my lord Theseus, and deliberate about what is best for your house!

HIPPOLYTUS

I heard your cry and came in haste, father. But what it was that brought forth your groan, I do not know but would gladly hear from your lips.

He sees the corpse of Phaedra.

But what can this be? I see your wife, father, dead. This causes me the greatest astonishment. Just now I left her, and it was no long time ago that she was looking on this light of day. What has happened to her? How did she die? Father, I want to learn this from you. *(Theseus is silent.)* What, silent? Silence is no use in misfortune. [For the heart that longs to hear all things is proved greedy in misfortune as well.] It is not right to hide your troubles from those who are your kin, no, more than kin, father.

THESEUS

O foolish mankind, so often missing the mark, why do you teach crafts numberless and contrive and invent all things when there is one thing you do not understand and have not hunted after, how to teach the senseless to be sensible!

HIPPOLYTUS

That is a formidable expert you mention, who is able to force insensate fools to show sense. But since these fine-spun disputations of yours, father, are unseasonable, I

---

903 ὅτῳ στένεις ἔπι Diggle: ἐφ᾽ ᾧτινι στένεις fere C
908 χρόνος παλαιὸς Lehrs: χρόνον παλαιὸν C
912–13 del. Barrett

δέδοικα μή σου γλῶσσ᾽ ὑπερβάλλῃ κακοῖς.

ΘΗΣΕΥΣ

925 φεῦ, χρῆν βροτοῖσι τῶν φίλων τεκμήριον
σαφές τι κεῖσθαι καὶ διάγνωσιν φρενῶν,
ὅστις τ᾽ ἀληθής ἐστιν ὅς τε μὴ φίλος,
δισσάς τε φωνὰς πάντας ἀνθρώπους ἔχειν,
τὴν μὲν δικαίαν, τὴν δ᾽ ὅπως ἐτύγχανεν,
930 ὡς ἡ φρονοῦσα τἄδικ᾽ ἐξηλέγχετο
πρὸς τῆς δικαίας, κοὐκ ἂν ἠπατώμεθα.

ΙΠΠΟΛΥΤΟΣ

ἀλλ᾽ ἦ τις ἐς σὸν οὖς με διαβαλὼν ἔχει
φίλων, νοσοῦμεν δ᾽ οὐδὲν ὄντες αἴτιοι;
ἔκ τοι πέπληγμαι· σοὶ γὰρ ἐκπλήσσουσί με
935 λόγοι, παραλλάσσοντες ἔξεδροι φρενῶν.

ΘΗΣΕΥΣ

φεῦ τῆς βροτείας—ποῖ προβήσεται;—φρενός.
τί τέρμα τόλμης καὶ θράσους γενήσεται;
εἰ γὰρ κατ᾽ ἀνδρὸς βίοτον ἐξογκώσεται,
ὁ δ᾽ ὕστερος τοῦ πρόσθεν εἰς ὑπερβολὴν
940 πανοῦργος ἔσται, θεοῖσι προσβαλεῖν χθονὶ
ἄλλην δεήσει γαῖαν ἣ χωρήσεται
τοὺς μὴ δικαίους καὶ κακοὺς πεφυκότας.
σκέψασθε δ᾽ ἐς τόνδ᾽, ὅστις ἐξ ἐμοῦ γεγὼς
ᾔσχυνε τἀμὰ λέκτρα κἀξελέγχεται
945 πρὸς τῆς θανούσης ἐμφανῶς κάκιστος ὤν.
δεῖξον δ᾽, ἐπειδή γ᾽ ἐς μίασμ᾽ ἐλήλυθα,

fear that your misfortunes have caused your tongue to run amok.

THESEUS

Oh, there ought to be for mortals some reliable test for friends, some way to know their minds, which of them is a true friend and which is not, and each man ought to have two voices, the one a voice of justice, the other whatever he chanced to have, so that the voice that thinks unjust thoughts would be convicted of falsehood by the just voice, and in this way we should never be deceived!

HIPPOLYTUS

But has one of my kin been slandering me in your ear and are my fortunes ill though I have done nothing wrong? I am astonished. Your words, cast adrift from all sense, astonish me.

THESEUS

Oh, the heart of mortals, how far will it go? What limit can be set to audacity and brazenness? If it grows great in the course of a man's life, and he who comes after overtops his predecessor in knavery, the gods will have to add another land to the world to hold the criminal and the vile!

Look at this man! He was born from my loins, and yet he disgraced my bed and is clearly convicted of utter baseness by the dead woman here!

Hippolytus turns away.

Come, show your face to your father, eye to eye, since in

---

931 fort. δικαίας· οὐκ
946 ἐλήλυθα Musgrave: -θας C

τὸ σὸν πρόσωπον δεῦρ' ἐναντίον πατρί.
σὺ δὴ θεοῖσιν ὡς περισσὸς ὢν ἀνὴρ
ξύνει; σὺ σώφρων καὶ κακῶν ἀκήρατος;
950 οὐκ ἂν πιθοίμην τοῖσι σοῖς κόμποις ἐγὼ
θεοῖσι προσθεὶς ἀμαθίαν φρονεῖν κακῶς.
ἤδη νυν αὔχει καὶ δι' ἀψύχου βορᾶς
σίτοις καπήλευ' Ὀρφέα τ' ἄνακτ' ἔχων
βάκχευε πολλῶν γραμμάτων τιμῶν καπνούς·
955 ἐπεί γ' ἐλήφθης. τοὺς δὲ τοιούτους ἐγὼ
φεύγειν προφωνῶ πᾶσι· θηρεύουσι γὰρ
σεμνοῖς λόγοισιν, αἰσχρὰ μηχανώμενοι.

τέθνηκεν ἥδε· τοῦτό σ' ἐκσώσειν δοκεῖς;
ἐν τῷδ' ἁλίσκῃ πλεῖστον, ὦ κάκιστε σύ·
960 ποῖοι γὰρ ὅρκοι κρείσσονες, τίνες λόγοι
τῆσδ' ἂν γένοιντ' ἄν, ὥστε σ' αἰτίαν φυγεῖν;
μισεῖν σε φήσεις τήνδε, καὶ τὸ δὴ νόθον
τοῖς γνησίοισι πολέμιον πεφυκέναι;
κακὴν ἄρ' αὐτὴν ἔμπορον βίου λέγεις,
965 εἰ δυσμενείᾳ σῇ τὰ φίλτατ' ὤλεσεν.
ἀλλ' ὡς τὸ μῶρον ἀνδράσιν μὲν οὐκ ἔνι,
γυναιξὶ δ' ἐμπέφυκεν; οἶδ' ἐγὼ νέους
οὐδὲν γυναικῶν ὄντας ἀσφαλεστέρους,
ὅταν ταράξῃ Κύπρις ἡβῶσαν φρένα·

---

[a] Those who have committed terrible crimes are thought to contaminate those who looked at them or came into close contact with them. Since, however, Theseus has already looked at his son, there is no reason for him not to continue to do so.

any case I have already involved myself in pollution.[a] Are
you, then, the companion of the gods, as a man beyond
the common? Are you the chaste one, untouched by evil?
Your vauntings will never persuade me to be so wrong-
headed as to impute folly to the gods. Continue then your
confident boasting, adopt a meatless diet and play the
showman with your food, make Orpheus your lord and
engage in mystic rites, holding the vaporings of many
books in honor![b] For you have been found out. To all I
give the warning: avoid men like this. For they make you
their prey with their holy-sounding words while they con-
trive deeds of shame.

She is dead. Do you think this will save you? This is
the fact that most serves to convict you, villainous man!
For what oaths, what arguments, could be more powerful
than she is, to win you acquittal on the charge? Will you
claim that she hated you and that the bastard is always
regarded as an enemy to the true-born? You make her a
poor merchant of her own life, then, if she destroyed what
was most precious to herself[c] for enmity of you. But will
you say that folly is not to be found in men but is native to
women? I know young men who are no more stable than
women when Cypris stirs their young hearts to confusion.

[b] Theseus compares Hippolytus to the Orphics, an ascetic
religious sect that ate a vegetarian diet and had a reputation for
hypocrisy.
[c] Her life. The trade Theseus here cannot imagine is in fact
close to the one Phaedra chose, though in exchange for her life
she won not only Hippolytus' punishment but also the rescue of
her own good name.

970 τὸ δ' ἄρσεν αὐτοὺς ὠφελεῖ προσκείμενον.
      νῦν οὖν—τί ταῦτα σοῖς ἁμιλλῶμαι λόγοις
      νεκροῦ παρόντος μάρτυρος σαφεστάτου;
      ἔξερρε γαίας τῆσδ' ὅσον τάχος φυγάς,
      καὶ μήτ' Ἀθήνας τὰς θεοδμήτους μόλῃς
975 μήτ' εἰς ὅρους γῆς ἧς ἐμὸν κρατεῖ δόρυ.
      εἰ γὰρ παθών γέ σου τάδ' ἡσσηθήσομαι,
      οὐ μαρτυρήσει μ' Ἴσθμιος Σίνις ποτὲ
      κτανεῖν ἑαυτὸν ἀλλὰ κομπάζειν μάτην,
      οὐδ' αἱ θαλάσσῃ σύννομοι Σκιρωνίδες
980 φήσουσι πέτραι τοῖς κακοῖς μ' εἶναι βαρύν.

ΧΟΡΟΣ
      οὐκ οἶδ' ὅπως εἴποιμ' ἂν εὐτυχεῖν τινα
      θνητῶν· τὰ γὰρ δὴ πρῶτ' ἀνέστραπται πάλιν.

ΙΠΠΟΛΥΤΟΣ
      πάτερ, μένος μὲν ξύντασίς τε σῶν φρενῶν
      δεινή· τὸ μέντοι πρᾶγμ', ἔχον καλοὺς λόγους,
985 εἴ τις διαπτύξειεν οὐ καλὸν τόδε.
      ἐγὼ δ' ἄκομψος εἰς ὄχλον δοῦναι λόγον,
      ἐς ἥλικας δὲ κὠλίγους σοφώτερος·
      ἔχει δὲ μοῖραν καὶ τόδ'· οἱ γὰρ ἐν σοφοῖς
      φαῦλοι παρ' ὄχλῳ μουσικώτεροι λέγειν.
990 ὅμως δ' ἀνάγκη, ξυμφορᾶς ἀφιγμένης,
      γλῶσσάν μ' ἀφεῖναι. πρῶτα δ' ἄρξομαι λέγειν
      ὅθεν μ' ὑπῆλθες πρῶτον ὡς διαφθερῶν
      οὐκ ἀντιλέξοντ'. εἰσορᾷς φάος τόδε
      καὶ γαῖαν· ἐν τοῖσδ' οὐκ ἔνεστ' ἀνὴρ ἐμοῦ,

218

But their standing as males serves them well.

And so now—but why do I wage this contest against your words when this corpse, witness most reliable, lies near? Go forth from this land at once into exile, and come no more either to god-built Athens or to the borders of any land ruled by my spear! For if I am to be bested by you when you have done this to me, Isthmian Sinis shall no longer attest that I killed him but say it was an idle boast, and the Skironian rocks near the sea shall deny that I am a scourge to evildoers!

CHORUS LEADER

I do not know how I could say that any mortal enjoys good fortune. For what is noblest is now overthrown.

HIPPOLYTUS

Father, the anger and vehemence of your heart is dreadful. Yet though the case you argue provides such persuasive arguments, it is not persuasive in fact if one examines it closely. I am not skilled in making speeches to a crowd but have more ability to address my age-mates and the few. This too is as fate wills it, for those who are of no account among the wise are often more inspired speakers before the multitude. Yet since disaster has come upon me, I must loosen my tongue. I shall begin to speak from the point where you first attacked me, expecting you would destroy me with not a word to say in reply. You see the light of the sun, you see the earth. Upon this sun-lit

---

983 ξύντασίς Herwerden: ξύστ- C
993 οὐκ Markland: κοὐκ C

995 οὐδ' ἦν σὺ μὴ φῇς, σωφρονέστερος γεγώς.
ἐπίσταμαι γὰρ πρῶτα μὲν θεοὺς σέβειν
φίλοις τε χρῆσθαι μὴ ἀδικεῖν πειρωμένοις
ἀλλ' οἷσιν αἰδὼς μήτ' ἐπαγγέλλειν κακὰ
μήτ' ἀνθυπουργεῖν αἰσχρὰ τοῖσι χρωμένοις,
1000 οὐκ ἐγγελαστὴς τῶν ὁμιλούντων, πάτερ,
ἀλλ' αὐτὸς οὐ παροῦσι κἀγγὺς ὢν φίλοις.
ἑνὸς δ' ἄθικτος, ᾧ με νῦν ἔχειν δοκεῖς·
λέχους γὰρ ἐς τόδ' ἡμέρας ἁγνὸν δέμας·
οὐκ οἶδα πρᾶξιν τήνδε πλὴν λόγῳ κλύων
1005 γραφῇ τε λεύσσων· οὐδὲ ταῦτα γὰρ σκοπεῖν
πρόθυμός εἰμι, παρθένον ψυχὴν ἔχων.
    καὶ δὴ τὸ σῶφρον τοὐμὸν οὐ πείθει σ'· ἴτω·
δεῖ δή σε δεῖξαι τῷ τρόπῳ διεφθάρην.
πότερα τὸ τῆσδε σῶμ' ἐκαλλιστεύετο
1010 πασῶν γυναικῶν; ἢ σὸν οἰκήσειν δόμον
ἔγκληρον εὐνὴν προσλαβὼν ἐπήλπισα;
[μάταιος ἄρ' ἦν, οὐδαμοῦ μὲν οὖν φρενῶν.
ἀλλ' ὡς τυραννεῖν ἡδὺ τοῖσι σώφροσιν;
ἥκιστ', ἐπεί τοι τὰς φρένας διέφθορεν
1015 θνητῶν ὅσοισιν ἀνδάνει μοναρχία.]
ἐγὼ δ' ἀγῶνας μὲν κρατεῖν Ἑλληνικοὺς
πρῶτος θέλοιμ' ἄν, ἐν πόλει δὲ δεύτερος
σὺν τοῖς ἀρίστοις εὐτυχεῖν ἀεὶ φίλοις·
πράσσειν τε γὰρ πάρεστι, κίνδυνός τ' ἀπὼν
1020 κρείσσω δίδωσι τῆς τυραννίδος χάριν.
    ἐν οὐ λέλεκται τῶν ἐμῶν, τὰ δ' ἄλλ' ἔχεις·
εἰ μὲν γὰρ ἦν μοι μάρτυς οἷός εἰμ' ἐγὼ

earth there is no man—deny it though you may—more
chaste than I. I know how to reverence the gods and how
to make friends of those who try to commit no wrong,
friends who scruple to give evil orders and to render base
services to those in their company. I am no mocker of my
companions, father, but the same man to friends both
absent and present. By one thing I am untouched, the
very thing in which you think you have convicted me: to
this very moment my body is untainted by love. I do not
know this act save by report or seeing it in painting. I am
not eager to look at it either, since I have a virgin soul.

But suppose that my chastity does not persuade you. I
waive the point. You ought then to show how I was cor-
rupted. Did her body surpass all other women's in
beauty? Or did I hope that by taking an heiress as mis-
tress I would succeed to your house? [I was foolish then,
nay completely out of my mind. But will you say that to
be king is a tempting pleasure even to the virtuous? Not
at all, since kingly power has corrupted the minds of all
those who love it.] I for my part would wish to be first in
the Greek games but in the city to be second and to enjoy
continuous good fortune with noble friends. For not only
is there scope for accomplishment, but the absence of
danger yields a greater pleasure than being king.

One more point remains to be made, you have heard
all else. If I had a witness to what manner of man I am

---

998 ἐπαγγέλλειν Milton: ἀπαγγ- C

1007 ἴτω Murray: ἴσως C

1012–15 in suspicionem voc. Barrett

1014 ἥκιστ', ἐπεί τοι Barrett: ἥκιστά γ', εἰ μὴ C

καὶ τῆσδ' ὁρώσης φέγγος ἠγωνιζόμην,
ἔργοις ἂν εἶδες τοὺς κακοὺς διεξιών·
1025 νῦν δ' ὅρκιόν σοι Ζῆνα καὶ πέδον χθονὸς
ὄμνυμι τῶν σῶν μήποθ' ἅψασθαι γάμων
μηδ' ἂν θελῆσαι μηδ' ἂν ἔννοιαν λαβεῖν.
ἦ τἄρ' ὀλοίμην ἀκλεὴς ἀνώνυμος
[ἄπολις ἄοικος, φυγὰς ἀλητεύων χθόνα,]
1030 καὶ μήτε πόντος μήτε γῆ δέξαιτό μου
σάρκας θανόντος, εἰ κακὸς πέφυκ' ἀνήρ.
τί δ' ἥδε δειμαίνουσ' ἀπώλεσεν βίον
οὐκ οἶδ', ἐμοὶ γὰρ οὐ θέμις πέρα λέγειν·
ἐσωφρόνησε δ' οὐκ ἔχουσα σωφρονεῖν,
1035 ἡμεῖς δ' ἔχοντες οὐ καλῶς ἐχρώμεθα.

ΧΟΡΟΣ
ἀρκοῦσαν εἶπας αἰτίας ἀποστροφὴν
ὅρκους παρασχών, πίστιν οὐ σμικράν, θεῶν.

ΘΗΣΕΤΣ
ἆρ' οὐκ ἐπῳδὸς καὶ γόης πέφυχ' ὅδε,
ὃς τὴν ἐμὴν πέποιθεν εὐοργησίᾳ
1040 ψυχὴν κρατήσειν, τὸν τεκόντ' ἀτιμάσας;

ΙΠΠΟΛΥΤΟΣ
καὶ σοῦ γε ταὐτὰ κάρτα θαυμάζω, πάτερ·
εἰ γὰρ σὺ μὲν παῖς ἦσθ', ἐγὼ δὲ σὸς πατήρ,
ἔκτεινά τοί σ' ἂν κοὐ φυγαῖς ἐζημίουν,
εἴπερ γυναικὸς ἠξίους ἐμῆς θιγεῖν.

ΘΗΣΕΤΣ
1045 ὡς ἄξιον τόδ' εἶπας. οὐχ οὕτω θανῇ

and if I were pleading my case while *she* was still alive,
your careful investigation would have discovered in very
truth who is the guilty party. As things stand, I swear by
Zeus, god of oaths, and by the earth beneath me that I
never touched your wife, never wished to, never had the
thought. May I perish with no name or reputation, [citi-
less, homeless, wandering the earth an exile,] and may
neither sea nor earth receive my corpse if I am guilty!
What the fear was that made her take her life I do not
know, for it would not be right for me to speak further.
But she showed chastity, though she could not be chaste,
while I, who could, have used it to my hurt.

CHORUS LEADER
You have made a sufficient rebuttal of the charge against
you in swearing by the gods, no slight assurance.

THESEUS
Is this man not a chanter of spells and a charlatan? He is
confident that by his calm temper he will overmaster my
soul, though he has dishonored the father who begot him.

HIPPOLYTUS
I feel the same great wonder at you, father. For if you
were my son and I your father, I would not have banished
but killed you, if you had dared to touch my wife.

THESEUS
How like you these words are! Not thus will you die,

---

¹⁰²⁹ del. Valckenaer
¹⁰³² τί Bothe: εἰ C

223

ὥσπερ σὺ σαυτῷ τόνδε προύθηκας νόμον·
ταχὺς γὰρ Ἅιδης ῥᾷστον ἀνδρὶ δυστυχεῖ·
ἀλλ' ἐκ πατρῴας φυγὰς ἀλητεύων χθονός
[ξένην ἐπ' αἶαν λυπρὸν ἀντλήσεις βίον·
μισθὸς γὰρ οὗτός ἐστιν ἀνδρὶ δυσσεβεῖ].

1050

ΙΠΠΟΛΥΤΟΣ
οἴμοι, τί δράσεις; οὐδὲ μηνυτὴν χρόνον
δέξῃ καθ' ἡμῶν, ἀλλά μ' ἐξελᾷς χθονός;

ΘΗΣΕΥΣ
πέραν γε Πόντου καὶ τόπων Ἀτλαντικῶν,
εἴ πως δυναίμην, ὡς σὸν ἐχθαίρω κάρα.

ΙΠΠΟΛΥΤΟΣ
1055 οὐδ' ὅρκον οὐδὲ πίστιν οὐδὲ μάντεων
φήμας ἐλέγξας ἄκριτον ἐκβαλεῖς με γῆς;

ΘΗΣΕΥΣ
ἡ δέλτος ἥδε κλῆρον οὐ δεδεγμένη
κατηγορεῖ σου πιστά· τοὺς δ' ὑπὲρ κάρα
φοιτῶντας ὄρνις πόλλ' ἐγὼ χαίρειν λέγω.

ΙΠΠΟΛΥΤΟΣ
1060 ὦ θεοί, τί δῆτα τοὐμὸν οὐ λύω στόμα,
ὅστις γ' ὑφ' ὑμῶν, οὓς σέβω, διόλλυμαι;
οὐ δῆτα· πάντως οὐ πίθοιμ' ἂν οὕς με δεῖ,
μάτην δ' ἂν ὅρκους συγχέαιμ' οὓς ὤμοσα.

1046 del. Wheeler
1049–50 del. Weil (1050 Nauck): cf. 898
1060 λύω Elmsley: λύσω C

according to the rule you have just laid down for your-self—for swift death is a mercy for a man in misfortune—but as a wanderer from your ancestral land. [On foreign soil you will drain to the dregs a life of misery. For that is the penalty for an impious man.]

HIPPOLYTUS

Ah, what do you mean to do? Will you not even wait for Time to give evidence about me but banish me from the land?

THESEUS

Yes, beyond the Euxine Sea and the Pillars of Atlas, if I could, so much do I hate you!

HIPPOLYTUS

Will you also not examine my oath and sworn testimony or the words of seers? Will you banish me without a trial?

THESEUS

This tablet contains no divination by lot, and its charge against you is convincing. As for the birds that fly above my head, I bid them good day!

HIPPOLYTUS

O gods, why do I not then open my mouth, seeing that I am being done to death by you towards whom I am show-ing piety? But no, I would not convince those I must and would break for nothing the oath I swore.

ΘΗΣΕΥΣ

οἴμοι, τὸ σεμνὸν ὥς μ' ἀποκτενεῖ τὸ σόν.
1065 οὐκ εἶ πατρῴας ἐκτὸς ὡς τάχιστα γῆς;

ΙΠΠΟΛΥΤΟΣ

ποῖ δῆθ' ὁ τλήμων τρέψομαι; τίνος ξένων
δόμους ἔσειμι, τῇδ' ἐπ' αἰτίᾳ φυγών;

ΘΗΣΕΥΣ

ὅστις γυναικῶν λυμεῶνας ἥδεται
ξένους κομίζων καὶ ξυνοικούρους κακῶν.

ΙΠΠΟΛΥΤΟΣ

1070 αἰαῖ, πρὸς ἧπαρ· δακρύων ἐγγὺς τόδε,
εἰ δὴ κακός γε φαίνομαι δοκῶ τε σοί.

ΘΗΣΕΥΣ

τότε στενάζειν καὶ προγιγνώσκειν σ' ἐχρῆν
ὅτ' ἐς πατρῴαν ἄλοχον ὑβρίζειν ἔτλης.

ΙΠΠΟΛΥΤΟΣ

ὦ δώματ', εἴθε φθέγμα γηρύσαισθέ μοι
1075 καὶ μαρτυρήσαιτ' εἰ κακὸς πέφυκ' ἀνήρ.

ΘΗΣΕΥΣ

ἐς τοὺς ἀφώνους μάρτυρας φεύγεις σοφῶς·
τὸ δ' ἔργον οὐ λέγον σε μηνύει κακόν.

ΙΠΠΟΛΥΤΟΣ

φεῦ·
εἴθ' ἦν ἐμαυτὸν προσβλέπειν ἐναντίον
στάνθ', ὡς ἐδάκρυσ' οἷα πάσχομεν κακά.

THESEUS

Oh! Your holy manner will be the death of me! Leave
your father's land at once!

HIPPOLYTUS

Where am I to turn, unhappy man that I am? What host's
house shall I enter when I am exiled on this charge?

THESEUS

Someone's who likes to entertain seducers of their wives
and men who keep at home plotting evil!

HIPPOLYTUS

Oh! That stroke cut me to the heart! It is nearly enough
to make me weep if I am regarded as base and seem so to
you.

THESEUS

The time for groans and forethought was when you dared
to commit outrage against your father's wife!

HIPPOLYTUS

O house, would that you could utter speech on my behalf
and bear me witness whether I am base!

THESEUS

How clever of you to take refuge in witnesses that are
dumb, while the facts, mute as they are, betray your base-
ness!

HIPPOLYTUS

Oh! Oh! Would that I could stand apart and look at
myself so that I might weep at the misfortunes I am suf-
fering!

ΘΗΣΕΥΣ

1080 πολλῷ γε μᾶλλον σαυτὸν ἤσκησας σέβειν
ἢ τοὺς τεκόντας ὅσια δρᾶν δίκαιος ὤν.

ΙΠΠΟΛΥΤΟΣ

ὦ δυστάλαινα μῆτερ, ὦ πικραὶ γοναί·
μηδείς ποτ᾽ εἴη τῶν ἐμῶν φίλων νόθος.

ΘΗΣΕΥΣ

οὐχ ἕλξετ᾽ αὐτόν, δμῶες; οὐκ ἀκούετε
1085 πάλαι ξενοῦσθαι τόνδε προυννέποντά με;

ΙΠΠΟΛΥΤΟΣ

κλαίων τις αὐτῶν ἆρ᾽ ἐμοῦ γε θίξεται·
σὺ δ᾽ αὐτός, εἴ σοι θυμός, ἐξώθει χθονός.

ΘΗΣΕΥΣ

δράσω τάδ᾽, εἰ μὴ τοῖς ἐμοῖς πείσῃ λόγοις·
οὐ γάρ τις οἶκτος σῆς μ᾽ ὑπέρχεται φυγῆς.

ΙΠΠΟΛΥΤΟΣ

1090 ἄραρεν, ὡς ἔοικεν· ὦ τάλας ἐγώ,
ὡς οἶδα μὲν ταῦτ᾽, οἶδα δ᾽ οὐχ ὅπως φράσω.
ὦ φιλτάτη μοι δαιμόνων Λητοῦς κόρη,
σύνθακε, συγκύναγε, φευξούμεσθα δὴ
κλεινὰς Ἀθήνας. ἀλλὰ χαιρέτω πόλις
1095 καὶ γαῖ᾽ Ἐρεχθέως· ὦ πέδον Τροζήνιον,
ὡς ἐγκαθηβᾶν πόλλ᾽ ἔχεις εὐδαίμονα,
χαῖρ᾽· ὕστατον γάρ σ᾽ εἰσορῶν προσφθέγγομαι.
ἴτ᾽, ὦ νέοι μοι τῆσδε γῆς ὁμήλικες,
προσείπαθ᾽ ἡμᾶς καὶ προπέμψατε χθονός·
1100 ὡς οὔποτ᾽ ἄλλον ἄνδρα σωφρονέστερον

THESEUS

You are far more practiced in worshiping yourself than in being just and acting piously toward your father.

HIPPOLYTUS

O unhappy mother, O unwelcome birth, never may any friend of mine have a bastard's life!

THESEUS

Drag him away, servants! Have you not heard me long since proclaim him an exile?

HIPPOLYTUS

Any of them who touches me shall regret it. Rather you yourself, if you have the heart to, cast me forth from the land.

THESEUS

I shall if you do not obey my words. No pity for your exile moves my heart.

HIPPOLYTUS

My fate, it seems, is fixed. O how luckless I am, seeing that I know the truth but not how I may tell it! Dearest of gods to me, daughter of Leto, you I have sat with, you I have hunted with, I shall leave glorious Athens as an exile. Now farewell, city and land of Erechtheus! O land of Trozen, how many are the blessings you have for a young man! Farewell: this is my last look at you and my last greeting!

Come, you my young age-mates of this land, bid me farewell and speed me from the land! For you will never

ὄψεσθε, κεἰ μὴ ταῦτ' ἐμῷ δοκεῖ πατρί.

ΧΟΡΟΣ

στρ. α

ἦ μέγα μοι τὰ θεῶν μελεδήμαθ', ὅταν φρένας ἔλθῃ,
1105 λύπας παραιρεῖ· ξύνεσιν δέ τις ἐλπίδι κεύθων
λείπεται ἔν τε τύχαις θνατῶν καὶ ἐν ἔργμασι λεύσσων·
ἄλλα γὰρ ἄλλοθεν ἀμεί-
βεται, μετὰ δ' ἵσταται ἀνδράσιν αἰὼν
1110 πολυπλάνητος αἰεί.

ἀντ. α

εἴθε μοι εὐξαμένᾳ θεόθεν τάδε μοῖρα παράσχοι,
τύχαν μετ' ὄλβου καὶ ἀκήρατον ἄλγεσι θυμόν·
1115 δόξα δὲ μήτ' ἀτρεκὴς μήτ' αὖ παράσημος ἐνείη,
ῥᾴδια δ' ἤθεα τὸν αὔ-
ριον μεταβαλλομένα χρόνον αἰεὶ
βίον συνευτυχοίην.

στρ. β
1120 οὐκέτι γὰρ καθαρὰν φρέν' ἔχω, παρὰ δ' ἐλπίδ' ἃ
λεύσσω,
ἐπεὶ τὸν Ἑλλανίας φανερώτατον ἀστέρα γαίας
εἴδομεν εἴδομεν ἐκ πατρὸς ὀργᾶς
1125 ἄλλαν ἐπ' αἶαν ἱέμενον.
ὦ ψάμαθοι πολιήτιδος ἀκτᾶς,

1105 τις Barrett: τιν' C
1106 λείπεται Barrett: λείπομαι C
1121 παρὰ δ' ἐλπίδ' ἃ Musgrave: παρὰ δ' ἐλπίδα vel παρ'
ἐλπίδα C
1123 ἀστέρα γαίας Hartung e Σ: ἀστέρ' Ἀθήνας fere C

see a man more chaste than I, even though my father
thinks not so.

*Exit HIPPOLYTUS and the young members of the crowd by
Eisodos A. Exit THESEUS into the palace.*

CHORUS[a]

Whenever thoughts about the gods come into my mind,
they greatly relieve my pain. But anyone who hopes for
understanding fails to find it as he looks amid the fortunes
and the deeds of mortals. From one quarter comes one
thing and from another another, and men's life is a shift-
ing thing, ever unstable.

O that in answer to my prayer destiny might give me
this gift from the gods, a fate that is blessed and a heart
untouched by sorrow! No mind unswervingly obdurate
would I have, nor yet again one false-struck, but changing
my pliant character ever for the morrow may I share its
happiness my whole life through!

For my mind is no longer untroubled: beyond all
expectation are the things I behold. We have seen
Greece's brightest star, have seen him go forth sped by his
father's wrath to another land. O sands of our city's shore,

---

[a] The manuscripts make the Chorus use a masculine partici-
ple of themselves in the first and second strophe. A. W. Verrall
assigned these strophes to the Chorus of servants and the anti-
strophes to the main Chorus, but A. Sommerstein, *BICS* 35
(1988), 35–9, has shown the extreme unlikelihood of this solu-
tion. I have adopted Barrett's emendations in the first strophe
and Musgrave's in the second, but corruption may well be
deeper.

ὦ δρυμὸς ὄρεος ὅθι κυνῶν
ὠκυπόδων μέτα θῆρας ἔναιρεν
1130   Δίκτυνναν ἀμφὶ σεμνάν.

ἀντ. β

οὐκέτι συζυγίαν πώλων Ἐνετᾶν ἐπιβάσῃ
τὸν ἀμφὶ Λίμνας τρόχον κατέχων ποδὶ γυμνάδος ἵππου·
1135   μοῦσα δ᾽ ἄυπνος ὑπ᾽ ἄντυγι χορδᾶν
λήξει πατρῷον ἀνὰ δόμον·
ἀστέφανοι δὲ κόρας ἀνάπαυλαι
Λατοῦς βαθεῖαν ἀνὰ χλόαν·
1140   νυμφιδία δ᾽ ἀπόλωλε φυγᾷ σᾷ
λέκτρων ἅμιλλα κούραις.

ἐπῳδ.

ἐγὼ δὲ σᾷ δυστυχίᾳ
δάκρυσιν διοίσω
πότμον ἄποτμον· ὦ τάλαινα μᾶτερ,
1145   ἔτεκες ἀνόνατα· φεῦ·
μανίω θεοῖσιν.
ἰὼ ἰώ·
συζύγιαι Χάριτες, τί τὸν τάλαν᾽ ἐκ πατρίας γᾶς
οὐδὲν ἄτας αἴτιον
1150   πέμπετε τῶνδ᾽ ἀπ᾽ οἴκων;

— καὶ μὴν ὀπαδὸν Ἱππολύτου τόνδ᾽ εἰσορῶ
σπουδῇ σκυθρωπὸν πρὸς δόμους ὁρμώμενον.

1127 ὄρεος post Wilamowitz Diggle: ὄρειος C
1128–9 μέτα θῆρας ἔναιρεν Blomfield: ἐπέβας θεᾶς μέτα
θῆρας ἐναίρων C

232

O mountain thickets where with his swift hounds he slew the wild beasts in company with holy Dictynna!

No more shall you mount behind a pair of Venetian horses and tread the race course about the Mere with the feet of your racing steeds. The music that never slept beneath the frame of the lyre strings shall cease in your father's house. Bare of garlands will be the resting places of Leto's daughter in the deep greenwood. The rivalry of maidens to be your bride has been brought to an end by your exile.

But I for my part because of your misfortune shall live out in tears an unhappy fate.[a] O unhappy mother, it was to no purpose that you bore him. Oh, I am angry with the gods! Ye Graces that dance your round, why do you send the poor man, guilty of no mad deed, from his father's land and from this house?

Enter as MESSENGER *one of Hippolytus' men by Eisodos A.*

CHORUS LEADER

But look, I see a servant of Hippolytus, with gloomy face, rushing toward the house!

[a] Or "will spread abroad your unhappy fate with tears at your misfortune."

[1134] Λίμναν Diggle   γυμνάδος ἵππου Musgrave: -δας ἵππους C

ΑΓΓΕΛΟΣ

ποῖ γῆς ἄνακτα τῆσδε Θησέα μολὼν
εὕροιμ' ἄν, ὦ γυναῖκες; εἴπερ ἴστε μοι
1155 σημήνατ'· ἆρα τῶνδε δωμάτων ἔσω;

ΧΟΡΟΣ

ὅδ' αὐτὸς ἔξω δωμάτων πορεύεται.

ΑΓΓΕΛΟΣ

Θησεῦ, μερίμνης ἄξιον φέρω λόγον
σοὶ καὶ πολίταις οἵ τ' Ἀθηναίων πόλιν
ναίουσι καὶ γῆς τέρμονας Τροζηνίας.

ΘΗΣΕΥΣ

1160 τί δ' ἔστι; μῶν τις συμφορὰ νεωτέρα
δισσὰς κατείληφ' ἀστυγείτονας πόλεις;

ΑΓΓΕΛΟΣ

Ἱππόλυτος οὐκέτ' ἔστιν, ὡς εἰπεῖν ἔπος·
δέδορκε μέντοι φῶς ἐπὶ σμικρᾶς ῥοπῆς.

ΘΗΣΕΥΣ

πρὸς τοῦ; δι' ἔχθρας μῶν τις ἦν ἀφιγμένος
1165 ὅτου κατῄσχυν' ἄλοχον ὡς πατρὸς βίᾳ;

ΑΓΓΕΛΟΣ

οἰκεῖος αὐτὸν ὤλεσ' ἁρμάτων ὄχος
ἀραί τε τοῦ σοῦ στόματος, ἃς σὺ σῷ πατρὶ
πόντου κρέοντι παιδὸς ἠράσω πέρι.

ΘΗΣΕΥΣ

ὦ θεοί, Πόσειδόν θ'· ὡς ἄρ' ἦσθ' ἐμὸς πατὴρ
1170 ὀρθῶς, ἀκούσας τῶν ἐμῶν κατευγμάτων.

MESSENGER

Women, where must I go to find Theseus, this land's king? If you know, tell me. Is he in the palace?

Enter THESEUS from the palace.

CHORUS LEADER

Here he comes out of the house.

MESSENGER

Theseus, I bring you news that will cause solicitude to you and all the citizens who dwell in Athens and in the land of Trozen.

THESEUS

What is it? Has some recent disaster seized the two neighboring cities?

MESSENGER

Hippolytus is dead, as good as dead; he still has life but by a slender thread.

THESEUS

At whose hand? Could it be that someone whose wife he ravished as he did his father's became his enemy?

MESSENGER

His own chariot destroyed him, and the curses of your mouth which you uttered against your son to your father, lord of the sea.

THESEUS

(stretching out his hands, palms upward, in prayer) Merciful gods! So after all you are truly my father, Poseidon,

---

[1169] fort. θεοί. Πόσειδον [θ’]

πῶς καὶ διώλετ'; εἰπέ, τῷ τρόπῳ Δίκης
ἔπαισεν αὐτὸν ῥόπτρον αἰσχύναντά με;

ΑΓΓΕΛΟΣ

ἡμεῖς μὲν ἀκτῆς κυμοδέγμονος πέλας
ψήκτραισιν ἵππων ἐκτενίζομεν τρίχας
1175 κλαίοντες· ἦλθε γάρ τις ἄγγελος λέγων
ὡς οὐκέτ' ἐν γῇ τῇδ' ἀναστρέψοι πόδα
Ἱππόλυτος, ἐκ σοῦ τλήμονας φυγὰς ἔχων.
ὁ δ' ἦλθε ταὐτὸν δακρύων ἔχων μέλος
ἡμῖν ἐπ' ἀκτάς, μυρία δ' ὀπισθόπους
1180 φίλων ἅμ' ἔστειχ' ἡλίκων <θ'> ὁμήγυρις.
χρόνῳ δὲ δή ποτ' εἶπ' ἀπαλλαχθεὶς γόων·
Τί ταῦτ' ἀλύω; πειστέον πατρὸς λόγοις.
ἐντύναθ' ἵππους ἅρμασι ζυγηφόρους,
δμῶες, πόλις γὰρ οὐκέτ' ἔστιν ἥδε μοι.
1185 τοὐνθένδε μέντοι πᾶς ἀνὴρ ἠπείγετο,
καὶ θᾶσσον ἢ λέγοι τις ἐξηρτυμένας
πώλους παρ' αὐτὸν δεσπότην ἐστήσαμεν.
μάρπτει δὲ χερσὶν ἡνίας ἀπ' ἄντυγος,
αὐταῖσιν ἀρβύλαισιν ἁρμόσας πόδας.
1190 καὶ πρῶτα μὲν θεοῖς εἶπ' ἀναπτύξας χέρας·
Ζεῦ, μηκέτ' εἴην εἰ κακὸς πέφυκ' ἀνήρ·
αἴσθοιτο δ' ἡμᾶς ὡς ἀτιμάζει πατὴρ
ἤτοι θανόντας ἢ φάος δεδορκότας.
κἂν τῷδ' ἐπῆγε κέντρον ἐς χεῖρας λαβὼν
1195 πώλοις ἁμαρτῇ· πρόσπολοι δ' ὑφ' ἅρματος
πέλας χαλινῶν εἱπόμεσθα δεσπότῃ
τὴν εὐθὺς Ἄργους κἀπιδαυρίας ὁδόν.

since you heard my prayer! How did he perish? Tell me,
how did the cudgel of Justice strike him for dishonoring
me?

MESSENGER

We were scraping and combing the horses' coats near the
wave-beaten shore and weeping at our task. For a mes-
senger had come saying that Hippolytus would no longer
tread the soil of this land, being sent into miserable exile
by you. Then he came, singing the same tearful burden,
to join us at the shore, and a countless throng of friends
and age-mates at his heels came with him. When some
time had passed, he ceased his lamenting and said, "Why
should I be distraught at this? I must obey my father's
words. Servants, get the yoke-horses ready for my char-
iot, for no longer is this my city."

Thereupon every man worked in haste, and more
quickly than one could describe we set the horses in their
gear beside the master. He seized the reins from the
chariot rail and fitted his feet right into the footstalls.
First he spread his hands palms upward in prayer to the
gods and said, "O Zeus, may I no longer live if I am guilty!
But whether I am dead or look on the light may my father
come to know that he dishonors me!"

So saying he took the whip into his hand and applied it
to his horses all together. We servants, on the ground
beside the chariot, accompanied our master, keeping
abreast of his bridle, along the road that makes straight
for Argos and Epidaurus.

1179 ἀκτάς Kirchhoff: -αῖς C   1180 <θ'> Markland
1184 fort. ἐστὶν ἥδ' ἐμή

ἐπεὶ δ' ἔρημον χῶρον εἰσεβάλλομεν,
ἀκτή τις ἔστι τοὐπέκεινα τῆσδε γῆς
1200 πρὸς πόντον ἤδη κειμένη Σαρωνικόν.
ἔνθεν τις ἠχὼ χθόνιος, ὡς βροντὴ Διός,
βαρὺν βρόμον μεθῆκε, φρικώδη κλυεῖν·
ὀρθὸν δὲ κρᾶτ' ἔστησαν οὖς τ' ἐς οὐρανὸν
ἵπποι, παρ' ἡμῖν δ' ἦν φόβος νεανικὸς
1205 πόθεν ποτ' εἴη φθόγγος. ἐς δ' ἁλιρρόθους
ἀκτὰς ἀποβλέψαντες ἱερὸν εἴδομεν
κῦμ' οὐρανῷ στηρίζον, ὥστ' ἀφῃρέθη
Σκίρωνος ἀκτὰς ὄμμα τοὐμὸν εἰσορᾶν,
ἔκρυπτε δ' Ἰσθμὸν καὶ πέτραν Ἀσκληπιοῦ.
1210 κἄπειτ' ἀνοιδῆσάν τε καὶ πέριξ ἀφρὸν
πολὺν καχλάζον ποντίῳ φυσήματι
χωρεῖ πρὸς ἀκτὰς οὗ τέθριππος ἦν ὄχος.
αὐτῷ δὲ σὺν κλύδωνι καὶ τρικυμίᾳ
κῦμ' ἐξέθηκε ταῦρον, ἄγριον τέρας·
1215 οὗ πᾶσα μὲν χθὼν φθέγματος πληρουμένη
φρικῶδες ἀντεφθέγγετ', εἰσορῶσι δὲ
κρεῖσσον θέαμα δεργμάτων ἐφαίνετο.
εὐθὺς δὲ πώλοις δεινὸς ἐμπίπτει φόβος.
καὶ δεσπότης μὲν ἱππικοῖσιν ἤθεσιν
1220 πολὺς ξυνοικῶν ἥρπασ' ἡνίας χεροῖν,
ἕλκει δέ, κώπην ὥστε ναυβάτης ἀνήρ,
ἱμᾶσιν ἐς τοὔπισθεν ἀρτήσας δέμας·
αἱ δ' ἐνδακοῦσαι στόμια πυριγενῆ γνάθοις
βίᾳ φέρουσιν, οὔτε ναυκλήρου χερὸς
1225 οὔθ' ἱπποδέσμων οὔτε κολλητῶν ὄχων

238

When we struck deserted country, there is a headland beyond our territory, lying out towards what is at that point the Saronic gulf. There a great noise in the earth, like Zeus's thunder, roared heavily—it made one shudder to hear it! The horses pricked up their heads and ears to heaven, while we servants were taken with a violent fear, wondering where this voice came from. When we turned our eyes to the sea-beaten beach, we saw an unearthly wave, its peak fixed in the heavens, so great that my eye was robbed of the sight of Skiron's coast, and the Isthmus and Asclepius' cliff were hid from view. And then as the sea-surge made it swell and seethe up much foam all about, it came toward the shore where the four-horse chariot was. With its very swell and surge the wave put forth a monstrous, savage bull. The whole land was filled with its bellowing and gave back unearthly echoes, and as we looked on it the sight was too great for our eyes to bear. At once a terrible panic fell upon the horses. My master, who had lived long with the ways of horses, seized the reins in his hands and pulled them, as a sailor pulls an oar, letting his body hang backwards from the straps. But they took the fire-wrought bit in their teeth and carried him against his will, paying no heed to their captain's hand or the harness or the tight-glued chariot. If he held

μεταστρέφουσαι. κεἰ μὲν ἐς τὰ μαλθακὰ
γαίας ἔχων οἴακας εὐθύνοι δρόμον,
προυφαίνετ' ἐς τὸ πρόσθεν, ὥστ' ἀναστρέφειν,
ταῦρος, φόβῳ τέτρωρον ἐκμαίνων ὄχον·
1230 εἰ δ' ἐς πέτρας φέροιντο μαργῶσαι φρένας,
σιγῇ πελάζων ἄντυγι ξυνείπετο,
ἐς τοῦθ' ἕως ἔσφηλε κἀνεχαίτισεν
ἁψῖδα πέτρῳ προσβαλὼν ὀχήματος.
σύμφυρτα δ' ἦν ἅπαντα· σύριγγές τ' ἄνω
1235 τροχῶν ἐπήδων ἀξόνων τ' ἐνήλατα,
αὐτὸς δ' ὁ τλήμων ἡνίαισιν ἐμπλακεὶς
δεσμὸν δυσεξέλικτον ἕλκεται δεθείς,
σποδούμενος μὲν πρὸς πέτραις φίλον κάρα
θραύων τε σάρκας, δεινὰ δ' ἐξαυδῶν κλύειν·
1240 Στῆτ', ὦ φάτναισι ταῖς ἐμαῖς τεθραμμέναι,
μή μ' ἐξαλείψητ'· ὦ πατρὸς τάλαιν' ἀρά.
τίς ἄνδρ' ἄριστον βούλεται σῶσαι παρών;
πολλοὶ δὲ βουληθέντες ὑστέρῳ ποδὶ
ἐλειπόμεσθα. χὠ μὲν ἐκ δεσμῶν λυθεὶς
1245 τμητῶν ἱμάντων οὐ κάτοιδ' ὅτῳ τρόπῳ
πίπτει, βραχὺν δὴ βίοτον ἐμπνέων ἔτι·
ἵπποι δ' ἔκρυφθεν καὶ τὸ δύστηνον τέρας
ταύρου λεπαίας οὐ κάτοιδ' ὅποι χθονός.
δοῦλος μὲν οὖν ἔγωγε σῶν δόμων, ἄναξ,
1250 ἀτὰρ τοσοῦτόν γ' οὐ δυνήσομαί ποτε,
τὸν σὸν πιθέσθαι παῖδ' ὅπως ἐστὶν κακός,
οὐδ' εἰ γυναικῶν πᾶν κρεμασθείη γένος
καὶ τὴν ἐν Ἴδῃ γραμμάτων πλήσειέ τις
πεύκην· ἐπεί νιν ἐσθλὸν ὄντ' ἐπίσταμαι.

the helm and directed their course toward the softer ground, the bull appeared before him to turn them back, maddening with fear the four-horse team. But if they rushed with maddened senses into the rocks, it drew near and silently accompanied the chariot until it upset and overthrew it, striking its wheel rims on a rock. All was confusion: the wheels' naves and the axle pins were leaping into the air, and the poor man himself, entangled in the reins, bound in a bond he could not untie, was dragged along, his head being smashed against the rocks and flesh being torn, uttering things dreadful to hear: "Stay, horses my mangers have nourished, do not blot me out! O wretched curse of my father! Who will stand by the best of men and save him?"

Many of us would have, but we were outsped, and our feet lagged behind. He was cut loose from the reins of leather and fell upon the ground I know not how, with scarcely any breath of life still in him. The horses vanished and so too did the monstrous bull to some place I know not where in that rocky land.

I am, I know, a slave of your house, my lord, but I shall never be able to believe that your son is guilty, not even if the whole female sex should hang themselves and fill with letters tablets made from all the pine wood that grows upon Mount Ida! For I know that he is good.

EURIPIDES

ΧΟΡΟΣ

1255 αἰαῖ, κέκρανται συμφορὰ νέων κακῶν,
οὐδ᾽ ἔστι μοίρας τοῦ χρεών τ᾽ ἀπαλλαγή.

ΘΗΣΕΤΣ

μίσει μὲν ἀνδρὸς τοῦ πεπονθότος τάδε
λόγοισιν ἥσθην τοῖσδε· νῦν δ᾽ αἰδούμενος
θεούς τ᾽ ἐκεῖνόν θ᾽, οὕνεκ᾽ ἐστὶν ἐξ ἐμοῦ,
1260 οὔθ᾽ ἥδομαι τοῖσδ᾽ οὔτ᾽ ἐπάχθομαι κακοῖς.

ΑΓΓΕΛΟΣ

πῶς οὖν; κομίζειν, ἢ τί χρὴ τὸν ἄθλιον
δράσαντας ἡμᾶς σῇ χαρίζεσθαι φρενί;
φρόντιζ᾽· ἐμοῖς δὲ χρώμενος βουλεύμασιν
οὐκ ὠμὸς ἐς σὸν παῖδα δυστυχοῦντ᾽ ἔσῃ.

ΘΗΣΕΤΣ

1265 κομίζετ᾽ αὐτόν, ὡς ἰδὼν ἐν ὄμμασιν
1267 λόγοις τ᾽ ἐλέγξω δαιμόνων τε συμφοραῖς
1266 τὸν τἄμ᾽ ἀπαρνηθέντα μὴ χρᾶναι λέχη.

ΧΟΡΟΣ

σὺ τὰν θεῶν ἄκαμπτον φρένα καὶ βροτῶν
ἄγεις, Κύπρι, σὺν δ᾽ ὁ ποι-
1270 κιλόπτερος ἀμφιβαλὼν
ὠκυτάτῳ πτερῷ.
ποτᾶται δὲ γαῖαν εὐάχητόν θ᾽
ἁλμυρὸν ἐπὶ πόντον,
θέλγει δ᾽ Ἔρως ᾧ μαινομένᾳ κραδίᾳ
1275 πτανὸς ἐφορμάσῃ χρυσοφαῆς <στίλβων>

HIPPOLYTUS

CHORUS LEADER

Alas! New misfortunes have been brought to pass, and there is no escape from fate and destiny!

THESEUS

For hatred of the man who has suffered these things I took pleasure at your words. But now in respect for the gods and for him, since he is my son, I feel neither pleasure nor pain at these misfortunes.

MESSENGER

How shall we act? Shall we bring the unhappy man here, or what shall we do, to please your heart? Think this out: but if you take my advice, you will not be savage toward your son in his misfortune.

THESEUS

Bring him so that I may look him in the face and with my words and the misfortunes sent by the gods give him the lie, the man who denies he violated my bed.

Exit MESSENGER by Eisodos A.

CHORUS

You lead captive the unyielding hearts of the gods, Cypris, and of men, and with you, surrounding you with his swift pinions, is he of the gleaming wings. Eros flies over the earth and over the loud-roaring salt sea, he bewitches the one upon whose love-maddened heart, winged and gold-

---

1266–7 inverso ordine pars codd.
1272 δὲ Seidler: δ' ἐπὶ vel ἐπὶ C
1275 <στίλβων> Diggle

φύσιν ὀρεσκόων σκύμνων πελαγίων θ᾿
ὅσα τε γᾶ τρέφει
τά τ᾿ αἰθόμενος ἅλιος δέρκεται
1280 ἄνδρας τε· συμπάντων βασιληίδα τι-
μάν, Κύπρι, τῶνδε μόνα κρατύνεις.

ΑΡΤΕΜΙΣ

σὲ τὸν εὐπατρίδην Αἰγέως κέλομαι
παῖδ᾿ ἐπακοῦσαι·
1285 Λητοῦς δὲ κόρη σ᾿ Ἄρτεμις αὐδῶ.
Θησεῦ, τί τάλας τοῖσδε συνήδῃ,
παῖδ᾿ οὐχ ὁσίως σὸν ἀποκτείνας
ψευδέσι μύθοις ἀλόχου πεισθεὶς
ἀφανῆ; φανερὰν δ᾿ ἔσχεθες ἄτην.
1290 πῶς οὐχ ὑπὸ γῆς τάρταρα κρύπτεις
δέμας αἰσχυνθείς,
ἢ πτηνὸν ἄνω μεταβὰς βίοτον
πήματος ἔξω πόδα τοῦδ᾿ ἀνέχεις;
ὡς ἔν γ᾿ ἀγαθοῖς ἀνδράσιν οὔ σοι
1295 κτητὸν βιότου μέρος ἐστίν.

ἄκουε, Θησεῦ, σῶν κακῶν κατάστασιν.
καίτοι προκόψω γ᾿ οὐδέν, ἀλγυνῶ δέ σε·
ἀλλ᾿ ἐς τόδ᾿ ἦλθον, παιδὸς ἐκδεῖξαι φρένα
τοῦ σοῦ δικαίαν, ὡς ὑπ᾿ εὐκλείας θάνῃ,
1300 καὶ σῆς γυναικὸς οἶστρον ἢ τρόπον τινὰ
γενναιότητα· τῆς γὰρ ἐχθίστης θεῶν
ἡμῖν ὅσαισι παρθένειος ἡδονὴ
δηχθεῖσα κέντροις παιδὸς ἠράσθη σέθεν.

gleaming, he flies; he bewitches the whelps of the mountain and those of the sea, what the earth brings forth and what the blazing sun looks down upon, and likewise mortal men. Over all these, Cypris, you alone hold royal sway.

ARTEMIS *appears on the* theologeion *above the* skene.

ARTEMIS

Nobly born son of Aegeus! Listen, I command you! It is I, Artemis, Leto's daughter, who address you. Why, unhappy man, do you take joy in these things? You have killed your son in godless fashion, persuaded of things unseen by the false words of your wife. But all too clearly seen is the ruin you have won for yourself! You should hide yourself beneath the earth's depths in shame or change your life for that of a bird above and take yourself out of this pain! In life lived among good men you have no share.

Hear, Theseus, the state of your misfortunes. And yet I accomplish nothing by this, and merely cause you grief. But it was for this purpose that I came, to make plain that your son's heart is guiltless so that he may die with a good name, make plain, too, the maddened frenzy of your wife or, if I may call it so, her nobility. For she was stung by the goad of that goddess most hated by us who take pleasure in virginity and fell in love with your son. When

---

¹²⁷⁷ σκύμνων Wilamowitz: σκυλάκων C   ¹²⁷⁹ τά τ' Wecklein: τὰν C   αἰθόμενος ἅλιος Wilamowitz: ἄλ- αἰ- fere C   ¹²⁸⁰ συμπάντων Dindorf: σ. δὲ vel σ. τε vel σ. γε C   ¹²⁸⁹ ἔσχεθες Markland: ἔσχες C   ¹²⁹² πτηνὸν Valckenaer: -ὸς C   ¹³⁰² ὅσαις τε Weil

γνώμῃ δὲ νικᾶν τὴν Κύπριν πειρωμένη
1305 τροφοῦ διώλετ' οὐχ ἑκοῦσα μηχαναῖς,
ἣ σῷ δι' ὅρκων παιδὶ σημαίνει νόσον.
ὁ δ', ὥσπερ οὖν δίκαιον, οὐκ ἐφέσπετο
λόγοισιν, οὐδ' αὖ πρὸς σέθεν κακούμενος
ὅρκων ἀφεῖλε πίστιν, εὐσεβὴς γεγώς.
1310 ἡ δ' εἰς ἔλεγχον μὴ πέσῃ φοβουμένη
ψευδεῖς γραφὰς ἔγραψε καὶ διώλεσεν
δόλοισι σὸν παῖδ', ἀλλ' ὅμως ἔπεισέ σε.

ΘΗΣΕΥΣ

οἴμοι.

ΑΡΤΕΜΙΣ

δάκνει σε, Θησεῦ, μῦθος; ἀλλ' ἔχ' ἥσυχος,
τοὐνθένδ' ἀκούσας ὡς ἂν οἰμώξῃς πλέον.
1315 ἆρ' οἶσθα πατρὸς τρεῖς ἀρὰς ἔχων σαφεῖς;
ὧν τὴν μίαν παρεῖλες, ὦ κάκιστε σύ,
ἐς παῖδα τὸν σόν, ἐξὸν εἰς ἐχθρῶν τινα.
πατὴρ μὲν οὖν σοι πόντιος φρονῶν καλῶς
ἔδωχ' ὅσονπερ χρῆν, ἐπείπερ ᾔνεσεν·
1320 σὺ δ' ἔν τ' ἐκείνῳ κἀν ἐμοὶ φαίνῃ κακός,
ὃς οὔτε πίστιν οὔτε μάντεων ὄπα
ἔμεινας, οὐκ ἤλεγξας, οὐ χρόνῳ μακρῷ
σκέψιν παρέσχες, ἀλλὰ θᾶσσον ἤ σ' ἐχρῆν
ἀρὰς ἐφῆκας παιδὶ καὶ κατέκτανες.

ΘΗΣΕΥΣ

δέσποιν', ὀλοίμην.

she attempted to conquer Cypris by her resolve, she was destroyed all unwitting by the contrivances of her nurse, who told your son under oath of her malady. He, as was right, did not fall in with her words, nor yet again, godly man that he is, did he break the firm bond of his oath, though he was reviled by you. Phaedra, fearing lest she be put to the proof, wrote a false letter and destroyed your son by guile, and though it was a lie, she persuaded you.

THESEUS

O woe!

ARTEMIS

Does this tale sting you, Theseus? Hold your peace so that you may hear the rest and groan the more. Do you know that you were given by your father three curses certain of fulfillment? One of these you took, base man, to use against your son when you could have used it against an enemy. Your father, the sea lord, kindly disposed as he was toward you, granted what he had to grant seeing that he had promised. But in his sight and in mine you are proved base since you did not wait either for confirmation or for the word of a prophet, you did not put the charge to the proof nor grant to Time the right to investigate it, but more rashly than you ought you let loose this curse upon your son and killed him.

THESEUS

Lady, let me die!

ΑΡΤΕΜΙΣ

1325   δείν' ἔπραξας, ἀλλ' ὅμως
ἔτ' ἔστι καί σοι τῶνδε συγγνώμης τυχεῖν·
Κύπρις γὰρ ἤθελ' ὥστε γίγνεσθαι τάδε,
πληροῦσα θυμόν. θεοῖσι δ' ὧδ' ἔχει νόμος·
οὐδεὶς ἀπαντᾶν βούλεται προθυμίᾳ
1330 τῇ τοῦ θέλοντος, ἀλλ' ἀφιστάμεσθ' ἀεί.
ἐπεί, σάφ' ἴσθι, Ζῆνα μὴ φοβουμένη
οὐκ ἄν ποτ' ἦλθον ἐς τόδ' αἰσχύνης ἐγὼ
ὥστ' ἄνδρα πάντων φίλτατον βροτῶν ἐμοὶ
θανεῖν ἐᾶσαι. τὴν δὲ σὴν ἁμαρτίαν
1335 τὸ μὴ εἰδέναι μὲν πρῶτον ἐκλύει κάκης·
ἔπειτα σὴ θανοῦσ' ἀνήλωσεν γυνὴ
λόγων ἐλέγχους, ὥστε σὴν πεῖσαι φρένα.
    μάλιστα μέν νυν σοὶ τάδ' ἔρρωγεν κακά,
λύπη δὲ κἀμοί· τοὺς γὰρ εὐσεβεῖς θεοὶ
1340 θνήσκοντας οὐ χαίρουσι· τούς γε μὴν κακοὺς
αὐτοῖς τέκνοισι καὶ δόμοις ἐξόλλυμεν.

ΧΟΡΟΣ

καὶ μὴν ὁ τάλας ὅδε δὴ στείχει,
σάρκας νεαρὰς ξανθόν τε κάρα
διαλυμανθείς. ὦ πόνος οἴκων,
1345 οἷον ἐκράνθη δίδυμον μελάθροις
πένθος θεόθεν καταληπτόν.

ΙΠΠΟΛΥΤΟΣ

αἰαῖ αἰαῖ·
δύστηνος ἐγώ, πατρὸς ἐξ ἀδίκου

HIPPOLYTUS

ARTEMIS

You have done dreadful things, but for all that it is still possible for you to win pardon for these deeds of yours. It was Cypris, sating her anger, who willed that things should happen thus. Among the gods the custom is this: no god will cross the will of another, but we all stand aside. For you can be sure that if I had not been afraid of Zeus, I would never have endured such disgrace as to allow the man I love most among mortals to die. Ignorance acquits your mistakes of baseness, and further your wife by dying made it impossible to test her words, and thus she persuaded your mind.

It is chiefly upon you that these misfortunes break, but I too feel grief. The gods do not rejoice at the death of the godly, but the wicked we destroy, children, house, and all.

Enter HIPPOLYTUS *by Eisodos A supported by his servants.*

CHORUS LEADER

Look, here comes the unhappy man, his young flesh and golden head all mangled. Oh, what trouble has afflicted this house! What a double grief has been brought to pass for it, seizing it by the will of heaven!

HIPPOLYTUS

What agony! Wretched man that I am, I am shamefully

1336 σὴ Wilamowitz: δ' ἡ C
1348 ἐξ] fort. ὡς

χρησμοῖς ἀδίκοις διελυμάνθην.
1350 ἀπόλωλα τάλας, οἴμοι μοι.
διά μου κεφαλῆς ᾄσσουσ' ὀδύναι,
κατὰ δ' ἐγκέφαλον πηδᾷ σφάκελος.
σχές, ἀπειρηκὸς σῶμ' ἀναπαύσω.
ἒ ἔ·
1355 ὦ στυγνὸν ὄχημ' ἵππειον, ἐμῆς
βόσκημα χερός,
διά μ' ἔφθειρας, κατὰ δ' ἔκτεινας.
φεῦ φεῦ· πρὸς θεῶν, ἀτρέμα, δμῶες,
χροὸς ἑλκώδους ἅπτεσθε χεροῖν.
1360 τίς ἐφέστηκεν δεξιὰ πλευροῖς;
πρόσφορά μ' αἴρετε, σύντονα δ' ἕλκετε
τὸν κακοδαίμονα καὶ κατάρατον
πατρὸς ἀμπλακίαις. Ζεῦ Ζεῦ, τάδ' ὁρᾷς;
ὅδ' ὁ σεμνὸς ἐγὼ καὶ θεοσέπτωρ,
1365 ὅδ' ὁ σωφροσύνῃ πάντας ὑπερσχών,
προῦπτον ἐς Ἅιδην στείχω, κατ' ἄκρας
ὀλέσας βίοτον, μόχθους δ' ἄλλως
τῆς εὐσεβίας
εἰς ἀνθρώπους ἐπόνησα.

1370 αἰαῖ αἰαῖ·
καὶ νῦν ὀδύνα μ' ὀδύνα βαίνει·
μέθετέ με τάλανα,
καί μοι θάνατος παιὰν ἔλθοι.
προσαπόλλυτέ μ' ὄλλυτε τὸν δυσδαί-
1375 μον'· <ὑπ'> ἀμφιτόμου λόγχας ἔραμαι

treated by the unjust utterance of an unjust father! I am
gone, alas, alas! Pains dart through my head and spasms
leap in my brain! *(to one of his servants)* Stop, so that I
may rest my exhausted body! O agony! O hateful horses
my own hand has fed, you have destroyed me, have killed
me! Oh! Oh! I beg you by the gods, servants, handle my
wounded flesh gently! Who is standing at my right side?
Lift me carefully, draw me with muscles ever tensed, me
the wretch, cursed by his father's misdeed! Zeus, Zeus,
do you mark this? Here am I, the holy and god-revering
one, the man who surpassed all men in chastity, plainly
going to my death! I have lost my life utterly, and all in
vain have been my labors of piety toward men.

(sung) O agony! And now the pain, the pain, comes
over me! Let me go, wretched man that I am, and may
death come to me as healer! Kill me, kill the wretch that
is me! I long to be cut in half by a two-edged blade and to

1365 ὑπερσχών Valckenaer: ὑπερέχων fere C
1375 <ὑπ'> Willink

διαμοιρᾶσθαι κατά τ᾽ εὐνᾶσαι
τὸν ἐμὸν βίοτον.
ὦ πατρὸς ἐμοῦ δύστανος ἀρά·
μιαιφόνον τι σύγγονον
1380 παλαιῶν προγεννη-
τόρων ἐξορίζεται
κακὸν οὐδὲ μένει,
ἔμολέ τ᾽ ἐπ᾽ ἐμέ—τί ποτε, τὸν οὐ-
δὲν ὄντ᾽ ἐπαίτιον κακῶν;
ἰώ μοί μοι·
1385 τί φῶ; πῶς ἀπαλλά-
ξω βιοτὰν ἐμὰν
τοῦδ᾽ ἀνάλγητον πάθους;
εἴθε με κοιμάσειε τὸν
δυσδαίμον᾽ Ἅιδα μέλαι-
να νύκτερός τ᾽ ἀνάγκα.

ΑΡΤΕΜΙΣ

ὦ τλῆμον, οἵᾳ συμφορᾷ συνεζύγης·
1390 τὸ δ᾽ εὐγενές σε τῶν φρενῶν ἀπώλεσεν.

ΙΠΠΟΛΥΤΟΣ

ἔα·
ὦ θεῖον ὀσμῆς πνεῦμα· καὶ γὰρ ἐν κακοῖς
ὢν ᾐσθόμην σου κἀνεκουφίσθην δέμας·
ἔστ᾽ ἐν τόποισι τοισίδ᾽ Ἄρτεμις θεά.

ΑΡΤΕΜΙΣ

ὦ τλῆμον, ἔστι, σοί γε φιλτάτη θεῶν.

lay my life to rest. O ill-fated curse of my father! Some bloodstained calamity within the family, committed by ancestors long dead, breaks forth and does not stay, and it has come against me. Why, when I am guilty of no wrong? Alas! What am I to say? How free my life painlessly of this disaster? O that the dark necessity of death's night would lay me, unhappy man, to rest!

ARTEMIS

O poor man, to what a calamity you are yoked! Yet it was the nobility of your mind that destroyed you.

HIPPOLYTUS

But what is this? O breath of divine fragrance! Though I am in misfortune I feel your presence and my body's pain is lightened. The goddess Artemis is in this place!

ARTEMIS

Poor one, she is, dearest of gods to you.

1376 διαμοιρᾶσθαι Valckenaer: -ᾶσαι C   κατά Herwerden: διά C
1381 μένει Wilamowitz: μέλλει C
1386 ἀνάλγητον Weil: -ήτου C

ΙΠΠΟΛΥΤΟΣ

1395   ὁρᾷς με, δέσποιν', ὡς ἔχω, τὸν ἄθλιον;

ΑΡΤΕΜΙΣ

ὁρῶ· κατ' ὄσσων δ' οὐ θέμις βαλεῖν δάκρυ.

ΙΠΠΟΛΥΤΟΣ

οὐκ ἔστι σοι κυναγὸς οὐδ' ὑπηρέτης.

ΑΡΤΕΜΙΣ

οὐ δῆτ'· ἀτάρ μοι προσφιλής γ' ἀπόλλυσαι.

ΙΠΠΟΛΥΤΟΣ

οὐδ' ἱππονώμας οὐδ' ἀγαλμάτων φύλαξ.

ΑΡΤΕΜΙΣ

1400   Κύπρις γὰρ ἡ πανοῦργος ὧδ' ἐμήσατο.

ΙΠΠΟΛΥΤΟΣ

ὤμοι, φρονῶ δὴ δαίμον' ἥ μ' ἀπώλεσεν.

ΑΡΤΕΜΙΣ

τιμῆς ἐμέμφθη, σωφρονοῦντι δ' ἤχθετο.

ΙΠΠΟΛΥΤΟΣ

τρεῖς ὄντας ἡμᾶς ὤλεσ', ᾔσθημαι, μία.

ΑΡΤΕΜΙΣ

πατέρα γε καὶ σὲ καὶ τρίτην ξυνάορον.

ΙΠΠΟΛΥΤΟΣ

1405   ᾤμωξα τοίνυν καὶ πατρὸς δυσπραξίας.

1403 ὤλεσ', ᾔσθημαι, μία Valckenaer: ὤλεσ' ᾔσθημαι Κύ-
πρις a: ὤλεσεν μία Κύπρις b
1404 γε Kirchhoff: τε a: om. b

HIPPOLYTUS
Do you see me, lady, see my wretched state?

ARTEMIS
Yes, but the law forbids my shedding tears.

HIPPOLYTUS
No more do you have your huntsman and your servant!

ARTEMIS
No, but though you die, I love you still.

HIPPOLYTUS
No one to tend your horses or your statue!

ARTEMIS
No, for knavish Cypris willed it so.

HIPPOLYTUS
Ah, now I learn the power that has destroyed me!

ARTEMIS
The slight to her honor galled her, and she hated your chastity.

HIPPOLYTUS
One power destroyed us three, I see it now.

ARTEMIS
Your father, you, and Theseus' wife the third.

HIPPOLYTUS
Therefore I groan for Theseus' fate as well.

ΑΡΤΕΜΙΣ

ἐξηπατήθη δαίμονος βουλεύμασιν.

ΙΠΠΟΛΥΤΟΣ

ὦ δυστάλας σὺ τῆσδε συμφορᾶς, πάτερ.

ΘΗΣΕΥΣ

ὄλωλα, τέκνον, οὐδέ μοι χάρις βίου.

ΙΠΠΟΛΥΤΟΣ

στένω σε μᾶλλον ἢ 'μὲ τῆς ἁμαρτίας.

ΘΗΣΕΥΣ

1410 εἰ γὰρ γενοίμην, τέκνον, ἀντὶ σοῦ νεκρός.

ΙΠΠΟΛΥΤΟΣ

ὦ δῶρα πατρὸς σοῦ Ποσειδῶνος πικρά.

ΘΗΣΕΥΣ

ὡς μήποτ' ἐλθεῖν ὤφελ' ἐς τοὐμὸν στόμα.

ΙΠΠΟΛΥΤΟΣ

τί δ'; ἔκτανές τἄν μ', ὡς τότ' ἦσθ' ὠργισμένος.

ΘΗΣΕΥΣ

δόξης γὰρ ἦμεν πρὸς θεῶν ἐσφαλμένοι.

ΙΠΠΟΛΥΤΟΣ

φεῦ·
1415 εἴθ' ἦν ἀραῖον δαίμοσιν βροτῶν γένος.

ΑΡΤΕΜΙΣ

ἔασον· οὐ γὰρ οὐδὲ γῆς ὑπὸ ζόφον
θεᾶς ἄτιμοι Κύπριδος ἐκ προθυμίας
ὀργαὶ κατασκήψουσιν ἐς τὸ σὸν δέμας,

ARTEMIS
He was deceived, a god contrived it so.

HIPPOLYTUS
How great, unhappy father, your misfortune!

THESEUS
I am gone, my son, I have no joy in life.

HIPPOLYTUS
For your mistake I pity you more than me.

THESEUS
Would I could die, my son, instead of you!

HIPPOLYTUS
Poseidon your father's gifts, what woe they brought!

THESEUS
Would that the curse had never come to my lips!

HIPPOLYTUS
You would have killed me still, such was your anger.

THESEUS
Yes, for the gods had robbed me of my wits.

HIPPOLYTUS
Oh! Would that the race of men could curse the gods![a]

ARTEMIS
Let be! For though you are in the gloom under the earth, even so you will get revenge for the wrath that has fallen against you by Cypris' design, and this will be the reward

---

[a] A dying man's curse was believed to be efficacious, but the gods are exempt from its effects.

σῆς εὐσεβείας κἀγαθῆς φρενὸς χάριν·
1420 ἐγὼ γὰρ αὐτῆς ἄλλον ἐξ ἐμῆς χερὸς
ὃς ἂν μάλιστα φίλτατος κυρῇ βροτῶν
τόξοις ἀφύκτοις τοῖσδε τιμωρήσομαι.
σοὶ δ᾽, ὦ ταλαίπωρ᾽, ἀντὶ τῶνδε τῶν κακῶν
τιμὰς μεγίστας ἐν πόλει Τροζηνίᾳ
1425 δώσω· κόραι γὰρ ἄζυγες γάμων πάρος
κόμας κεροῦνταί σοι, δι᾽ αἰῶνος μακροῦ
πένθη μέγιστα δακρύων καρπουμένῳ.
ἀεὶ δὲ μουσοποιὸς ἐς σὲ παρθένων
ἔσται μέριμνα, κοὐκ ἀνώνυμος πεσὼν
1430 ἔρως ὁ Φαίδρας ἐς σὲ σιγηθήσεται.

σὺ δ᾽, ὦ γεραιοῦ τέκνον Αἰγέως, λαβὲ
σὸν παῖδ᾽ ἐν ἀγκάλαισι καὶ προσέλκυσαι·
ἄκων γὰρ ὤλεσάς νιν, ἀνθρώποισι δὲ
θεῶν διδόντων εἰκὸς ἐξαμαρτάνειν.
1435 καὶ σοὶ παραινῶ πατέρα μὴ στυγεῖν σέθεν,
Ἱππόλυτ᾽· ἔχει γὰρ μοῖραν ᾗ διεφθάρης.
καὶ χαῖρ᾽· ἐμοὶ γὰρ οὐ θέμις φθιτοὺς ὁρᾶν
οὐδ᾽ ὄμμα χραίνειν θανασίμοισιν ἐκπνοαῖς·
ὁρῶ δέ σ᾽ ἤδη τοῦδε πλησίον κακοῦ.

ΙΠΠΟΛΥΤΟΣ

1440 χαίρουσα καὶ σὺ στεῖχε, παρθέν᾽ ὀλβία·
μακρὰν δὲ λείπεις ῥᾳδίως ὁμιλίαν.
λύω δὲ νεῖκος πατρὶ χρῃζούσης σέθεν·
καὶ γὰρ πάροιθε σοῖς ἐπειθόμην λόγοις.
αἰαῖ, κατ᾽ ὄσσων κιγχάνει μ᾽ ἤδη σκότος·
1445 λαβοῦ, πάτερ, μου καὶ κατόρθωσον δέμας.

of your piety and goodness. That mortal of hers she loves
the most I shall punish with these inescapable arrows shot
from my hand. To you, unhappy man, I shall grant, in
recompense for these sorrows, supreme honors in the
land of Trozen. Unmarried girls before their marriage
will cut their hair for you, and over the length of ages you
will harvest the deep mourning of their tears. The prac-
ticed skill of poetry sung by maidens will for ever make
you its theme, and Phaedra's love for you shall not fall
nameless and unsung.

But you, child of old Aegeus, take your son in your
arms and embrace him. For you were not responsible for
killing him, and when the gods so ordain, it is to be
expected that men will make disastrous mistakes. As for
you, Hippolytus, I urge you not to hate your father. For
the manner of your death is set by fate. Farewell: it is not
lawful for me to look upon the dead or to defile my sight
with the last breath of the dying. And I see that you are
already near that misfortune.

Exit ARTEMIS.

HIPPOLYTUS

And farewell to you in your going, blessed maiden! Yet
how easily you leave our long friendship! Still, at your
bidding I end my quarrel with my father. For in times
past too I obeyed your words.

Oh, oh! Darkness is coming down upon my eyes!
Take me, father, and lay my body straight!

[1427] καρπουμένῳ Valckenaer: -ούμεναι vel -ουμένα C
[1436] ἔχει J. U. Powell cl. 988: ἔχεις C

ΘΗΣΕΥΣ

οἴμοι, τέκνον, τί δρᾷς με τὸν δυσδαίμονα;

ΙΠΠΟΛΥΤΟΣ

ὄλωλα καὶ δὴ νερτέρων ὁρῶ πύλας.

ΘΗΣΕΥΣ

ἦ τὴν ἐμὴν ἄναγνον ἐκλιπὼν χέρα;

ΙΠΠΟΛΥΤΟΣ

οὐ δῆτ᾽, ἐπεί σε τοῦδ᾽ ἐλευθερῶ φόνου.

ΘΗΣΕΥΣ

1450   τί φῄς; ἀφίῃς αἵματός μ᾽ ἐλεύθερον;

ΙΠΠΟΛΥΤΟΣ

τὴν τοξόδαμνον Ἄρτεμιν μαρτύρομαι.

ΘΗΣΕΥΣ

ὦ φίλταθ᾽, ὡς γενναῖος ἐκφαίνῃ πατρί.

ΙΠΠΟΛΥΤΟΣ

ὦ χαῖρε καὶ σύ, χαῖρε πολλά μοι, πάτερ.

ΘΗΣΕΥΣ

οἴμοι φρενὸς σῆς εὐσεβοῦς τε κἀγαθῆς.

ΙΠΠΟΛΥΤΟΣ

1455   τοιῶνδε παίδων γνησίων εὔχου τυχεῖν.

ΘΗΣΕΥΣ

μή νυν προδῷς με, τέκνον, ἀλλὰ καρτέρει.

ΙΠΠΟΛΥΤΟΣ

κεκαρτέρηται τἄμ᾽· ὄλωλα γάρ, πάτερ.
κρύψον δέ μου πρόσωπον ὡς τάχος πέπλοις.

THESEUS
Alas, my son, what are you doing to me?

HIPPOLYTUS
I am gone. I see the gates of the Underworld!

THESEUS
And will you leave me with my hands unclean?

HIPPOLYTUS
Oh no, for of this murder I acquit you.

THESEUS
What is this you say? You set me free of murder?

HIPPOLYTUS
The conquering bow of Artemis be my witness!

THESEUS
How noble you are to your father, dearest son!

HIPPOLYTUS
I wish you, father, plenteous joy as well!

THESEUS
Oh, what a noble, godly heart is lost!

HIPPOLYTUS
Pray that your true-born sons may be as good!

THESEUS
Do not desert me, son, but struggle on!

HIPPOLYTUS
My struggle is over, father: I am gone. Cover my face,
and quickly, with my garments!

He falls silent. Theseus covers his face.

ΘΗΣΕΥΣ

ὦ κλείν' Ἐρεχθέως Παλλάδος θ' ὁρίσματα,
1460 οἵου στερήσεσθ' ἀνδρός. ὦ τλήμων ἐγώ,
ὡς πολλά, Κύπρι, σῶν κακῶν μεμνήσομαι.

ΧΟΡΟΣ

κοινὸν τόδ' ἄχος πᾶσι πολίταις
ἦλθεν ἀέλπτως.
πολλῶν δακρύων ἔσται πίτυλος·
1465 τῶν γὰρ μεγάλων ἀξιοπενθεῖς
φῆμαι μᾶλλον κατέχουσιν.

1459 Ἐρεχθέως Stockert: Ἀθῆναι a: Ἀθηνῶν b

HIPPOLYTUS

THESEUS

Glorious territory of Erechtheus and Pallas, what a man you have been bereft of! Unhappy me, how well I shall remember, Cypris, the woes you have brought to pass!

Exit THESEUS into the palace, accompanied by servants carrying the body of his son.

CHORUS LEADER

This grief has come unlooked for upon all the citizens in common. Floods of tears shall come over us again and again. For tales of grief about the great have greater power to move.

Exit CHORUS by Eisodos B.

ANDROMACHE

INTRODUCTION

Andromache was produced sometime around 425. A *scholion* on line 445 says that the play was not produced in Athens, which is probably an inference from the absence of an entry "Euripides, *Andromache*" in the *didaskaleiai* that Aristotle or his pupils copied from the public records of the Dionysia. From the same *scholion* we learn that the Hellenistic scholar Callimachus noted that the play, in a copy or copies known to him, bore the name Democrates. Whether we must conclude that it was put on in Athens but under another poet's name, or that it was put on elsewhere, or both, we cannot tell.

The play dramatizes the aftermath of the Trojan War. Like several of Euripides' extant plays, it combines two stories that have no necessary connection with one another—the story of Hermione's and Menelaus' attempted murder of Andromache and the story of Orestes' murder of Neoptolemus and marriage to Hermione—and hence it has no single central character or center of interest.

The scene is set in Thetideion, the part of Thessaly where Achilles' son Neoptolemus lives, not far from Phthia, where his grandfather Peleus is king. Long ago Peleus had been given the goddess Thetis as his wife and had become the father of Achilles, the noblest warrior of the Greeks. Achilles perished at Troy, slain by Paris and Apollo. After helping to capture Troy, Neoptolemus had come home with Andromache, widow of Hector, the most valiant of the Trojans. The Greeks had given her to him as a prize of honor, and she became his mistress, bearing him a son. (In the play, the son is nameless, but it will be convenient to call him Molossus, as the mythological tradition does.) Andromache has passed from a life of royalty to one of slavery, and her only hope of ameliorating her ruined fortunes lies in Neoptolemus and the son she has by him. But Neoptolemus, out of a desire for legitimate heirs, has married Hermione, daughter of Menelaus and Helen, and the wife is persecuting the mistress and her son. During Neoptolemus' absence on a trip to Delphi—he has gone there to offer amends to Apollo for an earlier visit, when he had demanded satisfaction from the god for killing his father Achilles—Hermione has summoned her father from Sparta, and the two of them are attempting to murder Andromache and Molossus. Andromache at the beginning of the action has taken refuge at the altar of Thetis and is safe there for the moment. But Menelaus finds Molossus and, bringing the child captive before his mother, tells her that either she must surrender and be killed or he will kill her son. She surrenders to save Molossus' life; then Menelaus announces that his promise to spare Molossus in no way binds Hermione. Andromache and Molossus are just about to be put to death when Peleus arrives and sends Menelaus packing.

At this point, the Andromache and Hermione story, which may be Euripides' own invention, intersects with another known to us from Delphic myth, the murder of

Neoptolemus at Delphi. Hermione emerges from the house desperate at the thought that she will have to face her husband Neoptolemus without her father's support. Suddenly her cousin Orestes appears, seemingly in answer to her prayers. He claims at first that he is merely passing through Thessaly and has stopped to see how his cousin is faring. He listens to her recital of the plan to murder Andromache and Molossus and how it failed. Then he reveals that he already knows of Hermione's trouble and has come to take her away and marry her. (She had been promised to him before the war.) Only when they are already on their way does Orestes reveal that he has set in motion a plot to ambush Neoptolemus at Delphi.

After their departure, Peleus comes back to investigate a rumor that Hermione has left her husband's house. The Chorus confirm this and then warn him that Neoptolemus is in mortal danger at Delphi. Peleus dispatches a slave to warn him, but before he can leave, a messenger comes with the news that Neoptolemus has been treacherously slain. Orestes had spread the rumor that Neoptolemus had come to plunder Delphi, and he was murdered in the temple precincts. Peleus is prostrated by the news: the only son of his only son is dead, and his line is all but extinct.

Then the goddess Thetis appears in the role of *deus ex machina* to bring consolation to her former husband and to prophesy the future for him, Andromache, and Molossus. He should not grieve for his grandson's death, she says, for death is a debt all must pay. As for his line being extinct, it lives on in Molossus. Andromache, now free from slavery, will marry Priam's son Helenus and dwell in

269

Molossia, and Molossus himself will be the first of a long and blessed dynasty to rule over that part of Greece. Peleus is destined to become an immortal god and to dwell with her for all time as her husband. He will even see Achilles, who lives on as a hero. The Chorus end the play with lines repeated from *Alcestis* on the unexpectedness of what the gods bring to pass.

Few of Euripides' plays equal *Andromache* in the depiction of the multiple and contrary vicissitudes of fortune. The characters may be divided into sympathetic (the Trojan Andromache, the Thessalians Peleus and Neoptolemus) and unsympathetic (the Spartan Hermione and her father Menelaus, and the Argive Orestes). Both groups experience rapid and unexpected reversals of fortune. Andromache's fortunes sink ever lower as she gives up her life to save her son only to be told that she has been tricked and both will be killed. Then Peleus intervenes, rescuing her from imminent death and overturning the fortunes of the Spartan party. Hermione, despairing for her life, is rescued by Orestes, who deals a cruel blow to Peleus' fortunes. Last, Thetis announces a happy future for the sympathetic characters. All this amply justifies the five choral lines with which the play ends, describing the surprises the gods have in store for mortals.

The play also dramatizes important contrasts. Andromache, Peleus, and Neoptolemus, on the one hand, are brave, forthright, heroic, concerned for their posterity, and believers in *phusis* (nature, inborn character) and moral excellence. Hermione, Menelaus, and Orestes, on the other, are cowardly, deceitful, concerned only with their own satisfaction and careless of the future, and convinced that the intellectual virtues of cleverness and *didache* (teaching, training) hold the key to success in the world. Neoptolemus' marriage to Hermione was an unnatural alliance between members of different groups, and Peleus had warned him against it. It brought misery to Andromache and her son, and it was finally dissolved by the violence of Orestes.

Orestes is not the sole contriver, though, for both he and the messenger make it clear that Apollo had a hand in killing Neoptolemus, even though Neoptolemus had returned to make amends. The role of Apollo seems to reflect discredit upon the god, but the ancients may have felt differently. They had no notion that repentance made things between a man and a god all right again. That Apollo should punish Neoptolemus for his insolence, even if he said he was sorry, would not have seemed out of character for an Olympian god. Orestes had called on Apollo the Healer (line 900) to grant "a release from these troubles," and that is arguably what he does for everyone concerned. The two groups are forcibly disjoined, Andromache is set free, and Neoptolemus makes a heroic end worthy of the son of Achilles, fighting off his cowardly attackers single-handed until the god intervenes. In light of Thetis' remarks about the provident care of the gods for the line of Peleus and of Troy, it is possible to interpret Apollo's action as a blessing in heavy disguise. We are left at the end of the play with the sense that its chaotic and unexpected happenings are part of a divine plan no human mind could have foreseen. Such, Euripides says, are the dealings of the gods with mortals.

SELECT BIBLIOGRAPHY

Editions

D. Bassi (Milan, 1933).
P. T. Stevens (Oxford, 1971).
A. Garzya (Leipzig, 1978).

Literary criticism

K. M. Aldrich, *The* Andromache *of Euripides* (Lincoln, 1961).

E. K. Borthwick, "Trojan Leap and Pyrrhic Dance in Euripides' *Andromache*," *JHS* 87 (1967), 18–23.

A. P. Burnett, *Catastrophe Survived* (Oxford, 1971), chapter 6.

D. J. Conacher, *Euripidean Drama: Myth, Theme, and Structure* (Toronto, 1967), chapter 9.

J. Fontenrose, *The Cult and Myth of Pyrros at Delphi* (Berkeley and Los Angeles, 1960).

P. D. Kovacs, *The* Andromache *of Euripides: An Interpretation* (Chico, Calif., 1980).

A. Lesky, "Der Ablauf der Handlung in der *Andromache* des Euripides," *Anz. Akad. Wien* 84 (1947), 99ff, rpt. in his *Gesammelte Schriften* (Bern, 1966), pp. 144–55.

Dramatis Personae

ΑΝΔΡΟΜΑΧΗ	ANDROMACHE, widow of Hector and slave of Neoptolemus
ΘΕΡΑΠΑΙΝΑ	MAIDSERVANT, slave once of Andromache , now of Neoptolemus
ΧΟΡΟΣ	CHORUS of local Thessalian women
ΕΡΜΙΟΝΗ	HERMIONE, daughter of Menelaus and wife of Neoptolemus
ΜΕΝΕΛΑΟΣ	MENELAUS, King of Sparta
ΠΑΙΣ	BOY, son of Andromache and Neoptolemus
ΠΗΛΕΥΣ	PELEUS, grandfather of Neoptolemus and father of Achilles
ΤΡΟΦΟΣ	NURSE, servant of Hermione
ΟΡΕΣΤΗΣ	ORESTES, cousin of Hermione
ΑΓΓΕΛΟΣ	MESSENGER, one of Neoptolemus' retinue
ΘΕΤΙΣ	THETIS, sea goddess, wife of Peleus and mother of Achilles

A Note on Staging

The *skene* represents Neoptolemus' house in Thetideion, not far from Pharsalia in Thessaly. In the *orchestra* is an altar and shrine to Thetis. Eisodos A represents the road to Pharsalia and is also the route used by Menelaus, Orestes, and Hermione to return to Sparta. Eisodos B leads to Delphi.

273

ΑΝΔΡΟΜΑΧΗ

Ἀσιάτιδος γῆς σχῆμα, Θηβαία πόλι,
ὅθεν ποθ' ἕδνων σὺν πολυχρύσῳ χλιδῇ
Πριάμου τύραννον ἑστίαν ἀφικόμην
δάμαρ δοθεῖσα παιδοποιὸς Ἕκτορι,
5   ζηλωτὸς ἔν γε τῷ πρὶν Ἀνδρομάχη χρόνῳ,
νῦν δ', εἴ τις ἄλλη, δυστυχεστάτη γυνή
[ἐμοῦ πέφυκεν ἢ γενήσεταί ποτε]·
ἥτις πόσιν μὲν Ἕκτορ' ἐξ Ἀχιλλέως
θανόντ' ἐσεῖδον, παῖδά θ' ὃν τίκτω πόσει
10   ῥιφθέντα πύργων Ἀστυάνακτ' ἀπ' ὀρθίων,
ἐπεὶ τὸ Τροίας εἷλον Ἕλληνες πέδον·
αὐτὴ δὲ δούλη τῶν ἐλευθερωτάτων
οἴκων νομισθεῖσ' Ἑλλάδ' εἰσαφικόμην
τῷ νησιώτῃ Νεοπτολέμῳ δορὸς γέρας
15   δοθεῖσα λείας Τρωικῆς ἐξαίρετον.
Φθίας δὲ τῆσδε καὶ πόλεως Φαρσαλίας
σύγχορτα ναίω πεδί', ἵν' ἡ θαλασσία
Πηλεῖ ξυνῴκει χωρὶς ἀνθρώπων Θέτις
φεύγουσ' ὅμιλον· Θεσσαλὸς δέ νιν λεὼς

---

7 om. Π, iam del. Valckenaer

274

ANDROMACHE

Enter ANDROMACHE *from the house. She takes her place as a suppliant at the altar of Thetis in the* orchestra.

ANDROMACHE
Glory of Asia, city of Thebe![a] It was from you that I once came, dowered with golden luxury, to the royal house of Priam, given to Hector as lawful wife for the bearing of his children—I, Andromache, in days gone by a woman to be envied, but now, if ever woman was, the paragon of misery. I saw my husband Hector killed at the hands of Achilles and beheld Astyanax, the son I bore my husband, hurled from the high battlements when the Greeks had captured the land of Troy. I myself, who belonged to a house most free, became a slave and was brought to Greece, given as the choicest of the Trojan spoil to the islander[b] Neoptolemus as his prize of war. I live now in these lands that border on Phthia and the city of Pharsalia, lands where the sea goddess Thetis, far from the haunts of men and fleeing their company, lived as wife

[a] City in Mysia in Asia Minor, ruled by Andromache's father, Eëtion.

[b] Neoptolemus was born on the island of Scyros.

275

20 Θετίδειον αὐδᾷ θεᾶς χάριν νυμφευμάτων.
ἔνθ' οἶκον ἔσχε τόνδε παῖς Ἀχιλλέως,
Πηλέα δ' ἀνάσσειν γῆς ἐᾷ Φαρσαλίας,
ζῶντος γέροντος σκῆπτρον οὐ θέλων λαβεῖν.
κἀγὼ δόμοις τοῖσδ' ἄρσεν' ἐντίκτω κόρον,
25 πλαθεῖσ' Ἀχιλλέως παιδί, δεσπότῃ δ' ἐμῷ.
καὶ πρὶν μὲν ἐν κακοῖσι κειμένην ὅμως
ἐλπίς μ' ἀεὶ προσῆγε σωθέντος τέκνου
ἀλκήν τιν' εὑρεῖν κἀπικούρησιν κακῶν·
ἐπεὶ δὲ τὴν Λάκαιναν Ἑρμιόνην γαμεῖ
30 τοὐμὸν παρώσας δεσπότης δοῦλον λέχος,
κακοῖς πρὸς αὐτῆς σχετλίοις ἐλαύνομαι.
λέγει γὰρ ὥς νιν φαρμάκοις κεκρυμμένοις
τίθημ' ἄπαιδα καὶ πόσει μισουμένην,
αὐτὴ δὲ ναίειν οἶκον ἀντ' αὐτῆς θέλω
35 τόνδ', ἐκβαλοῦσα λέκτρα τἀκείνης βίᾳ·
ἁγὼ τὸ πρῶτον οὐχ ἑκοῦσ' ἐδεξάμην,
νῦν δ' ἐκλέλοιπα· Ζεὺς τάδ' εἰδείη μέγας,
ὡς οὐχ ἑκοῦσα τῷδ' ἐκοινώθην λέχει.
ἀλλ' οὔ σφε πείθω, βούλεται δέ με κτανεῖν,
40 πατήρ τε θυγατρὶ Μενέλεως συνδρᾷ τάδε.
καὶ νῦν κατ' οἴκους ἔστ', ἀπὸ Σπάρτης μολὼν
ἐπ' αὐτὸ τοῦτο· δειματουμένη δ' ἐγὼ
δόμων πάροικον Θέτιδος εἰς ἀνάκτορον
θάσσω τόδ' ἐλθοῦσ', ἤν με κωλύσῃ θανεῖν.
45 Πηλεύς τε γάρ νιν ἔκγονοί τε Πηλέως
σέβουσιν, ἑρμήνευμα Νηρῇδος γάμων.
ὃς δ' ἔστι παῖς μοι μόνος, ὑπεκπέμπω λάθρᾳ

with Peleus. The people of Thessaly call the place The-
tideion in honor of the goddess' marriage. Here Achilles'
son made his home, allowing Peleus to rule over the land
of Pharsalia: he was unwilling to take the scepter during
the old man's lifetime. In this house I have given birth to
a manchild, lying with Achilles' son, my master.

Formerly, though I was sunk in misery, the hope
always drew me to him that if the child lived I would find
some kind of help and defense from misfortune. But ever
since my master married Hermione, spurning my servile
bed, I have been hounded by cruel abuse from her. She
says that with secret drugs I make her childless and hated
by her husband, and that I wish to take her place in the
house, forcibly casting her out as wife. I took this bed
unwillingly to begin with, and now I have relinquished it.[a]
Great Zeus be my witness that it was against my will that I
became sharer in this bed! But I cannot persuade her of
this, and she wants to kill me. Menelaus her father is his
daughter's accomplice in this scheme, and he is now
residing in the house, having come from Sparta for this
very purpose. I in fear have come and taken my seat at
this shrine of Thetis near the house in the hope that it
may save me from death. For Peleus and Peleus' off-
spring honor it as a monument to their marriage tie with
the Nereid.

My only child I have sent secretly to another house,

[a] She means not that she has broken off relations with Neop-
tolemus (which is not in her power as a slave to do), but that she
has left the house to become a suppliant.

---

25 δ' Elmsley: τ' C   27 προῆγε Reiske
28 κακῶν a: δόμων b: δόμον Kovacs

ἄλλους ἐς οἴκους, μὴ θάνῃ φοβουμένη.
ὁ γὰρ φυτεύσας αὐτὸν οὔτ᾽ ἐμοὶ πάρα
50 προσωφελῆσαι παιδί τ᾽ οὐδέν ἐστ᾽, ἀπὼν
Δελφῶν κατ᾽ αἶαν, ἔνθα Λοξίᾳ δίκην
δίδωσι μανίας, ἣν ποτ᾽ ἐς Πυθὼ μολὼν
ᾔτησε Φοῖβον πατρὸς οὗ κτείνει δίκην,
εἴ πως τὰ πρόσθε σφάλματ᾽ ἐξαιτούμενος
55 θεὸν παράσχοιτ᾽ ἐς τὸ λοιπὸν εὐμενῆ.

ΘΕΡΑΠΑΙΝΑ

δέσποιν᾽, ἐγώ τοι τοὔνομ᾽ οὐ φεύγω τόδε
καλεῖν σ᾽, ἐπείπερ καὶ κατ᾽ οἶκον ἠξίουν
τὸν σόν, τὸ Τροίας ἡνίκ᾽ ᾠκοῦμεν πέδον.
εὔνους δ᾽ ἐκεῖ σοι ζῶντί τ᾽ ἦ τῷ σῷ πόσει,
60 καὶ νῦν φέρουσά σοι νέους ἥκω λόγους,
φόβῳ μέν, εἴ τις δεσποτῶν αἰσθήσεται,
οἴκτῳ δὲ τῷ σῷ· δεινὰ γὰρ βουλεύεται
Μενέλαος ἐς σὲ παῖς θ᾽, ἅ σοι φυλακτέα.

ΑΝΔΡΟΜΑΧΗ

ὦ φιλτάτη σύνδουλε (σύνδουλος γὰρ εἶ
65 τῇ πρόσθ᾽ ἀνάσσῃ τῇδε, νῦν δὲ δυστυχεῖ),
τί δρῶσι; ποίας μηχανὰς πλέκουσιν αὖ,
κτεῖναι θέλοντες τὴν παναθλίαν ἐμέ;

ΘΕΡΑΠΑΙΝΑ

τὸν παῖδά σου μέλλουσιν, ὦ δύστηνε σύ,
κτείνειν, ὃν ἔξω δωμάτων ὑπεξέθου.

52 ᾗ Reiske
59 δ᾽ ἐκεῖ Badham: δὲ καὶ C

for fear that he will be killed. His father is not here to protect me and is no use to his son since he is away in the land of Delphi. There he is offering amends to Apollo for his madness—he once went to Pytho and asked Phoebus for satisfaction for his father Achilles, whom the god had killed—in the hope that by begging forgiveness for his previous sin he might win the god's favor for the future.

Enter MAIDSERVANT *from the house.*

MAIDSERVANT
Mistress, I do not shrink from calling you this name since it was the name I thought it right to use in your house when we lived in the land of Troy. I was well disposed toward you there and to your husband while he lived, and now I have come to you with bad news, in fear that one of my masters might see me but pitying you: Menelaus and his daughter are planning dreadful things against you. You must be on your guard.

ANDROMACHE
Dearest fellow slave (for you are fellow slave to me, once your queen but now in misery), what are they doing? What kind of plots are they weaving this time in their desire to kill me in my utter wretchedness?

MAIDSERVANT
They are about to kill your son, unhappy woman, whom you sent secretly out of the house.

ΑΝΔΡΟΜΑΧΗ

70 οἴμοι· πέπυσθον τὸν ἐμὸν ἔκθετον γόνον;
πόθεν ποτ'; ὦ δύστηνος, ὡς ἀπωλόμην.

ΘΕΡΑΠΑΙΝΑ

οὐκ οἶδ', ἐκείνων δ' ᾐσθόμην ἐγὼ τάδε.
φροῦδος δ' ἐπ' αὐτὸν Μενέλεως δόμων ἄπο.

ΑΝΔΡΟΜΑΧΗ

ἀπωλόμην ἄρ'. ὦ τέκνον, κτενοῦσί σε
75 δισσοὶ λαβόντες γῦπες, ὁ δὲ κεκλημένος
πατὴρ ἔτ' ἐν Δελφοῖσι τυγχάνει μένων.

ΘΕΡΑΠΑΙΝΑ

δοκῶ γὰρ οὐκ ἂν ὧδέ σ' ἂν πράσσειν κακῶς
κείνου παρόντος· νῦν δ' ἔρημος εἶ φίλων.

ΑΝΔΡΟΜΑΧΗ

οὐδ' ἀμφὶ Πηλέως ἦλθεν ὡς ἥξοι φάτις;

ΘΕΡΑΠΑΙΝΑ

80 γέρων ἐκεῖνος ὥστε σ' ὠφελεῖν παρών.

ΑΝΔΡΟΜΑΧΗ

καὶ μὴν ἔπεμψ' ἐπ' αὐτὸν οὐχ ἅπαξ μόνον.

ΘΕΡΑΠΑΙΝΑ

μῶν οὖν δοκεῖς σου φροντίσαι τιν' ἀγγέλων;

ΑΝΔΡΟΜΑΧΗ

πόθεν; θέλεις οὖν ἄγγελος σύ μοι μολεῖν;

ΘΕΡΑΠΑΙΝΑ

τί δῆτα φήσω χρόνιος οὖσ' ἐκ δωμάτων;

ANDROMACHE

ANDROMACHE

Oh me! Have they found the son I sent into hiding? How could they have done so? Oh I am undone and in utter misery!

MAIDSERVANT

I do not know how, but I learned this from *them*. Menelaus has left the house to fetch him.

ANDROMACHE

Then I am done for. O my son, those two vultures will take you and kill you, while the man who is called your father tarries in Delphi!

MAIDSERVANT

Yes, I do not think that you would be in such sorry plight if he were present. But as it is you are bereft of friends.

ANDROMACHE

Is there also no word of Peleus' coming?

MAIDSERVANT

He is too old to help you even if he were here.

ANDROMACHE

And yet I sent a message to him more than once.

MAIDSERVANT

Do you suppose any of your messengers cared about you?

ANDROMACHE

Of course not! Will you then go as my messenger?

MAIDSERVANT

What shall I say to excuse my long absence from home?

---

[70] πέπυσθον Nauck: πέπυσται C, quo servato ante h. v. 73 trai. Radermacher

ΑΝΔΡΟΜΑΧΗ

85 πολλὰς ἂν εὕροις μηχανάς· γυνὴ γὰρ εἶ.

ΘΕΡΑΠΑΙΝΑ

κίνδυνος· Ἑρμιόνη γὰρ οὐ σμικρὸν φύλαξ.

ΑΝΔΡΟΜΑΧΗ

ὁρᾷς; ἀπαυδᾷς ἐν κακοῖς φίλοισι σοῖς.

ΘΕΡΑΠΑΙΝΑ

οὐ δῆτα· μηδὲν τοῦτ' ὀνειδίσῃς ἐμοί.
ἀλλ' εἶμ', ἐπεί τοι κοὐ περίβλεπτος βίος
90 δούλης γυναικός, ἤν τι καὶ πάθω κακόν.

ΑΝΔΡΟΜΑΧΗ

χώρει νυν· ἡμεῖς δ' οἷσπερ ἐγκείμεσθ' ἀεὶ
θρήνοισι καὶ γόοισι καὶ δακρύμασιν
πρὸς αἰθέρ' ἐκτενοῦμεν· ἐμπέφυκε γὰρ
γυναιξὶ τέρψις τῶν παρεστώτων κακῶν
95 ἀνὰ στόμ' αἰεὶ καὶ διὰ γλώσσης ἔχειν.
πάρεστι δ' οὐχ ἓν ἀλλὰ πολλά μοι στένειν,
πόλιν πατρῴαν τὸν θανόντα θ' Ἕκτορα
στερρόν τε τὸν ἐμὸν δαίμον' ᾧ συνεζύγην
δούλειον ἦμαρ ἐσπεσοῦσ' ἀναξίως.
100 χρὴ δ' οὔποτ' εἰπεῖν οὐδέν' ὄλβιον βροτῶν,
πρὶν ἂν θανόντος τὴν τελευταίαν ἴδῃς
ὅπως περάσας ἡμέραν ἥξει κάτω.

Ἰλίῳ αἰπεινᾷ Πάρις οὐ γάμον ἀλλά τιν' ἄταν

---

86 σμικρὸν tamquam ex cod. Kirchhoff: σμικρὸς a:
σμικρὰ b

282

ANDROMACHE

ANDROMACHE

You will find many ruses: you are a woman.

MAIDSERVANT

It is a dangerous job. Hermione is no slacker as guard.

ANDROMACHE

You see? You are failing your friends in their misfortune!

MAIDSERVANT

Not at all: don't reproach me with that! I will go, since in any case if something happens to me the life of a slave is not much to envy.

Exit MAIDSERVANT *by Eisodos A.*

ANDROMACHE

Go then! For my part I shall fill heaven at great length with the laments and groans and tears to which my whole life is devoted. It is natural for women to get pleasure from their present misfortunes, by constantly having them on their lips. I have many things, not one, to lament, my native land, the death of Hector, and the hard lot to which I have been yoked when I was cast undeservedly into slavery. One should never call any mortal happy until he dies and you can see how he has completed his last day and gone below.

    (sung)[a] For lofty Troy it was not as bride but as mad

[a] This lament is unique, for only here in tragedy is the elegiac meter used. See D. L. Page, "The Elegiacs in Euripides' *Andromache*," in *Greek Poetry and Life: Essays Presented to Gilbert Murray* (Oxford, 1936), pp. 206–30.

---

[102] ἥκει Herwerden

ἀγάγετ᾽ εὐναίαν ἐς θαλάμους Ἑλέναν.
105 ἆς ἕνεκ᾽, ὦ Τροία, δορὶ καὶ πυρὶ δηιάλωτον
εἷλέ σ᾽ ὁ χιλιόναυς Ἑλλάδος ὀξὺς Ἄρης
καὶ τὸν ἐμὸν μελέας πόσιν Ἕκτορα, τὸν περὶ τείχη
εἵλκυσε διφρεύων παῖς ἁλίας Θέτιδος·
αὐτὰ δ᾽ ἐκ θαλάμων ἀγόμαν ἐπὶ θῖνα θαλάσσας,
110 δουλοσύναν στυγερὰν ἀμφιβαλοῦσα κάρᾳ.
πολλὰ δὲ δάκρυά μοι κατέβα χροός, ἁνίκ᾽ ἔλειπον
ἄστυ τε καὶ θαλάμους καὶ πόσιν ἐν κονίαις.
ὤμοι ἐγὼ μελέα, τί μ᾽ ἐχρῆν ἔτι φέγγος ὁρᾶσθαι
Ἑρμιόνας δούλαν; ἇς ὕπο τειρομένα
115 πρὸς τόδ᾽ ἄγαλμα θεᾶς ἱκέτις περὶ χεῖρε βαλοῦσα
τάκομαι ὡς πετρίνα πιδακόεσσα λιβάς.

ΧΟΡΟΣ

στρ. α

ὦ γύναι, ἃ Θέτιδος δάπεδον καὶ ἀνάκτορα θάσσεις
δαρὸν οὐδὲ λείπεις,
Φθιὰς ὅμως ἔμολον ποτὶ σὰν Ἀσιήτιδα γένναν,
120 εἴ τί σοι δυναίμαν
ἄκος τῶν δυσλύτων πόνων τεμεῖν,
οἵ σε καὶ Ἑρμιόναν ἔριδι στυγερᾷ συνέκλῃσαν,
τλᾶμον, ἀμφὶ λέκτρων
διδύμων, ἐπίκοινον ἔχουσαν
125 ἄνδρα, παῖδ᾽ Ἀχιλλέως.

ἀντ. α

γνῶθι τύχαν, λόγισαι τὸ παρὸν κακὸν εἰς ὅπερ ἥκεις.
δεσπόταις ἁμιλλᾷ

ruin that Paris brought Helen into his bedchamber! For
her sake the keen warcraft of Greece, its ships a thousand
strong, captured you, O Troy, sacked you with fire and
sword, and killed Hector, husband to my unlucky self!
The son of the sea goddess Thetis dragged him behind his
chariot as he rode about the walls of Troy. I myself was
led off from my chamber to the seashore, wrapping hate-
ful slavery as a covering about my head. Many were the
tears that rolled down my cheeks when I left city and
home and husband lying in the dust! Oh, unhappy me,
why should I still look on the light as Hermione's slave?
Oppressed by her I have come as suppliant to this statue
of the goddess and thrown my arms about it, melting in
tears like some gushing spring high up on a cliff.

Enter women of Phthia as CHORUS *by Eisodos A.*

CHORUS
Woman, seated all this time upon the floor of Thetis'
shrine, never leaving it: though I am a Phthian, I have
come to you, child of Asia, in the hope that I might be
able to find a remedy for your troubles so hard to cure,
troubles that have joined you, unhappy woman, and
Hermione in hateful quarrel about a double marriage,
since you share a husband, the son of Achilles.

Know your fate, consider the present ill-fortune into
which you have come. Do you wrangle with your masters

---

[106] ὀξὺς Schaefer (cf. *Hcld.* 290): ὠκὺς C
[124–5] ἔχουσαν ἄνδρα Diggle: ἐοῦσαν ἀμφὶ C

Ἰλιὰς οὖσα κόρα Λακεδαίμονος ἐγγενέταισιν;
λεῖπε δεξίμηλον

130 δόμον τᾶς ποντίας θεοῦ. τί σοι
καιρὸς ἀτυζομένᾳ δέμας αἰκέλιον καταλείβειν
δεσποτᾶν ἀνάγκαις;
τὸ κρατοῦν δέ σ' ἔπεισι. τί μόχθον
οὐδὲν οὖσα μοχθεῖς;

στρ. β

135 ἀλλ' ἴθι λεῖπε θεᾶς Νηρηίδος ἀγλαὸν ἕδραν,
γνῶθι δ' οὖσ' ἐπὶ ξένας
δμωὶς ἀπ' ἀλλοτρίας
πόλεος, ἔνθ' οὐ φίλων τιν' εἰσορᾷς
σῶν, ὦ δυστυχεστάτα,

140 <ὦ> παντάλαινα νύμφα.

ἀντ. β

οἰκτροτάτα γὰρ ἔμοιγ' ἔμολες, γύναι Ἰλιάς, οἴκους
δεσποτᾶν ἐμῶν· φόβῳ δ'
ἡσυχίαν ἄγομεν
(τὸ δὲ σὸν οἴκτῳ φέρουσα τυγχάνω)

145 μὴ παῖς τᾶς Διὸς κόρας
σοί μ' εὖ φρονοῦσαν εἰδῇ.

ΕΡΜΙΟΝΗ

κόσμον μὲν ἀμφὶ κρατὶ χρυσέας χλιδῆς
στολμόν τε χρωτὸς τόνδε ποικίλων πέπλων
οὐ τῶν Ἀχιλλέως οὐδὲ Πηλέως ἄπο

150 δόμων ἀπαρχὰς δεῦρ' ἔχουσ' ἀφικόμην,
ἀλλ' ἐκ Λακαίνης Σπαρτιάτιδος χθονὸς
Μενέλαος ἡμῖν ταῦτα δωρεῖται πατὴρ

when you are a woman of Troy and they were born in Sparta? The sea goddess' shrine, receiver of sacrifices—leave it behind! What profit is it for you in your distress to mar your body with weeping because of your masters' hard constraints? Their forcible hand will come upon you: why do you toil in vain, powerless as you are?

But come, leave the bright seat of the Nereid, recognize that you stand, a slave woman from another land, on foreign soil where you see none of your friends, O woman most luckless, most wretched.

In my eyes you were much to be pitied when you came, woman of Troy, to the house of my lords. But I hold my peace from fear (though in fact I pity your lot) lest the child of Zeus's daughter learn that I wish you well.

Enter from the house HERMIONE, *impressively dressed and bejewelled.*

HERMIONE

The luxurious gold that adorns my head and neck and the spangled gown that graces my body—I did not bring these here as the first fruits of the house of Achilles or of Peleus: my father Menelaus gave them to me from the

---

[130] τί Musgrave: τίς C

[137] ἀπ' Murray: ἐπ' C

[140] <ὦ> Triclinius: πα<σᾶ>ν τάλαινα Wilamowitz

[142] ἐμῶν· φόβῳ δ' Nauck: δ' ἐμῶν φόβῳ C

πολλοῖς σὺν ἕδνοις, ὥστ' ἐλευθεροστομεῖν.
[ὑμᾶς μὲν οὖν τοῖσδ' ἀνταμείβομαι λόγοις.]
155　σὺ δ' οὖσα δούλη καὶ δορίκτητος γυνὴ
δόμους κατασχεῖν ἐκβαλοῦσ' ἡμᾶς θέλεις
τούσδε, στυγοῦμαι δ' ἀνδρὶ φαρμάκοισι σοῖς,
νηδὺς δ' ἀκύμων διὰ σέ μοι διόλλυται·
δεινὴ γὰρ ἠπειρῶτις ἐς τὰ τοιάδε
160　ψυχὴ γυναικῶν· ὧν ἐπισχήσω σ' ἐγώ,
κοὐδέν σ' ὀνήσει δῶμα Νηρῇδος τόδε,
οὐ βωμὸς οὐδὲ ναός, ἀλλὰ κατθανῇ.
ἢν δ' οὖν βροτῶν τίς σ' ἢ θεῶν σῶσαι θέλῃ,
δεῖ σ' ἀντὶ τῶν πρὶν ὀλβίων φρονημάτων
165　πτῆξαι ταπεινὴν προσπεσεῖν τ' ἐμὸν γόνυ,
σαίρειν τε δῶμα τοὐμὸν ἐκ χρυσηλάτων
τευχέων χερὶ σπείρουσαν Ἀχελῴου δρόσον
γνῶναί θ' ἵν' εἶ γῆς. οὐ γάρ ἐσθ' Ἕκτωρ τάδε,
οὐ Πρίαμος οὐδὲ χρυσός, ἀλλ' Ἑλλὰς πόλις.
170　ἐς τοῦτο δ' ἥκεις ἀμαθίας, δύστηνε σύ,
ἢ παιδὶ πατρὸς ὃς σὸν ὤλεσεν πόσιν
τολμᾷς ξυνεύδειν καὶ τέκν' αὐθεντῶν πάρα
τίκτειν. τοιοῦτον πᾶν τὸ βάρβαρον γένος·
πατήρ τε θυγατρὶ παῖς τε μητρὶ μείγνυται
175　κόρη τ' ἀδελφῷ, διὰ φόνου δ' οἱ φίλτατοι
χωροῦσι, καὶ τῶνδ' οὐδὲν ἐξείργει νόμος.
ἃ μὴ παρ' ἡμᾶς ἔσφερ'· οὐδὲ γὰρ καλὸν
δυοῖν γυναικοῖν ἄνδρ' ἕν' ἡνίας ἔχειν,
ἀλλ' ἐς μίαν βλέποντες εὐναίαν Κύπριν
180　στέργουσιν, ὅστις μὴ κακῶς οἰκεῖν θέλῃ.

city of Sparta together with a large dowry, and therefore I
may speak my mind. [So it is with these words that I reply
to all of you.]

But though you are a slave woman won by the spear,
you mean to throw me out of this house and take posses-
sion of it: because of your drugs I am hated by my hus-
band, and my womb is perishing unfruitful because of
you. The minds of Asian women are skilled at such
things. But I shall foil your plan: the temple of the
Nereid here, its altar and its sanctuary, will do you no
good, but you will die. If some god or mortal means to
save your life, you must cease from those rich, proud
thoughts you once had and cower in humility, fall at my
feet, and sweep my house, scattering Achelous' water by
hand from my gold-wrought vessels, and know where in
the world you are. There is no Hector here, no Priam or
his gold: this is a Greek city. Yet you, unhappy creature,
are so far gone in folly that you bring yourself to sleep
with the son of the man who killed your husband and to
bear children to a family that has killed your kin. That is
the way all barbarians are: father lies with daughter, son
with mother, and sister with brother, nearest kin murder
each other, and no law prevents any of this. Do not intro-
duce such customs into our city. For it is also not right for
one man to hold the reins of two women. Rather, every-
one who wants to live decently is content to look to a
single mate for his bed.

---

[154] del. Hunger
[172] αὐθεντῶν Heiland: αὐθέντου C

ΧΟΡΟΣ

ἐπίφθονόν τι χρῆμα θηλείας φρενὸς
καὶ ξυγγάμοισι δυσμενὲς μάλιστ' ἀεί.

ΑΝΔΡΟΜΑΧΗ

φεῦ φεῦ·
κακόν γε θνητοῖς τὸ νέον ἔν τε τῷ νέῳ
185   τὸ μὴ δίκαιον ὅστις ἀνθρώπων ἔχει.
ἐγὼ δὲ ταρβῶ μὴ τὸ δουλεύειν μέ σοι
λόγων ἀπώσῃ πόλλ' ἔχουσαν ἔνδικα,
ἢν δ' αὖ κρατήσω, μὴ 'πὶ τῷδ' ὄφλω βλάβην·
οἱ γὰρ πνέοντες μεγάλα τοὺς κρείσσους λόγους
190   πικρῶς φέρουσι τῶν ἐλασσόνων ὕπο.
ὅμως δ' ἐμαυτὴν οὐ προδοῦσ' ἁλώσομαι.
    εἴπ', ὦ νεᾶνι, τῷ σ' ἐχεγγύῳ λόγῳ
πεισθεῖσ' ἀπωθῶ γνησίων νυμφευμάτων;
[ὡς ἡ Λάκαινα τῶν Φρυγῶν μείων πόλις,
195   τύχῃ θ' ὑπερθεῖ, κἄμ' ἐλευθέραν ὁρᾷς;]
199   πότερον ἵν' αὐτὴ παῖδας ἀντὶ σοῦ τέκω
200   δούλους ἐμαυτῇ τ' ἀθλίαν ἐφολκίδα;
196   ἢ τῷ νέῳ τε καὶ σφριγῶντι σώματι
πόλεως τε μεγέθει καὶ φίλοις ἐπηρμένη
198   οἶκον κατασχεῖν τὸν σὸν ἀντὶ σοῦ θέλω;
201   ἢ τοὺς ἐμούς τις παῖδας ἐξανέξεται
Φθίας τυράννους ὄντας, ἢν σὺ μὴ τέκῃς.
φιλοῦσι γάρ μ' Ἕλληνες Ἕκτορός γ' ἄπο.
αὐτή τ' ἀμαυρὰ κοὐ τύραννος ἦ Φρυγῶν;
205   οὐκ ἐξ ἐμῶν σε φαρμάκων στυγεῖ πόσις

ANDROMACHE

CHORUS LEADER

The mind of a woman is a jealous thing and always ill-disposed toward rivals in marriage.

ANDROMACHE

How true it is that youth is a great curse to mankind, especially those of the young who practice injustice! I am afraid that my being your slave will prevent me from speaking, even though my case is strong, and that if I win the argument I may for that very reason suffer harm. Those whose pride is great do not take kindly to hearing superior arguments from their inferiors. Nonetheless I shall not be guilty of betraying my cause.

Tell me, young woman, what was the reliable argument that persuaded me to deprive you of your lawful due as a wife? [Is it that Sparta is a lesser city than Troy, that my fortune surpasses yours, and that you see in me a free woman?] Was it in order that I might bear children instead of you, slaves and miserable dependents to myself? Or is it that, emboldened by a body in the bloom of youth, by the greatness of my city and the support of friends, I mean to possess your house instead of you? Of course people will put up with *my* children as the royal family of Phthia if you do not bear any! For the Greeks love me for Hector's sake! And am I myself obscure and not one of Troy's royal family?

No, it is not because of any drugs of mine that your

---

[190] ἄπο Hermann

[194-5] del., 199–200 ante 196 trai. Kovacs, *HSCP* 81 (1977), 137–48: tradita defendit Goebel, *CP* 84 (1989), 32–5

[203] γ' Jacobs: τ' C, quo servato lac. post h. v. stat. Dindorf

ἀλλ' εἰ ξυνεῖναι μὴ 'πιτηδεία κυρεῖς.
φίλτρον δὲ καὶ τόδ'· οὐ τὸ κάλλος, ὦ γύναι,
ἀλλ' ἀρεταὶ τέρπουσι τοὺς ξυνευνέτας.
σὺ δ' ἤν τι κνισθῇς, ἡ Λάκαινα μὲν πόλις

210 μέγ' ἐστί, τὴν δὲ Σκῦρον οὐδαμοῦ τίθης,
πλουτεῖς δ' ἐν οὐ πλουτοῦσι· Μενέλεως δέ σοι
μείζων Ἀχιλλέως. ταῦτά τοί σ' ἔχθει πόσις.
χρὴ γὰρ γυναῖκα, κἂν κακῷ πόσει δοθῇ,
στέργειν ἅμιλλάν τ' οὐκ ἔχειν φρονήματος.

215 εἰ δ' ἀμφὶ Θρήκην τὴν χιόνι κατάρρυτον
τύραννον ἔσχες ἄνδρ', ἵν' ἐν μέρει λέχος
δίδωσι πολλαῖς εἷς ἀνὴρ κοινούμενος,
ἔκτεινας ἂν τάσδ'; εἶτ' ἀπληστίαν λέχους
πάσαις γυναιξὶ προστιθεῖσ' ἂν ηὑρέθης.

220 αἰσχρόν γε· καίτοι χεῖρον ἀρσένων νόσον
ταύτην νοσοῦμεν, ἀλλὰ προύστημεν καλῶς.
ὦ φίλταθ' Ἕκτορ, ἀλλ' ἐγὼ τὴν σὴν χάριν
σοὶ καὶ ξυνήρων, εἴ τί σε σφάλλοι Κύπρις,
καὶ μαστὸν ἤδη πολλάκις νόθοισι σοῖς

225 ἐπέσχον, ἵνα σοι μηδὲν ἐνδοίην πικρόν.
καὶ ταῦτα δρῶσα τῇ ἀρετῇ προσηγόμην
πόσιν· σὺ δ' οὐδὲ ῥανίδ' ὑπαιθρίας δρόσου
τῷ σῷ προσίζειν ἀνδρὶ δειμαίνουσ' ἐᾷς.
μὴ τὴν τεκοῦσαν τῇ φιλανδρίᾳ, γύναι,

230 ζήτει παρελθεῖν· τῶν κακῶν γὰρ μητέρων
φεύγειν τρόπους χρὴ τέκν' ὅσοις ἔνεστι νοῦς.

215 τὴν χιόνι Blaydes: χιόνι τὴν C

husband dislikes you but because you are not fit to live with. For this too is a love-charm: it is not beauty but goodness that gives a husband pleasure. But if *you* get angry, you argue that Sparta is a great city and Scyros[a] is of no account, that you are a rich woman living in the midst of the poor, and that Menelaus is a greater man than Achilles. It is for this that your husband hates you. A woman, even if given in marriage to a low-born husband, must respect him and not contend with him in pride.

If you had married a king in snow-clad Thrace, where one husband shares his bed in turn among many women, would you have killed them? If so, you would have clearly branded all women with insatiable lust. This is a disgraceful thing. We women suffer worse from this disease than men, but we do well to veil it decently from sight.

Dearest Hector, I even went so far as to help you in your amours, if Aphrodite ever tripped you up, and I often gave the breast to your bastards in order that I might show you no bitterness. By doing this I won my husband's love with my goodness. But you in your fear will not let so much as a drop of water from the open sky fall on your husband. Do not seek to surpass your mother in her man-loving ways, woman. All children who have sense must avoid the paths their wayward mothers went.

[a] See note to line 14 above.

ΧΟΡΟΣ

δέσποιν', ὅσον σοι ῥᾳδίως παρίσταται,
τοσόνδε πείθου τῇδε συμβῆναι λόγοις.

ΕΡΜΙΟΝΗ

τί σεμνομυθεῖς κἀς ἀγῶν' ἔρχῃ λόγων,
235 ὡς δὴ σὺ σώφρων, τἀμὰ δ' οὐχὶ σώφρονα;

ΑΝΔΡΟΜΑΧΗ
236 οὔκουν ἐφ' οἷς γε νῦν καθέστηκας λόγοις.

ΕΡΜΙΟΝΗ
251 ἐκεῖνο λέξον οὗπερ οὕνεκ' ἐστάλην.

ΑΝΔΡΟΜΑΧΗ
252 λέγω σ' ἐγὼ νοῦν οὐκ ἔχειν ὅσον σ' ἔδει.

ΕΡΜΙΟΝΗ
237 ὁ νοῦς ὁ σός μοι μὴ ξυνοικοίη, γύναι.

ΑΝΔΡΟΜΑΧΗ

νέα πέφυκας καὶ λέγεις αἰσχρῶν πέρι.

ΕΡΜΙΟΝΗ

σὺ δ' οὐ λέγεις γε, δρᾷς δέ μ' εἰς ὅσον δύνᾳ.

ΑΝΔΡΟΜΑΧΗ
240 οὐκ αὖ σιωπῇ Κύπριδος ἀλγήσεις πέρι;

ΕΡΜΙΟΝΗ

τί δ'; οὐ γυναιξὶ ταῦτα πρῶτα πανταχοῦ;

235 fort. δὴ φρονοῦσα; τἄμ' ἄρ'
251-2 huc trai. Lee
241 post h. v. lac. stat. Kovacs

294

CHORUS LEADER

My lady, to the extent that you are able to without vexation, to that extent take my advice and come to some agreement with her.

HERMIONE

Why do you take this lofty tone and enter into a contest of words with me, as if you are modest while I am not?

ANDROMACHE

You modest? Not at least to judge from your talk!

HERMIONE

Say now the words I came to you to hear.

ANDROMACHE

I say you do not have the sense you ought.

HERMIONE

What you call sense—never, woman, may it come to dwell under my roof!

ANDROMACHE

You are young and you speak of shameful things.

HERMIONE

And you, though you do not speak of them, do them against me with all your might!

ANDROMACHE

Will you not suffer in silence your troubles in love?

HERMIONE

What? Is not this the first interest of women everywhere?

<ΑΝΔΡΟΜΑΧΗ

οὔκ, ἤν γε μή τις μάργος οὖσα τυγχάνῃ.

ΕΡΜΙΟΝΗ

ἀλλ' οὐ τὰ Κύπριδος δῶρα σεμνὰ καὶ καλά;>

ΑΝΔΡΟΜΑΧΗ

καλῶς γε χρωμέναισιν· εἰ δὲ μή, οὐ καλά.

ΕΡΜΙΟΝΗ

οὐ βαρβάρων νόμοισιν οἰκοῦμεν πόλιν.

ΑΝΔΡΟΜΑΧΗ

κἀκεῖ τά γ' αἰσχρὰ κἀνθάδ' αἰσχύνην ἔχει.

ΕΡΜΙΟΝΗ

245 σοφὴ σοφὴ σύ· κατθανεῖν δ' ὅμως σε δεῖ.

ΑΝΔΡΟΜΑΧΗ

ὁρᾷς ἄγαλμα Θέτιδος ἐς σ' ἀποβλέπον;

ΕΡΜΙΟΝΗ

μισοῦν γε πατρίδα σὴν Ἀχιλλέως φόνῳ.

ΑΝΔΡΟΜΑΧΗ

Ἑλένη νιν ὤλεσ', οὐκ ἐγώ, μήτηρ γε σή.

ΕΡΜΙΟΝΗ

ἦ καὶ πρόσω γὰρ τῶν ἐμῶν ψαύσεις κακῶν;

ΑΝΔΡΟΜΑΧΗ

250 ἰδοὺ σιωπῶ κἀπιλάζυμαι στόμα.

[242] καλῶς a: ναί, καλῶς b   fort. χρωμένοισιν
[248] γε Aldina: δὲ C

ANDROMACHE

<ANDROMACHE

No, not unless the woman is a wanton.

HERMIONE

But are not the gifts of Aphrodite a holy and honorable
thing?>

ANDROMACHE

Yes, for those who make honorable use of them. Other-
wise, they are not.

HERMIONE

We do not live in this city according to barbarian customs.

ANDROMACHE

What's shameful is shameful, here as well as there.

HERMIONE

You're clever, clever! Still, you must be killed.

ANDROMACHE

Do you see Thetis' image, looking at you?

HERMIONE

Yes, hating your country for the death of Achilles.

ANDROMACHE

Helen caused his death, not I: it was *your* mother.

HERMIONE

Are you going to keep on probing my woes?

ANDROMACHE

There, I'm silent and hold my tongue.

ΕΡΜΙΟΝΗ

253 λείψεις τόδ' ἁγνὸν τέμενος ἐναλίας θεοῦ;

ΑΝΔΡΟΜΑΧΗ

εἰ μὴ θανοῦμαί γ'· εἰ δὲ μή, οὐ λείψω ποτέ.

ΕΡΜΙΟΝΗ

255 ὡς τοῦτ' ἄραρε, κοὐ μενῶ πόσιν μολεῖν.

ΑΝΔΡΟΜΑΧΗ

ἀλλ' οὐδ' ἐγὼ μὴν πρόσθεν ἐκδώσω μέ σοι.

ΕΡΜΙΟΝΗ

πῦρ σοι προσοίσω, κοὐ τὸ σὸν προσκέψομαι, . . .

ΑΝΔΡΟΜΑΧΗ

σὺ δ' οὖν κάταιθε· θεοὶ γὰρ εἴσονται τάδε.

ΕΡΜΙΟΝΗ

. . . καὶ χρωτὶ δεινῶν τραυμάτων ἀλγηδόνας.

ΑΝΔΡΟΜΑΧΗ

260 σφάζ', αἵματου θεᾶς βωμόν, ἢ μέτεισί σε.

ΕΡΜΙΟΝΗ

ὦ βάρβαρον σὺ θρέμμα καὶ σκληρὸν θράσος,
ἐγκαρτερεῖς δὴ θάνατον; ἀλλ' ἐγώ σ' ἕδρας
ἐκ τῆσδ' ἑκοῦσαν ἐξαναστήσω τάχα·
τοιόνδ' ἔχω σου δέλεαρ. ἀλλὰ γὰρ λόγους
265 κρύψω, τὸ δ' ἔργον αὐτὸ σημανεῖ τάχα.
κάθησ' ἑδραία· καὶ γὰρ εἰ πέριξ σ' ἔχοι
τηκτὸς μόλυβδος, ἐξαναστήσω σ' ἐγὼ
πρὶν ᾧ πέποιθας παῖδ' Ἀχιλλέως μολεῖν.

ANDROMACHE

HERMIONE
This sacred shrine of the sea goddess, will you leave it?

ANDROMACHE
If I am not to die: otherwise never.

HERMIONE
My mind is fixed. I shall not wait for my husband.

ANDROMACHE
But neither will I surrender before he comes.

HERMIONE
I'll set fire upon you, paying you no heed, . . .

ANDROMACHE
Burn on! The gods will know who is to blame!

HERMIONE
. . . and on your flesh the pain of terrible wounds!

ANDROMACHE
Slay me, bloody the goddess' altar! She'll pursue you!

HERMIONE
O barbarian creature, bold as brass, do you defy death?
Yet I shall soon make you leave this seat willingly: such is
the lure I possess to entice you. But I will say no more,
the event itself will soon make all plain. Sit on! For even
if molten lead all about you should hold you fast, I shall
make you get up before Achilles' son comes, in whom you
trust.

Exit HERMIONE into the house.

ΑΝΔΡΟΜΑΧΗ

πέποιθα. δεινὸν δ' ἑρπετῶν μὲν ἀγρίων
270 ἄκη βροτοῖσι θεῶν καταστῆσαί τινα,
ὃ δ' ἔστ' ἐχίδνης καὶ πυρὸς περαιτέρω
οὐδεὶς γυναικὸς φάρμακ' ἐξηύρηκέ πω
[κακῆς· τοσοῦτόν ἐσμεν ἀνθρώποις κακόν].

ΧΟΡΟΣ

στρ. α

ἦ μεγάλων ἀχέων ἄρ' ὑπῆρξεν, ὅτ' Ἰδαίαν
275 ἐς νάπαν ἦλθ', ὁ Μαί-
ας τε καὶ Διὸς τόκος,
τρίπωλον ἅρμα δαιμόνων
ἄγων τὸ καλλιζυγές,
ἔριδι στυγερᾷ κεκορυθμένον εὐμορφίας
280 σταθμοὺς ἐπὶ βούτας,
βοτῆρά τ' ἀμφὶ μονότροπον νεανίαν
ἔρημόν θ' ἑστιοῦχον αὐλάν.

ἀντ. α

ταὶ δ' ἐπεὶ ὑλόκομον νάπος ἤλυθον οὐρειᾶν
285 πιδάκων νίψαν αἰ-
γλᾶντα σώματα ῥοαῖς,
ἔβαν δὲ Πριαμίδαν ὑπερ-
βολαῖς λόγων δυσφρόνων
παραβαλλόμεναι, δολίοις δ' ἕλε Κύπρις λόγοις,
290 τερπνοῖς μὲν ἀκοῦσαι,
πικρὰν δ' <ἔχουσι> σύγχυσιν βίου πόλει
ταλαίνᾳ περγάμοις τε Τροίας.

300

ANDROMACHE

Yes, in him I trust! It is strange that some god has given man remedies against snakes of the wild, yet where something worse than snake or fire is concerned, no one has yet found the specific against a woman [, a bad one: such a great bane we are to mankind].

CHORUS

Great were the woes—I see it now—that the son of Maia and of Zeus[a] set in motion when he came to Ida's glen with the goddesses three, a lovely team beneath a lovely yoke, helmeted for the contest of beauty, to the shepherd lodge, the solitary young shepherd, and his lonely hearth and home.

When they came to the shady vale, they bathed their radiant bodies in the water of mountain springs. Then they went to the son of Priam vying with each other in excesses of spiteful speech. Aphrodite with deceptive words won the day, words delightful to hear but entailing bitter destruction for the luckless city and citadel of Troy.

---

[a] Hermes, who escorted Hera, Athena, and Aphrodite to Paris to judge their beauty.

---

271 ὃ Seager: ἅ C

273 del. Cobet

280 βούτας Schoene: -τα C

289 δολίοις δ' ἕλε Κύπρις λόγοις Murray: Κύπρις εἷλε λόγοις δολίοις C

291 <ἔχουσι> Jackson   πόλει Jackson: Φρυγῶν πόλει C

στρ. β

εἰ γὰρ ὑπὲρ κεφαλὰν ἔβαλεν κακὸν
ἁ τεκοῦσά νιν μόρον
295 πρὶν Ἰδαῖον κατοικίσαι λέπας,
ὅτε νιν παρὰ θεσπεσίῳ δάφνᾳ
βόασε Κασσάνδρα κτανεῖν,
μεγάλαν Πριάμου πόλεως λώβαν.
τίν' οὐκ ἐπῆλθε, ποῖον οὐκ ἐλίσσετο
300 δαμογερόντων βρέφος φονεύειν;

ἀντ. β

οὔτ' ἂν ἐπ' Ἰλιάσι ζυγὸν ἤλυθε
δούλιον σύ τ' ἄν, γύναι,
τυράννων ἔσχες ἂν δόμων ἕδρας·
παρέλυσε δ' ἂν Ἑλλάδος ἀλγεινοὺς
305 οὓς ἀμφὶ Τρωίαν πόνους
δεκέτεις ἀλάληντο νέοι λόγχαις,
λέχη τ' ἔρημ' ἂν οὔποτ' ἐξελείπετο
καὶ τεκέων ὀρφανοὶ γέροντες.

ΜΕΝΕΛΑΟΣ

ἥκω λαβὼν σὸν παῖδ', ὃν εἰς ἄλλους δόμους
310 λάθρᾳ θυγατρὸς τῆς ἐμῆς ὑπεξέθου.
σὲ μὲν γὰρ ηὔχεις θεᾶς βρέτας σώσειν τόδε,
τοῦτον δὲ τοὺς κρύψαντας· ἀλλ' ἐφηυρέθης
ἧσσον φρονοῦσα τοῦδε Μενέλεω, γύναι.
κεἰ μὴ τόδ' ἐκλιποῦσ' ἐρημώσεις πέδον,
315 ὅδ' ἀντὶ τοῦ σοῦ σώματος σφαγήσεται.
ταῦτ' οὖν λογίζου, πότερα κατθανεῖν θέλεις

Would that the mother who bore him had cast him over her head to an evil end before he came to dwell on a ridge of Ida! Beside the prophetic laurel Cassandra shrieked, bidding her kill the child, great destroyer of Priam's city. Whom did she not approach, which of the city's elders did she not beg to kill the child?

Slavery's yoke would not have come upon the women of Troy and you, woman, would still occupy a royal house. She would have loosed Hellas from grievous toils of ten years' roaming the young men endured in war at Troy. And marriage beds would never have been left desolate nor old men bereft of their children.

Enter by Eisodos A MENELAUS *in armor with his retinue, leading Andromache's son.*

MENELAUS

I have come with your son, whom you sent for safety to another house without my daughter's knowledge. You expected that this statue would save your life and that those who hid him would save his. But it has turned out, woman, that you were less astute than Menelaus here. And if you do not leave this precinct, this boy will be slaughtered in place of you. So consider this, whether

---

293 εἰ γὰρ Paley: ἀλλ' εἴθ' fere C

294 μόρον Hermann: Πάριν C

302 σύ τ' ἄν Pflugk: οὔτ' ἄν σὺ C

303 fort. εἶχες

305 οὓς ἀμφὶ Τρωίαν πόνους post Headlam Murray: μόχθους οὓς ἀμφὶ Τροίαν fere C

311 σώσειν Dobree: σῶσαι C

ἢ τόνδ' ὀλέσθαι σῆς ἁμαρτίας ὕπερ,
ἣν εἰς ἔμ' ἔς τε παῖδ' ἐμὴν ἁμαρτάνεις.

ΑΝΔΡΟΜΑΧΗ

ὦ δόξα δόξα, μυρίοισι δὴ βροτῶν
320   οὐδὲν γεγῶσι βίοτον ὤγκωσας μέγαν.
[εὔκλεια δ' οἷς μέν ἐστ' ἀληθείας ὕπο
εὐδαιμονίζω· τοὺς δ' ὑπὸ ψευδῶν ἔχειν
οὐκ ἀξιώσω, πλὴν τύχῃ φρονεῖν δοκεῖν.]
σὺ δὴ στρατηγῶν λογάσιν Ἑλλήνων ποτὲ
325   Τροίαν ἀφείλου Πρίαμον, ὧδε φαῦλος ὤν;
ὅστις θυγατρὸς ἀντίπαιδος ἐκ λόγων
τοσόνδ' ἔπνευσας καὶ γυναικὶ δυστυχεῖ
δούλῃ κατέστης εἰς ἀγῶν'· οὐκ ἀξιῶ
οὔτ' οὖν σὲ Τροίας οὔτε σοῦ Τροίαν ἔτι.
330   [ἔξωθέν εἰσιν οἱ δοκοῦντες εὖ φρονεῖν
λαμπροί, τὰ δ' ἔνδον πᾶσιν ἀνθρώποις ἴσοι,
πλὴν εἴ τι πλούτῳ· τοῦτο δ' ἰσχύει μέγα.
Μενέλαε, φέρε δὴ διαπεράνωμεν λόγους·
τέθνηκα τῇ σῇ θυγατρὶ καί μ' ἀπώλεσεν·
335   μιαιφόνον μὲν οὐκέτ' ἂν φύγοι μύσος.
ἐν τοῖς δὲ πολλοῖς καὶ σὺ τόνδ' ἀγωνιῇ
φόνον· τὸ συνδρῶν γάρ σ' ἀναγκάσει χρέος.
ἢν δ' οὖν ἐγὼ μὲν μὴ θανεῖν ὑπεκδράμω,
τὸν παῖδά μου κτενεῖτε; κᾆτα πῶς πατὴρ
340   τέκνου θανόντος ῥᾳδίως ἀνέξεται;
οὐχ ὧδ' ἄνανδρον αὐτὸν ἡ Τροία καλεῖ·
ἀλλ' εἰσὶν οἷ χρή, Πηλέως γὰρ ἄξια

you prefer to die or to have this boy killed for the wrongs
you are committing against me and against my daughter.

O renown, renown, countless are the mortals, worthless
men in themselves, whose lives you have puffed to great-
ness! [Those who receive a good name at the hands of
truth I count blessed, while those who derive it from
falsehood I will not deem worthy of it, except that chance
makes them seem intelligent.] Did you, who are such a
petty creature, once serve as general over Greece's troops
and wrest Troy away from Priam? Yet at the word of your
daughter, a mere child, you come in great pride and enter
the fray against a poor slave woman! I regard you no
longer as worthy of Troy or Troy as worthy of you. [It is
from without that those with the reputation for wisdom
are splendid, while from within they are no more than the
rest of humanity except in wealth: yet wealth has great
power. Menelaus, come now, let us converse. Suppose I
have died at your daughter's hand and she has destroyed
me. From that point on she will not escape the pollution
of murder. But in the eyes of the majority you also will be
on trial for this murder, for your complicity will make you
so against your will. But if I escape death, will you kill my
son? And then how will his father cheerfully put up with
his son being killed? Troy does not call him such a cow-
ard. But he will go to all necessary lengths and will make
it clear that his conduct is worthy of Peleus and of his

321–3 del. Hartung
330–51 del. Kovacs (330–2 iam Dobree, 333 Wilamowitz)
337 fort. χερός

πατρός τ' Ἀχιλλέως ἔργα δρῶν φανήσεται,
ὥσει δὲ σὴν παῖδ' ἐκ δόμων· σὺ δ' ἐκδιδοὺς
345 ἄλλῳ τί λέξεις; πότερον ὡς κακὸν πόσιν
φεύγει τὸ ταύτης σῶφρον; ἀλλ' οὐ πείσεται.
γαμεῖ δὲ τίς νιν; ἢ σφ' ἄνανδρον ἐν δόμοις
χήραν καθέξεις πολιόν; ὦ τλήμων ἀνήρ,
κακῶν τοσούτων οὐχ ὁρᾷς ἐπιρροάς;
350 πόσας ἂν εὐνὰς θυγατέρ' ἠδικημένην
βούλοι' ἂν εὑρεῖν ἢ παθεῖν ἁγὼ λέγω;]
οὐ χρὴ 'πὶ μικροῖς μεγάλα πορσύνειν κακὰ
οὐδ', εἰ γυναῖκές ἐσμεν ἀτηρὸν κακόν,
ἄνδρας γυναιξὶν ἐξομοιοῦσθαι φύσιν.
355 ἡμεῖς γὰρ εἰ σὴν παῖδα φαρμακεύομεν
καὶ νηδὺν ἐξαμβλοῦμεν, ὡς αὕτη λέγει,
ἑκόντες οὐκ ἄκοντες, οὐδὲ βώμιοι
πίτνοντες, αὐτοὶ τὴν δίκην ὑφέξομεν
ἐν σοῖσι γαμβροῖς, οἷσιν οὐκ ἐλάσσονα
360 βλάβην ὀφείλω προστιθεῖσ' ἀπαιδίαν.
ἡμεῖς μὲν οὖν τοιοίδε· τῆς δὲ σῆς φρενός,
ἕν σου δέδοικα· διὰ γυναικείαν ἔριν
καὶ τὴν τάλαιναν ὤλεσας Φρυγῶν πόλιν.

ΧΟΡΟΣ

ἄγαν ἔλεξας ὡς γυνὴ πρὸς ἄρσενας,
<τὸ δ' ὀξύθυμον τὴν διάγνωσιν κρατεῖ>
365 καί σου τὸ σῶφρον ἐξετόξευσεν φρενός.

ΜΕΝΕΛΑΟΣ

γύναι, τάδ' ἐστὶ σμικρὰ καὶ μοναρχίας

father Achilles and will expel your daughter from the
house. And if you try to marry her to another husband,
what will you say? That her virtuous nature recoiled from
a bad husband? But he will not believe you. Who will
marry her? Or will you keep her gray-headed and with-
out a mate in your own house? O unhappy man, do you
not see what disasters are rushing upon you? How many
marriage beds would you not see your daughter wronged
in rather than suffer what I am describing?] You should
not repay trifling injuries with great, nor, if we women are
a ruinous evil, should you men imitate our nature. For of
my own accord, willingly and taking no refuge at an altar,
I shall stand trial to determine whether I am poisoning
your daughter and making her womb infertile, as she
claims. My judge shall be your son-in-law, for in his eyes
no less than yours I deserve punishment if I afflict him
with childlessness. Such then am I, but as for your
nature, there is one thing I fear: it was in a quarrel about
a woman that you also destroyed unhappy Troy.

CHORUS LEADER

You have spoken too much as a woman to a man. <Anger
has overcome your good sense> and hurled forth sober
judgment from your mind.

MENELAUS

Woman, these things are, as you say, trifles and not worthy

---

[346] ἀλλ᾽ οὐ πείσεται Pflugk: ἀλλὰ ψεύσεται C
[364] post h.v. lac. stat. Page, suppl. Diggle

οὐκ ἄξι᾿, ὡς φῄς, τῆς ἐμῆς οὐδ᾿ Ἑλλάδος.
εὖ δ᾿ ἴσθ᾿, ὅτου τις τυγχάνει χρείαν ἔχων,
τοῦτ᾿ ἔσθ᾿ ἑκάστῳ μεῖζον ἢ Τροίαν ἑλεῖν.
370 κἀγὼ θυγατρί (μεγάλα γὰρ κρίνω τάδε,
λέχους στέρεσθαι) σύμμαχος καθίσταμαι.
τὰ μὲν γὰρ ἄλλα δεύτερ᾿ ἂν πάσχῃ γυνή,
ἀνδρὸς δ᾿ ἁμαρτάνουσ᾿ ἁμαρτάνει βίου.
δούλων δ᾿ ἐκεῖνον τῶν ἐμῶν ἄρχειν χρεὼν
375 καὶ τῶν ἐκείνου τοὺς ἐμοὺς ἡμᾶς τε πρός·
φίλων γὰρ οὐδὲν ἴδιον, οἵτινες φίλοι
ὀρθῶς πεφύκασ᾿, ἀλλὰ κοινὰ χρήματα.
μένων δὲ τοὺς ἀπόντας, εἰ μὴ θήσομαι
τἄμ᾿ ὡς ἄριστα, φαῦλός εἰμι κοὐ σοφός.
380 ἀλλ᾿ ἐξανίστω τῶνδ᾿ ἀνακτόρων θεᾶς·
ὡς, ἢν θάνῃς σύ, παῖς ὅδ᾿ ἐκφεύγει μόρον,
σοῦ δ᾿ οὐ θελούσης κατθανεῖν τόνδε κτενῶ.
δυοῖν δ᾿ ἀνάγκη θατέρῳ λιπεῖν βίον.

ΑΝΔΡΟΜΑΧΗ

οἴμοι, πικρὰν κλήρωσιν αἵρεσίν τέ μοι
385 βίου καθίστης· καὶ λαχοῦσά γ᾿ ἀθλία
καὶ μὴ λαχοῦσα δυστυχὴς καθίσταμαι.
    ὦ μεγάλα πράσσων αἰτίας σμικρᾶς πέρι,
πιθοῦ· τί καίνεις μ᾿; ἀντὶ τοῦ; ποίαν πόλιν
προύδωκα; τίνα σῶν ἔκτανον παίδων ἐγώ;
390 ποῖον δ᾿ ἔπρησα δῶμ᾿; ἐκοιμήθην βίᾳ
σὺν δεσπόταισι· κᾆτ᾿ ἔμ᾿, οὐ κεῖνον κτενεῖς,
τὸν αἴτιον τῶνδ᾿, ἀλλὰ τὴν ἀρχὴν ἀφεὶς
πρὸς τὴν τελευτὴν ὑστέραν οὖσαν φέρῃ;

of my kingly power or of Greece. But make no mistake, whatever an individual happens to desire, that becomes for him a goal greater than the conquest of Troy. I have come to the aid of my daughter, for I think it is a serious matter to be deprived of one's mate. Any other misfortunes a woman may suffer are secondary, but if she loses her husband she loses her life. Neoptolemus must rule over my slaves, while my daughter (and I with her) must rule over his: friends who are truly friends have no private property but hold all things in common. And if I do not set my own affairs in the best order possible while awaiting those who are absent, I am useless and no wise man.

But get up from this temple of the goddess, since if you die, this boy will escape death, but if you refuse, I will kill him. One of the pair of you must leave this life.

ANDROMACHE

Oh, how painful is the drawing of lots, the choice between lives, you set before me! If I win my life, it means misery, if I lose it, disaster!

Mover of mountains because of trifles, do as I ask! Why do you kill me? For what reason? What city have I betrayed? Which of your children have I killed? What house of yours have I set fire to? I went to bed against my will with my master: will you then kill me rather than him, the one who is to blame? Will you let go the cause and attack the effect that came after?

---

[372] ἂν Musgrave: ἃν C

οἴμοι κακῶν τῶνδ'· ὦ τάλαιν' ἐμὴ πατρίς,
395 ὡς δεινὰ πάσχω. τί δέ με καὶ τεκεῖν ἐχρῆν
396 ἄχθος τ' ἐπ' ἄχθει τῷδε προσθέσθαι διπλοῦν;
404 τί δῆτά μοι ζῆν ἡδύ; πρὸς τί χρὴ βλέπειν;
405 πρὸς τὰς παρούσας ἢ παρελθούσας τύχας;
399 ἥτις σφαγὰς μὲν Ἕκτορος τροχηλάτους
400 κατεῖδον οἰκτρῶς τ' Ἴλιον πυρούμενον,
αὐτὴ δὲ δούλη ναῦς ἐπ' Ἀργείων ἔβην
κόμης ἐπισπασθεῖσ'· ἐπεὶ δ' ἀφικόμην
403 Φθίαν, φονεῦσιν Ἕκτορος νυμφεύομαι.
397 ἀτὰρ τί ταῦτα δύρομαι, τὰ δ' ἐν ποσὶν
398 οὐκ ἐξικμάζω καὶ λογίζομαι κακά;
406 εἷς παῖς ὅδ' ἦν μοι λοιπὸς ὀφθαλμὸς βίου·
τοῦτον κτανεῖν μέλλουσιν οἷς δοκεῖ τάδε.
οὐ δῆτα τοὐμοῦ γ' οὕνεκ' ἀθλίου βίου·
ἐν τῷδε μὲν γὰρ ἐλπίς, εἰ σωθήσεται,
410 ἐμοὶ δ' ὄνειδος μὴ θανεῖν ὑπὲρ τέκνου.
ἰδού, προλείπω βωμὸν ἥδε χειρία
σφάζειν φονεύειν δεῖν ἀπαρτῆσαι δέρην.
ὦ τέκνον, ἡ τεκοῦσά σ', ὡς σὺ μὴ θάνῃς,
στείχω πρὸς Ἅιδην· ἢν δ' ὑπεκδράμῃς μόρον,
415 μέμνησο μητρός, οἷα τλᾶσ' ἀπωλόμην,
καὶ πατρὶ τῷ σῷ διὰ φιλημάτων ἰὼν
δάκρυά τε λείβων καὶ περιπτύσσων χέρας
λέγ' οἷ' ἔπραξα. πᾶσι δ' ἀνθρώποις ἄρ' ἦν
ψυχὴ τέκν'· ὅστις δ' αὔτ' ἄπειρος ὢν ψέγει,
420 ἧσσον μὲν ἀλγεῖ, δυστυχῶν δ' εὐδαιμονεῖ.

O misery! My unhappy fatherland, what suffering is mine! Why did I need to give birth and double the burden I bear? How can life be sweet for me? To what shall I look? To my past or my present fate? I saw Hector dragged to death behind a chariot and Troy put piteously to the torch, and I myself went, pulled by the hair, as a slave to the Argive ships. And when I came to Phthia, I was wedded to Hector's murderers. Yet why do I lament these things but not drain to their last drop the misfortunes immediately before me? My son here was the only light my life possessed: those who think it best are about to kill him. But no, not if my poor life can prevent it! If he survives he bears my hopes, while not to die for my child would be a reproach to me.

She leaves the altar and puts her arms about her son.

There, I leave the altar and am in your hands, to slaughter, murder, imprison, or hang. My child, I, your mother, go to the world below so that you may not die. If you escape death, remember the sufferings your mother endured and the death I died. Kiss your father and embrace him and tell him in tears what I have done. All mankind, it seems, find children their very life. Whoever has no children and disparages them, though he may have less pain, has sorry happiness.

397–8 hos vv. et 404–5 invicem trai. Musgrave
397 ταῦτα δύρομαι Porson: ταῦτ᾽ ὀδύρομαι C

ΧΟΡΟΣ

ᾤκτιρ' ἀκούσασ'· οἰκτρὰ γὰρ τὰ δυστυχῆ
βροτοῖς ἅπασι, κἂν θυραῖος ὢν κυρῇ.
ἐς ξύμβασιν δ' ἐχρῆν σε παῖδα σὴν ἄγειν,
Μενέλαε, καὶ τήνδ', ὡς ἀπαλλαχθῇ πόνων.

ΜΕΝΕΛΑΟΣ

425   λάβεσθέ μοι τῆσδ', ἀμφελίξαντες χέρας,
δμῶες· λόγους γὰρ οὐ φίλους ἀκούσεται.
      ἔχω σ'· ἵν' ἁγνὸν βωμὸν ἐκλίποις θεᾶς,
προύτεινα παιδὸς θάνατον, ᾧ σ' ὑπήγαγον
ἐς χεῖρας ἐλθεῖν τὰς ἐμὰς ἐπὶ σφαγήν.
430   καὶ τἀμφὶ σοῦ μὲν ὧδ' ἔχοντ' ἐπίστασο·
τὰ δ' ἀμφὶ παιδὸς τοῦδε παῖς ἐμὴ κρινεῖ,
ἤν τε κτανεῖν νιν ἤν τε μὴ κτανεῖν θέλῃ.
ἀλλ' ἕρπ' ἐς οἴκους τούσδ', ἵν' εἰς ἐλευθέρους
δούλη γεγῶσα μηκέθ' ὑβρίζειν μάθῃς.

ΑΝΔΡΟΜΑΧΗ

435   οἴμοι· δόλῳ μ' ὑπῆλθες, ἠπατήμεθα.

ΜΕΝΕΛΑΟΣ

κήρυσσ' ἅπασιν· οὐ γὰρ ἐξαρνούμεθα.

ΑΝΔΡΟΜΑΧΗ

ἦ ταῦτ' ἐν ὑμῖν τοῖς παρ' Εὐρώτᾳ σοφά;

ΜΕΝΕΛΑΟΣ

κἀν τοῖς γε Τροίᾳ, τοὺς παθόντας ἀντιδρᾶν.

---

423 παῖδα σὴν Kirchhoff: σὴν παῖδ' a: σήν γε παῖδ' b: καὶ
σὴν παῖδ' c   427 ἔχω Jackson: ἐγώ C

ANDROMACHE

CHORUS LEADER

I hear and feel pity. For misery evokes pity from all mortals, even if the sufferer is no kin. But you, Menelaus, must bring your daughter and this woman to an agreement so that she may escape misfortune.

MENELAUS

Seize her, slaves, bind her hands! For the words she hears will not be welcome.

The slaves seize and bind her.

I've got you! To make you leave the goddess' shrine, I threatened you with the death of your son, and by this means I induced you to surrender and be put to death. That is the way things stand, you may be quite sure, with you. As to your son, my daughter shall decide whether she wants to kill him or not. But go into the house here so that you may learn, slave that you are, to commit no further outrages against the free.

ANDROMACHE

Oh, you have tricked me, I have been deceived!

MENELAUS

Tell the world! I shall not deny it.

ANDROMACHE

Do you dwellers by the Eurotas find this clever?

MENELAUS

Yes, just as do dwellers in Troy: it is called revenge.

---

[434] μηκέθ' Paley: μήποθ'
[438] κἂν Kirchhoff: καὶ C

ΑΝΔΡΟΜΑΧΗ

τὰ θεῖα δ' οὐ θεῖ' οὐδ' ἔχειν ἡγῇ δίκην;

ΜΕΝΕΛΑΟΣ

440 ὅταν τάδ' ᾖ, τότ' οἴσομεν· σὲ δὲ κτενῶ.

ΑΝΔΡΟΜΑΧΗ

ἦ καὶ νεοσσὸν τόνδ', ὑπὸ πτερῶν σπάσας;

ΜΕΝΕΛΑΟΣ

οὐ δῆτα· θυγατρὶ δ', ἢν θέλῃ, δώσω κτανεῖν.

ΑΝΔΡΟΜΑΧΗ

οἴμοι· τί δῆτά σ' οὐ καταστένω, τέκνον;

ΜΕΝΕΛΑΟΣ

οὔκουν θρασεῖά γ' αὐτὸν ἐλπὶς ἀμμένει.

ΑΝΔΡΟΜΑΧΗ

445 ὦ πᾶσιν ἀνθρώποισιν ἔχθιστοι βροτῶν
Σπάρτης ἔνοικοι, δόλια βουλευτήρια,
ψευδῶν ἄνακτες, μηχανορράφοι κακῶν,
ἑλικτὰ κοὐδὲν ὑγιὲς ἀλλὰ πᾶν πέριξ
φρονοῦντες, ἀδίκως εὐτυχεῖτ' ἀν' Ἑλλάδα.
450 τί δ' οὐκ ἐν ὑμῖν ἐστιν; οὐ πλεῖστοι φόνοι;
οὐκ αἰσχροκερδεῖς, οὐ λέγοντες ἄλλα μὲν
γλώσσῃ, φρονοῦντες δ' ἄλλ' ἐφευρίσκεσθ' ἀεί;
ὄλοισθ'. ἐμοὶ μὲν θάνατος οὐχ οὕτω βαρὺς
ὅς σοι δέδοκται· κεῖνα γάρ μ' ἀπώλεσεν,
455 ὅθ' ἡ τάλαινα πόλις ἀνηλώθη Φρυγῶν
πόσις θ' ὁ κλεινός, ὅς σε πολλάκις δορὶ
ναύτην ἔθηκεν ἀντὶ χερσαίου κακόν.

444 ἀμμένει Nauck: ἀναμένει C

ANDROMACHE
Are not the gods divine, do you not think they punish?

MENELAUS
I'll endure that when it comes. Meanwhile I shall kill you.

ANDROMACHE
And kill this young bird, tearing him from beneath my wings?

MENELAUS
Heavens no! I leave *his* death to my daughter!

ANDROMACHE
Ah, ah! Why should I not lament your fate, my son?

MENELAUS
The prospects that await him are certainly not bright.

ANDROMACHE
Dwellers in Sparta, most hateful of mortals in the eyes of all mankind, treacherous plotters, masters of the lie, weavers of deadly wiles, whose thoughts are always devious, nothing that is sound, but all that is twisted, how unjust is the prosperity you enjoy in Greece! What crime is not to be found in your midst? Are there not countless murders? Are you not constantly being unmasked as greedy for gain, with one thing on your lips and another in your heart? My curse upon you! I do not find so heavy the death-sentence you have passed on me. That day brought my life to an end when the unhappy city of Troy was destroyed and my glorious husband killed, my husband whose spear often changed you from a coward on

---

454 ὃς Lenting: ὡς C

νῦν δ' ἐς γυναῖκα γοργὸς ὁπλίτης φανεὶς
κτείνεις μ'. ἀπόκτειν'· ὡς ἀθώπευτόν γέ σε
460 γλώσσης ἀφήσω τῆς ἐμῆς καὶ παῖδα σήν.
ἐπεὶ σὺ μὲν πέφυκας ἐν Σπάρτῃ μέγας,
ἡμεῖς δὲ Τροίᾳ γ'. εἰ δ' ἐγὼ πράσσω κακῶς,
μηδὲν τόδ' αὔχει· καὶ σὺ γὰρ πράξειας ἄν.

ΧΟΡΟΣ

στρ. α
465 οὐδέποτε δίδυμα λέκτρ' ἐπαινέσω βροτῶν
οὐδ' ἀμφιμάτορας κόρους,
ἔριν μελάθρων δυσμενεῖς τε λύπας·
μίαν μοι στεργέτω πόσις γάμοις
470 ἀκοινώνητον ἁμὸς εὐνάν.

ἀντ. α
οὐδέ γ' ἄρα πόλεσι δίπτυχοι τυραννίδες
μιᾶς ἀμείνονες φέρειν,
475 ἄχθος τ' ἐπ' ἄχθει καὶ στάσιν πολίταις·
τεκόντοιν θ' ὕμνον ἐργάταιν δυοῖν
ἔριν Μοῦσαι φιλοῦσι κραίνειν.

στρ. β
πνοαὶ δ' ὅταν φέρωσι ναυτίλους θοαί,
480 κατὰ πηδαλίων διδύμα πραπίδων γνώμα
σοφῶν τε πλῆθος ἀθρόον ἀσθενέστερον
φαυλοτέρας φρενὸς αὐτοκρατοῦς.
ἑνὸς ἄρ' ἄνυσις ἀνά τε μέλαθρα

---

467 ἔριν μελάθρων Reiske: ἔριδας οἴκων C: ἐρινὺν οἴκων
Wecklein   470 ἁμὸς Herwerden: ἀνδρὸς C

land to one on shipboard.[a] And now you appear against a woman in grim warrior garb and are killing me! Kill on! For I shall leave you without uttering one word of truckling flattery to you or your daughter. Though you are great in Sparta, yet I was great in Troy, and if my fortune now is evil, do not make this your boast: yours may be so as well.

Exit MENELAUS *with retinue,* ANDROMACHE, *and Boy into the house.*

CHORUS
Never shall I praise doubleness of marriage among mortals or sons with two mothers. It is strife and hateful pain for a house. May my husband be content in marriage with a single mate and a bed unshared!

For cities, likewise, double kingship[b] is worse than single to endure, grief piled on grief for the citizens and the cause of faction. When two poets produce a hymn, the Muses are wont to work strife between them.

When swift breezes are hurtling sailors along, a double intelligence at the helm and a throng of wise men conjoined is not as effective as a lesser mind with full authority. The execution of affairs in house and in city must

---

[a] I.e. Hector forced Menelaus to take refuge on his ship.

[b] Perhaps an allusion to Sparta, which had two kings in historical times.

---

471 γ’ ἄρα Stinton: γὰρ ἐν C
475 στάσιν Diggle: στάσις C
476 τεκόντοιν θ’ ὕμνον Goram: τεκτόνοιν θ’ ὕμνοιν (vel -οι vel -οις) fere C   480 πηδάλιον Reiske
483 ἄρ’ ἄνυσις Diggle: ἁ δύνασις C

κατά τε πόλιας, ὁπόταν εὑ-
485 ρεῖν θέλωσι καιρόν.

ἀντ. β

ἔδειξεν ἁ Λάκαινα τοῦ στρατηλάτα
Μενέλα· διὰ γὰρ πυρὸς ἦλθ' ἑτέρῳ λέχει,
κτείνει δὲ τὰν τάλαιναν Ἰλιάδα κόραν
490 παῖδά τε δύσφρονος ἀμφ' ἔριδος.
ἄθεος ἄνομος ἄχαρις ὁ φόνος·
ἔτι σε, πότνια, μετατροπὰ
τῶνδ' ἔπεισιν ἔργων.

— καὶ μὴν ἐσορῶ τόδε σύγκρατον
495 ζεῦγος πρὸ δόμων ψήφῳ θανάτου
κατακεκριμένον.
δύστηνε γύναι, τλῆμον δὲ σὺ παῖ,
μητρὸς λεχέων ὃς ὑπερθνῄσκεις
οὐδὲν μετέχων
500 οὐδ' αἴτιος ὢν βασιλεῦσιν.

ΑΝΔΡΟΜΑΧΗ

στρ.

ἅδ' ἐγὼ χέρας αἱματη-
ρὰς βρόχοισι κεκλημένα
πέμπομαι κατὰ γαίας.

ΠΑΙΣ

μᾶτερ μᾶτερ, ἐγὼ δὲ σᾷ
505 πτέρυγι συγκαταβαίνω.

490 ἀμφ' ἔριδος Hermann: ἔριδος ὕπερ C

belong to a single man if men wish to find their true
advantage.

This is proved by the Spartan woman, daughter of
Menelaus the commander. She raged like fire against her
rival and is putting to death the poor Trojan girl and her
son because of hateful strife. Godless, lawless, graceless
is this murder. Some day, my lady, retribution for these
deeds will come upon you!

Enter from the house ANDROMACHE *and* BOY, *bound, fol-
lowed by* MENELAUS *and his retinue. Menelaus holds a
drawn sword.*

CHORUS LEADER
Look, I see this pair close joined, before the palace under
sentence of death. Poor woman! And you, my child, how
luckless you are, put to death because of your mother's
bed, though you have no share of blame in the eyes of our
masters!

ANDROMACHE[a]
Here am I, hands bloodied with the tight bonds about
them, being sent down to death!

BOY
Mother, O mother, under your wing I go down as well!

[a] From here until 544 Andromache and the Boy sing, and
Menelaus' replies are spoken or chanted anapests.

504n Παῖς Murray: Μολοττός C

ΑΝΔΡΟΜΑΧΗ

θῦμα δάιον, ὦ χθονὸς
Φθίας κράντορες.

ΠΑΙΣ

ὦ πάτερ,
μόλε φίλοις ἐπίκουρος.

ΑΝΔΡΟΜΑΧΗ

510 κείσῃ δή, τέκνον ὦ φίλος,
μαστοῖς ματέρος ἀμφὶ σᾶς
νεκρὸς ὑπὸ χθονὶ σὺν νεκρῷ <τε>.

ΠΑΙΣ

ὤμοι μοι, τί πάθω; τάλας
δῆτ' ἐγὼ σύ τε, μᾶτερ.

ΜΕΝΕΛΑΟΣ

515 ἴθ' ὑποχθόνιοι· καὶ γὰρ ἀπ' ἐχθρῶν
ἥκετε πύργων. δύο δ' ἐκ δισσαῖν
θνήσκετ' ἀνάγκαιν· σὲ μὲν ἡμετέρα
ψῆφος ἀναιρεῖ, παῖδα δ' ἐμὴ παῖς
τόνδ' Ἑρμιόνη· καὶ γὰρ ἀνοία
520 μεγάλη λείπειν ἐχθροὺς ἐχθρῶν,
ἐξὸν κτείνειν
καὶ φόβον οἴκων ἀφελέσθαι.

ΑΝΔΡΟΜΑΧΗ

ἀντ.

ὦ πόσις πόσις, εἴθε σὰν
χεῖρα καὶ δόρυ σύμμαχον
525 κτησαίμαν, Πριάμου παῖ.

ANDROMACHE

ANDROMACHE
This is a cruel sacrifice, O rulers of Phthia!

BOY
Father, come and help those you love!

ANDROMACHE
Dear child, you will lie below dead with your dead mother, next to her breast!

BOY
Ah me! What will become of me? Unhappy are we, you and I, mother!

MENELAUS
Go down to the Underworld! For it is from an enemy city that you have come. The two of you die by two votes: it is my sentence that puts you to death, while your son's death is the work of my daughter Hermione. It is sheer folly to leave alive enemies, the offspring of enemies, when by killing them you can free your house from fear.

ANDROMACHE
O husband, husband, Priam's son, how I wish I could gain your hand and spear as ally!

---

512 <τε> Aldina

ΠΑΙΣ

δύστανος, τί δ' ἐγὼ μόρου
παράτροπον μέλος εὕρω;

ΑΝΔΡΟΜΑΧΗ

λίσσου γούνασι δεσπότου
χρίμπτων, ὦ τέκνον.

ΠΑΙΣ

530   ὦ φίλος
φίλος, ἄνες θάνατόν μοι.

ΑΝΔΡΟΜΑΧΗ

λείβομαι δάκρυσιν κόρας,
στάζω λισσάδος ὡς πέτρας
λιβὰς ἀνάλιος, ἁ τάλαινα.

ΠΑΙΣ

535   ὤμοι μοι, τί δ' ἐγὼ κακῶν
μῆχος ἐξανύσωμαι;

ΜΕΝΕΛΑΟΣ

τί με προσπίτνεις, ἁλίαν πέτραν
ἢ κῦμα λιταῖς ὡς ἱκετεύων;
τοῖς γὰρ ἐμοῖσιν γέγον' ὠφελία,
540   σοὶ δ' οὐδὲν ἔχω φίλτρον, ἐπεί τοι
μέγ' ἀναλώσας ψυχῆς μόριον
Τροίαν εἷλον καὶ μητέρα σήν·
ἧς ἀπολαύων
Ἅιδην χθόνιον καταβήσῃ.

ANDROMACHE

BOY

Unhappy mother, what song shall I find to ward off death?

ANDROMACHE

Plead with your master, touching his knees, my child!

He kneels before Menelaus.

BOY

Dear friend, dear friend, spare my life!

ANDROMACHE

My eyes are bathed in tears, I pour them forth, unlucky woman, as a spring in a sunless place sends its water down a smooth cliff.

BOY

O alas! How long must I suffer pain?

MENELAUS

Why do you fall before me, entreating me when I am like some sea-beaten cliff or ocean wave? I help my kin, but I have no cause to love you since I expended a great part of my soul in capturing Troy and with it your mother. It is thanks to her that you now go down to the Underworld!

Enter by Eisodos A PELEUS, helped by the Maidservant sent by Andromache.

ΧΟΡΟΣ

545 καὶ μὴν δέδορκα τόνδε Πηλέα πέλας,
σπουδῇ τιθέντα δεῦρο γηραιὸν πόδα.

ΠΗΛΕΥΣ

ὑμᾶς ἐρωτῶ τόν τ᾽ ἐφεστῶτα σφαγῇ,
τί ταῦτα, πῶς ταῦτ᾽; ἐκ τίνος λόγου νοσεῖ
δόμος; τί πράσσετ᾽ ἄκριτα μηχανώμενοι;
550 Μενέλα᾽, ἐπίσχες· μὴ τάχυν᾽ ἄνευ δίκης.
ἡγοῦ σὺ θᾶσσον, οὐ γὰρ ὡς ἔοικέ μοι
σχολῆς τόδ᾽ ἔργον, ἀλλ᾽ ἀνηβητηρίαν
ῥώμην με καιρὸς λαμβάνειν, εἴπερ ποτέ.
πρῶτον μὲν οὖν κατ᾽ οὖρον ὥσπερ ἱστίοις
555 ἐμπνεύσομαι τῇδ᾽· εἰπέ, τίνι δίκῃ χέρας
βρόχοισιν ἐκδήσαντες οἵδ᾽ ἄγουσί σε
καὶ παῖδ᾽; ὕπαρνος γάρ τις οἷς ἀπόλλυσαι,
ἡμῶν ἀπόντων τοῦ τε κυρίου σέθεν.

ΑΝΔΡΟΜΑΧΗ

οἶδ᾽, ὦ γεραιέ, σὺν τέκνῳ θανουμένην
560 ἄγουσί μ᾽ οὕτως ὡς ὁρᾷς. τί σοι λέγω;
οὐ γὰρ μιᾶς σε κληδόνος προθυμίᾳ
μετῆλθον ἀλλὰ μυρίων ὑπ᾽ ἀγγέλων.
ἔριν δὲ τὴν κατ᾽ οἶκον οἶσθά που κλύων
τῆς τοῦδε θυγατρός, ὧν τ᾽ ἀπόλλυμαι χάριν.
565 καὶ νῦν με βωμοῦ Θέτιδος, ἣ τὸν εὐγενῆ
ἔτικτέ σοι παῖδ᾽, ἣν σὺ θαυμαστὴν σέβεις,
ἄγουσ᾽ ἀποσπάσαντες, οὔτε τῳ δίκῃ
κρίναντες οὔτε τοὺς ἀπόντας ἐκ δόμων

CHORUS LEADER

But look, I see Peleus not far off, hastening his aged steps hither.

PELEUS

You men there, I ask you, and you who are overseeing this slaughter: what is going on, how has it come about? What is the cause of the house's sickness? What are you doing plotting death without trial? Menelaus, stop! Do not hasten on an unjust course!

(to Maidservant) Lead me on more quickly, for this is not, I think, the task of a leisured moment: it is time now, if ever, to recover the strength of my youth. First I shall blow a favoring breeze on this woman's sails: tell me, on what charge do these men bind your hands fast in bonds and lead you and your son off? For you are being put to death like some ewe with her lamb while I and your master are away.

ANDROMACHE

These men, old sir, are taking me and my son away to die, just as you see. What am I to tell you? It was not by a single eager summons that I sent for you but by countless messengers. No doubt you have heard of the contentious rivalry of this man's daughter in our house and why I am being killed. Now they are taking me away and have dragged me off from the altar of Thetis, who bore you your noble son and whom you hold in reverence. They did not try me on any charge or wait for the arrival of

---

553 με καιρὸς Paley: μ' ἐπαινῶ vel ἐπαινῶ C
557 οἷς Hartung: ὣς C
568 οὔτε Lenting: οὐδὲ C

μείναντες, ἀλλὰ τὴν ἐμὴν ἐρημίαν
570 γνόντες τέκνου τε τοῦδ᾽, ὃν οὐδὲν αἴτιον
μέλλουσι σὺν ἐμοὶ τῇ ταλαιπώρῳ κτανεῖν.
    ἀλλ᾽ ἀντιάζω σ᾽, ὦ γέρον, τῶν σῶν πάρος
πίτνουσα γονάτων—χειρὶ δ᾽ οὐκ ἔξεστί μοι
τῆς σῆς λαβέσθαι φιλτάτης γενειάδος—
575 ῥῦσαί με πρὸς θεῶν· εἰ δὲ μή, θανούμεθα
αἰσχρῶς μὲν ὑμῖν, δυστυχῶς δ᾽ ἐμοί, γέρον.

ΠΗΛΕΥΣ

χαλᾶν κελεύω δεσμὰ πρὶν κλαίειν τινά,
καὶ τῆσδε χεῖρας διπτύχους ἀνιέναι.

ΜΕΝΕΛΑΟΣ

ἐγὼ δ᾽ ἀπαυδῶ, τἄλλα τ᾽ οὐχ ἥσσων σέθεν
580 καὶ τῆσδε πολλῷ κυριώτερος γεγώς.

ΠΗΛΕΥΣ

πῶς; ἦ τὸν ἁμὸν οἶκον οἰκήσεις μολὼν
δεῦρ᾽; οὐχ ἅλις σοι τῶν κατὰ Σπάρτην κρατεῖν;

ΜΕΝΕΛΑΟΣ

εἷλόν νιν αἰχμάλωτον ἐκ Τροίας ἐγώ.

ΠΗΛΕΥΣ

οὑμὸς δέ γ᾽ αὐτὴν ἔλαβε παῖς παιδὸς γέρας.

ΜΕΝΕΛΑΟΣ

585 οὔκουν ἐκείνου τἀμὰ τἀκείνου τ᾽ ἐμά;

ΠΗΛΕΥΣ

δρᾶν <γ᾽> εὖ, κακῶς δ᾽ οὔ, μηδ᾽ ἀποκτείνειν βίᾳ.

[586] δρᾶν Lascaris: ναί, δρᾶν C   <γ᾽> Lenting

those who are abroad since they knew my weakness and that of this child here. They are about to kill him, guiltless though he is, along with me, his unhappy mother.

She falls to the ground before Peleus.

But I entreat you, old sir, falling before your knees—for I cannot touch your beloved chin with my hand—save me, in the gods' name! Otherwise I shall die, sir, with disgrace to your family and misery for me.

PELEUS
(to the servants holding Andromache and the Boy) I order you to loosen her bonds and to release this woman's hands before someone pays for this!

MENELAUS
And I say don't, and I am in other ways your superior and have much more authority over her.

PELEUS
What? Will you come here and run my household? Is it not enough to lord it over Sparta?

MENELAUS
It was I who took her captive from Troy.

PELEUS
Yes, but my grandson received her as his prize of valor.

MENELAUS
Are not my possessions his and his mine?

PELEUS
Yes, to treat well, not ill, and not to kill by the sword.

EURIPIDES

ΜΕΝΕΛΑΟΣ

ὡς τήνδ' ἀπάξεις οὔποτ' ἐξ ἐμῆς χερός.

ΠΗΛΕΥΣ

σκήπτρῳ γε τῷδε σὸν καθαιμάξας κάρα.

ΜΕΝΕΛΑΟΣ

ψαῦσόν θ', ἵν' εἰδῇς, καὶ πέλας πρόσελθέ μου.

ΠΗΛΕΥΣ

590   σὺ γὰρ μετ' ἀνδρῶν, ὦ κάκιστε κὰκ κακῶν;
        [σοὶ ποῦ μέτεστιν ὡς ἐν ἀνδράσιν λόγου;]
        ὅστις πρὸς ἀνδρὸς Φρυγὸς ἀφῃρέθης λέχος,
        ἄκληστ' †ἄδουλα δώμαθ' ἑστίας† λιπών,
        ὡς δὴ γυναῖκα σώφρον' ἐν δόμοις ἔχων
595   πασῶν κακίστην. οὐδ' ἂν εἰ βούλοιτό τις
        σώφρων γένοιτο Σπαρτιατίδων κόρη·
        αἳ ξὺν νέοισιν ἐξερημοῦσαι δόμους
        γυμνοῖσι μηροῖς καὶ πέπλοις ἀνειμένοις
        δρόμους παλαίστρας τ' οὐκ ἀνασχετῶς ἐμοὶ
600   κοινὰς ἔχουσι. κᾆτα θαυμάζειν χρεὼν
        εἰ μὴ γυναῖκας σώφρονας παιδεύετε;
        Ἑλένην ἐρέσθαι χρὴ τάδ', ἥτις ἐκ δόμων
        τὸν σὸν λιποῦσα Φίλιον ἐξεκώμασεν
        νεανίου μετ' ἀνδρὸς εἰς ἄλλην χθόνα.
605   κἄπειτ' ἐκείνης οὕνεχ' Ἑλλήνων ὄχλον
        τοσόνδ' ἀθροίσας ἤγαγες πρὸς Ἴλιον;
        ἣν χρῆν σ' ἀποπτύσαντα μὴ κινεῖν δόρυ,

588 γε Lenting: δὲ fere C   καθαιμάξας Pflugk: -ξω C

328

MENELAUS

Know this: you will never take her from my hand!

PELEUS

Yes I will, when I have bloodied your head with this scepter!

MENELAUS

Come over here and touch me: you'll find out!

PELEUS

What, do you belong with the men then, you utter coward? [How do you have any claim to esteem among men?] You were deprived of your wife by a mere Phrygian since you left your house unlocked and unguarded, believing you had a chaste wife in your house, when in fact she was the most wanton of women. Not even if she wanted to could a Spartan girl be chaste. They leave their houses in the company of young men, with bare thighs and loosened tunics, and in a fashion I cannot stand they share the same running tracks and wrestling places with them. After that is it any wonder that you do not bring up women to be chaste? You should ask Helen this question: she left your house behind and your Kindred Zeus[a] and went off on a revel with a young man to another country. Was it for *her* sake, then, that you mustered such a great throng and took them to Troy? You ought to have spat her

---

[a] Zeus Philios, Zeus of Kindred, is the patron of all ties of affection.

---

591 v. del. Herwerden
592 ἀφῃρέθης Kovacs: ἀπηλλάγης C
599 ἀνασχετῶς Naber: -τοὺς vel -τὰς C

κακὴν ἐφευρόντ', ἀλλ' ἐᾶν αὐτοῦ μένειν
μισθόν τε δόντα μήποτ' εἰς οἴκους λαβεῖν.
610 ἀλλ' οὔτι ταύτῃ σὸν φρόνημ' ἐπούρισας,
ψυχὰς δὲ πολλὰς κἀγαθὰς ἀπώλεσας
παίδων τ' ἄπαιδας γραῦς ἔθηκας ἐν δόμοις
πολιούς τ' ἀφείλου πατέρας εὐγενῆ τέκνα.
ὧν εἷς ἐγὼ δύστηνος· αὐθέντην δέ σε
615 μιάστορ' ὥς τιν' ἐσδέδορκ' Ἀχιλλέως.
ὃς οὐδὲ τρωθεὶς ἦλθες ἐκ Τροίας μόνος,
κάλλιστα τεύχη δ' ἐν καλοῖσι σάγμασιν
ὅμοι' ἐκεῖσε δεῦρό τ' ἤγαγες πάλιν.
κἀγὼ μὲν ηὔδων τῷ γαμοῦντι μήτε σοὶ
620 κῆδος ξυνάψαι μήτε δώμασιν λαβεῖν
κακῆς γυναικὸς πῶλον· ἐκφέρουσι γὰρ
μητρῷ' ὀνείδη. τοῦτο καὶ σκοπεῖτέ μοι,
μνηστῆρες, ἐσθλῆς θυγατέρ' ἐκ μητρὸς λαβεῖν.
   πρὸς τοῖσδε δ' εἰς ἀδελφὸν οἷ' ἐφύβρισας,
625 σφάξαι κελεύσας θυγατέρ' εὐηθέστατα·
οὕτως ἔδεισας μὴ οὐ κακὴν δάμαρτ' ἔχοις;
ἑλὼν δὲ Τροίαν (εἶμι γὰρ κἀνταῦθά σοι)
οὐκ ἔκτανες γυναῖκα χειρίαν λαβών,
ἀλλ', ὡς ἐσεῖδες μαστόν, ἐκβαλὼν ξίφος
630 φίλημ' ἐδέξω, προδότιν αἰκάλλων κύνα,
ἥσσων πεφυκὼς Κύπριδος, ὦ κάκιστε σύ.
κἄπειτ' ἐς οἴκους τῶν ἐμῶν ἐλθὼν τέκνων
πορθεῖς ἀπόντων, καὶ γυναῖκα δυστυχῆ
κτείνεις ἀτίμως παῖδά θ', ὃς κλαίοντά σε
635 καὶ τὴν ἐν οἴκοις σὴν καταστήσει κόρην,

away without stirring a single spear once you had discovered her betrayal, should have let her stay in Troy, should have paid her a wage and never taken her back! But your mind did not make in this direction: rather, you lost lives many and brave, left old women at home bereft of their sons, and robbed gray-headed fathers of their noble children. Of these fathers I, unlucky man, am one, and I regard you as the murderer of Achilles, stained with defilement. You alone came back from Troy without a scratch, and you took your fine armor in its fine case to Troy and brought it back in the same condition. I told Neoptolemus when he was about to marry not to make a marriage alliance with you or take into his house the foal of such a base mother. For such daughters reproduce their mothers' faults. Take heed, suitors, to get the daughter of a good mother!

Furthermore, what an outrage you committed against your brother, ordering him to kill his daughter most foolishly! Were you so afraid that you would not recover your worthless wife? And when you had taken Troy (for I shall go there also in my argument), you did not kill your wife when you had her in your power, but when you saw her breasts, you threw away your sword and kissed the traitorous bitch and fawned on her, proving no match, coward that you are, for Aphrodite's power. On top of this you come into the house of my grandson and plunder it in his absence and commit dishonorable murder on a poor woman and a boy. This boy will make you smart for it, you and your daughter in the house, though he be three times

κεἰ τρὶς νόθος πέφυκε· πολλάκις δέ τοι
ξηρὰ βαθεῖαν γῆν ἐνίκησε σπορᾷ,
νόθοι τε πολλοὶ γνησίων ἀμείνονες.
ἀλλ᾽ ἐκκομίζου παῖδα. κύδιον βροτοῖς
640   πένητα χρηστὸν ἢ κακὸν καὶ πλούσιον
γαμβρὸν πεπᾶσθαι καὶ φίλον· σὺ δ᾽ οὐδὲν εἶ.

ΧΟΡΟΣ

σμικρᾶς ἀπ᾽ ἀρχῆς νεῖκος ἀνθρώποις μέγα
γλῶσσ᾽ ἐκπορίζει· τοῦτο δ᾽ οἱ σοφοὶ βροτῶν
ἐξευλαβοῦνται, μὴ φίλοις τεύχειν ἔριν.

ΜΕΝΕΛΑΟΣ

645   τί δῆτ᾽ ἂν εἴποις τοὺς γέροντας ὡς σοφοί,
647   ὅτ᾽ ὢν σὺ Πηλεὺς καὶ πατρὸς κλεινοῦ γεγὼς
646   κἀς τοὺς φρονεῖν δοκοῦντας Ἕλλησίν ποτε
κῆδος συνάψας, αἰσχρὰ μὲν σαυτῷ λέγεις
ἡμῖν δ᾽ ὀνείδη διὰ γυναῖκα βάρβαρον,
650   ἣν χρῆν σ᾽ ἐλαύνειν τήνδ᾽ ὑπὲρ Νείλου ῥοὰς
ὑπέρ τε Φᾶσιν, κἀμὲ παρακαλεῖν ἅμα,
οὖσαν μὲν ἠπειρῶτιν, οὗ πεσήματα
πλεῖσθ᾽ Ἑλλάδος πέπτωκε δοριπετῆ νεκρῶν,
τοῦ σοῦ τε παιδὸς αἵματος κοινουμένην.
655   [Πάρις γάρ, ὃς σὸν παῖδ᾽ ἔπεφν᾽ Ἀχιλλέα,
Ἕκτορος ἀδελφὸς ἦν, δάμαρ δ᾽ ἥδ᾽ Ἕκτορος.]
καὶ τῇδέ γ᾽ εἰσέρχῃ σὺ ταὐτὸν ἐς στέγος
καὶ ξυντράπεζον ἀξιοῖς ἔχειν βίον,

647 ante 646 trai. Kovacs
646 κἀς Kovacs: καὶ C

bastard. For just as stony ground often surpasses deep soil in its produce, so bastards are often better men than legitimate sons. But take your daughter away. It is more creditable for mortals to have relations and friends who are poor and honest rather than rich and base. And you are a nobody!

CHORUS LEADER

From trivial causes the tongue brings about great quarrels for men. Mortals who are wise take care not to wrangle with their kin.

MENELAUS

How can one maintain that old men are wise, when you, Peleus, son of a famous father[a] and connected by marriage with those who were once renowned among the Greeks for wisdom,[b] utter words that are disgraceful to yourself and reproachful to me on account of a barbarian woman? You ought to be driving her off to a place beyond the Nile or the Phasis—and asking for my help at it too—since she is from Asia, where so many Greeks fell in battle, and she shares in the death of your son. [For Paris, who slew your son Achilles, was Hector's brother, and she was Hector's wife.] Yet you share the same roof with her, you think it right to have her at your table, and

[a] Aeacus, son of Zeus, who was famed for his justice and became one of the judges in the Underworld.

[b] I.e. himself, since he was the leader of the Trojan expedition.

---

651 ἅμα Schenkl: ἀεί C
655–6 del. Nauck

τίκτειν δ' ἐν οἴκοις παῖδας ἐχθίστους ἐᾷς.
660 κἀγὼ προνοίᾳ τῇ τε σῇ κἀμῇ, γέρον,
κτανεῖν θέλων τήνδ' ἐκ χερῶν ἁρπάζομαι.
καίτοι φέρ'· ἅψασθαι γὰρ οὐκ αἰσχρὸν λόγου·
ἦν παῖς μὲν ἡμὴ μὴ τέκῃ, ταύτης δ' ἄπο
βλάστωσι παῖδες, τούσδε γῆς Φθιώτιδος
665 στήσεις τυράννους, βάρβαροι δ' ὄντες γένος
Ἕλλησιν ἄρξουσ'; εἶτ' ἐγὼ μὲν οὐ φρονῶ
μισῶν τὰ μὴ δίκαια, σοὶ δ' ἔνεστι νοῦς;
[κἀκεῖνο νῦν ἄθρησον· εἰ σὺ παῖδα σὴν
δούς τῳ πολιτῶν, εἶτ' ἔπασχε τοιάδε,
670 σιγῇ καθῆσ' ἄν; οὐ δοκῶ· ξένης δ' ὕπερ
τοιαῦτα λάσκεις τοὺς ἀναγκαίους φίλους;
καὶ μὴν ἴσον γ' ἀνήρ τε καὶ γυνὴ στένει
ἀδικουμένη πρὸς ἀνδρός· ὡς δ' αὔτως ἀνὴρ
γυναῖκα μωραίνουσαν ἐν δόμοις ἔχων.
675 καὶ τῷ μὲν ἔστιν ἐν χεροῖν μέγα σθένος,
τῇ δ' ἐν γονεῦσι καὶ φίλοις τὰ πράγματα.
οὔκουν δίκαιον τοῖς γ' ἐμοῖς ἐπωφελεῖν;]
γέρων γέρων εἶ. τὴν δ' ἐμὴν στρατηγίαν
λέγων ἔμ' ὠφελοῖς ἂν ἢ σιγῶν πλέον.
680 Ἑλένη δ' ἐμόχθησ' οὐχ ἑκοῦσ' ἀλλ' ἐκ θεῶν,
καὶ τοῦτο πλεῖστον ὠφέλησεν Ἑλλάδα·
ὅπλων γὰρ ὄντες καὶ μάχης ἄιστορες
ἔβησαν ἐς τἀνδρεῖον· ἡ δ' ὁμιλία
πάντων βροτοῖσι γίγνεται διδάσκαλος.
685 εἰ δ' ἐς πρόσοψιν τῆς ἐμῆς ἐλθὼν ἐγὼ
γυναικὸς ἔσχον μὴ κτανεῖν, ἐσωφρόνουν.

you allow her to give birth in your house to children who
are your bitterest enemies. When I, in forethought for
you and for me, try to kill her, she is snatched from my
hands. Yet come now (it is no shame to touch on this
point): if my daughter is childless and this woman has
children, will you set them up as kings over the land of
Phthia, and will they, barbarians by birth, rule over
Greeks? Can you maintain after this that I, who hate
what is not proper, am lacking in judgment, while it is you
that have sense? [Now consider this point too. If you had
given your daughter to one of your fellow citizens and she
had suffered this kind of treatment, would you sit by in
silence? I do not think so. Yet do you, on behalf of a for-
eigner, shout such things at your close kin? Further, a
woman groans as much as a man when she is wronged by
her mate; so too a man groans when he has a wayward
wife in his house. The man's strength lies in his hands,
while the woman's interests are defended by her parents
and kin. Am I not right then to come to the aid of my
own?] You are an old, old man. And when you mention
my generalship, you help my case more than by saying
nothing. Helen got into trouble not of her own accord
but by the will of the gods, and this was of very great ben-
efit to Hellas. For the Greeks, who were ignorant of
weapons and battle, proceeded to deeds of valor: associa-
tion is the teacher of all things to mortals. But if I fore-
bore to kill my wife, when I came face to face with her,

---

660 κἀγὼ Kirchhoff: ἀγὼ C
664 τούσδε Brunck: τῆσδε C
668–77 del. Hirzel
672 στένει Bothe: σθένει C

οὐδ' ἂν σὲ Φῶκον ἤθελον κατακτανεῖν.

   ταῦτ' εὖ φρονῶν σ' ἐπῆλθον, οὐκ ὀργῆς χάριν·
ἦν δ' ὀξυθυμῇ, σοὶ μὲν ἡ γλωσσαλγία
690   μείζων, ἐμοὶ δὲ κέρδος ἡ προμηθία.

ΧΟΡΟΣ

παύσασθον ἤδη—λῷστα γὰρ μακρῷ τάδε—
λόγων ματαίων, μὴ δύο σφαλῆθ' ἅμα.

ΠΗΛΕΥΣ

οἴμοι, καθ' Ἑλλάδ' ὡς κακῶς νομίζεται·
ὅταν τροπαῖα πολεμίων στήσῃ στρατός,
695   οὐ τῶν πονούντων τοὔργον ἡγοῦνται τόδε,
ἀλλ' ὁ στρατηγὸς τὴν δόκησιν ἄρνυται,
ὃς εἷς μετ' ἄλλων μυρίων πάλλων δόρυ,
οὐδὲν πλέον δρῶν ἑνός, ἔχει πλείω λόγον.
[σεμνοὶ δ' ἐν ἀρχαῖς ἥμενοι κατὰ πτόλιν
700   φρονοῦσι δήμου μεῖζον, ὄντες οὐδένες·
οἱ δ' εἰσὶν αὐτῶν μυρίῳ σοφώτεροι,
εἰ τόλμα προσγένοιτο βούλησίς θ' ἅμα.]
ὡς καὶ σὺ σός τ' ἀδελφὸς ἐξωγκωμένοι
Τροίᾳ κάθησθε τῇ τ' ἐκεῖ στρατηγίᾳ,
705   μόχθοισιν ἄλλων καὶ πόνοις ἐπηρμένοι.
δείξω δ' ἐγώ σοι μὴ τὸν Ἰδαῖον Πάριν
μείζω νομίζειν Πηλέως ἐχθρόν ποτε,
εἰ μὴ φθερῇ τῆσδ' ὡς τάχιστ' ἀπὸ στέγης
καὶ παῖς ἄτεκνος, ἣν ὅ γ' ἐξ ἡμῶν γεγὼς

₆₈₉ ὀξυθυμῇ Cobet: -θυμῆς C
_{699–702} del. Busche

that was self-control. I could wish that you had not killed Phocus either.[a]

I have confronted you on these points in good will toward you, not out of anger. But if you show a hot temper, you only make yourself more hoarse, whereas my forethought is a gain to me.

CHORUS LEADER
Cease from these foolish words, both of you—this is by far the best course—lest you fall together.

PELEUS
Oh, how perverse customs are in Greece! When the army sets up trophies over an enemy, people do not regard this as the deed of those who have done the work. Instead the general receives the honor. He brandished his spear as one man among countless others and did no more than a single warrior, yet he gets more credit. [And sitting arrogantly in office in the city they think grander thoughts than the common people, though they are worthless. The people would be far superior to them in wisdom if they acquired daring and will.] It is in this fashion that you and your brother sit puffed up over Troy and your generalship there, made arrogant by the toils and labors of others. But I will teach you not to regard Paris of Ida a greater enemy than Peleus unless you clear off from this house at once, you and your barren daughter! My grandson will

[a] Peleus and his brother Telamon killed their half-brother Phocus, son of Aeacus by a nymph.

---

709 ὅ γ' L. Dindorf: ὅδ' C

710 ἐλᾷ δι' οἴκων τῶνδ' ἐπισπάσας κόμης,
    εἰ στερρὸς οὖσα μόσχος οὐκ ἀνέξεται
    τίκτοντας ἄλλους, οὐκ ἔχουσ' αὐτὴ τέκνα.
    ἀλλ', εἰ τὸ κείνης δυστυχεῖ παίδων πέρι,
    ἄπαιδας ἡμᾶς δεῖ καταστῆναι τέκνων;
715 φθείρεσθε τῆσδε, δμῶες, ὡς ἂν ἐκμάθω
    εἴ τίς με λύειν τῆσδε κωλύσει χέρας.

    ἔπαιρε σαυτήν· ὡς ἐγὼ καίπερ τρέμων
    πλεκτὰς ἱμάντων στροφίδας ἐξανήσομαι.
    ὧδ', ὦ κάκιστε, τῆσδ' ἐλυμήνω χέρας;
720 βοῦν ἢ λέοντ' ἤλπιζες ἐντείνειν βρόχοις;
    ἢ μὴ ξίφος λαβοῦσ' ἀμυνάθοιτό σε
    ἔδεισας; ἕρπε δεῦρ' ὑπ' ἀγκάλας, βρέφος,
    ξύλλυε δεσμὰ μητρός· ἐν Φθίᾳ σ' ἐγὼ
    θρέψω μέγαν τοῖσδ' ἐχθρόν. εἰ δ' ἀπῆν δορὸς
725 τοῖς Σπαρτιάταις δόξα καὶ μάχης ἀγών,
    τἄλλ' ὄντες ἴστε μηδενὸς βελτίονες.

                    ΧΟΡΟΣ
    ἀνειμένον τι χρῆμα πρεσβυτῶν γένος
    καὶ δυσφύλακτον ὀξυθυμίας ὕπο.

                    ΜΕΝΕΛΑΟΣ
    ἄγαν προνωπὴς ἐς τὸ λοιδορεῖν φέρῃ·
730 ἐγὼ δὲ πρὸς βίαν μὲν ἐς Φθίαν μολὼν
    οὔτ' οὖν τι δράσω φλαῦρον οὔτε πείσομαι.
    καὶ νῦν μέν—οὐ γὰρ ἄφθονον σχολὴν ἔχω—
    ἄπειμ' ἐς οἴκους· ἔστι γάρ τις οὐ πρόσω
    Σπάρτης πόλις τις, ἢ πρὸ τοῦ μὲν ἦν φίλη,

speed her through this house, grasping her by the hair, if she, sterile heifer that she is, cannot put up with others' having children because she herself has none. Just because she has had bad luck in regard to children, must we be bereft of offspring? Away from this woman, slaves, so that I may learn whether anyone means to prevent me from loosening her hands.

(to Andromache) Raise yourself up! *(Andromache rises to her feet.)* Though I tremble with age, I will loosen the plaited thongs. *(to Menelaus)* Did you, villain, disfigure her hands so cruelly? Was it a bull or a lion you thought you were tying up with these knots? Or were you afraid that she might take a sword and avenge herself on you? Come here under my arms, boy, and help me to untie your mother's bonds. In Phthia I shall rear you to be a great enemy to these people. If you Spartans were not renowned for war and battle strife, you may be sure that in other respects you are no one's superior.

CHORUS LEADER

Old men are a thing unrestrained and are hard to control because of their quick tempers.

MENELAUS

You fly too readily into abusive talk. For my part, I shall not come to Phthia and do anything demeaning by force, nor will I have it done to me. For the present, since I do not have unlimited time, I will go home. There is a city not far off from Sparta which previously was friendly

---

⁷¹⁰ τῶνδ᾽ Musgrave: τήνδ᾽ vel τῆσδ᾽ C

⁷¹¹ εἰ Wilamowitz: ἢ C

⁷²³ δεσμὰ μητρός Heath: μητρὸς δεσμά C

735 νῦν δ' ἐχθρὰ ποιεῖ· τῇδ' ἐπεξελθεῖν θέλω
στρατηλατήσας χὐποχείριον λαβεῖν.
ὅταν δὲ τἀκεῖ θῶ κατὰ γνώμην ἐμήν,
ἥξω· παρὼν δὲ πρὸς παρόντας ἐμφανῶς
γαμβροὺς διδάξω καὶ διδάξομαι λόγους.
740 κἂν μὲν κολάζῃ τήνδε καὶ τὸ λοιπὸν ᾖ
σώφρων καθ' ἡμᾶς, σώφρον' ἀντιλήψεται,
θυμούμενος δὲ τεύξεται θυμουμένων
[ἔργοισι δ' ἔργα διάδοχ' ἀντιλήψεται].
τοὺς σοὺς δὲ μύθους ῥᾳδίως ἐγὼ φέρω·
745 σκιὰ γὰρ ἀντίστοιχος ὢς φωνὴν ἔχεις,
ἀδύνατος οὐδὲν ἄλλο πλὴν λέγειν μόνον.

ΠΗΛΕΥΣ

ἡγοῦ τέκνον μοι δεῦρ' ὑπ' ἀγκάλαις σταθείς,
σύ τ', ὦ τάλαινα· χείματος γὰρ ἀγρίου
τυχοῦσα λιμένας ἦλθες εἰς εὐηνέμους.

ΑΝΔΡΟΜΑΧΗ

750 ὦ πρέσβυ, θεοί σοι δοῖεν εὖ καὶ τοῖσι σοῖς,
σώσαντι παῖδα κἀμὲ τὴν δυσδαίμονα.
ὅρα δὲ μὴ νῷν εἰς ἐρημίαν ὁδοῦ
πτήξαντες οἵδε πρὸς βίαν ἄγωσί με,
γέροντα μὲν σ' ὁρῶντες, ἀσθενῆ δ' ἐμὲ
755 καὶ παῖδα τόνδε νήπιον· σκόπει τάδε,
μὴ νῦν φυγόντες εἶθ' ἁλῶμεν ὕστερον.

ΠΗΛΕΥΣ

οὐ μὴ γυναικῶν δειλὸν εἰσοίσεις λόγον;
χώρει· τίς ὑμῶν ἅψεται; κλαίων ἄρα

but now is hostile. I mean to lead my army and attack it and make it our subject. But when I have arranged matters there to my satisfaction, I shall return. Man to man with my son-in-law I shall instruct and be instructed. If he punishes her and in future shows moderation toward us, he shall receive moderation in return. But if he shows anger, anger shall be his reward [and he shall get deeds successive to his deeds]. As for *your* words, I bear them with patience. For like a shadow that walks, you have a voice but are powerless to do anything but speak.

Exit MENELAUS with his retinue by Eisodos A.

PELEUS

My son, take your place below my arm and lead me, and you likewise, poor woman. For though you have run into a fierce storm, you have come to a harbor sheltered from the wind.

ANDROMACHE

Old sir, may the gods grant blessing to you and to yours for saving my child and his luckless mother! But look out: these men may be crouching in ambush where the road is deserted and may take me off by force, seeing that you are old, I am weak, and this boy a mere babe. Take care lest we escape now only to be captured later!

PELEUS

No more of woman's craven speech! March on! Who will touch you? He that does so shall smart for it! For by the

---

735 τῇδ' Diggle: τήνδ' C
743 del. Valckenaer

ψαύσει. θεῶν γὰρ οὕνεχ᾽ ἱππικοῦ τ᾽ ὄχλου
760 πολλῶν θ᾽ ὁπλιτῶν ἄρχομεν Φθίαν κάτα·
ἡμεῖς δ᾽ ἔτ᾽ ὀρθοὶ κοὐ γέροντες, ὡς δοκεῖς,
ἀλλ᾽ ἔς γε τοιόνδ᾽ ἄνδρ᾽ ἀποβλέψας μόνον
τροπαῖον αὐτοῦ στήσομαι, πρέσβυς περ ὤν.
πολλῶν νέων γὰρ καὶ γέρων εὔψυχος ὢν
765 κρείσσων· τί γὰρ δεῖ δειλὸν ὄντ᾽ εὐσωματεῖν;

ΧΟΡΟΣ

στρ.

ἦ μὴ γενοίμαν ἢ πατέρων ἀγαθῶν
εἴην πολυκτήτων τε δόμων μέτοχος.
770 εἴ τι γὰρ πάσχοι τις ἀμήχανον, ἀλκᾶς
οὐ σπάνις εὐγενέταις,
κηρυσσομένοισι δ᾽ ἀπ᾽ ἐσθλῶν δωμάτων
τιμὰ καὶ κλέος· οὔτοι λείψανα τῶν ἀγαθῶν
ἀνδρῶν ἀφαιρεῖται χρόνος· ἁ δ᾽ ἀρετὰ
775 καὶ θανοῦσι λάμπει.

ἀντ.

κρεῖσσον δὲ νίκαν μὴ κακόδοξον ἔχειν
780 ἢ ξὺν φθόνῳ σφάλλειν δυνάμει τε δίκαν.
ἡδὺ μὲν γὰρ αὐτίκα τοῦτο βροτοῖσιν,
ἐν δὲ χρόνῳ τελέθει
ξηρὸν καὶ ὀνείδεσιν ἔγκειται δόμων.
785 ταύταν ᾔνεσα ταύταν καὶ σέβομαι βιοτάν,
μηδὲν δίκας ἔξω κράτος ἐν θαλάμοις
καὶ πόλει δύνασθαι.

ἐπῳδ.

790 ὦ γέρον Αἰακίδα,

gods' grace I rule over a great army of cavalry and foot soldiers in Phthia. And I myself still stand erect and am no graybeard, as you suppose. I have only to cast a cross glance at that sort of man to send him flying, old man though I am. Even a graybeard, if he be brave, is more than a match for many young men. What use is bodily vigor if one is a coward?

Exit PELEUS, ANDROMACHE, BOY, and Maidservant by Eisodos A.

CHORUS

Noble birth be mine and membership in a house of great wealth, or no birth at all! For if hard misfortune comes, the nobly born have no lack of defense. Those whom the herald proclaims as descendants of noble houses have honor and fame. Time does not efface what noble men leave behind, and their prowess shines forth even when they are dead.

It is better to win a victory without dishonor than to overthrow justice by the odious use of power. For a victory over justice is sweet to mortals at first, but in time it withers and presses hard upon the guilty with disgrace to his house. This life I praise and honor, to hold no power in private or public that goes beyond justice's bounds.

O aged son of Aeacus, I am convinced that with your

---

763 αὐτὸς Wilamowitz

764 καὶ . . . ὢν Wecklein: κἂν . . . ᾖ C

770 γὰρ Dindorf: γὰρ ἂν C

784 δόμος Diggle: δόμῳ Stevens

785 σέβομαι Herwerden: φέρομαι C

πείθομαι καὶ σὺν Λαπίθαισί σε Κενταύ-
ροις ὁμιλῆσαι δορὶ
κλεινοτάτῳ· καὶ ἐπ' Ἀργῴου δορὸς ἄξενον ὑγρὰν
795 ἐκπερᾶσαι ποντιᾶν Ξυμπληγάδων
κλεινὰν ἐπὶ ναυστολίαν,
Ἰλιάδα τε πόλιν ὅτε <τὸ> πάρος
εὐδόκιμον ὁ Διὸς ἶνις ἀμφέβαλε φόνῳ,
800 κοινὰν τὰν εὔκλειαν ἔχοντ'
Εὐρώπαν ἀφικέσθαι.

ΤΡΟΦΟΣ

ὦ φίλταται γυναῖκες, ὡς κακὸν κακῷ
διάδοχον ἐν τῇδ' ἡμέρᾳ πορσύνεται.
δέσποινα γὰρ κατ' οἶκον, Ἑρμιόνην λέγω,
805 πατρός τ' ἐρημωθεῖσα συννοίᾳ θ' ἅμα
οἷον δέδρακεν ἔργον, Ἀνδρομάχην κτανεῖν
καὶ παῖδα βουλεύσασα, κατθανεῖν θέλει,
πόσιν τρέμουσα, μὴ ἀντὶ τῶν δεδραμένων
ἐκ τῶνδ' ἀτίμως δωμάτων ἀποσταλῇ
810 [ἢ κατθάνῃ κτείνουσα τοὺς οὐ χρὴ κτανεῖν].
μόλις δέ νιν θέλουσαν ἀρτῆσαι δέρην
εἴργουσι φύλακες δμῶες ἔκ τε δεξιᾶς
ξίφη καθαρπάζουσιν ἐξαιρούμενοι.
οὕτω μεταλγεῖ καὶ τὰ πρὶν δεδραμένα
815 ἔγνωκε πράξασ' οὐ καλῶς. ἐγὼ μὲν οὖν
δέσποιναν εἴργουσ' ἀγχόνης κάμνω, φίλαι·
ὑμεῖς δὲ βᾶσαι τῶνδε δωμάτων ἔσω

791 σε Musgrave: σε καὶ vel τε καὶ fere C

344

illustrious spear you joined battle at the side of the Lap-
iths against the Centaurs, that on the ship Argo you
passed through the inhospitable waters of the seaborne
Symplegades on a voyage of fame, and when on that ear-
lier day the son of Zeus[a] encircled with destruction the
glorious city of Troy, you came back to Europe with a
share of high renown!

Enter Hermione's NURSE *from the house.*

NURSE

My dear ladies, how disaster follows upon disaster this
day! For my mistress within the house, Hermione that is,
deserted by her father and at the same time aware of what
a dreadful thing she has done in plotting to kill Andro-
mache and her son, wants to die. She is afraid that her
husband may punish her for what she has done by send-
ing her away in disgrace from this house [or put her to
death for trying to kill those she should not]. She tried to
hang herself and was barely prevented by the slaves who
guarded her, and they also took a sword from her right
hand. So great is the regret she feels after the fact: she
has learned that her previous deeds were not well done. I
for my part am weary with restraining my mistress from
hanging herself, my friends. But I ask you to go into this

---

[a] Heracles, who waged an earlier war against Troy.

---

797 <τὸ> Hermann
799 εὐδόκιμον Hermann: -ος C
810 del. Cobet
814 μεταλγεῖ Σ sicut coni. Nauck: μέγ' ἀλγεῖ C

θανάτου νιν ἐκλύσασθε· τῶν γὰρ ἠθάδων
φίλων νέοι μολόντες εὐπιθέστεροι.

ΧΟΡΟΣ

820 καὶ μὴν ἐν οἴκοις προσπόλων ἀκούομεν
βοὴν ἐφ' οἷσιν ἦλθες ἀγγέλλουσα σύ.
δείξειν δ' ἔοικεν ἡ τάλαιν' ὅσον στένει
πράξασα δεινά· δωμάτων γὰρ ἐκπερᾷ
φεύγουσα χεῖρας προσπόλων πόθῳ θανεῖν.

ΕΡΜΙΟΝΗ

στρ. α

825 ἰώ μοί μοι·
σπάραγμα κόμας ὀνύχων τε
δάι' ἀμύγματα θήσομαι.

ΤΡΟΦΟΣ

ὦ παῖ, τί δράσεις; σῶμα σὸν καταικιῇ;

ΕΡΜΙΟΝΗ

ἀντ. α

αἰαῖ αἰαῖ·
830 ἔρρ' αἰθέριον πλοκάμων ἐ-
μῶν ἄπο, λεπτόμιτον φάρος.

ΤΡΟΦΟΣ

τέκνον, κάλυπτε στέρνα, σύνδησον πέπλους.

house and save her from death. For newcomers are more persuasive than old friends.

Shouting is heard within.

CHORUS LEADER
There, inside the house we hear the servants shouting over what you have come to tell us.

Enter HERMIONE from the house followed by servants.

But it is likely that the poor woman will show clearly how much she laments over the terrible deeds she has done. For here she comes out of the house, fleeing the hands of her servants and longing to die.

HERMIONE[a]
O alas, alas! I shall tear my hair and furrow my cheeks with my nails!

NURSE
My child, what will you do? Disfigure your body?

HERMIONE
Oh, oh! Leave my head, into the air with you, veil of fine-spun threads!

She casts her veil away.

NURSE
Child, cover your breasts, fasten your gown together!

[a] From here to 865 Hermione's words are sung while the Nurse replies in spoken trimeters.

ΕΡΜΙΟΝΗ

στρ. β

τί δέ με δεῖ στέρνοις καλύπτειν πέπλους;
δῆλα καὶ ἀμφιφανῆ καὶ ἄκρυπτα δε-
835 δράκαμεν πόσιν.

ΤΡΟΦΟΣ

ἀλγεῖς φόνον ῥάψασα συγγάμῳ σέθεν;

ΕΡΜΙΟΝΗ

ἀντ. β

κατὰ μὲν οὖν τόλμας στένω δαΐας,
ἃν ῥέξ᾽ ἁ κατάρατος ἐγὼ κατά-
ρατος ἀνθρώποις.

ΤΡΟΦΟΣ

840 συγγνώσεταί σοι τήνδ᾽ ἁμαρτίαν πόσις.

ΕΡΜΙΟΝΗ

τί μοι ξίφος ἐκ χερὸς ἠγρεύσω;
ἀπόδος, ὦ φίλος, ἀπόδος, ἵν᾽ ἀνταίαν
ἐρείσω πλαγάν· τί με βρόχων εἴργεις;

ΤΡΟΦΟΣ

845 ἀλλ᾽ εἴ σ᾽ ἀφείην μὴ φρονοῦσαν, ὡς θάνῃς;

ΕΡΜΙΟΝΗ

οἴμοι πότμου.
ποῦ μοι πυρὸς φίλα φλόξ;
ποῦ δ᾽ ἐκ πέτρας ἀερθῶ,
<ἢ> κατὰ πόντον ἢ καθ᾽ ὕλαν ὀρέων,
850 ἵνα θανοῦσα νερτέροισιν μέλω;

HERMIONE

What use to cover my breasts with my gown? Bare, clear to the eye and never to be hid are the deeds I have done to my husband!

NURSE

Are you in pain because you plotted murder against your rival?

HERMIONE

Even more: I groan for my murderous deed of daring, the deed I did, I the accursed, accursed in the eyes of men!

NURSE

Your husband will forgive you this misstep.

HERMIONE

Why did you snatch the sword from my hand? Give it back, my friend, give it back so that I may strike a blow to my heart! Why do you stay me from the noose?

NURSE

But if I let you go to your death when you are out of your mind, what then?

HERMIONE

Alas for my fate! Where is the flame of fire my heart longs for? Where shall I hurl myself aloft from a cliff, either at the sea's edge or in the mountain woods, so that I may die and those below may take me into their care?

---

^{833} με δεῖ στέρνοις Diggle: με δεῖ στέρνα vel με στέρνα C
^{837} τόλμας στένω δαΐας Bothe: στένω δαΐας τόλμας C
^{838} ῥέξ' Burges: ἔρεξα C ^{848} ἐκ Usener: εἰς C
^{849} <ᾗ> Seidler

EURIPIDES

ΤΡΟΦΟΣ

τί ταῦτα μοχθεῖς; συμφοραὶ θεήλατοι
πᾶσιν βροτοῖσιν ἢ τότ' ἦλθον ἢ τότε.

ΕΡΜΙΟΝΗ

ἔλιπες ἔλιπες, ὦ πάτερ, ἐπακτίαν
855 μονάδ' ἔρημον οὖσαν ἐνάλου κώπας.
ὀλεῖ ὀλεῖ με· τᾷδ' οὐκέτ' ἐνοικήσω
νυμφιδίῳ στέγᾳ.
τίνος ἄγαλμα θεῶν ἱκέτις ὁρμαθῶ;
860 ἢ δούλα δούλας γόνασι προσπέσω;
Φθιάδος ἐκ γᾶς
κυανόπτερος ὄρνις ἀρθείην,
πευκᾶεν σκάφος ᾇ διὰ κυανέ-
ας ἐπέρασεν ἀκτάς,
865 πρωτόπλοος πλάτα.

ΤΡΟΦΟΣ

ὦ παῖ, τὸ λίαν οὔτ' ἐκεῖν' ἐπήνεσα,
ὅτ' ἐς γυναῖκα Τρῳάδ' ἐξημάρτανες,
οὔτ' αὖ τὸ νῦν σου δεῖμ' ὃ δειμαίνεις ἄγαν.
οὐχ ὧδε κῆδος σὸν διώσεται πόσις
870 φαύλοις γυναικὸς βαρβάρου πεισθεὶς λόγοις.
οὐ γάρ τί σ' αἰχμάλωτον ἐκ Τροίας ἔχει,
ἀλλ' ἀνδρὸς ἐσθλοῦ παῖδα σὺν πολλοῖς λαβὼν
ἕδνοισι πόλεώς τ' οὐ μέσως εὐδαίμονος.
πατὴρ δέ σ' οὐχ ὧδ' ὡς σὺ δειμαίνεις, τέκνον,
875 προδοὺς ἐάσει δωμάτων τῶνδ' ἐκπεσεῖν.
ἀλλ' εἴσιθ' εἴσω μηδὲ φαντάζου δόμων

NURSE

Why do you grieve this way? Misfortunes sent by the gods come to all mortals late or soon.

HERMIONE

You have left me, father, left me all alone on the shore with no seagoing craft! He will kill me, kill me! No more shall I dwell in this bridal house of mine! To what god's statue shall I run as suppliant? Or shall I fall as a slave before the knees of a slave? O that I could soar out of the land of Phthia to the place where the ship of pine, first bark that ever sailed, passed through the Symplegades!

NURSE

My child, I did not praise your extreme behavior when you committed your crime against the woman of Troy, nor yet again do I praise your present excessive fear. Your husband will not, as you think, end his marriage to you, won over by the words of a barbarian woman, words that count for little. You are not his as a prisoner taken from Troy: he has received you with a large dowry, and you are the daughter of a man of importance and come from a city of no ordinary prosperity. Your father will not, as you fear, abandon you and allow you to be banished from this house. But go inside and do not show yourself in front of

---

855 μονάδ᾽ Seidler: ὡσεὶ μ- C   ἐνάλου Seidler: ἐναλίου C

856 ὀλεῖ ὀλεῖ με· τᾷδ᾽ οὐκέτ᾽ ἐνοικήσω Seidler: ὀλεῖ μ᾽ ὀλεῖ με δηλαδὴ πόσις· οὐκέτι τᾷδ᾽ ἐνοικήσω C

859 ἄγαλμα θεῶν Jacobs: ἀγαλμάτων C

862 ἀρθείην Stevens: εἴθ᾽ εἴην C

863 πευκᾶεν Bothe: ἢ πευκᾶεν C   ᾷ Bothe: ἂ C

πάροιθε τῶνδε, μή τιν' αἰσχύνην λάβῃς
[πρόσθεν μελάθρων τῶνδ' ὁρωμένη, τέκνον].

ΧΟΡΟΣ

καὶ μὴν ὅδ' ἀλλόχρως τις ἔκδημος ξένος
880   σπουδῇ πρὸς ἡμᾶς βημάτων πορεύεται.

ΟΡΕΣΤΗΣ

ξέναι γυναῖκες, ἦ τάδ' ἔστ' Ἀχιλλέως
παιδὸς μέλαθρα καὶ τυραννικαὶ στέγαι;

ΧΟΡΟΣ

ἔγνως· ἀτὰρ δὴ πυνθάνῃ τίς ὢν τάδε;

ΟΡΕΣΤΗΣ

Ἀγαμέμνονός τε καὶ Κλυταιμήστρας τόκος,
885   ὄνομα δ' Ὀρέστης· ἔρχομαι δὲ πρὸς Διὸς
μαντεῖα Δωδωναῖ'. ἐπεὶ δ' ἀφικόμην
Φθίαν, δοκεῖ μοι ξυγγενοῦς μαθεῖν περὶ
γυναικός, εἰ ζῇ κεὐτυχοῦσα τυγχάνει
ἡ Σπαρτιᾶτις Ἑρμιόνη· τηλουρὰ γὰρ
890   ναίουσ' ἀφ' ἡμῶν πεδί' ὅμως ἐστὶν φίλη.

ΕΡΜΙΟΝΗ

ὦ ναυτίλοισι χείματος λιμὴν φανεὶς
Ἀγαμέμνονος παῖ, πρός σε τῶνδε γουνάτων
οἴκτιρον ἡμᾶς ὧν ἐπισκοπεῖς τύχας,
πράσσοντας οὐκ εὖ. στεμμάτων δ' οὐχ ἥσσονας
895   σοῖς προστίθημι γόνασιν ὠλένας ἐμάς.

878 del. Bothe
880 βημάτων Brunck: δωμάτων C

the house lest you disgrace yourself [being seen in front of these halls, my daughter].

Enter ORESTES *in traveling costume by Eisodos B.*

CHORUS LEADER
Look, here comes a foreigner, a man of different hue from ourselves, hastening toward us with speedy step.

ORESTES
Ladies who dwell in this foreign land, is this the house of Achilles' son and his royal residence?

CHORUS LEADER
It is. But who are you that ask this?

ORESTES
I am the son of Agamemnon and Clytaemestra, and my name is Orestes. I am going to the oracle of Zeus at Dodona. But since I have arrived in Phthia, I have decided to learn whether my kinswoman Hermione of Sparta is alive and doing well. For though the land she dwells in is far off, she is nevertheless dear to me.

Hermione kneels before Orestes and grasps his knees.

HERMIONE
O haven from storm appearing to sailors, son of Agamemnon, I beg you by your knees, have pity on me for the plight you see me in: my fortunes are not good! I place my arms, which are as good as suppliant garlands, about your knees!

EURIPIDES

ΟΡΕΣΤΗΣ

ἔα·
τί χρῆμα; μῶν ἐσφάλμεθ' ἢ σαφῶς ὁρῶ
δόμων ἄνασσαν τῶνδε Μενέλεω κόρην;

ΕΡΜΙΟΝΗ

ἥνπερ μόνην γε Τυνδαρὶς τίκτει γυνὴ
Ἑλένη κατ' οἴκους πατρί· μηδὲν ἀγνόει.

ΟΡΕΣΤΗΣ

900 ὦ Φοῖβ' ἀκέστορ, πημάτων δοίης λύσιν.
τί χρῆμα; πρὸς θεῶν ἢ βροτῶν πάσχεις κακά;

ΕΡΜΙΟΝΗ

τὰ μὲν πρὸς ἡμῶν, τὰ δὲ πρὸς ἀνδρὸς ὅς μ' ἔχει,
τὰ δ' ἐκ θεῶν του· πανταχῇ δ' ὀλώλαμεν.

ΟΡΕΣΤΗΣ

τίς οὖν ἂν εἴη μὴ 'πεφυκότων γέ πω
905 παίδων γυναικὶ συμφορὰ πλὴν ἐς λέχος;

ΕΡΜΙΟΝΗ

τοῦτ' αὐτὸ καὶ νοσοῦμεν· εὖ μ' ὑπηγάγου.

ΟΡΕΣΤΗΣ

ἄλλην τιν' εὐνὴν ἀντὶ σοῦ στέργει πόσις;

ΕΡΜΙΟΝΗ

τήν <γ'> αἰχμάλωτον Ἕκτορος ξυνευνέτιν.

ΟΡΕΣΤΗΣ

κακόν γ' ἔλεξας, δίσσ' ἕν' ἄνδρα ἔχειν λέχη.

897 τῶνδε Brunck: τήνδε C

ORESTES

Ah! What is this? Am I mistaken, or do I truly see this
house's lady, Menelaus' daughter?

HERMIONE

Yes, the only child Helen, daughter of Tyndareus, bore to
my father in their house. You may be quite sure.

ORESTES

O Phoebus, healer god, give us an end to these troubles!
What is the matter? Is it by gods or mortals that you are
being ill-treated?

HERMIONE

In part it is my doing, in part my husband's, and in part
one of the gods is to blame. Yet I am wholly undone.

ORESTES

What other misfortune could there be to a woman who
has not yet borne children than one affecting her mar-
riage bed?

HERMIONE

It is just this that is my trouble. You prompt me well.

ORESTES

Your husband loves another in your stead?

HERMIONE

Yes, the captive slave that once was Hector's wife.

ORESTES

Your words spell bane, one man who has two women!

---

908 ⟨γ'⟩ Diggle   909 δίσσ' ἔν' ἄνδρα Grotius: ἔν' ἄνδρα
δίσσ' vel ἄνδρ' ἔνα δίσσ' C

ΕΡΜΙΟΝΗ

910 τοιαῦτα ταῦτα. κᾆτ᾽ ἔγωγ᾽ ἠμυνάμην.

ΟΡΕΣΤΗΣ

μῶν ἐς γυναῖκ᾽ ἔρραψας οἷα δὴ γυνή;

ΕΡΜΙΟΝΗ

φόνον γ᾽ ἐκείνῃ καὶ τέκνῳ νοθαγενεῖ.

ΟΡΕΣΤΗΣ

κἄκτεινας, ἤ τις συμφορά σ᾽ ἀφείλετο;

ΕΡΜΙΟΝΗ

γέρων γε Πηλεύς, τοὺς κακίονας σέβων.

ΟΡΕΣΤΗΣ

915 σοὶ δ᾽ ἦν τις ὅστις τοῦδ᾽ ἐκοινώνει φόνου;

ΕΡΜΙΟΝΗ

πατήρ γ᾽ ἐπ᾽ αὐτὸ τοῦτ᾽ ἀπὸ Σπάρτης μολών.

ΟΡΕΣΤΗΣ

κἄπειτα τοῦ γέροντος ἡσσήθη χερί;

ΕΡΜΙΟΝΗ

αἰδοῖ γε· καί μ᾽ ἔρημον οἴχεται λιπών.

ΟΡΕΣΤΗΣ

συνῆκα· ταρβεῖς τοῖς δεδραμένοις πόσιν.

ΕΡΜΙΟΝΗ

920 ἔγνως· ὀλεῖ γάρ μ᾽ ἐνδίκως. τί δεῖ λέγειν;
ἀλλ᾽ ἄντομαί σε Δία καλοῦσ᾽ ὁμόγνιον,
πέμψον με χώρας τῆσδ᾽ ὅποι προσωτάτω
ἢ πρὸς πατρῷον μέλαθρον· ὡς δοκοῦσί γε

ANDROMACHE

HERMIONE

How right you are! And then I took revenge.

ORESTES

Did you perchance plot against her like a woman?

HERMIONE

Yes, death for her and for her bastard son.

ORESTES

Did you kill them, or did some mischance prevent you?

HERMIONE

Old Peleus stopped me, favoring the lowly.

ORESTES

But was there one who shared this murder with you?

HERMIONE

My father, come from Sparta for this purpose.

ORESTES

Yet he was bested by an old man's hand?

HERMIONE

Yes, by his sense of shame—and then he left me!

ORESTES

I see: for what you've done you fear your husband.

HERMIONE

Yes. For he will be within his rights to kill me. What use
to speak of it? But I entreat you in the name of Kindred
Zeus, escort me to a place far away from this land or to my
father's house! For this house seems to take voice and

δόμοι τ' ἐλαύνειν φθέγμ' ἔχοντες οἵδε με,
925 μισεῖ τε γαῖα Φθιάς. εἰ δ' ἥξει πάρος
Φοίβου λιπὼν μαντεῖον ἐς δόμους πόσις,
κτενεῖ μ' ἐπ' αἰσχίστοισιν, ἢ δουλεύσομεν
νόθοισι λέκτροις ὧν ἐδέσποζον πρὸ τοῦ.

ΟΡΕΣΤΗΣ
πῶς οὖν τάδ', ὡς εἴποι τις, ἐξημάρτανες;

ΕΡΜΙΟΝΗ
930 κακῶν γυναικῶν εἴσοδοί μ' ἀπώλεσαν,
αἵ μοι λέγουσαι τούσδ' ἐχαύνωσαν λόγους·
Σὺ τὴν κακίστην αἰχμάλωτον ἐν δόμοις
δούλην ἀνέξῃ σοι λέχους κοινουμένην;
μὰ τὴν ἄνασσαν, οὐκ ἂν ἔν γ' ἐμοῖς δόμοις
935 βλέπουσ' ἂν αὐγὰς τἄμ' ἐκαρποῦτ' ἂν λέχη.
κἀγὼ κλυοῦσα τούσδε Σειρήνων λόγους
[σοφῶν πανούργων ποικίλων λαλημάτων]
ἐξηνεμώθην μωρίᾳ. τί γάρ μ' ἐχρῆν
πόσιν φυλάσσειν, ᾗ παρῆν ὅσων ἔδει;
940 πολὺς μὲν ὄλβος, δωμάτων δ' ἠνάσσομεν,
παῖδας δ' ἐγὼ μὲν γνησίους ἔτικτον ἄν,
ἡ δ' ἡμιδούλους τοῖς ἐμοῖς νοθαγενεῖς.
ἀλλ' οὔποτ' οὔποτ' (οὐ γὰρ εἰσάπαξ ἐρῶ)
χρὴ τούς γε νοῦν ἔχοντας, οἷς ἔστιν γυνή,
945 πρὸς τὴν ἐν οἴκοις ἄλοχον ἐσφοιτᾶν ἐᾶν
γυναῖκας· αὗται γὰρ διδάσκαλοι κακῶν·
ἡ μέν τι κερδαίνουσα συμφθείρει λέχος,
ἡ δ' ἀμπλακοῦσα συννοσεῖν αὑτῇ θέλει,

drive me forth, and the land of Phthia hates me. And if my husband leaves the oracle of Phoebus and comes home before I leave, he will kill me amidst great disgrace or I shall be a slave to the concubine who was once my slave.

ORESTES

How then did you come to commit these grave sins, as someone might call them?

HERMIONE

My undoing was bad women coming into the house. They puffed me up in folly by speaking in this vein: "Will you put up with this wretched captive in your house sharing in your marriage bed? By the goddess,[a] in my house she would not have taken her pleasure of my husband and lived to see the light!"

I listened to these Sirens' words [, these clever, knavish, deceitful chatterers,] and became inflated with foolish thoughts. What necessity was there to keep such a watch on my husband when I had all I needed? I had great wealth, I was mistress in the house, and I would have borne legitimate children, while she would have borne bastards with half-slave parentage to serve my children. But never, never (for I say it again and again) should husbands who have sense allow women to come to visit their wives in the house! They are the ones who teach evil. One woman corrupts a friend's marriage with an eye to gain, while another who has slipped from virtue

---

[a] Presumably Hera as goddess of marriage.

---

924 τ' Bothe: γ' vel μ' C
937 del. Nauck

πολλαὶ δὲ μαργότητι· κἀντεῦθεν δόμοι
950 νοσοῦσιν ἀνδρῶν. πρὸς τάδ' εὖ φυλάσσετε
κλήθροισι καὶ μοχλοῖσι δωμάτων πύλας·
ὑγιὲς γὰρ οὐδὲν αἱ θύραθεν εἴσοδοι
δρῶσιν γυναικῶν, ἀλλὰ πολλὰ καὶ κακά.

ΧΟΡΟΣ

ἄγαν ἐφῆκας γλῶσσαν ἐς τὸ σύμφυτον.
955 συγγνωστὰ μέν νυν σοὶ τάδ', ἀλλ' ὅμως χρεὼν
κοσμεῖν γυναῖκας τὰς γυναικείας νόσους.

ΟΡΕΣΤΗΣ

σοφόν τι χρῆμα τοῦ διδάξαντος βροτοὺς
λόγους ἀκούειν τῶν ἐναντίων πάρα.
ἐγὼ γὰρ εἰδὼς τῶνδε σύγχυσιν δόμων
960 ἔριν τε τὴν σὴν καὶ γυναικὸς Ἕκτορος
φυλακὰς ἔχων ἔμιμνον, εἴτ' αὐτοῦ μενεῖς
εἴτ' ἐκφοβηθεῖσ' αἰχμαλωτίδος φόνῳ
γυναικὸς οἴκων τῶνδ' ἀπηλλάχθαι θέλεις.
ἦλθον δὲ σὰς μὲν οὐ σέβων ἐπιστολάς,
965 εἰ δ' ἐνδιδοίης, ὥσπερ ἐνδίδως, λόγον
πέμψων σ' ἀπ' οἴκων τῶνδ'. ἐμὴ γὰρ οὖσα πρὶν
σὺν τῷδε ναίεις ἀνδρὶ σοῦ πατρὸς κάκῃ,
ὃς πρὶν τὰ Τροίας ἐσβαλεῖν ὁρίσματα
γυναῖκ' ἐμοί σε δοὺς ὑπέσχεθ' ὕστερον
970 τῷ νῦν σ' ἔχοντι, Τρῳάδ' εἰ πέρσοι πόλιν.
ἐπεὶ δ' Ἀχιλλέως δεῦρ' ἐνόστησεν γόνος,
σῷ μὲν συνέγνων πατρί, τὸν δ' ἐλισσόμην
γάμους ἀφεῖναι σούς, ἐμὰς λέγων τύχας

wants company in her vice, while many act from sheer
lewdness. That is the source of the disease in the houses
of men. In view of this, guard well with bolt and bar the
gates of your houses! For visits of women from outside
cause nothing good but only trouble aplenty.

CHORUS LEADER
You have hurled your tongue too violently at your own
sex. To be sure, this is pardonable in your case, but still
women ought to cover up women's frailties.

ORESTES
Wise was the advice of him who taught men to listen to
reports from their enemies. Because I had learned of the
turmoil in this house and the strife between you and Hec-
tor's wife, I kept watch waiting to see whether you would
remain here or, frightened by the murderous attempt on
the slave woman, would wish to leave this house. It was
not out of respect for any commands of yours that I came,
but so that if you should give me the chance to talk to you,
as you are now doing, I might escort you from this house.
For you were mine to begin with, and you are married to
Neoptolemus only by the baseness of your father. Before
he attacked Troy, he gave you to me to be my wife, but
later he promised you to your present husband as a
reward if he sacked Troy. When Achilles' son came home
to this land, I was forgiving toward your father, but I
begged Neoptolemus to relinquish his marriage to you. I

---

955 μέν νυν Canter: μὲν οὖν C
966 πέμψων Heath: πέμψω C

καὶ τὸν παρόντα δαίμον', ὡς φίλων μὲν ἂν

975 γήμαιμ' ἀπ' ἀνδρῶν, ἔκτοθεν δ' οὐ ῥᾳδίως,
φεύγων ἀπ' οἴκων ἃς ἐγὼ φεύγω φυγάς.
ὁ δ' ἦν ὑβριστὴς ἔς τ' ἐμῆς μητρὸς φόνον
τάς θ' αἱματωποὺς θεὰς ὀνειδίζων ἐμοί.
κἀγὼ ταπεινὸς ὢν τύχαις ταῖς οἴκοθεν

980 ἤλγουν μὲν ἤλγουν, συμφοραῖς δ' ἐνειχόμην
σῶν δὲ στερηθεὶς ᾠχόμην ἄκων γάμων.
νῦν οὖν, ἐπειδὴ περιπετεῖς ἔχεις τύχας
καὶ ξυμφορὰν τήνδ' ἐσπεσοῦσ' ἀμηχανεῖς,
ἄξω σ' ἐς οἴκους καὶ πατρὸς δώσω χερί.

985 τὸ συγγενὲς γὰρ δεινόν, ἔν τε τοῖς κακοῖς
οὐκ ἔστιν οὐδὲν κρεῖσσον οἰκείου φίλου.

ΕΡΜΙΟΝΗ

νυμφευμάτων μὲν τῶν ἐμῶν πατὴρ ἐμὸς
μέριμναν ἕξει, κοὐκ ἐμὸν κρίνειν τόδε.
ἀλλ' ὡς τάχιστα τῶνδέ μ' ἔκπεμψον δόμων,

990 μὴ φθῇ σε προσβὰς δῶμα καί μ' ἑλὼν πόσις
ἢ πρέσβυς οἴκους μ' ἐξερημοῦσαν μαθὼν
Πηλεὺς μετέλθῃ πωλικοῖς διώγμασιν.

ΟΡΕΣΤΗΣ

θάρσει γέροντος χεῖρα· τὸν δ' Ἀχιλλέως
μηδὲν φοβηθῇς παῖδ', ὅσ' εἰς ἔμ' ὕβρισεν.

995 τοία γὰρ αὐτῷ μηχανὴ πεπλεγμένη
βρόχοις ἀκινήτοισιν ἕστηκεν φόνου
πρὸς τῆσδε χειρός· ἣν πάρος μὲν οὐκ ἐρῶ,

980 ἐνειχόμην Barnes: ἠνειχ- C

362

told him of my evil fortunes and my present fate, how I could marry the daughter of a kinsman but only with difficulty one from outside, since I was in exile from my home. But he was insulting and berated me for the murder of my mother and the goddesses whose eyes drip blood.[a] Humiliated as I was because of my troubles at home, though I grieved greatly, nevertheless I was in the grip of disaster and went off robbed of you as my wife, though much against my will. But now, since your fortunes are in ruins and you have fallen into this calamity and are helpless, I shall take you home and restore you to your father's hand. For the tie of blood is strangely powerful, and in the hour of misfortune there is nothing better than a friend who is kin.

HERMIONE

My father shall take care of my marriage: it is not for me to decide this. But remove me quickly from this house so that my husband may not arrive home first and catch me, or old Peleus learn that I am abandoning the house and come after me with horses in hot pursuit.

ORESTES

Forget the old man's interference. And do not fear the son of Achilles, for all his insolence toward me. Such is the cunningly wrought trap, its snare fixed and immovable, that stands in his path. I shall not reveal this trap

---

[a] The Erinyes, who pursued Orestes for the murder of his mother.

---

981 fort. τε
990 σε Stevens: με C   μ' ἑλὼν F. W. Schmidt: μολὼν C
994 ὅσ' Bothe: ὃς C

τελουμένων δὲ Δελφὶς εἴσεται πέτρα.
ὁ μητροφόντης δ', ἢν δορυξένων ἐμῶν
1000 μείνωσιν ὅρκοι Πυθικὴν ἀνὰ χθόνα,
δείξω γαμεῖν σφε μηδέν' ὧν ἐχρῆν ἐμέ.
πικρῶς δὲ πατρὸς φόνιον αἰτήσει δίκην
ἄνακτα Φοῖβον· οὐδέ νιν μετάστασις
γνώμης ὀνήσει θεῷ διδόντα νῦν δίκας,
1005 ἀλλ' ἔκ τ' ἐκείνου διαβολαῖς τε ταῖς ἐμαῖς
κακῶς ὀλεῖται· γνώσεται δ' ἔχθραν θεοῦ.
ἐχθρῶν γὰρ ἀνδρῶν μοῖραν εἰς ἀναστροφὴν
δαίμων δίδωσι κοὐκ ἐᾷ φρονεῖν μέγα.

ΧΟΡΟΣ

στρ. α
1010 ὦ Φοῖβε πυργώσας τὸν ἐν Ἰλίῳ εὐτειχῆ πάγον
καὶ πόντιε κυανέαις ἵπποις διφρεύ-
ων ἅλιον πέλαγος,
τίνος οὕνεκ' ἄτιμον ὀργά-
1015 ας χέρα τεκτοσύνας Ἐ-
νυαλίῳ δοριμήστορι προσθέν-
τες τάλαιναν τάλαι-
ναν μεθεῖτε Τροίαν;

ἀντ. α
πλείστους δ' ἐπ' ἀκταῖσιν Σιμοεντίσιν εὐίππους ὄχους
1020 ἐζεύξατε καὶ φονίους ἀνδρῶν ἁμίλ-
λας ἔθετ' ἀστεφάνους·
ἀπὸ δὲ φθίμενοι βεβᾶσιν
Ἰλιάδαι βασιλῆες,
1025 οὐδ' ἔτι πῦρ ἐπιβώμιον ἐν Τροί-

beforehand, but the cliff of Delphi shall come to know of my plans as they are brought to fulfillment. I, the matricide, provided the oaths of my allies in Delphi hold fast, shall teach him not to marry a bride that is rightfully mine. His demand to Lord Apollo for satisfaction for his father's death shall prove costly to him. His change of heart shall do him no good as the god punishes him. Thanks to Apollo and my accusations he will die a painful death, and he shall learn what the enmity of the god is like. For a divinity overturns the fortunes of his enemies and does not allow them to be proud.

Exit ORESTES *and* HERMIONE *by Eisodos B,* NURSE *into the house.*

CHORUS

O Phoebus, who built high the fair-walled rock of Troy, and you, Lord of the Deep, who ride your chariot with wave-dark horses over the briny sea, why did you deprive your hand of its cunning craftsmanship,[a] and put it at the service of Ares, Lord of the Spear, and thereby let slip luckless, luckless Troy?

Many were the chariots with lovely horses that you caused to be yoked by the banks of the Simois, many the deadly contests of men, with no garlands for the victor, that you established. Dead and gone are the kings descended from Ilus, and no more does the fire gleam on

---

[a] Apollo and Poseidon both helped build Troy.

1001 δείξω Herwerden: δείξει C   1002 πικρὰν Cobet
1006 θεοῦ Kirchhoff: ἐμὴν a: ἐμοὶ b (cf. 1005)
1014 ὀργάνας Kovacs: ὀργάναν C

365

ᾳ θεοῖσιν λέλαμ-
πεν καπνῷ θυώδει.

στρ. β

βέβακε δ' Ἀτρείδας ἀλόχου παλάμαις,
αὐτά τ' ἐναλλάξασα φόνον θανάτου
1030   πρὸς τέκνων ἐπηῦρεν.
θεοῦ θεοῦ νῦν κέλευσμ' ἐπεστράφη
μαντόσυνον, ὅτε νιν Ἀργόθεν πορευθεὶς
Ἀγαμεμνόνιος κέλωρ, ἀδύτων ἐπιβὰς
1035   ἵκετ', ὧν ματρὸς φονεύς.
ὦ δαῖμον, ὦ Φοῖβε, πῶς πείθομαι;

ἀντ. β

πολλαὶ δ' ἀν' Ἑλλάνων ἀγόρους στοναχὰς
μέλποντο δυστάνων λεχέων ἄλοχοι,
1040   ἐκ δ' ἔλειπον οἴκους
πρὸς ἄλλον εὐνάτορ'. οὐχὶ σοὶ μόνᾳ
δύσφρονες ἐπέπεσον, οὐ φίλοισι, λῦπαι·
νόσον Ἑλλὰς ἔτλα, νόσον· διέβα δὲ Φρυγῶν
1045   καὶ πρὸς εὐκάρπους γύας
σκηπτὸς σταλάσσων <ὅδ'> Ἅιδα φόνον.

ΠΗΛΕΥΣ

Φθιώτιδες γυναῖκες, ἱστοροῦντί μοι
σημήνατ'· ᾐσθόμην γὰρ οὐ σαφῆ λόγον
ὡς δώματ' ἐκλιποῦσα Μενέλεω κόρη
1050   φρούδη τάδ'· ἥκω δ' ἐκμαθεῖν σπουδὴν ἔχων
εἰ ταῦτ' ἀληθῆ· τῶν γὰρ ἐκδήμων φίλων
δεῖ τοὺς κατ' οἶκον ὄντας ἐκπονεῖν τύχας.

[1029] θανάτου Stevens: θανάτῳ C

the altars of the gods in Troy or its smoke of incense rise.

Dead is Atreus' son by the hand of his wife, and she in her turn received death, in exchange for his murder, at the hands of her children. But now the god's oracular commandment has come again when the son of Agamemnon, come from Argos and standing in the god's inmost shrine, approached him in supplication, his mother's blood on his hands. O god, O Phoebus, how can I believe it?

Many in the gathering places of the Greeks are the wives who sang dirges for their luckless husbands and left their homes to share another's bed. Not on you alone[a] or on your kin have cruel griefs fallen. It is a plague Greece has suffered, a plague! Yet also to the fertile fields of the Phrygians did this pestilence pass, dripping deadly gore.

Enter PELEUS *with retinue by Eisodos A.*

PELEUS

Women of Phthia, tell me the answer to my question: I have heard an indistinct rumor that Menelaus' daughter has left the house and is gone, and I came here eager to learn whether this is true. For those who are at home must be solicitous of the fortunes of their loved ones abroad.

---

[a] These words could be addressed either to Hermione or to Andromache.

1030 ἐπηῦρεν Herwerden: ἀπηύρα C
1031 νῦν Kovacs: νιν C
1035 ἵκετ᾽ ὤν Wilamowitz: κτεάνων C
1039 λεχέων Heath: τεκέων vel τοκέων C
1046 <ὅδ᾽> Wilamowitz   φόνον] fort. δρόσον

EURIPIDES

ΧΟΡΟΣ

Πηλεῦ, σαφῶς ἤκουσας· οὐδ' ἐμοὶ καλὸν
κρύπτειν ἐν οἷς παροῦσα τυγχάνω κακοῖς·
1055 βασίλεια γὰρ τῶνδ' οἴχεται φυγὰς δόμων.

ΠΗΛΕΥΣ

τίνος φόβου τυχοῦσα; διαπέραινέ μοι.

ΧΟΡΟΣ

πόσιν τρέμουσα, μὴ δόμων νιν ἐκβάλῃ.

ΠΗΛΕΥΣ

μῶν ἀντὶ παιδὸς θανασίμων βουλευμάτων;

ΧΟΡΟΣ

ναί, καὶ γυναικὸς αἰχμαλωτίδος φόνῳ.

ΠΗΛΕΥΣ

1060 σὺν πατρὶ δ' οἴκους ἢ τίνος λείπει μέτα;

ΧΟΡΟΣ

Ἀγαμέμνονός νιν παῖς βέβηκ' ἄγων χθονός.

ΠΗΛΕΥΣ

ποίαν περαίνων ἐλπίδ'; ἢ γῆμαι θέλων;

ΧΟΡΟΣ

καὶ σῷ γε παιδὸς παιδὶ πορσύνων μόρον.

ΠΗΛΕΥΣ

κρυπτὸς καταστὰς ἢ κατ' ὄμμ' ἐλθὼν μάχῃ;

ΧΟΡΟΣ

1065 ἁγνοῖς ἐν ἱεροῖς Λοξίου Δελφῶν μέτα.

1054 οἷς παροῦσα Wecklein: οἷσπερ οὖσα C

368

CHORUS LEADER

Peleus, the rumor you heard was true, and it is not right
for me to conceal the troubles I find myself neighbor to:
the queen has gone off in flight from this house.

PELEUS

In fear of what? Finish your story.

CHORUS LEADER

Afraid that her husband might expel her from this house.

PELEUS

For plotting to kill the boy, perhaps?

CHORUS LEADER

Yes, and because she tried to murder the slave woman.

PELEUS

With whom did she leave home? Was it her father?

CHORUS LEADER

It was Agamemnon's son who took her away.

PELEUS

In hope of what? Meaning to marry her?

CHORUS LEADER

Yes, and contriving death against your grandson.

PELEUS

Crouching in ambush or in open battle?

CHORUS LEADER

With the help of Delphians in Loxias' sacred shrine.

---

¹⁰⁵⁹ φόνῳ Lenting: φόβῳ C
¹⁰⁶³ σῷ Lobeck: σοῦ C

369

EURIPIDES

ΠΗΛΕΥΣ

οἴμοι· τόδ' ἤδη δεινόν. οὐχ ὅσον τάχος
χωρήσεταί τις Πυθικὴν πρὸς ἑστίαν
καὶ τἀνθάδ' ὄντα τοῖς ἐκεῖ λέξει φίλοις,
πρὶν παῖδ' Ἀχιλλέως κατθανεῖν ἐχθρῶν ὕπο;

ΑΓΓΕΛΟΣ

1070 ὤμοι μοι·
οἵας ὁ τλήμων ἀγγελῶν ἥκω τύχας
σοί τ', ὦ γεραιέ, καὶ φίλοισι δεσπότου.

ΠΗΛΕΥΣ

αἰαῖ· πρόμαντις θυμὸς ὥς τι προσδοκᾷ.

ΑΓΓΕΛΟΣ

οὐκ ἔστι σοι παῖς παιδός, ὡς μάθῃς, γέρον
Πηλεῦ· τοιάσδε φασγάνων πληγὰς ἔχει
1075 Δελφῶν ὑπ' ἀνδρῶν καὶ Μυκηναίου ξένου.

ΧΟΡΟΣ

ἆ ἆ, τί δράσεις, ὦ γεραιέ; μὴ πέσῃς·
ἔπαιρε σαυτόν.

ΠΗΛΕΥΣ

οὐδέν εἰμ'· ἀπωλόμην.
φρούδη μὲν αὐδή, φροῦδα δ' ἄρθρα μου κάτω.

ΑΓΓΕΛΟΣ

ἄκουσον, εἰ σοὶ καὶ φίλοις ἀμυναθεῖν
1080 χρήζεις, τὸ πραχθέν, σὸν κατορθώσας δέμας.

1075 om. a, praebet b, del. Wecklein
1079 σοὶ καὶ Jackson: καὶ σοῖς C

PELEUS

Oh, oh, this is dreadful! Someone go with all speed to the Pythian altar and report what has happened here to our friends there before Achilles' son is killed by his enemies!

Enter MESSENGER by Eisodos B.

MESSENGER

Ah me! What terrible news have I, unlucky man, come bearing for you, old sir, and for those who love my master!

PELEUS

Oh no! My prophetic heart foretells disaster!

MESSENGER

To tell you my news, aged Peleus, your grandson is dead: such are the sword thrusts he has received from the men of Delphi and the stranger from Mycenae.

Peleus staggers backwards.

CHORUS LEADER

Oh, oh, what are you doing, old sir? Do not fall! Hold yourself up!

PELEUS

I am dead, I am destroyed! I cannot speak, my limbs no longer hold me up!

MESSENGER

If you wish to assist yourself and your kin, stand and listen to what has happened.

ΠΗΛΕΥΣ

ὦ μοῖρα, γήρως ἐσχάτοις πρὸς τέρμασιν
οἵα με τὸν δύστηνον ἀμφιβᾶσ' ἔχεις.
πῶς δ' οἴχεταί μοι παῖς μόνου παιδὸς μόνος;
σήμαιν'· ἀκοῦσαι δ' οὐκ ἀκούσθ' ὅμως θέλω.

ΑΓΓΕΛΟΣ

1085 ἐπεὶ τὸ κλεινὸν ἤλθομεν Φοίβου πέδον,
τρεῖς μὲν φαεννὰς ἡλίου διεξόδους
θέᾳ διδόντες ὄμματ' ἐξεπίμπλαμεν.
καὶ τοῦθ' ὕποπτον ἦν ἄρ'· ἐς δὲ συστάσεις
κύκλους τ' ἐχώρει λαὸς οἰκήτωρ θεοῦ.

1090 Ἀγαμέμνονος δὲ παῖς διαστείχων πόλιν
ἐς οὗς ἑκάστῳ δυσμενεῖς ηὔδα λόγους·
Ὁρᾶτε τοῦτον, ὃς διαστείχει θεοῦ
χρυσοῦ γέμοντα γύαλα, θησαυροὺς βροτῶν,
τὸ δεύτερον παρόντ' ἐφ' οἷσι καὶ πάρος

1095 δεῦρ' ἦλθε, Φοίβου ναὸν ἐκπέρσαι θέλων;
κἀκ τοῦδ' ἐχώρει ῥόθιον ἐν πόλει κακόν,
ἀρχαὶ δ' ἐπληροῦντ' ἐς τὰ βουλευτήρια,
ἰδίᾳ θ' ὅσοι θεοῦ χρημάτων ἐφέστασαν
φρουρὰν ἐτάξαντ' ἐν περιστύλοις δόμοις.

1100 ἡμεῖς δὲ μῆλα, φυλλάδος Παρνασίας
παιδεύματ', οὐδὲν τῶνδέ πω πεπυσμένοι,
λαβόντες ᾖμεν ἐσχάραις τ' ἐφέσταμεν
σὺν προξένοισι μάντεσίν τε Πυθικοῖς.
καί τις τόδ' εἶπεν· Ὦ νεανία, τί σοι

1105 θεῷ κατευξώμεσθα; τίνος ἥκεις χάριν;

PELEUS

Ah fate, how you have overwhelmed me, unhappy man
that I am, on the farthest edge of old age! But how did
the only son of my only son perish? Though the news is
past all hearing, I wish to hear.

MESSENGER

When we had come to Phoebus' glorious land, we spent
three shining circuits of the sun in looking around and
took our fill of gazing. This, it seems, caused suspicion:
the people who dwell in the god's land gathered in knots
and circles. The son of Agamemnon went through the
city and spoke in each man's ear these hostile words: "Do
you see this man, who makes his way through the god's
gold-laden precincts, the treasuries given by mortals? He
has come here a second time for the same purpose as
before and means to plunder the temple of Phoebus."
Thereafter an angry clamor ran through the city. The
authorities streamed into the council chamber, and those
who had charge of the god's property privately posted a
watch in the pillared halls. We, not yet knowing anything
of this, took sheep, nurslings of the grass of Parnassus,
and went on our way and stood next to the altars together
with Delphian officials and diviners. Someone said,
"Young man, what shall we ask from the god on your

1097 δ' Blaydes: τ' C   τὰ Wecklein: τε C

ὁ δ' εἶπε· Φοίβῳ τῆς πάροιθ' ἁμαρτίας
δίκας παρασχεῖν βουλόμεσθ'· ᾔτησα γὰρ
πατρός ποτ' αὐτὸν αἵματος δοῦναι δίκην.
κἀνταῦθ' Ὀρέστου μῦθος ἰσχύων μέγα
1110 ἐφαίνεθ', ὡς ψεύδοιτο δεσπότης ἐμός,
ἥκων ἐπ' αἰσχροῖς. ἔρχεται δ' ἀνακτόρων
κρηπῖδος ἐντός, ὡς πάρος χρηστηρίων
εὔξαιτο Φοίβῳ· τυγχάνει δ' ἐν ἐμπύροις·
τῷ δὲ ξιφήρης ἆρ' ὑφειστήκει λόχος
1115 δάφνῃ σκιασθείς· ὧν Κλυταιμήστρας τόκος
εἷς ἦν ἁπάντων τῶνδε μηχανορράφος.
χὠ μὲν κατ' ὄμμα στὰς προσεύχεται θεῷ·
οἱ δ' ὀξυθήκτοις φασγάνοις ὡπλισμένοι
κεντοῦσ' ἀτευχῆ παῖδ' Ἀχιλλέως λάθρᾳ.
1120 χωρεῖ δὲ πρύμναν· οὐ γὰρ ἐς καιρὸν τυπεὶς
ἐτύγχαν'· ἐξέλκει δὲ κἀκ παραστάδος
κρεμαστὰ τεύχη πασσάλων καθαρπάσας
ἔστη 'πὶ βωμοῦ γοργὸς ὁπλίτης ἰδεῖν,
βοᾷ δὲ Δελφῶν παῖδας ἱστορῶν τάδε·
1125 Τίνος μ' ἕκατι κτείνετ' εὐσεβεῖς ὁδοὺς
ἥκοντα; ποίας ὄλλυμαι πρὸς αἰτίας;
τῶν δ' οὐδὲν οὐδεὶς μυρίων ὄντων πέλας
ἐφθέγξατ', ἀλλ' ἔβαλλον ἐκ χειρῶν πέτροις.
πυκνῇ δὲ νιφάδι πάντοθεν σποδούμενος
1130 προύτεινε τεύχη κἀφυλάσσετ' ἐμβολὰς
ἐκεῖσε κἀκεῖσ' ἀσπίδ' ἐκτείνων χερί.
ἀλλ' οὐδὲν ἧνον ἀλλὰ πόλλ' ὁμοῦ βέλη,
οἰστοί, μεσάγκυλ' ἔκλυτοί τ' ἀμφώβολοι

behalf? Why have you come here?" And he replied, "I want to give satisfaction to Phoebus for my earlier sin. For I once demanded that the god pay the penalty for my father's death." At that point it was clear that Orestes' story was having a great effect, the story that my master was lying and had come for a disgraceful purpose. He went up the steps and into the temple in order that before the shrine he might offer prayer to Phoebus. He happened to be engaged in making burnt offerings. But there were, it turned out, armed men lying in ambush for him, hidden by the shadow of laurel branches, and the son of Clytaemestra was the sole contriver of all these doings. Neoptolemus stood in full view and prayed to the god, but they, armed with sharp swords, stabbed from their hiding place at the unprotected son of Achilles. He gave ground (for he was not mortally wounded) and drew his sword, and snatching down from its nail on the temple wall armor that hung there, he took his stand upon the altar, a warrior terrible to look upon, and shouted this question to the sons of Delphi, "Why do you try to kill me on an errand of piety? For what reason am I being done to death?" But though a throng stood nearby, none of his attackers made any reply but instead pelted him with stones. Battered by a thick snowfall of missiles from all sides, he used his armor as defense and warded off their attack by holding his shield now here, now there. His attackers made no progress, but their many missiles

---

1121 κἀκ Wecklein: καὶ C

1132 ἦνον Borthwick: ἦνεν C: fort. ἀλλ᾽ οὐκ ἀνῆκαν

σφαγῆς ἐχώρουν βουπόροι ποδῶν πάρος.
1135 δεινὰς δ᾽ ἂν εἶδες πυρρίχας φρουρουμένου
βέλεμνα παιδός. ὡς δέ νιν περισταδὸν
κύκλῳ κατεῖχον οὐ διδόντες ἀμπνοάς,
βωμοῦ κενώσας δεξίμηλον ἐσχάραν,
τὸ Τρωικὸν πήδημα πηδήσας ποδοῖν
1140 χωρεῖ πρὸς αὐτούς· οἱ δ᾽ ὅπως πελειάδες
ἱέρακ᾽ ἰδοῦσαι πρὸς φυγὴν ἐνώτισαν.
πολλοὶ δ᾽ ἔπιπτον μιγάδες ἔκ τε τραυμάτων
αὐτοί θ᾽ ὑφ᾽ αὑτῶν στενοπόρους κατ᾽ ἐξόδους,
κραυγὴ δ᾽ ἐν εὐφήμοισι δύσφημος δόμοις
1145 πέτραισιν ἀντέκλαγξ᾽· ἐν εὐδίᾳ δέ πως
ἔστη φαεννοῖς δεσπότης στίλβων ὅπλοις,
πρὶν δή τις ἀδύτων ἐκ μέσων ἐφθέγξατο
δεινόν τι καὶ φρικῶδες, ὦρσε δὲ στρατὸν
στρέψας πρὸς ἀλκήν. ἔνθ᾽ Ἀχιλλέως πίτνει
1150 παῖς ὀξυθήκτῳ πλευρὰ φασγάνῳ τυπεὶς
[Δελφοῦ πρὸς ἀνδρός, ὅσπερ αὐτὸν ὤλεσεν]
πολλῶν μετ᾽ ἄλλων· ὡς δὲ πρὸς γαῖαν πίτνει,
τίς οὐ σίδηρον προσφέρει, τίς οὐ πέτρον,
βάλλων ἀράσσων; πᾶν δ᾽ ἀνήλωται δέμας
1155 τὸ καλλίμορφον τραυμάτων ὑπ᾽ ἀγρίων.
νεκρὸν δὲ δή νιν κείμενον βωμοῦ πέλας
ἐξέβαλον ἐκτὸς θυοδόκων ἀνακτόρων.
ἡμεῖς δ᾽ ἀναρπάσαντες ὡς τάχος χεροῖν
κομίζομέν νίν σοι κατοιμῶξαι γόοις
1160 κλαῦσαί τε, πρέσβυ, γῆς τε κοσμῆσαι τάφῳ.
τοιαῦθ᾽ ὁ τοῖς ἄλλοισι θεσπίζων ἄναξ,

together, arrows, javelins, and double-pointed ox-piercing spits snatched from the slaughter of victims, fell in front of his feet. You would have seen the young man dance a jig[a] in deadly earnest as he kept warding off the weapons. But when they encircled him and gave him no space to breathe, he left the altar hearth, where sacrifice is received, leaping his famous Trojan leap, and charged at them. Like doves that have seen a hawk, they turned and fled. And many fell, both from the wounds he gave them and from those they gave one another in the narrow gateway. In those holy precincts an unholy cry arose and smote the rocky cliffs. In the calm that somehow ensued, my master stood still, the brilliance of his gleaming weapons about him, until from the inmost shrine some voice uttered a sound dreadful and chilling and roused the army, turning them toward battle. Then it was that the son of Achilles fell, struck in his side with a sharp sword [by the Delphian who slew him], but many others fell too. When he collapsed to the ground, what man of them did not bring sword or rock and strike him? His whole fair form was rent with terrible wounds. They hurled his corpse, which had fallen near the altar, out of the shrine fragrant with incense. We quickly took him up in our arms and brought him back for you to mourn him, old sir, and give him burial.

This was the way the god who prophesies to others,

[a] Lit. "a terrible pyrrhic dance," a sort of military exercise that derives its name from Neoptolemus' other name, Pyrrhus.

1148 τι Lenting: τε C
1151 del. Hartung (ὅσπερ . . . ἄλλων del. Hermann)

EURIPIDES

ὁ τῶν δικαίων πᾶσιν ἀνθρώποις κριτής,
δίκας διδόντα παῖδ' ἔδρασ' Ἀχιλλέως.
ἐμνημόνευσε δ' ὥσπερ ἄνθρωπος κακὸς
1165 παλαιὰ νείκη· πῶς ἂν οὖν εἴη σοφός;

ΧΟΡΟΣ

καὶ μὴν ὅδ' ἄναξ ἤδη φοράδην
Δελφίδος ἐκ γῆς δῶμα πελάζει.
τλήμων ὁ παθών, τλήμων δέ, γέρον,
καὶ σύ· δέχῃ γὰρ τὸν Ἀχίλλειον
1170 σκύμνον ἐς οἴκους οὐχ ὡς σὺ θέλεις,
αὐτός τε κακοῖς
εἰς ἓν μοίρας συνέκυρσας.

ΠΗΛΕΥΣ

στρ. α

ὤμοι ἐγώ, κακὸν οἷον ὁρῶ τόδε
καὶ δέχομαι χερὶ δώμασιν ἀμοῖς.
1175 ἰώ μοί μοι, αἰαῖ,
ὦ πόλι Θεσσαλίας, διολώλαμεν,
οἰχόμεθ'· οὐκέτι μοι γένος, οὐ τέκνα λείπεται οἴκοις·
ὦ σχέτλιος παθέων <ἄρ'> ἐγώ· φίλον
1180 ἐς τίνα βάλλων τέρψομαι αὐγάς;
ὦ φίλιον στόμα καὶ γένυ καὶ χέρες,
εἴθε σ' ὑπ' Ἰλίῳ ἤναρε δαίμων
Σιμοεντίδα παρ' ἀκτάν.

1171 κακοῖς Koerner: κακοῖς πήμασι κύρσας C
1176 Θεσσαλίας Hermann: -ία C
1177 οὐ τέκνα Nauck: οὐκέτι μοι τέκνα fere C

378

ANDROMACHE

who judges what is right for all mankind, has treated
Achilles' son when he offered amends. Like a base mortal, he remembered old quarrels. How then can he be
wise?

Enter by Eisodos B a procession carrying the body of
Neoptolemus.

CHORUS LEADER

See, here is our lord, his body carried home from the land
of Delphi. Luckless is the dead man, luckless likewise,
old sir, are you. How unlike your hopes is this homecoming of Achilles' son, and you yourself have met with the
same fate as the wicked.

PELEUS[a]

Ah me, what disaster is this I see and take in my hands
into my house! Oh, alas! O city of Thessaly, I am undone,
I am finished, none of my race, no children, are left for
me in my house! Oh how wretched misfortune has made
me! To what friend shall I look for consolation? O face
that I love and knees and hands, would that a god had
killed you beneath Troy's walls by the bank of the Simois!

---

[a] From here to 1230 Peleus' words are sung and the Chorus'
words sometimes spoken (1184–5, 1208, 1218, 1221), sometimes
sung (1197–8, 1214–5), and sometimes chanted (1226–30).

1179 <ἄρ'> Hermann
1179–80 φίλον / ἐς τίνα βάλλων τέρψομαι αὐγάς Hermann:
ἐς τίνα / δὴ φίλον αὐγὰς βαλὼν τέρψομαι C

ΧΟΡΟΣ

οὗτός τ' ἂν ὡς ἐκ τῶνδ' ἐτιμᾶτ' ἄν, γέρον,
1185 θανών, τὸ σόν τ' ἦν ὧδ' ἂν εὐτυχέστερον.

ΠΗΛΕΥΣ

ἀντ. α

ὦ γάμος, ὦ γάμος, ὃς τάδε δώματα
καὶ πόλιν ὤλεσας ὤλεσας ἁμάν.
αἰαῖ, ἒ ἔ, ὦ παῖ·
μήποτε σῶν λεχέων τὸ δυσώνυμον
1190 †ὤφελ' ἐμὸν γένος ἐς τέκνα καὶ δόμον ἀμφιβαλέσθαι
Ἑρμιόνας Ἀίδαν ἐπὶ σοί, τέκνον,†
ἀλλὰ κεραυνῷ πρόσθεν ὀλέσθαι·
μηδ' ἐπὶ τοξοσύνᾳ φονίῳ πατρὸς
1195 αἷμα τὸ διογενές ποτε Φοῖβον
βροτὸς ἐς θεὸν ἀνάψαι.

ΧΟΡΟΣ

στρ. β

ὀττοτοτοτοῖ, θανόντα δεσπόταν γόοις
νόμῳ τῷ νερτέρων κατάρξω.

ΠΗΛΕΥΣ

1200 ὀττοτοτοτοῖ, διάδοχά <σοι> τάλας ἐγὼ
γέρων καὶ δυστυχὴς δακρύω.

ΧΟΡΟΣ

θεοῦ γὰρ αἶσα, θεὸς ἔκρανε συμφοράν.

1185 τ' L. Dindorf: δ' C
1187 ὤλεσας ὤλεσας ἁμάν Hermann: ἐμὰν ὤλεσας C

CHORUS LEADER

In that case he would have been honored in death, and
your life would be more fortunate.

PELEUS

O marriage, marriage, you have destroyed my house,
destroyed my city! Alas, my child! Would that you had
not cast upon our family and house this ill-famed mar-
riage and on yourself a union with Hermione that was
death, my son! Would you had perished ere then by the
lightning-bolt! And how I wish that you, a mortal, had
never fastened upon Phoebus, a god, the death by his
murderous archery of your Zeus-descended father!

CHORUS

O grief! I shall begin my lament for my perished lord
with the strain reserved for the dead.

PELEUS

O grief! In my turn I, unhappy man, old and luckless,
take up the lament.

CHORUS

A god caused this doom, a god made this disaster.

1190–1 fort. ἐς γένος ἡμῖν καὶ δόμον ὤφελες ἀμφιβαλέσθαι
/ σοί τ' Ἀίδα γάμον Ἑρμιόνας, τέκνον
1195 Φοῖβον ed. Hervag.2: -ον C
1200 <σοι> Wilamowitz

ΠΗΛΕΥΣ

1205 ὦ φίλος, δόμον ἔλιπες ἔρημον,
[ὤμοι μοι, ταλαίπωρον ἐμὲ]
γέροντ' ἄπαιδα νοσφίσας.

ΧΟΡΟΣ

θανεῖν θανεῖν σε, πρέσβυ, χρῆν πάρος τέκνων.

ΠΗΛΕΥΣ

οὐ σπαράξομαι κόμαν,
1210 οὐκ ἐμῷ 'πιθήσομαι
κάρᾳ κτύπημα χειρὸς ὀλοόν; ὦ πόλις,
διπλῶν τέκνων μ' ἐστέρησε Φοῖβος.

ΧΟΡΟΣ

ἀντ. β

ὦ κακὰ παθὼν ἰδών τε δυστυχὲς γέρον,
1215 τίν' αἰῶν' ἐς τὸ λοιπὸν ἕξεις;

ΠΗΛΕΥΣ

ἄτεκνος ἔρημος, οὐκ ἔχων πέρας κακῶν
διαντλήσω πόνους ἐς Ἅιδαν.

ΧΟΡΟΣ

μάτην δέ σ' ἐν γάμοισιν ὤλβισαν θεοί.

ΠΗΛΕΥΣ

ἀμπτάμενα φροῦδα πάντ' ἐκεῖνα
1220 κόμπων μεταρσίων πρόσω.

ΧΟΡΟΣ

μόνος μόνοισιν ἐν δόμοις ἀναστρέφῃ.

PELEUS

You have left the house bereft, dear child, [oh, alas, unhappy me,] and robbed an old man of his children!

CHORUS

To die, to die before your children do—this would have been right!

PELEUS

Shall I not rend my hair, not strike upon my head a hand's destructive blow? O my city, of two offspring has Phoebus bereft me!

CHORUS

O luckless old man, who have seen and suffered pain, what life will be yours in time to come?

PELEUS

Childless and bereft, with no limit set to misfortune, I shall drain misery to the dregs until my death!

CHORUS

It was for nothing that the gods blessed you in marriage.

PELEUS

All that blessedness is flown, sped beyond the reach of high-flying boasts.

CHORUS

Lonely in a lonely house you dwell.

ΠΗΛΕΥΣ

οὐκέτ᾽ εἴμ᾽, οἴμοι, πόλις,
σκῆπτρά τ᾽ ἐρρέτω τάδε·
σύ τ᾽, ὦ κατ᾽ ἄντρα νύχια Νηρέως κόρα,
1225 πανώλεθρόν μ᾽ ὄψεαι πίτνοντα.

ΧΟΡΟΣ

ἰὼ ἰώ·
τί κεκίνηται, τίνος αἰσθάνομαι
θείου; κοῦραι, λεύσσετ᾽ ἀθρήσατε·
δαίμων ὅδε τις λευκὴν αἰθέρα
πορθμευόμενος τῶν ἱπποβότων
1230 Φθίας πεδίων ἐπιβαίνει.

ΘΕΤΙΣ

Πηλεῦ, χάριν σοι τῶν πάρος νυμφευμάτων
ἥκω Θέτις λιποῦσα Νηρέως δόμους.
καὶ πρῶτα μέν σοι τοῖς παρεστῶσιν κακοῖς
μηδέν τι λίαν δυσφορεῖν παρήνεσα·
1235 κἀγὼ γάρ, ἣν ἄκλαυτ᾽ ἐχρῆν τίκτειν τέκνα,
1254 θεὰν γεγῶσαν καὶ θεοῦ πατρὸς τέκος,
1236 ἀπώλεσ᾽ ἐκ σοῦ παῖδα τὸν ταχὺν πόδας
Ἀχιλλέα τεκοῦσα πρῶτον Ἑλλάδος.
    ὧν δ᾽ οὕνεκ᾽ ἦλθον σημανῶ, σὺ δ᾽ ἐνδέχου.
τὸν μὲν θανόντα τόνδ᾽ Ἀχιλλέως γόνον
1240 θάψον πορεύσας Πυθικὴν πρὸς ἐσχάραν,
Δελφοῖς ὄνειδος, ὡς ἀπαγγέλλῃ τάφος

1222 οὐκέτ᾽ εἴμ᾽, οἴμοι Jackson: οὐκέτι μοι vel οὔτε μοι
C   πόλις Hermann: πόλις πόλις C

PELEUS

O city, I am dead! Farewell, my scepter! *(He throws his scepter to the ground.)* And you, Nereid[a] in your dark cave, shall see me fallen into utter destruction.

Enter THETIS *aloft on the* mechane.

CHORUS LEADER

But look, what is this motion, what divinity do I see? Look, women, see! Here is a deity riding through the bright air and alighting on the ground of horse-pasturing Phthia!

THETIS

Peleus, because of the marriage bed we once shared I, Thetis, have left the house of Nereus and come here. First I counsel you not to be too much cast down by your present misfortunes. For even I, who ought to have borne children I need not weep for, since I am a goddess and have a god for my father, have lost the child I had from you, Achilles, the swift of foot, whom I bore to be the noblest of the Greeks.

But listen and I shall tell you why I have come. Take the son of Achilles, who lies here slain, to the altar of Delphi and there bury him, a reproach to the Delphians, so that his grave may proclaim that he was violently slain by

---

[a] Thetis.

1223 τάδε Kirchhoff: τάδ' ἐπὶ γαῖαν C
1225 πίτνοντα Seidler: πίτνοντα πρὸς γᾶν C
1231 σοι Platt: σῶν C
1254 huc trai. Jackson   θεὰν γεγῶσαν Jackson: -ὰ -σα C

φόνον βίαιον τῆς Ὀρεστείας χερός·
γυναῖκα δ' αἰχμάλωτον, Ἀνδρομάχην λέγω,
Μολοσσίαν γῆν χρὴ κατοικῆσαι, γέρον,
1245 Ἑλένῳ συναλλαχθεῖσαν εὐναίοις γάμοις,
καὶ παῖδα τῆσδε, τῶν ἀπ' Αἰακοῦ μόνον
λελειμμένον δή. βασιλέα δ' ἐκ τοῦδε χρὴ
ἄλλον δι' ἄλλου διαπερᾶν Μολοσσίας
εὐδαιμονοῦντας· οὐ γὰρ ὧδ' ἀνάστατον
1250 γένος γενέσθαι δεῖ τὸ σὸν κἀμόν, γέρον,
Τροίας τε· καὶ γὰρ θεοῖσι κἀκείνης μέλει,
καίπερ πεσούσης Παλλάδος προθυμίᾳ.
1253 σὲ δ', ὡς ἂν εἰδῇς τῆς ἐμῆς εὐνῆς χάριν,
1255 κακῶν ἀπαλλάξασα τῶν βροτησίων
ἀθάνατον ἄφθιτόν τε ποιήσω θεόν.
κἄπειτα Νηρέως ἐν δόμοις ἐμοῦ μέτα
τὸ λοιπὸν ἤδη θεὸς συνοικήσεις θεᾷ·
ἔνθεν κομίζων ξηρὸν ἐκ πόντου πόδα
1260 τὸν φίλτατόν σοι παῖδ' ἐμοί τ' Ἀχιλλέα
ὄψῃ δόμους ναίοντα νησιωτικοὺς
Λευκὴν κατ' ἀκτὴν ἐντὸς ἀξένου πόρου.
ἀλλ' ἕρπε Δελφῶν ἐς θεόδμητον πόλιν
νεκρὸν κομίζων τόνδε, καὶ κρύψας χθονὶ
1265 ἐλθὼν παλαιᾶς χοιράδος κοῖλον μυχὸν
Σηπιάδος ἵζου· μίμνε δ' ἔστ' ἂν ἐξ ἁλὸς
λαβοῦσα πεντήκοντα Νηρήδων χορὸν
ἔλθω κομιστήν σου· τὸ γὰρ πεπρωμένον
δεῖ σ' ἐκκομίζειν, Ζηνὶ γὰρ δοκεῖ τάδε.

the hand of Orestes. As for the captive woman, Andromache that is, she must migrate to the land of the Molossians and be married to Helenus, and with her must go her son, the last of the line of Aeacus. It is fated that his descendants in unbroken succession will rule over Molossia in blessedness. For, old sir, it was not to be that your race and mine should be so laid waste, nor that of Troy, for Troy too is in the gods' care although it fell by the will of Pallas. As for yourself, in order that you may feel grateful for your marriage to me, I shall set you free from mortal woe and make you a god, deathless and exempt from decay. And then you shall dwell with me in the house of Nereus, god with goddess, for all time to come. From there, as you walk dry-shod out of the deep, you will see your beloved son and mine, Achilles, dwelling in his island home on the strand of Leuke in the Sea Inhospitable.[a] But go to the god-built city of Delphi with the body of this man, and when you have laid him in earth, go to the hollow cave on the ancient promontory of Sepias and sit. Wait there until I come from the sea with a chorus of fifty Nereids to escort you. You must carry out the course that fate prescribes, for this is the will of Zeus.

---

[a] A tradition going back to the epic poet Arctinus said that Achilles' ghost haunted the island of Leuke, opposite the mouth of the Danube in the Euxine Sea.

1246 τῆσδε Mastronarde: τόνδε C
1248 Μολοσσίας Lenting: -ίαν C
1254 vide post 1235
1262 ἀξένου Cobet: εὐξείνου C

EURIPIDES

1270   παῦσαι δὲ λύπης τῶν τεθνηκότων ὕπερ·
        πᾶσιν γὰρ ἀνθρώποισιν ἥδε πρὸς θεῶν
        ψῆφος κέκρανται κατθανεῖν τ᾽ ὀφείλεται.

ΠΗΛΕΥΣ

        ὦ πότνι᾽, ὦ γενναῖα συγκοιμήματα,
        Νηρέως γένεθλον, χαῖρε· ταῦτα δ᾽ ἀξίως
1275   σαυτῆς τε ποιεῖς καὶ τέκνων τῶν ἐκ σέθεν.
        παύω δὲ λύπην σοῦ κελευούσης, θεά,
        καὶ τόνδε θάψας εἶμι Πηλίου πτυχάς,
        οὗπερ σὸν εἷλον χερσὶ κάλλιστον δέμας.
        κᾆτ᾽ οὐ γαμεῖν δῆτ᾽ ἔκ τε γενναίων χρεὼν
1280   δοῦναί τ᾽ ἐς ἐσθλούς, ὅστις εὖ βουλεύεται,
        κακῶν δὲ λέκτρων μὴ ᾽πιθυμίαν ἔχειν,
        μηδ᾽ εἰ ζαπλούτους οἴσεται φερνὰς δόμοις;
        [οὐ γάρ ποτ᾽ ἂν πράξειαν ἐκ θεῶν κακῶς.]

ΧΟΡΟΣ

        πολλαὶ μορφαὶ τῶν δαιμονίων,
1285   πολλὰ δ᾽ ἀέλπτως κραίνουσι θεοί·
        καὶ τὰ δοκηθέντ᾽ οὐκ ἐτελέσθη,
        τῶν δ᾽ ἀδοκήτων πόρον ηὗρε θεός.
        τοιόνδ᾽ ἀπέβη τόδε πρᾶγμα.

        1279–82 del. Stevens, defendit Sommerstein *CQ* 38 (1988),
243–6
        1283 del. Hartung
        1284–8 del. Hartung, defendit Roberts, *CQ* 37 (1987), 51–64

Cease your grieving for the dead. For this is the judgment that stands over all mortals, and death is their debt to pay.

Exit THETIS by the mechane.

PELEUS

O lady, O noble sharer of my bed, daughter of Nereus, farewell! Your conduct is worthy of yourself and of the children sprung from you! I shall put an end to grief at your command, goddess, and when I have buried this man I shall go to the glens of Pelion where I took your fair form in my arms. Shall a man then not take a wife from a noble family and give his daughter in marriage to the great and good, if he has sense? Shall he not avoid desiring an ignoble wife even if she brings a rich dowry to the house? [Never shall they fare ill at the hands of the gods.]

Exit PELEUS with retinue, MESSENGER, and funeral procession by Eisodos B.

CHORUS LEADER

There are many shapes of divinity, and many things the gods accomplish against our expectation. What men look for is not brought to pass, but a god finds a way to achieve the unexpected. Such was the outcome of this story.

Exit CHORUS by Eisodos A.

HECUBA

INTRODUCTION

In his *Hecuba* Euripides has combined into one play two stories—the sacrifice of Polyxena by the Greeks and the murder of Polydorus by Polymestor—that have no necessary connection with each other except that both concern Hecuba. To be sure, he has done what he could to stitch them together, notably by having the ghost of Polydorus predict both of Hecuba's sorrows and by making the preparations for Polyxena's funeral the occasion for the discovery of Polydorus' body. But the stories remain distinct. This has troubled critics of the last two centuries, who have have had strict standards of artistic unity, and has led to the search for various other kinds of unity than that of action. It may be, however, that we should simply accept the fact that two stories have been put in the same play to variegate and enrich the theme of Hecuba's fall into misery. The Polyxena material can be viewed as a foil or preparation for the much more wrenching and horrific story of Polydorus' murder and Hecuba's revenge on his murderer.

The Polydorus story is introduced by the ghost of the boy himself, who speaks the prologue. He was the youngest of Priam's sons, too young to fight, and his father had sent him secretly to Thrace to be raised by the Thracian king Polymestor. With Polydorus came a great deal of gold, so that if Troy fell he would not lack for livelihood. After Troy's fall, Polymestor killed his young charge, seized his gold, and threw his body into the sea. Polydorus tells us that Hecuba is destined on this day to find his body and bury it, and that she is also fated to see the death of her daughter Polyxena.

After the prologue our attention is turned from Polydorus to Polyxena, whose sacrifice has just been decreed by the Greeks. Achilles' ghost has appeared to the Greeks as they were sailing homeward, and reproached them with ingratitude for leaving his tomb without its proper prize of honor. The Greeks in assembly debate the propriety of killing a royal captive to honor their comrade, and Odysseus, who argues that Greek interest requires the sacrifice, wins the day. When Odysseus arrives to take Polyxena away, Hecuba pleads with him to spare her, but in vain.

Hecuba then asks her daughter to plead. Polyxena refuses. As she sees it, life in her new circumstances is unworthy of her. She was born a princess and wants to die as one, not as a slave. She is led off to sacrifice, and in the next scene a report of her brave death is brought by the herald Talthybius.

After a choral ode a shrouded corpse is carried in. This is the body of Polydorus, but in a scene of carefully contrived pathos Hecuba first surmises that it is Polyxena, then Cassandra, before she learns the awful truth that it is her son, whom she had called "the last remaining anchor of my house" (80). This blow is more cruel than the death of Polyxena, for he was her youngest and the last of her sons still alive, and the man who killed him was no enemy Greek but a guest-friend she had trusted.

No sooner has she learned the truth than Agamemnon arrives to urge Hecuba to hurry up with the burial preparations for Polyxena. Hecuba tells him of the murder of her son by her guest-friend and appeals to him to punish the murderer. Her plea at first is unsuccessful, but Agamemnon at last agrees to help her. He allows her to send a servant through the camp to Polymestor with an enticing message to come with his sons.

Polymestor enters with his sons. He is a revoltingly hypocritical figure, and no one in the Athenian audience could doubt for a moment that his punishment is richly deserved. Hecuba plays upon his greed for money and entices him into the tent, where she claims she has hidden some gold. There the Trojan women pinion his arms and, after killing his sons before his eyes, blind him. He calls out in pain for the Greeks to help him, and Agamemnon enters, pretending shock at what has happened to Polymestor and offering to hear his case.

In the trial, Polymestor claims that he murdered Polydorus in furtherance of Greek interests, to prevent a resettling of Troy by a Priamid. In her rebuttal, Hecuba demonstrates that Polymestor, in defiance of laws human and divine, has killed his guest-friend out of mere greed. When both prosecutor and defendant have spoken, Agamemnon pronounces his verdict: Polymestor deserves the treatment he has received.

Thus far Hecuba's fate has illustrated to the full the theme of the mutability of human fortune. In speech after speech (e.g. 55–8, 231–3, 282–5, 583–4, 721–2, 956–60) Polydorus, Hecuba, the Chorus, and the seemingly pious but hypocritical Polymestor speak of Hecuba's fate as showing that the gods bring low what is mighty.

The decline of Hecuba's fortunes and the fall of Troy are repeatedly remarked on in this light, with occasional emphasis on the surprising and paradoxical way it was brought out (see especially 905–42). But the reverse of Polymestor's fortunes is equally awe-inspiring. He had every reason to think that his crime would remain undetected and no reason to think that Hecuba, even if she should discover what he had done, would be able to exact punishment from him. Hecuba's city no longer existed, and she herself was a slave in the power of others. Yet the plea of the murdered Polydorus for burial was heard by the gods, and his body was discovered. It would not be unduly rash to read in these events the hand of a punishing divinity. The gods have brought Hecuba low, but they do not allow her rights as guest-friend to Polymestor to be trampled on with impunity.

The end of the play contains a further surprise. Polymestor announces that he knows certain prophecies of Dionysus. Hecuba, he says, is destined to change into a hound, leap to her death from the mast of the ship, and give her name to a promontory in the Chersonese, Cynossema, "Hound's Grave," a mark for sailors to steer by. Cassandra will be cut down by Clytaemestra, who will murder Agamemnon as well. Agamemnon expresses his disbelief and orders Polymestor to be abandoned on a deserted isle. The winds are now favorable, and as they prepare to leave, Agamemnon utters the prayer that they will have a good journey and find all in good order at home. Neither prayer is destined to be fulfilled. In all versions of the story, the wind rises still further and wrecks much of the Greek fleet, and Agamemnon returns home only to be murdered by his wife and her lover. The Greeks, who destroyed Troy, will be destroyed in their turn. They are no exception to the rule of the mutability of all mortal fortunes.

Hecuba's metamorphosis into a hound is frequently interpreted as the physical manifestation of the loss of her humanity, the final judgment on the horrible revenge she exacted from Polymestor. But this is not an inevitable interpretation. Euripides often ends his plays by connecting his tragic figures with cult practices or geographical names in his audience's own world. The geographer Strabo refers to Cynossema and says it was also called Hecuba's Tomb, and it seems likely that the legend connecting Hecuba with this place was familiar to Euripides' audience. Euripides' treatment in 1259–74 does nothing to encourage us to view this metamorphosis, death, and burial as a judgment rather than as, say, a providential rescue of the Queen of Troy from a life of slavery or an award of posthumous fame.

SELECT BIBLIOGRAPHY

Editions

W. Hadley (Cambridge, 1894).
M. Tierney (Dublin, 1947).
S. G. Daitz (Leipzig, 1973).
C. Collard (Warminster, 1991).

Literary criticism

A. W. H. Adkins, "Basic Greek Values in Euripides' *Hecuba* and *Hercules Furens*," *CQ* 16 (1966), 193–219.
M. Heath, "'Iure Principem Locum Tenet': Euripides' *Hecuba*," *BICS* 34 (1987), 40–68.

D. Kovacs, *The Heroic Muse: Studies in the* Hippolytus *and* Hecuba *of Euripides* (Baltimore, 1987).

D. Lanza, "ΝΟΜΟΣ e ΙΣΟΝ in Euripide," *RFIC* 91 (1963), 416–39.

R. Meridor, "Hecuba's Revenge," *AJP* 96 (1978), 28–35.

——— "The Function of Polymestor's Crime in the *Hecuba* of Euripides," *Eranos* 81 (1983), 13–20.

J. Mossman, *Wild Justice: A Study in Euripides'* Hecuba (Oxford, 1995).

M. Nussbaum, *The Fragility of Goodness: Luck and Ethics in Greek Tragedy and Philosophy* (Cambridge, 1986), chapter 13.

Dramatis Personae

ΠΟΛΥΔΩΡΟΥ ΕΙΔΩΛΟΝ	GHOST OF POLYDORUS, son of Hecuba
ΕΚΑΒΗ	HECUBA, Queen of Troy
ΧΟΡΟΣ	CHORUS of Trojan women
ΠΟΛΥΞΕΝΗ	POLYXENA, daughter of Hecuba
ΟΔΥΣΣΕΥΣ	ODYSSEUS, King of Ithaca
ΤΑΛΘΥΒΙΟΣ	TALTHYBIUS, the Greek herald
ΘΕΡΑΠΑΙΝΑ	MAIDSERVANT of Hecuba
ΑΓΑΜΕΜΝΩΝ	AGAMEMNON, King of Mycenae
ΠΟΛΥΜΗΣΤΩΡ	POLYMESTOR, King of Thrace

A Note on Staging

The *skene* represents the tent of Agamemnon in the Greek encampment on the coast of Thrace. Eisodos A leads to the tents of the other Greek chiefs and to the seashore, Eisodos B to the inland regions of Thrace.

ΕΚΑΒΗ

ΠΟΛΥΔΩΡΟΥ ΕΙΔΩΛΟΝ

Ἥκω νεκρῶν κευθμῶνα καὶ σκότου πύλας
λιπών, ἵν' Ἅιδης χωρὶς ᾤκισται θεῶν,
Πολύδωρος, Ἑκάβης παῖς γεγὼς τῆς Κισσέως
Πριάμου τε πατρός, ὅς μ', ἐπεὶ Φρυγῶν πόλιν
5 κίνδυνος ἔσχε δορὶ πεσεῖν Ἑλληνικῷ,
δείσας ὑπεξέπεμψε Τρωικῆς χθονὸς
Πολυμήστορος πρὸς δῶμα Θρηκίου ξένου,
ὃς τήνδ' ἀρίστην Χερσονησίαν πλάκα
σπείρει, φίλιππον λαὸν εὐθύνων δορί.
10 πολὺν δὲ σὺν ἐμοὶ χρυσὸν ἐκπέμπει λάθρᾳ
πατήρ, ἵν', εἴ ποτ' Ἰλίου τείχη πέσοι,
τοῖς ζῶσιν εἴη παισὶ μὴ σπάνις βίου.
νεώτατος δ' ἦ Πριαμιδῶν, ὃ καί με γῆς
ὑπεξέπεμψεν· οὔτε γὰρ φέρειν ὅπλα
15 οὔτ' ἔγχος οἷός τ' ἦ νέῳ βραχίονι.
ἕως μὲν οὖν γῆς ὄρθ' ἔκειθ' ὁρίσματα

_____
8 τήνδ' Hermann: τὴν C

400

HECUBA

Enter POLYDORUS' GHOST on the theologeion *above the* skene.

POLYDORUS' GHOST

I have come from the hiding place of the dead and the gates of darkness, where Hades dwells apart from the other gods. I am Polydorus, son of Hecuba, Cisseus' daughter, and of Priam. When the city of the Phrygians[a] was in danger of falling to the Greek spear, Priam in fear sent me away secretly from the land of Troy to the house of his Thracian guest-friend, Polymestor, who sows this fertile plain of the Chersonese[b] and rules with his spear over a horse-loving folk. My father secretly sent a large sum of gold with me so that if some day the walls of Ilium should fall, his surviving sons would not lack the means to live. I was the youngest of Priam's sons, and it was for this reason that he sent me away secretly, for I could not wear the gear of war or wield a spear with my young arm.

As long as the land's boundary markers stood erect and

[a] The people of Troy (Ilium) are often called Phrygians in Greek poetry. Likewise the Greeks are called Danaans, Argives, and Achaeans.
[b] The Thracian Chersonese lies on the other side of the Hellespont from Troy.

πύργοι τ' ἄθραυστοι Τρωικῆς ἦσαν χθονὸς
Ἕκτωρ τ' ἀδελφὸς οὑμὸς εὐτύχει δορί,
καλῶς παρ' ἀνδρὶ Θρῃκὶ πατρῴῳ ξένῳ
20 τροφαῖσιν ὥς τις πτόρθος ηὐξόμην τάλας·
ἐπεὶ δὲ Τροία θ' Ἕκτορός τ' ἀπόλλυται
ψυχὴ πατρῴα θ' ἑστία κατεσκάφη
αὐτός τε βωμῷ πρὸς θεοδμήτῳ πίτνει
σφαγεὶς Ἀχιλλέως παιδὸς ἐκ μιαιφόνου,
25 κτείνει με χρυσοῦ τὸν ταλαίπωρον χάριν
ξένος πατρῷος καὶ κτανὼν ἐς οἶδμ' ἁλὸς
μεθῆχ', ἵν' αὐτὸς χρυσὸν ἐν δόμοις ἔχῃ.
κεῖμαι δ' ἐπ' ἀκταῖς, ἄλλοτ' ἐν πόντου σάλῳ,
πολλοῖς διαύλοις κυμάτων φορούμενος,
30 ἄκλαυτος ἄταφος· νῦν δ' ὑπὲρ μητρὸς φίλης
Ἑκάβης ἀίσσω, σῶμ' ἐρημώσας ἐμόν,
τριταῖον ἤδη φέγγος αἰωρούμενος,
ὅσονπερ ἐν γῇ τῇδε Χερσονησίᾳ
μήτηρ ἐμὴ δύστηνος ἐκ Τροίας πάρα.
35   πάντες δ' Ἀχαιοὶ ναῦς ἔχοντες ἥσυχοι
θάσσουσ' ἐπ' ἀκταῖς τῆσδε Θρῃκίας χθονός.
ὁ Πηλέως γὰρ παῖς ὑπὲρ τύμβου φανεὶς
κατέσχ' Ἀχιλλεὺς πᾶν στράτευμ' Ἑλληνικόν,
πρὸς οἶκον εὐθύνοντας ἐναλίαν πλάτην·
40 αἰτεῖ δ' ἀδελφὴν τὴν ἐμὴν Πολυξένην
τύμβῳ φίλον πρόσφαγμα καὶ γέρας λαβεῖν.
καὶ τεύξεται τοῦδ' οὐδ' ἀδώρητος φίλων
ἔσται πρὸς ἀνδρῶν· ἡ πεπρωμένη δ' ἄγει
θανεῖν ἀδελφὴν τῷδ' ἐμὴν ἐν ἥματι.

the towers of Troy were unscathed and Hector my brother was successful in battle, I grew up well tended like a sapling at the court of my father's Thracian guest-friend, though to my sorrow. But when Troy and the life of Hector were lost, and my father's hearth was overthrown, and he himself fell beside the god-built altar, slaughtered by the murderous son of Achilles, my father's guest-friend killed me, unluckly man that I was, for my gold, and having killed me cast my corpse into the billowing sea, so that he himself might keep the gold in his house. I lie now near the beach, now amid the high swell of the main, carried to and fro by the waves' constant ebb and flow, unwept, unburied. And now deserting my body I flit above the head[a] of Hecuba my mother, hovering aloft for three days now, the whole time my poor mother has been here in the Chersonese since she left Troy.

All the Achaeans, anchoring their ships, sit idle upon the shore of this land of Thrace. For Peleus' son Achilles appeared above his tomb and stopped the entire Greek fleet as they were steering their ships toward home, asking to receive my sister Polyxena as a special sacrifice for his tomb and a prize of honor. And get it he will: he will not be left without a gift by his friends. For fate is leading my sister to her death on this day. My mother shall

[a] In Homer and elsewhere in Greek literature, a ghost hovering above the head of someone asleep appears to him as a dream.

45 δυοῖν δὲ παίδοιν δύο νεκρὼ κατόψεται
μήτηρ, ἐμοῦ τε τῆς τε δυστήνου κόρης.
φανήσομαι γάρ, ὡς τάφου τλήμων τύχω,
δούλης ποδῶν πάροιθεν ἐν κλυδωνίῳ.
τοὺς γὰρ κάτω σθένοντας ἐξῃτησάμην
50 τύμβου κυρῆσαι κἀς χέρας μητρὸς πεσεῖν.
τοὐμὸν μὲν οὖν ὅσονπερ ἤθελον τυχεῖν
ἔσται· γεραιᾷ δ᾽ ἐκποδὼν χωρήσομαι
Ἑκάβῃ· περᾷ γὰρ ἥδ᾽ ὑπὸ σκηνῆς πόδα
Ἀγαμέμνονος, φάντασμα δειμαίνουσ᾽ ἐμόν.
φεῦ·
55 ὦ μῆτερ, ἥτις ἐκ τυραννικῶν δόμων
δούλειον ἦμαρ εἶδες, ὡς πράσσεις κακῶς
ὅσονπερ εὖ ποτ᾽· ἀντισηκώσας δέ σε
φθείρει θεῶν τις τῆς πάροιθ᾽ εὐπραξίας.

ΕΚΑΒΗ

ἄγετ᾽, ὦ παῖδες, τὴν γραῦν πρὸ δόμων,
60 ἄγετ᾽ ὀρθοῦσαι τὴν ὁμόδουλον,
Τρῳάδες, ὑμῖν, πρόσθε δ᾽ ἄνασσαν,
[λάβετε φέρετε πέμπετ᾽ ἀείρετέ μου]
γεραιᾶς χειρὸς προσλαζύμεναι·
65 κἀγὼ σκολιῷ σκίπωνι χερὸς
διερειδομένη σπεύσω βραδύπουν
ἤλυσιν ἄρθρων προτιθεῖσα.

ὦ στεροπὰ Διός, ὦ σκοτία νύξ,
τί ποτ᾽ αἴρομαι ἔννυχος οὕτω

see two corpses of two children, mine and her luckless daughter's. In order that I, poor wretch, may get burial, I shall appear in the sea swell before the feet of a slave girl. I have won permission from the powers below to pass into my mother's hands and receive burial. For my part, then, all that I wish for I shall have. But now I shall get out of the path of aged Hecuba, for she is coming out from the tent of Agamemnon, frightened at the sight of me in her dream. Ah! Dear mother, who have lived to see the day of slavery after life in a royal house, how sad your fortunes are, as sad now as once they were happy! Some god is ruining you in compensation for your former prosperity!

Exit POLYDORUS. Enter HECUBA from the skene *accompanied and supported by her former subjects.*

HECUBA

Daughters of Troy, my children, take the old woman out in front of her house, raise up and take your fellow slave, once your queen, [take, bear, send, lift me,] holding me fast by my aged hand. Leaning upon the crook of your arm as my staff, I shall hasten my limbs' slow-foot advance.

(*sung*) O gleam of Zeus's daylight, O black night, why is my heart so aflutter in the dark with fearful apparitions?

62–3 del. Bothe

70 δείμασι φάσμασιν; ὦ πότνια Χθών,
μελανοπτερύγων μᾶτερ ὀνείρων,
ἀποπέμπομαι ἔννυχον ὄψιν
[ἣν περὶ παιδὸς ἐμοῦ τοῦ σῳζομένου κατὰ Θρῄκην
75 ἀμφὶ Πολυξείνης τε φίλης θυγατρὸς δι' ὀνείρων
†εἶδον γὰρ φοβερὰν ὄψιν ἔμαθον ἐδάην†].
ὦ χθόνιοι θεοί, σώσατε παῖδ' ἐμόν,
80 ὃς μόνος οἴκων ἄγκυρ' ἔτ' ἐμῶν
τὰν χιονώδη Θρῄκαν κατέχει
ξείνου πατρίου φυλακαῖσιν.
ἔσται τι νέον·
ἥξει τι μέλος γοερὸν γοεραῖς.
85 οὔποτ' ἐμὰ φρὴν ὧδ' ἀλίαστον
φρίσσει ταρβεῖ.
ποῦ ποτε θείαν Ἑλένου ψυχὰν
καὶ Κασσάνδραν ἐσίδω, Τρωάδες,
ὥς μοι κρίνωσιν ὀνείρους;
90 [εἶδον γὰρ βαλιὰν ἔλαφον λύκου αἵμονι χαλᾷ
σφαζομέναν, ἀπ' ἐμῶν γονάτων σπασθεῖσαν ἀνοίκτως.]
καὶ τόδε δεῖμά μοι·
ἦλθ' ὑπὲρ ἄκρας τύμβου κορυφᾶς
φάντασμ' Ἀχιλέως· ᾔτει δὲ γέρας
95 τῶν πολυμόχθων τινὰ Τρωιάδων.
ἀπ' ἐμᾶς ἀπ' ἐμᾶς οὖν τόδε παιδὸς
πέμψατε, δαίμονες, ἱκετεύω.

73–8 del. Baier, Wilamowitz
85 ἀλίαστον Nauck: -ος C

O lady Earth, mother of black-winged dreams, I thrust from myself the vision of this night [which I saw in dreams concerning my son kept safe in Thrace and about Polyxena my dear daughter, for I saw, beheld, learned of a fearful vision]! O gods of the nether world, spare the life of my son! He is the last remaining anchor of my house and dwells in snowy Thrace in the keeping of his father's guest-friend. Some new sorrow shall come to pass. A tearful strain will come to those already in tears. Never has my heart been so unabatingly fearful and anxious. Where can I see Helenus, that prophetic soul, or Cassandra so that they may interpret my dreams? [For I saw a dappled doe, its throat being cut by the bloody paw of a wolf, torn pitilessly from my knees.] I have this fear as well: the ghost of Achilles came and stood above the peak of his tomb. And he kept asking for one of the trouble-laden daughters of Troy as a prize of honor. From my daughter, from my daughter, I entreat you, O gods, avert this fate!

Enter CHORUS of Trojan women by Eisodos A.

---

⁹⁰⁻⁷ del. Baier, Wilamowitz, 90–1 recte, 92–7 fort. recte

⁹¹ ἀνοίκτως Porson, glossemate ἀνηλεῶς fretus: ἀνάγκᾳ οἰκτρῶς C

⁹⁶ ἀπ’ ἐμᾶς ἀπ’ ἐμᾶς οὖν Bothe: ἀπ’ ἐμᾶς οὖν ἀπ’ ἐμᾶς C

ΧΟΡΟΣ

Ἑκάβη, σπουδῇ πρὸς σ᾽ ἐλιάσθην
τὰς δεσποσύνους σκηνὰς προλιποῦσ᾽,
100 ἵν᾽ ἐκληρώθην καὶ προσετάχθην
δούλη, πόλεως ἀπελαυνομένη
τῆς Ἰλιάδος, λόγχης αἰχμῇ
δοριθήρατος πρὸς Ἀχαιῶν,
οὐδὲν παθέων ἀποκουφίζουσ᾽
105 ἀλλ᾽ ἀγγελίας βάρος ἀραμένη
μέγα σοί τε, γύναι, κῆρυξ ἀχέων.
ἐν γὰρ Ἀχαιῶν πλήρει ξυνόδῳ
λέγεται δόξαι σὴν παῖδ᾽ Ἀχιλεῖ
σφάγιον θέσθαι. τύμβου δ᾽ ἐπιβὰς
110 οἶσθ᾽ ὅτε χρυσέοις ἐφάνη σὺν ὅπλοις,
τὰς ποντοπόρους δ᾽ ἔσχε σχεδίας
λαίφη προτόνοις ἐπερειδομένας,
τάδε θωύσσων· Ποῖ δή, Δαναοί,
τὸν ἐμὸν τύμβον
115 στέλλεσθ᾽ ἀγέραστον ἀφέντες;
πολλῆς δ᾽ ἔριδος συνέπαισε κλύδων,
δόξα δ᾽ ἐχώρει δίχ᾽ ἀν᾽ Ἑλλήνων
στρατὸν αἰχμητήν, τοῖς μὲν διδόναι
τύμβῳ σφάγιον, τοῖς δ᾽ οὐχὶ δοκοῦν.
120 ἦν δὲ τὸ μὲν σὸν σπεύδων ἀγαθὸν
τῆς μαντιπόλου Βάκχης ἀνέχων
λέκτρ᾽ Ἀγαμέμνων· τὼ Θησείδα δ᾽,
ὄζω Ἀθηνῶν, δισσῶν μύθων
ῥήτορες ἦσαν, γνώμῃ δὲ μιᾷ

HECUBA

CHORUS LEADER

Hecuba, I have slipped away to you in haste, leaving my master's tent, where I was assigned by lot and sent as a slave when I was carried off from the city of Ilium, a captive of the Achaean spear. I have not come to lighten any of your troubles but with a heavy burden of tidings, my lady, and as a messenger of grief. It is reported that in the full assembly of the Achaeans they have decided to sacrifice your daughter to Achilles. He appeared in his golden armor, you remember, standing upon his tomb, and checked the seagoing ships, their sails bellied out to their forestays,[a] shouting, "Where are you going, Danaans, leaving my tomb without its prize of honor?" Great waves of strife clashed together, and opinion was divided in the host of Greek spearmen, some thinking it best to give the tomb a victim, others dissenting. Furthering your interests was Agamemnon in loyalty to his mistress Cassandra, the inspired maenad.[b] But the sons of Theseus, two scions of Athens, although they made separate speeches,

---

[a] For the meaning of this phrase, see Diggle on *Phaethon* 86, Page, *Further Greek Epigrams*, p. 376. The ships were moving and had wind in their sails when Achilles' shouted accusation of ingratitude brought them to a halt. There is no evidence in the text that Achilles forced the Greeks to stay in the Chersonese by windlessness. The first mention of wind is line 900, where Agamemnon says that *the god* does not grant favorable breezes, and we are evidently meant to think of this as a new development.

[b] Agamemnon takes Polyxena's part because his mistress Cassandra is Hecuba's daughter and Polyxena's sister.

125 συνεχωρείτην, τὸν Ἀχίλλειον
τύμβον στεφανοῦν αἵματι χλωρῷ,
τὰ δὲ Κασσάνδρας λέκτρ' οὐκ ἐφάτην
τῆς Ἀχιλείας
πρόσθεν θήσειν ποτὲ λόγχης.
130 σπουδαὶ δὲ λόγων κατατεινομένων
ἦσαν ἴσαι πως, πρὶν ὁ ποικιλόφρων
κόπις ἡδυλόγος δημοχαριστὴς
Λαερτιάδης πείθει στρατιὰν
μὴ τὸν ἄριστον Δαναῶν πάντων
135 δούλων σφαγίων οὕνεκ' ἀπωθεῖν,
μηδέ τιν' εἰπεῖν παρὰ Φερσεφόνῃ
στάντα φθιμένων ὡς ἀχάριστοι
Δαναοὶ Δαναοῖς τοῖς οἰχομένοις
ὑπὲρ Ἑλλήνων
140 Τροίας πεδίων ἀπέβησαν.
ἥξει δ' Ὀδυσεὺς ὅσον οὐκ ἤδη
πῶλον ἀφέλξων σῶν ἀπὸ μαστῶν
ἔκ τε γεραιᾶς χερὸς ὁρμήσων.
ἀλλ' ἴθι ναούς, ἴθι πρὸς βωμούς,
145 [ἵζ' Ἀγαμέμνονος ἱκέτις γονάτων,]
κήρυσσε θεοὺς τούς τ' οὐρανίδας
τούς θ' ὑπὸ γαίας. ἢ γάρ σε λιταὶ
διακωλύσουσ' ὀρφανὸν εἶναι
παιδὸς μελέας ἢ δεῖ σ' ἐπιδεῖν
150 τύμβῳ προπετῆ φοινισσομένην
αἵματι παρθένον ἐκ χρυσοφόρου
δειρῆς νασμῷ μελαναυγεῖ.

yet were of a single mind, that the Greeks should crown
Achilles' tomb with fresh blood, and that they would
never set the love of Cassandra above Achilles' spear.
The warmth of debate on either side was about equal
until that wily knave, that honey-tongued demagogue
Odysseus, urged the army not to reject the most valiant of
all the Danaans merely to avoid shedding a slave's blood,
and said that none of the fallen should stand in Perse-
phone's realm and say that Greeks left the plains of Troy
without thanking Greeks who had died for Greeks.
Odysseus is coming at once to tear the foal from your
breast and rush her away from your aged embrace. But
go to the temples, go to the altars, [sit as a suppliant
before the knees of Agamemnon,] call upon the gods,
those of heaven and those beneath the earth! For either
your prayers will save you from the loss of your unlucky
daughter or you must look on as the girl falls bloodied
before the tomb, a dark stream of blood flowing from her
gold-decked throat.

---

[145] del. Heimsoeth
[147] γαίας Porson: γαῖαν C

EURIPIDES

EKABH

στρ.

 οἲ 'γὼ μελέα, τί ποτ' ἀπύσω;
155 ποίαν ἀχώ, ποῖον ὀδυρμόν,
 δειλαία δειλαίου γήρως
 <καὶ> δουλείας τᾶς οὐ τλατᾶς,
 τᾶς οὐ φερτᾶς; ὤμοι μοι.
 τίς ἀμύνει μοι; ποία γενεά,
160 ποία δὲ πόλις; φροῦδος πρέσβυς,
 φροῦδοι παῖδες.
 ποίαν ἢ ταύταν ἢ κείναν
 στείχω; ποῖ δὴ σωθῶ; ποῦ τις
 θεῶν ἢ δαίμων ἐπαρωγός;
165 ὦ κάκ' ἐνεγκοῦσαι
 Τρῳάδες, ὦ κάκ' ἐνεγκοῦσαι
 πήματ', ἀπωλέσατ' ὠλέσατ'· οὐκέτι μοι
 βίος ἀγαστὸς ἐν φάει.
 ὦ τλάμων ἄγησαί μοι πούς,
170 ἄγησαι τᾷ γηραιᾷ
 πρὸς τάνδ' αὐλάν. ὦ τέκνον, ὦ παῖ
 δυστανοτάτας ματέρος, ἔξελθ',
 ἔξελθ' οἴκων,
 ἄιε <σᾶς> ματέρος αὐδάν.

μεσῳδ.

175 ἰὼ τέκνον [ὡς εἰδῇς οἵαν οἵαν
 ἀίω φάμαν περὶ σᾶς ψυχᾶς].

412

HECUBA[a]

Ah me, what unhappiness is mine! What shall I utter, what sound, what cry of lamentation, since I am wretched with wretched old age and slavery unbearable, unendurable? Ah me! Who is my protector? What family, what city? Gone is my aged husband, gone are my children. What road shall I walk, this one or that? Where shall I reach safety? Where is there god or power to help me? Daughters of Troy, who have endured trouble, trouble, you have brought me destruction, destruction! No more is life in the light of day desirable to me!

She turns and moves toward the skene.

Lead me, unhappy feet, lead, I pray, the old woman toward the tent here! O daughter, O child of a mother most luckless, come forth, come forth from your lodging, hear the voice of your mother!

Hear me, daughter [, so that you may know what kind of report I have heard concerning your life]!

Enter POLYXENA *from the* skene.

[a] From here to line 215 Hecuba's and Polyxena's words are sung.

---

157 <καὶ> add. Triclinius
159 γενεά Porson: γέννα C
163 δὴ σωθῶ Diggle: δ' ἤσω C
171 γηραιᾷ Hermann: γραίᾳ C
174 <σᾶς> Dale
175 ἰὼ Reisig: ὦ C
175-6 ὡς . . . ψυχᾶς del. Hartung

ΠΟΛΥΞΕΝΗ

μᾶτερ μᾶτερ, τί βοᾷς; τί νέον
καρύξασ' οἴκων μ' ὥστ' ὄρνιν
θάμβει τῶνδ' ἐξέπταξας;

ΕΚΑΒΗ

180 ὤμοι μοι τέκνον.

ΠΟΛΥΞΕΝΗ

τί με δυσφημεῖς; φροίμιά μοι κακά.

ΕΚΑΒΗ

αἰαῖ σᾶς ψυχᾶς.

ΠΟΛΥΞΕΝΗ

ἐξαύδα· μὴ κρύψῃς δαρόν.
δειμαίνω δειμαίνω, μᾶτερ,
185 τί ποτ' ἀναστένεις.

ΕΚΑΒΗ

τέκνον τέκνον μελέας ματρός . . .

ΠΟΛΥΞΕΝΗ

τί τόδ' ἀγγέλλεις;

ΕΚΑΒΗ

. . . σφάξαι σ' Ἀργείων κοινὰ
συντείνει πρὸς τύμβον γνώμα
190 Πηλείᾳ γέννᾳ.

ΠΟΛΥΞΕΝΗ

οἴμοι, μᾶτερ, πῶς φθέγγῃ;
ἀμέγαρτα κακῶν μάνυσόν μοι,
μάνυσον, μᾶτερ.

POLYXENA

Mother, what are these cries? What news do you bring
that you scare me from this house in terror like a bird?

HECUBA

Alas, my child!

POLYXENA

Why do you address me with these ill-omened words?
They are the prelude to disaster.

HECUBA

Alas for your life!

POLYXENA

Speak out: hide it no longer! I am afraid, mother, afraid
to hear what it is you are lamenting!

HECUBA

Child, child of a luckless mother, . . .

POLYXENA

What is this news you bring?

HECUBA

. . . it is the common decree of the Argive army to sacrifice
you at the tomb of Peleus' son.

POLYXENA

Ah, mother, what do you mean? Tell me of this misery
unenviable, mother, tell me!

---

¹⁷⁷ μᾶτερ μᾶτερ Reisig: ἰὼ μ- μ- fere C
¹⁷⁹ τῶνδ' Reiske: τῷδ' C
¹⁸⁶ τέκνον τέκνον Hermann: ὦ τ- τ- fere C
¹⁹⁰ Πηλείᾳ Paley: Πηλείδα vel -είδου C

EURIPIDES

αὐδῶ, παῖ, δυσφήμους φήμας,
195 ἀγγέλλουσ' Ἀργείων δόξαι
ψήφῳ τᾶς σᾶς περὶ μοίρας.

ΠΟΛΥΞΕΝΗ

ἀντ.

ὦ δεινὰ παθοῦσ', ὦ παντλάμων,
ὦ δυστάνου, μᾶτερ, βιοτᾶς,
οἵαν οἵαν αὖ σοι λώβαν
200 <λώβαν> ἐχθίσταν ἀρρήταν τ'
ὦρσέν τις δαίμων· <ὤμοι.>
οὐκέτι σοι παῖς ἅδ' οὐκέτι δὴ
γήρᾳ δειλαία δειλαίῳ
συνδουλεύσω.
205 σκύμνον γάρ μ' ὥστ' οὐριθρέπταν
μόσχον δειλαία δειλαίαν
< . . . . > ἐσόψῃ
χειρὸς ἀναρπαστὰν
σᾶς ἄπο λαιμότομόν θ' Ἅιδα
γᾶς ὑποπεμπομέναν σκότον, ἔνθα νεκρῶν
210 μέτα τάλαινα κείσομαι.
καὶ σοῦ μέν, μᾶτερ, δυστάνου
κλαίω πανδύρτοις θρήνοις,
τοὐμοῦ δὲ βίου λώβαν λύμαν τ'
οὐ μέγα κλαίομαι, ἀλλὰ θανεῖν μοι
<τοῦ φέγγος ὁρᾶν>
215 πότμος κρείσσων ἐκύρησεν.

416

HECUBA

It is a tale of evil omen that I tell, my child, for I bring the news that the Argives have voted about your fate.

POLYXENA

O mother of terrible suffering, of utter wretchedness, of life ill-starred, what outrage, hateful and unspeakable, has some power roused once more against you! Ah me! No longer, no longer shall you in your wretched old age have your unhappy daughter to share in your slavery. For like the young of a wild beast of the mountain, a miserable calf, you in your misery < . . . . > shall see me torn from your arms and sent down with throat cut to Hades, to the darkness of the earth. There among the dead a wretched creature I shall lie. And it is for you, unhappy mother, that I weep with tearful lamentation, but the brutal outrage to my life—this I do not much lament, for death has come to me as a better fate <than life>.

Enter ODYSSEUS with retinue by Eisodos A.

---

196 μοίρας Page: μοι ψυχᾶς fere C

198 δύστανος Wecklein

200 <λώβαν> Hermann

201 <ὤμοι> Diggle

206 suspectus   post h. v. lac. indic. Murray

211 σοῦ Heimsoeth ex Σ: σὲ C

213 τοὐμοῦ . . . βίου Kovacs: τὸν ἐμὸν . . . βίον C

214 μέγα κλαίομαι Willink: μετακλαίομαι C   post h. v. lac. stat. Kovacs

215 πότμος Weil: ξυντυχία C

EURIPIDES

ΧΟΡΟΣ

καὶ μὴν Ὀδυσσεὺς ἔρχεται σπουδῇ ποδός,
Ἑκάβη, νέον τι πρὸς σὲ σημανῶν ἔπος.

ΟΔΥΣΣΕΥΣ

γύναι, δοκῶ μέν σ᾽ εἰδέναι γνώμην στρατοῦ
ψῆφόν τε τὴν κρανθεῖσαν, ἀλλ᾽ ὅμως φράσω·
220   ἔδοξ᾽ Ἀχαιοῖς παῖδα σὴν Πολυξένην
σφάξαι πρὸς ὀρθὸν χῶμ᾽ Ἀχιλλείου τάφου.
ἡμᾶς δὲ πομποὺς καὶ κομιστῆρας κόρης
τάσσουσιν εἶναι· θύματος δ᾽ ἐπιστάτης
ἱερεύς τ᾽ ἐπέσται τοῦδε παῖς Ἀχιλλέως.
225   οἶσθ᾽ οὖν ὃ δρᾶσον· μήτ᾽ ἀποσπασθῇς βίᾳ
μήτ᾽ ἐς χερῶν ἅμιλλαν ἐξέλθῃς ἐμοί·
γίγνωσκ᾽ ἀνάγκην καὶ παρουσίαν κακῶν
τῶν σῶν. σοφόν τοι κἀν κακοῖς ἃ δεῖ φρονεῖν.

ΕΚΑΒΗ

αἰαῖ· παρέστηχ᾽, ὡς ἔοικ᾽, ἀγὼν μέγας,
230   πλήρης στεναγμῶν οὐδὲ δακρύων κενός.
κἄγωγ᾽ ἄρ᾽ οὐκ ἔθνησκον οὗ μ᾽ ἐχρῆν θανεῖν,
οὐδ᾽ ὤλεσέν με Ζεύς, τρέφει δ᾽, ὅπως ὁρῶ
κακῶν κάκ᾽ ἄλλα μείζον᾽ ἡ τάλαιν᾽ ἐγώ.
εἰ δ᾽ ἔστι τοῖς δούλοισι τοὺς ἐλευθέρους
235   μὴ λυπρὰ μηδὲ καρδίας δηκτήρια
ἐξιστορῆσαι, †σοὶ μὲν εἰρῆσθαι† χρεών,
ἡμᾶς δ᾽ ἀκοῦσαι τοὺς ἐρωτῶντας τάδε.

ΟΔΥΣΣΕΥΣ

ἔξεστ᾽, ἐρώτα· τοῦ χρόνου γὰρ οὐ φθονῶ.

418

CHORUS LEADER

See! Here comes Odysseus with haste in his step,
Hecuba, to bring you fresh news.

ODYSSEUS

Lady, I think you know the will of the army and the vote
that was cast, but still I will tell you: the Argives have
resolved to slay your daughter Polyxena at the high burial
mound of Achilles' tomb. They have made me the escort
to fetch the girl. Presiding over this sacrifice as its priest
will be Achilles' son. Here then is what you must do: do
not make me tear her from you by force or try to fight me
hand to hand. Recognize that hard necessity is upon you
and that this is the hour of trouble for you. Even in
misfortune it is wise to take the attitude circumstance
requires.

HECUBA

O grief! It seems there is a great struggle at hand, one
full of groans and with no lack of tears! I did not die, it
now appears, when I ought to have died, and Zeus did not
kill me but keeps me alive, poor wretch, only to see new
misfortunes still greater than the old! But if slaves may
address to the free such questions as do not cause them
pain or sting their hearts, it is right for you to reply and
for us the askers to listen.

ODYSSEUS

It is permitted: ask your questions. I do not begrudge
you the time.

---

²²⁴ ἐπέσται Nauck: ἐπέστη C
²²⁷ γίγνωσκ' ἀνάγκην Herwerden: γίγνωσκε δ' ἀλκὴν C
²³⁶ σὲ μὲν ἀμείβεσθαι Herwerden

ΕΚΑΒΗ

οἶσθ' ἡνίκ' ἦλθες Ἰλίου κατάσκοπος
240   δυσχλαινίᾳ τ' ἄμορφος ὀμμάτων τ' ἄπο
φόνου σταλαγμοὶ σὴν κατέσταζον γένυν;

ΟΔΥΣΣΕΥΣ

οἶδ'· οὐ γὰρ ἄκρας καρδίας ἔψαυσέ μου.

ΕΚΑΒΗ

ἔγνω δέ σ' Ἑλένη καὶ μόνῃ κατεῖπ' ἐμοί;

ΟΔΥΣΣΕΥΣ

μεμνήμεθ' ἐς κίνδυνον ἐλθόντες μέγαν.

ΕΚΑΒΗ

245   ἦψω δὲ γονάτων τῶν ἐμῶν ταπεινὸς ὤν;

ΟΔΥΣΣΕΥΣ

246   ὥστ' ἐνθανεῖν γε σοῖς πέπλοισι χεῖρ' ἐμήν.

ΕΚΑΒΗ

249   τί δῆτ' ἔλεξας δοῦλος ὢν ἐμὸς τότε;

ΟΔΥΣΣΕΥΣ

250   πολλῶν λόγων εὑρήμαθ' ὥστε μὴ θανεῖν.

ΕΚΑΒΗ

247   ἔσωσα δῆτά σ' ἐξέπεμψά τε χθονός;

ΟΔΥΣΣΕΥΣ

248   ὥστ' εἰσορᾶν γε φέγγος ἡλίου τόδε.

245-51 hoc ordine pars codd.

HECUBA

Do you remember when you came to spy on Ilium, your appearance disfigured by tattered clothes and with blood dripping from your brow onto your chin?[a]

ODYSSEUS

I do. It touched me to my heart's core.

HECUBA

Did Helen recognize you and reveal you to me alone?

ODYSSEUS

I remember that I ran into grave danger.

HECUBA

And did you humbly touch my knees in supplication?

ODYSSEUS

So much so that my hand in the folds of your robe went numb.

HECUBA

What did you say when you were my slave on that occasion?

ODYSSEUS

All the words I could find to avoid being killed.

HECUBA

And did I spare your life and send you out of the country?

ODYSSEUS

Yes, and that is why today I am looking on the sun's light.

[a] In *Odyssey* 4.244–56 the story is told of Odysseus' coming to Troy as a spy, disguised by ragged clothing and self-inflicted wounds. In Homer's version only Helen realizes his identity.

ΕΚΑΒΗ

251 οὔκουν κακύνῃ τοῖσδε τοῖς βουλεύμασιν,
ὃς ἐξ ἐμοῦ μὲν ἔπαθες οἷα φῂς παθεῖν,
δρᾷς δ' οὐδὲν ἡμᾶς εὖ, κακῶς δ' ὅσον δύνᾳ;
ἀχάριστον ὑμῶν σπέρμ', ὅσοι δημηγόρους
255 ζηλοῦτε τιμάς· μηδὲ γιγνώσκοισθέ μοι,
οἳ τοὺς φίλους βλάπτοντες οὐ φροντίζετε,
ἢν τοῖσι πολλοῖς πρὸς χάριν λέγητέ τι.

ἀτὰρ τί δὴ σόφισμα τοῦθ' ἡγούμενοι
ἐς τήνδε παῖδα ψῆφον ὥρισαν φόνου;
260 πότερα τὸ χρή σφ' ἐπήγαγ' ἀνθρωποσφαγεῖν
πρὸς τύμβον, ἔνθα βουθυτεῖν μᾶλλον πρέπει;
ἢ τοὺς κτανόντας ἀνταποκτεῖναι θέλων
ἐς τήνδ' Ἀχιλλεὺς ἐνδίκως τείνει φόνον;
ἀλλ' οὐδὲν αὐτὸν ἥδε γ' εἴργασται κακόν.
265 [Ἑλένην νιν αἰτεῖν χρῆν τάφῳ προσφάγματα·
κείνη γὰρ ὤλεσέν νιν ἐς Τροίαν τ' ἄγει.]
εἰ δ' αἰχμαλώτων χρή τιν' ἔκκριτον θανεῖν
κάλλει θ' ὑπερφέρουσαν, οὐχ ἡμῶν τόδε·
ἡ Τυνδαρὶς γὰρ εἶδος ἐκπρεπεστάτη,
270 ἀδικοῦσά θ' ἡμῶν οὐδὲν ἧσσον ηὑρέθη.

τῷ μὲν δικαίῳ τόνδ' ἁμιλλῶμαι λόγον·
ἃ δ' ἀντιδοῦναι δεῖ σ' ἀπαιτούσης ἐμοῦ
ἄκουσον. ἥψω τῆς ἐμῆς, ὡς φῄς, χερὸς
καὶ τῆσδε γραίας προσπίτνων παρηίδος·
275 ἀνθάπτομαί σου τῶνδε τῶν αὐτῶν ἐγὼ
χάριν τ' ἀπαιτῶ τὴν τόθ' ἱκετεύω τέ σε,
μή μου τὸ τέκνον ἐκ χερῶν ἀποσπάσῃς

HECUBA

Is it not then utter baseness to put forward these propos-
als of yours? You have been treated by me as you admit
you were treated, yet you do me no good but instead all
the harm you can. An ungrateful lot you all are, who want
to be political leaders! Never may you be acquaintances
of mine! You do not care that you harm your friends pro-
vided that you say something to gratify the crowd!

But what cleverness did they imagine it was when they
passed a sentence of death against this girl? Was it Fate
that induced them to perform human sacrifice at a tomb,
a place where the sacrifice of a bull is more fitting? Or if
Achilles wished to pay back those who killed him, is it
right for him to murder *her*? She has done him no harm.
[He ought to be asking for Helen as a victim for his tomb.
For she caused his death by bringing him to Troy.] But if
it is necessary that of captives the choicest and most beau-
tiful be put to death, that honor does not belong to us.
Tyndareus' daughter Helen is the most outstanding in
beauty, and she has clearly done him no less harm than we
Trojans did.

Justice is the ground on which I make this plea. But
hear also what return you must make, since I am demand-
ing return, for kindness received. *(She supplicates
Odysseus, grasping his hand and chin.)* As you admit,
you fell in supplication before me and grasped my hand
and my aged cheek. I grasp you in the same way, and I
ask for the return of the favor I showed you then, and I
beg you: do not tear my child from my arms, do not kill

---

²⁶⁰ χρὴ Nauck: χρῆν C   ²⁶⁵⁻⁶ del. Kovacs
²⁷⁴ γραίας Valckenaer: γεραιᾶς vel γηρ- C

μηδὲ κτάνητε· τῶν τεθνηκότων ἅλις.
[ταύτῃ γέγηθα κἀπιλήθομαι κακῶν.
280 ἥδ' ἀντὶ πολλῶν ἐστί μοι παραψυχή,
πόλις, τιθήνη, βάκτρον, ἡγεμὼν ὁδοῦ.]
οὐ τοὺς κρατοῦντας χρὴ κρατεῖν ἃ μὴ χρεὼν
οὐδ' εὐτυχοῦντας εὖ δοκεῖν πράξειν ἀεί·
κἀγὼ γὰρ ἦ ποτ' ἀλλὰ νῦν οὐκ εἴμ' ἔτι,
285 τὸν πάντα δ' ὄλβον ἦμαρ ἕν μ' ἀφείλετο.

ἀλλ', ὦ φίλον γένειον, αἰδέσθητί με,
οἴκτιρον· ἐλθὼν δ' εἰς Ἀχαικὸν στρατὸν
παρηγόρησον ὡς ἀποκτείνειν φθόνος
γυναῖκας, ἃς τὸ πρῶτον οὐκ ἐκτείνατε
290 βωμῶν ἀποσπάσαντες ἀλλ' ᾠκτίρατε.
νόμος δ' ἐν ὑμῖν τοῖς τ' ἐλευθέροις ἴσος
καὶ τοῖσι δούλοις αἵματος κεῖται πέρι.
τὸ δ' ἀξίωμα, κἂν κακῶς λέγῃς, τὸ σὸν
πείσει· λόγος γὰρ ἔκ τ' ἀδοξούντων ἰὼν
295 κἀκ τῶν δοκούντων αὐτὸς οὐ ταὐτὸν σθένει.

ΧΟΡΟΣ
οὐκ ἔστιν οὕτω στερρὸς ἀνθρώπου φύσις
ἥτις γόων σῶν καὶ μακρῶν ὀδυρμάτων
κλύουσα θρήνους οὐκ ἂν ἐκβάλοι δάκρυ.

ΟΔΥΣΣΕΥΣ
Ἑκάβη, διδάσκου, μηδὲ τῷ θυμουμένῳ
300 τὸν εὖ λέγοντα δυσμενῆ ποιοῦ φρενί.
ἐγὼ τὸ μὲν σὸν σῶμ' ὑφ' οὗπερ εὐτύχουν
σῴζειν ἕτοιμός εἰμι κοὐκ ἄλλως λέγω·

her! Enough have been killed already! [I take joy in her and forget my troubles. She is a consolation to me for many things, she is my city, my nurse, my staff, my guide upon the road.] Those who have power ought not to exercise it wrongfully, nor when they are fortunate should they imagine that they will be so forever. I too was once someone of importance, but now I am so no longer: a single day has stolen all my happiness from me.

But, I beg you by your beard, have pity on me, have pity! Go to the Achaean army and deflect them from their purpose, tell them that it calls forth righteous anger to slay women you once spared out of pity when you took them from the altars. Moreover in your country there is a law laid down, the same for free men and slaves, concerning the shedding of blood. What is more, even if you speak without eloquence, your prestige will carry the day. For the same speech has quite a different force if it is spoken by a man of repute or by a nobody.

CHORUS LEADER

No nature is so unfeeling that it can hear your groans and your long lamentations without shedding a tear.

ODYSSEUS

Hecuba, hear what I have to teach you, and do not in anger make an enemy in your heart of one who gives you good advice. I am ready—I will not say otherwise—to save *your* life, since at your hands I enjoyed good fortune.

[279–81] del. Kovacs (279 iam Hartung cl. *Or.* 66)

[293] λέγῃς vertit Ennius, fr. 172 Jocelyn, coni. Muretus: -ῃ C

EURIPIDES

ἃ δ' εἶπον εἰς ἅπαντας οὐκ ἀρνήσομαι,
Τροίας ἁλούσης ἀνδρὶ τῷ πρώτῳ στρατοῦ
305 σὴν παῖδα δοῦναι σφάγιον ἐξαιτουμένῳ.
ἐν τῷδε γὰρ κάμνουσιν αἱ πολλαὶ πόλεις,
ὅταν τις ἐσθλὸς καὶ πρόθυμος ὢν ἀνὴρ
μηδὲν φέρηται τῶν κακιόνων πλέον.
ἡμῖν δ' Ἀχιλλεὺς ἄξιος τιμῆς, γύναι,
310 θανὼν ὑπὲρ γῆς Ἑλλάδος κάλλιστ' ἀνήρ.
οὔκουν τόδ' αἰσχρόν, εἰ βλέποντι μὲν φίλῳ
χρώμεσθ', ἐπεὶ δ' ὄλωλε μὴ χρώμεσθ' ἔτι;
εἶέν· τί δῆτ' ἐρεῖ τις, ἤν τις αὖ φανῇ
στρατοῦ τ' ἄθροισις πολεμίων τ' ἀγωνία;
315 πότερα μαχούμεθ' ἢ φιλοψυχήσομεν,
τὸν κατθανόνθ' ὁρῶντες οὐ τιμώμενον;
καὶ μὴν ἔμοιγε ζῶντι μὲν καθ' ἡμέραν
κεἰ σμίκρ' ἔχοιμι πάντ' ἂν ἀρκούντως ἔχοι·
τύμβον δὲ βουλοίμην ἂν ἀξιούμενον
320 τὸν ἐμὸν ὁρᾶσθαι· διὰ μακροῦ γὰρ ἡ χάρις.
  εἰ δ' οἰκτρὰ πάσχειν φῄς, τάδ' ἀντάκουέ μου·
εἰσὶν παρ' ἡμῖν οὐδὲν ἧσσον ἄθλιαι
γραῖαι γυναῖκες ἠδὲ πρεσβῦται σέθεν,
νύμφαι τ' ἀρίστων νυμφίων τητώμεναι,
325 ὧν ἥδε κεύθει σώματ' Ἰδαία κόνις.
τόλμα τάδ'. ἡμεῖς δ', εἰ κακῶς νομίζομεν
τιμᾶν τὸν ἐσθλόν, ἀμαθίαν ὀφλήσομεν·
οἱ βάρβαροι δὲ μήτε τοὺς φίλους φίλους
ἡγεῖσθε μήτε τοὺς καλῶς τεθνηκότας
330 θαυμάζεθ', ὡς ἂν ἡ μὲν Ἑλλὰς εὐτυχῇ,
ὑμεῖς δ' ἔχηθ' ὅμοια τοῖς βουλεύμασιν.

But I shall not unsay what I said to the whole assembly,
that since Troy has been captured, we ought to sacrifice
your daughter to the most valiant man in the army since
he has asked for her. It is exactly here that most cities get
into trouble, when a man who is both valiant and eager to
serve wins no greater prize of valor than his inferiors.
Achilles is worthy of honor in our eyes, lady, since he died
a most glorious death on behalf of the land of Greece. Is
it not a disgrace if we treat him as our friend while he
lives but after he is dead treat him so no longer? What
then will people say if occasion arises to muster the army
again and fight the enemy? Will we fight, or will we save
our skins since we notice that those who die receive no
honor? Besides, I at any rate would be satisfied in life if I
had only a little for my daily needs. But I would like to
see my tomb held worthy of honor: that is gratitude that
endures.

If you claim that your sufferings are worthy of pity,
hear what I have to say in reply. We have in Greece gray-
haired women and old men who are no less wretched
than yourself, and also brides bereft of their brave bride-
grooms, men whose bodies are covered by the soil of
Troy. You must bear up under this. As for us, if it is a bad
custom to honor the brave warrior, we will incur the
charge of hardheartedness. Continue, barbarian peoples,
not regarding your friends as friends and *not* honoring
those who have died noble deaths, so that Greece may
prosper while you enjoy the fate your principles deserve!

---

[320] τὸν ἐμὸν] στεφάνων Porson: στεφῶν Weil: τιμῶν Sakor-
raphos

EURIPIDES

ΧΟΡΟΣ

αἰαῖ· τὸ δοῦλον ὡς κακὸν πέφυκ' ἀεὶ
τολμᾷ θ' ἃ μὴ χρή, τῇ βίᾳ νικώμενον.

ΕΚΑΒΗ

ὦ θύγατερ, οὑμοὶ μὲν λόγοι πρὸς αἰθέρα
335 φροῦδοι μάτην ῥιφθέντες ἀμφὶ σοῦ φόνου·
σὺ δ', εἴ τι μείζω δύναμιν ἢ μήτηρ ἔχεις,
σπούδαζε πάσας ὥστ' ἀηδόνος στόμα
φθογγὰς ἱεῖσα, μὴ στερηθῆναι βίου.
πρόσπιπτε δ' οἰκτρῶς τοῦδ' Ὀδυσσέως γόνυ
340 καὶ πεῖθ' (ἔχεις δὲ πρόφασιν· ἔστι γὰρ τέκνα
καὶ τῷδε) τὴν σὴν ὥστ' ἐποικτῖραι τύχην.

ΠΟΛΥΞΕΝΗ

ὁρῶ σ', Ὀδυσσεῦ, δεξιὰν ὑφ' εἵματος
κρύπτοντα χεῖρα καὶ πρόσωπον ἔμπαλιν
στρέφοντα, μή σου προσθίγω γενειάδος.
345 θάρσει· πέφευγας τὸν ἐμὸν Ἱκέσιον Δία·
ὡς ἕψομαί γε τοῦ τ' ἀναγκαίου χάριν
θανεῖν τε χρῄζουσ'· εἰ δὲ μὴ βουλήσομαι,
κακὴ φανοῦμαι καὶ φιλόψυχος γυνή.
τί γάρ με δεῖ ζῆν; ᾗ πατὴρ μὲν ἦν ἄναξ
350 Φρυγῶν ἁπάντων· τοῦτό μοι πρῶτον βίου.
ἔπειτ' ἐθρέφθην ἐλπίδων καλῶν ὕπο
βασιλεῦσι νύμφη, ζῆλον οὐ σμικρὸν γάμων
ἔχουσ', ὅτου δῶμ' ἑστίαν τ' ἀφίξομαι·

CHORUS LEADER

Ah me! What an evil thing slavery always is! Slaves suffer injustice when violence overcomes them.

HECUBA

(releasing her suppliant grasp and rising to her feet)
Daughter, my speech pleading against your murder has been cast idly to the winds. But if you have any power greater than your mother's, spare no effort and utter like some nightingale all the notes within you so that you may not be robbed of life. Throw yourself heartrendingly at the knees of this man and try to win him over (you have a basis for your plea, for he has children too) so that he may take pity on your fate!

Odysseus turns his head away and covers his right hand in his garments.

POLYXENA

Odysseus, I see that you are hiding your right hand under your cloak and turning your face away so that I may not touch your chin. Courage! You have escaped from my Zeus of Suppliants![a] I shall follow you, both because I must do so and because I want to die. If I refuse to die, I will show myself to be a craven and cowardly woman. Why should I live? My father was king of all the Phrygians: that was how I started life. And then I was raised in high hopes that I would be the bride of royalty, and that it would be no small cause of rivalry whose hearth and

---

[a] Zeus Hikesios watches over suppliants, both those who take refuge at shrines and those who throw themselves at the knees of others. Refusing a request made by a suppliant was regarded as an offense against him.

δέσποινα δ' ἡ δύστηνος Ἰδαίαισιν ἢ
355 γυναιξί, παρθένοις τ' ἀπόβλεπτος μέτα,
ἴση θεοῖσι πλὴν τὸ κατθανεῖν μόνον.
νῦν δ' εἰμὶ δούλη. πρῶτα μέν με τοὔνομα
θανεῖν ἐρᾶν τίθησιν οὐκ εἰωθὸς ὄν·
ἔπειτ' ἴσως ἂν δεσποτῶν ὠμῶν φρένας
360 τύχοιμ' ἄν, ὅστις ἀργύρου μ' ὠνήσεται,
τὴν Ἕκτορός τε χἀτέρων πολλῶν κάσιν,
προσθεὶς δ' ἀνάγκην σιτοποιὸν ἐν δόμοις
σαίρειν τε δῶμα κερκίσιν τ' ἐφεστάναι
λυπρὰν ἄγουσαν ἡμέραν μ' ἀναγκάσει·
365 λέχη δὲ τἀμὰ δοῦλος ὠνητός ποθεν
χρανεῖ, τυράννων πρόσθεν ἠξιωμένα.
οὐ δῆτ'· ἀφίημ' ὀμμάτων ἐλευθέρων
φέγγος τόδ', Ἅιδη προστιθεῖσ' ἐμὸν δέμας.
ἄγ' οὖν μ', Ὀδυσσεῦ, καὶ διέργασαί μ' ἄγων·
370 οὔτ' ἐλπίδος γὰρ οὔτε του δόξης ὁρῶ
θάρσος παρ' ἡμῖν ὥς ποτ' εὖ πρᾶξαί με χρή.
μῆτερ, σὺ δ' ἡμῖν μηδὲν ἐμποδὼν γένῃ
λέγουσα μηδὲ δρῶσα, συμβούλου δέ μοι
θανεῖν πρὶν αἰσχρῶν μὴ κατ' ἀξίαν τυχεῖν.
375 ὅστις γὰρ οὐκ εἴωθε γεύεσθαι κακῶν
φέρει μέν, ἀλγεῖ δ' αὐχέν' ἐντιθεὶς ζυγῷ·
θανὼν δ' ἂν εἴη μᾶλλον εὐτυχέστερος
ἢ ζῶν· τὸ γὰρ ζῆν μὴ καλῶς μέγας πόνος.

ΧΟΡΟΣ

δεινὸς χαρακτὴρ κἀπίσημος ἐν βροτοῖς
380 ἐσθλῶν γενέσθαι, κἀπὶ μεῖζον ἔρχεται
τῆς εὐγενείας ὄνομα τοῖσιν ἀξίοις.

home I should grace. To the women of Troy I, ill-starred wretch, was their lady mistress, and in the company of the young girls I was conspicuous, like the gods in all but my mortality. But now I am a slave. First, the very word in its strangeness makes me long to die. Then perhaps I shall get a cruel-hearted master, who shall buy me for so much silver, me, the sister of Hector and many other noble brothers, and compel me to serve in the palace kitchen, to sweep the floors, and to tend the loom, living a life of misery. Some slave, bought from who knows where, will defile my bed, a bed once deemed worthy of royalty. It shall not be! From eyes still free I shut out the light of day and consign myself to the world below! Take me away, Odysseus, and in the taking end my life! For I see no encouraging hope or thought that I shall ever be happy. Mother, do not oppose me by word or deed, but rather share my wish that I should die before I meet with a disgrace my rank does not deserve. One who is unaccustomed to the experience of disaster, though he endures it, yet feels pain at putting his neck in the yoke. He will be luckier dead than alive, for life without honor is sore vexation.

CHORUS LEADER

How strangely unmistakable is the stamp of noble birth among mortals! More marvelous still is nobility's name in those worthy of it.

---

367 ἐλευθέρων Blomfield: ἐλεύθερον C

EURIPIDES

ΕΚΑΒΗ

καλῶς μὲν εἶπας, θύγατερ, ἀλλὰ τῷ καλῷ
λύπη πρόσεστιν. εἰ δὲ δεῖ τῷ Πηλέως
χάριν γενέσθαι παιδὶ καὶ ψόγον φυγεῖν
385 ὑμᾶς, Ὀδυσσεῦ, τήνδε μὲν μὴ κτείνετε,
ἡμᾶς δ' ἄγοντες πρὸς πυρὰν Ἀχιλλέως
κεντεῖτε, μὴ φείδεσθ'· ἐγὼ 'τεκον Πάριν,
ὃς παῖδα Θέτιδος ὤλεσεν τόξοις βαλών.

ΟΔΥΣΣΕΥΣ

οὐ σ', ὦ γεραιά, κατθανεῖν Ἀχιλλέως
390 φάντασμ' Ἀχαιοὺς ἀλλὰ τήνδ' ᾐτήσατο.

ΕΚΑΒΗ

ὑμεῖς δέ μ' ἀλλὰ θυγατρὶ συμφονεύσατε,
καὶ δὶς τόσον πῶμ' αἵματος γενήσεται
γαίᾳ νεκρῷ τε τῷ τάδ' ἐξαιτουμένῳ.

ΟΔΥΣΣΕΥΣ

ἅλις κόρης σῆς θάνατος, οὐ προσοιστέος
395 ἄλλος πρὸς ἄλλῳ· μηδὲ τόνδ' ὠφείλομεν.

ΕΚΑΒΗ

πολλή γ' ἀνάγκη θυγατρὶ συνθανεῖν ἐμέ.

ΟΔΥΣΣΕΥΣ

πῶς; οὐ γὰρ οἶδα δεσπότας κεκτημένος.

ΕΚΑΒΗ

ὅμοια· κισσὸς δρυὸς ὅπως τῆσδ' ἕξομαι.

ΟΔΥΣΣΕΥΣ

οὔκ, ἤν γε πείθῃ τοῖσι σοῦ σοφωτέροις.

432

HECUBA

That was nobly spoken, my daughter, but in that nobility
what sadness! Yet, Odysseus, if gratitude is to be shown
to the son of Peleus and you are to escape censure,
instead of killing her, take me to the grave of Achilles,
stab me and show no mercy. It was I who gave birth to
Paris, the man who killed Achilles with his arrow.

ODYSSEUS

Old woman, it is not your death that the ghost of Achilles
asked of the Achaeans but hers.

HECUBA

But at least kill me together with my daughter, and then
the earth and the dead man who asked for it will have
twice as much blood to drink!

ODYSSEUS

Your daughter's death is enough, and we should not pile
one death on another. Would that we had no need of this
death!

HECUBA

I absolutely *must* be killed with my daughter!

ODYSSEUS

Must? I am not aware that I have a master.

HECUBA

No matter: I shall cling to her like ivy to the oak.

ODYSSEUS

Not if you obey wiser heads than yours.

---

398 ὄμοια Reiske: ὁποῖα C

ΕΚΑΒΗ

400 ὡς τῆσδ᾽ ἑκοῦσα παιδὸς οὐ μεθήσομαι.

ΟΔΥΣΣΕΥΣ

ἀλλ᾽ οὐδ᾽ ἐγὼ μὴν τήνδ᾽ ἄπειμ᾽ αὐτοῦ λιπών.

ΠΟΛΥΞΕΝΗ

μῆτερ, πιθοῦ μοι· καὶ σύ, παῖ Λαερτίου,
χάλα τοκεῦσιν εἰκότως θυμουμένοις,
σύ τ᾽, ὦ τάλαινα, τοῖς κρατοῦσι μὴ μάχου.
405 βούλῃ πεσεῖν πρὸς οὖδας ἑλκῶσαί τε σὸν
γέροντα χρῶτα πρὸς βίαν ὠθουμένη
ἀσχημονῆσαί τ᾽ ἐκ νέου βραχίονος
σπασθεῖσ᾽, ἃ πείσῃ; μὴ σύ γ᾽· οὐ γὰρ ἄξιον.
ἀλλ᾽, ὦ φίλη μοι μῆτερ, ἡδίστην χέρα
410 δὸς καὶ παρειὰν προσβαλεῖν παρηίδι,
ὡς οὔποτ᾽ αὖθις ἀλλὰ νῦν πανύστατον
[ἀκτῖνα κύκλον θ᾽ ἡλίου προσόψομαι].
τέλος δέχῃ δὴ τῶν ἐμῶν προσφθεγμάτων·
414 ὦ μῆτερ ὦ τεκοῦσ᾽, ἄπειμι δὴ κάτω.

ΕΚΑΒΗ

417 οἰκτρὰ σύ, τέκνον, ἀθλία δ᾽ ἐγὼ γυνή.

ΠΟΛΥΞΕΝΗ

418 ἐκεῖ δ᾽ ἐν Ἅιδου κείσομαι χωρὶς σέθεν.

ΕΚΑΒΗ

419 οἴμοι· τί δράσω; ποῖ τελευτήσω βίον;

ΠΟΛΥΞΕΝΗ

420 δούλη θανοῦμαι, πατρὸς οὖσ᾽ ἐλευθέρου . . .

HECUBA
Be quite clear: I shall not willingly let her go.

ODYSSEUS
But I for my part will not go away and leave her here.

POLYXENA
Mother, be ruled by me. You, son of Laertes, be gentle
with my mother, who has cause for anger, and you,
unhappy mother, do not fight against your masters. Do
you want to be thrust aside by force, be thrown to the
ground, gash your aged flesh, and lose your dignity as you
are violently torn from me by a vigorous arm? This is
what will happen. Do not suffer such treatment: it is
beneath your dignity. Rather, dearest mother, give me
the hand I love and let me press my cheek against yours,
for never again shall I do so, this is the last time [I shall
look on the ray and the orb of the sun]. You hear the very
last words I shall speak to you. O mother who bore me, I
go to the world below!

HECUBA
Pitiable are you, my child, but I am in misery!

POLYXENA
There in the lower world I shall lie, separated from you.

HECUBA
Ah me! What am I to do? Where shall my life end?

POLYXENA
I shall die a slave, though my father was a free man . . .

---

[412] om. pars codd., del. Wecklein: cf. *Alc*. 207–8
[414-21] hoc ordine Diggle

ΕΚΑΒΗ

415 ὦ θύγατερ, ἡμεῖς δ' ἐν φάει δουλεύσομεν.

ΠΟΛΥΞΕΝΗ

416 . . . ἄνυμφος ἀνυμέναιος ὧν μ' ἐχρῆν τυχεῖν.

ΕΚΑΒΗ

421 ἡμεῖς δὲ πεντήκοντά γ' ἄμμοροι τέκνων.

ΠΟΛΥΞΕΝΗ

τί σοι πρὸς Ἕκτορ' ἢ γέροντ' εἴπω πόσιν;

ΕΚΑΒΗ

ἄγγελλε πασῶν ἀθλιωτάτην ἐμέ.

ΠΟΛΥΞΕΝΗ

ὦ στέρνα μαστοί θ', οἵ μ' ἐθρέψαθ' ἡδέως.

ΕΚΑΒΗ

425 ὦ τῆς ἀώρου θύγατερ ἀθλία τύχης.

ΠΟΛΥΞΕΝΗ

χαῖρ', ὦ τεκοῦσα, χαῖρε Κασσάνδρα τέ μοι . . .

ΕΚΑΒΗ

χαίρουσιν ἄλλοι, μητρὶ δ' οὐκ ἔστιν τόδε.

ΠΟΛΥΞΕΝΗ

. . . ὅ τ' ἐν φιλίπποις Θρῃξὶ Πολύδωρος κάσις.

ΕΚΑΒΗ

εἰ ζῇ γ'· ἀπιστῶ δ'· ὧδε πάντα δυστυχῶ.

ΠΟΛΥΞΕΝΗ

430 ζῇ καὶ θανούσης ὄμμα συγκλῄσει τὸ σόν.

---

425 ἀθλία Markland: -ας vel -ου C

436

HECUBA

I, daughter, shall be a slave among the living.

POLYXENA

. . . robbed of the bridegroom and wedding I should have had.

HECUBA

Yes, and I bereft of my fifty children.

POLYXENA

What message shall I take to Hector and to your aged husband?

HECUBA

Tell them that I am of all women the most miserable!

POLYXENA

O mother's breasts, that suckled me so sweetly!

HECUBA

O daughter, unlucky in your untimely fate!

POLYXENA

Farewell, mother, farewell also to Cassandra . . .

HECUBA

Others fare well, your mother cannot do so.

POLYXENA

. . . and also to my brother Polydorus among the horse-loving Thracians!

HECUBA

Yes, if he is alive. But I do not believe it: my misfortune is so complete.

POLYXENA

He is alive and will close your eyes when you die.

ΕΚΑΒΗ

τέθνηκ' ἔγωγε πρὶν θανεῖν κακῶν ὕπο.

ΠΟΛΥΞΕΝΗ

κόμιζ' Ὀδυσσεῦ μ' ἀμφιθεὶς κάρᾳ πέπλους
ὡς πρὶν σφαγῆναί γ' ἐκτέτηκα καρδίαν
θρήνοισι μητρὸς τήνδε τ' ἐκτήκω γόοις.
435   ὦ φῶς· προσειπεῖν γὰρ σὸν ὄνομ' ἔξεστί μοι,
μέτεστι δ' οὐδὲν πλὴν ὅσον χρόνον ξίφους
βαίνω μεταξὺ καὶ πυρᾶς Ἀχιλλέως.

ΕΚΑΒΗ

οἲ 'γώ, προλείπω· λύεται δέ μου μέλη.
ὦ θύγατερ, ἅψαι μητρός, ἔκτεινον χέρα,
440   δός, μὴ λίπῃς μ' ἄπαιδ'. ἀπωλόμην, φίλαι.
ὣς τὴν Λάκαιναν σύγγονον Διοσκόροιν
Ἑλένην ἴδοιμι· διὰ καλῶν γὰρ ὀμμάτων
αἴσχιστα Τροίαν εἷλε τὴν εὐδαίμονα.

ΧΟΡΟΣ

στρ. α

αὔρα, ποντιὰς αὔρα,
445   ἅτε ποντοπόρους κομί-
ζεις θοὰς ἀκάτους ἐπ' οἶδμα λίμνας,
ποῖ με τὰν μελέαν πορεύ-
σεις; τῷ δουλόσυνος πρὸς οἶ-
κον κτηθεῖσ' ἀφίξομαι; ἢ
450   Δωρίδος ὅρμον αἴας,
ἢ Φθιάδος, ἔνθα τὸν

---

432 κάρᾳ πέπλους Kirchhoff: κάρα πέπλοις C

438

HECUBA

I am already dead before my death, killed by my misfortunes.

POLYXENA

Wrap this garment about my head, Odysseus, and take me away, for the heart within me, before my slaughter, has been made to melt with the lamentations of my mother, and I melt her heart with mine. O sunlight! I have the power to speak your name but no share in you except for the brief time I walk from here to the sword and the pyre of Achilles!

Exit POLYXENA and ODYSSEUS with his retinue by Eisodos A.

HECUBA

Ah, ah! I am faint! My limbs are unstrung! Daughter, take hold of your mother, stretch out your hand, give it to me, do not leave me childless! My friends, my life is over! May I see that Spartan, Helen, sister of the Dioscuri, destroyed as I am! For with her fair eyes she foully ruined the happiness of Troy.

Hecuba lies on the ground and covers her head with her garments.

CHORUS

Breeze, breeze of the open main, conveyer of swift seagoing ships over the swelling deep, where will you take me in my misery? To whose house shall I pass as chattel slave? Shall I come to harbor in a Doric land? Or in

---

⁴⁴¹ ὡς Denniston

καλλίστων ὑδάτων πατέρα
φασὶν Ἀπιδανὸν πεδία λιπαίνειν,

ἀντ. α
455 ἢ νάσων, ἁλιήρει
κώπᾳ πεμπομέναν τάλαι-
ναν, οἰκτρὰν βιοτὰν ἔχουσαν οἴκοις,
ἔνθα πρωτόγονός τε φοῖ-
νιξ δάφνα θ᾽ ἱεροὺς ἀνέ-
460 σχε πτόρθους Λατοῖ φίλον ὠ-
δῖνος ἄγαλμα Δίας;
σὺν Δηλιάσιν τε κού-
ραισιν Ἀρτέμιδος θεᾶς
465 χρυσέαν τ᾽ ἄμπυκα τόξα τ᾽ εὐλογήσω;

στρ. β
ἢ Παλλάδος ἐν πόλει
τὰς καλλιδίφρους Ἀθα-
ναίας ἐν κροκέῳ πέπλῳ
ζεύξομαι ἆρα πώ-
470 λους ἐν δαιδαλέαισι ποι-
κίλλουσ᾽ ἀνθοκρόκοισι πή-
ναις ἢ Τιτάνων γενεάν,
τὰν Ζεὺς ἀμφιπύρῳ
κοιμίζει φλογμῷ Κρονίδας;

ἀντ. β
475 ὤμοι τεκέων ἐμῶν,
ὤμοι πατέρων χθονός θ᾽,
ἃ καπνῷ κατερείπεται
τυφομένα δορί-

Phthia where, men say, the Apidanos, father of waters
most lovely, makes all the plain rich?

Or to an island home, sped on my way in grief by an
oar plied in the brine, to spend a life of misery in the
house, there where the date palm, first of all its line, and
the laurel tree sent up their holy shoots as an adornment
dear to Leto to grace the birth of her children by Zeus?[a]
Shall I with the maidens of Delos sing in praise of the
golden headband and bow of the goddess Artemis?

Or shall I after all in the city of Pallas embroider in
Athena's saffron-colored gown[b] with threads of flowered
hue the yoking of her lovely chariot-mares or the race of
Titans, which Zeus, Cronus' son, laid low with his thun-
derbolts of double flame?

Alas for our children! Alas for our fathers and our
country! It lies a smoking ruin, overrun by the Argive

---

[a] The island is Delos. When Leto was about to give birth to
Apollo and Artemis, Zeus caused a date palm to spring up, whose
trunk Leto grasped during her birth pangs. The prominence of
Delos in this ode may reflect the reestablishment of the festival
of the Delia in 426/5: see Thucydides 3.104.

[b] At the great festival of the Panathenaea, in honor of the
city's tutelary deity, the goddess was presented with a new *pep-
los*, woven by the daughters of prominent citizens. Euripides
allows the chorus to ignore realism here in that slaves would have
had no part in the weaving.

---

460 φίλον Wecklein: φίλᾳ C

κτητος Ἀργείων· ἐγὼ δ'
480 ἐν ξείνᾳ χθονὶ δὴ κέκλη-
μαι δούλα, λιποῦσ' Ἀσίαν,
Εὐρώπας θεραπνᾶν
ἀλλάξασ' Ἅιδα θαλάμους.

ΤΑΛΘΥΒΙΟΣ

ποῦ τὴν ἄνασσαν δή ποτ' οὖσαν Ἰλίου
485 Ἑκάβην ἂν ἐξεύροιμι, Τρῳάδες κόραι;

ΧΟΡΟΣ

αὕτη πέλας σου νῶτ' ἔχουσ' ἐπὶ χθονί,
Ταλθύβιε, κεῖται συγκεκλημένη πέπλοις.

ΤΑΛΘΥΒΙΟΣ

ὦ Ζεῦ, τί λέξω; πότερά σ' ἀνθρώπους ὁρᾶν;
ἢ δόξαν ἄλλως τήνδε κεκτῆσθαι μάτην
490 [ψευδῆ, δοκοῦντας δαιμόνων εἶναι γένος],
τύχην δὲ πάντα τἀν βροτοῖς ἐπισκοπεῖν;
οὐχ ἥδ' ἄνασσα τῶν πολυχρύσων Φρυγῶν,
οὐχ ἥδε Πριάμου τοῦ μέγ' ὀλβίου δάμαρ;
καὶ νῦν πόλις μὲν πᾶσ' ἀνέστηκεν δορί,
495 αὐτὴ δὲ δούλη γραῦς ἄπαις ἐπὶ χθονὶ
κεῖται, κόνει φύρουσα δύστηνον κάρα.
φεῦ φεῦ· γέρων μέν εἰμ', ὅμως δέ μοι θανεῖν
εἴη πρὶν αἰσχρᾷ περιπεσεῖν τύχῃ τινί.
    ἀνίστασ', ὦ δύστηνε, καὶ μετάρσιον
500 πλευρὰν ἔπαιρε καὶ τὸ πάλλευκον κάρα.

490 del. Nauck

442

spear. I shall leave Asia behind and in a strange land bear
the name of slave, exchanging the chambers of the grave
for the dwelling places of Europe.

Enter TALTHYBIUS *by Eisodos A.*

TALTHYBIUS
Trojan women, where might I find Hecuba, once queen
of Ilium?

CHORUS LEADER
She lies at your feet, Talthybius, upon the ground,
wrapped in her garments.

TALTHYBIUS
O Zeus, what shall I say? That you watch over men? Or
that you have won the false reputation for doing so, [false,
supposing that the race of gods exist,] while chance in fact
governs all mortal affairs? Is this not the queen of Phry-
gia rich in gold, the wife of Priam the highly blessed?
And now her whole city has been devastated by the spear,
and she herself, a slave, old and childless, lies upon the
ground, defiling her luckless head in the dust. O the hor-
ror of it! Though I am an old man,[a] still I pray I may die
before I meet with such an ignominious fate!

Get up, unhappy woman, raise your limbs and snow-
white head from the ground.

Hecuba rises slowly to her feet.

---

[a] The old are here presumed to be eager for long life: cf.
Alcestis 669–71.

EURIPIDES

ΕΚΑΒΗ

ἔα· τίς οὗτος σῶμα τοὐμὸν οὐκ ἐᾷ
κεῖσθαι; τί κινεῖς μ᾽, ὅστις εἶ, λυπουμένην;

ΤΑΛΘΥΒΙΟΣ

Ταλθύβιος ἥκω Δαναϊδῶν ὑπηρέτης
[Ἀγαμέμνονος πέμψαντος, ὦ γύναι, μέτα].

ΕΚΑΒΗ

505   ὦ φίλτατ᾽, ἆρα κἄμ᾽ ἐπισφάξαι τάφῳ
δοκοῦν Ἀχαιοῖς ἦλθες; ὡς φίλ᾽ ἂν λέγοις.
σπεύδωμεν, ἐγκονῶμεν· ἡγοῦ μοι, γέρον.

ΤΑΛΘΥΒΙΟΣ

σὴν παῖδα κατθανοῦσαν ὡς θάψῃς, γύναι,
ἥκω μεταστείχων σε· πέμπουσιν δέ με
510   δισσοί τ᾽ Ἀτρεῖδαι καὶ λεὼς Ἀχαιικός.

ΕΚΑΒΗ

οἴμοι, τί λέξεις; οὐκ ἄρ᾽ ὡς θανουμένους
μετῆλθες ἡμᾶς ἀλλὰ σημανῶν κακά.
ὄλωλας, ὦ παῖ, μητρὸς ἁρπασθεῖσ᾽ ἄπο,
ἡμεῖς δ᾽ ἄτεκνοι τοὐπὶ σ᾽· ὦ τάλαιν᾽ ἐγώ.
515   πῶς καί νιν ἐξεπράξατ᾽; ἆρ᾽ αἰδούμενοι;
ἢ πρὸς τὸ δεινὸν ἤλθεθ᾽ ὡς ἐχθράν, γέρον,
κτείνοντες; εἰπέ, καίπερ οὐ λέξων φίλα.

ΤΑΛΘΥΒΙΟΣ

διπλᾶ με χρῄζεις δάκρυα κερδᾶναι, γύναι,
σῆς παιδὸς οἴκτῳ· νῦν τε γὰρ λέγων κακὰ

504 del. Jenni

444

HECUBA

Oh! Who is it that keeps my body from repose? Whoever you are, why do you disturb me in my pain?

TALTHYBIUS

I am Talthybius. I have come as the servant of the Greeks [at the summons, lady, of Agamemnon].

HECUBA

Most welcome of arrivals, have the Achaeans resolved to sacrifice me also on the tomb? Is this your errand? What grateful news that would be! Let us go quickly, lead the way, old sir!

TALTHYBIUS

Lady, your daughter has been killed, and I have come to fetch you so that you may bury her. The two sons of Atreus and the Achaean army have sent me.

HECUBA

Ah, what terrible news! So it was not to take me to my death that you have come but to tell me of misery! You are dead, my daughter, torn from your mother's embrace, and where you were concerned I am a childless woman! O misery! How in fact did you dispatch her? With respect? Or did you proceed to the deed of terror as if you were killing one you hated? Tell me, old man, though your words will not be welcome.

TALTHYBIUS

Lady, your request means that I must twice pay the penalty of tears shed in pity for your daughter. For in telling of her misfortune now I shall drench my face in

520 τέγξω τόδ᾽ ὄμμα πρὸς τάφῳ θ᾽ ὅτ᾽ ὤλλυτο.
παρῆν μὲν ὄχλος πᾶς Ἀχαϊκοῦ στρατοῦ
πλήρης πρὸ τύμβου σῆς κόρης ἐπὶ σφαγάς,
λαβὼν δ᾽ Ἀχιλλέως παῖς Πολυξένην χερὸς
ἔστησ᾽ ἐπ᾽ ἄκρου χώματος, πέλας δ᾽ ἐγώ·
525 λεκτοί τ᾽ Ἀχαιῶν ἔκκριτοι νεανίαι,
σκίρτημα μόσχου σῆς καθέξοντες χεροῖν,
ἕσποντο. πλῆρες δ᾽ ἐν χεροῖν λαβὼν δέπας
πάγχρυσον αἴρει χειρὶ παῖς Ἀχιλλέως
χοὰς θανόντι πατρί· σημαίνει δέ μοι
530 σιγὴν Ἀχαιῶν παντὶ κηρῦξαι στρατῷ.
κἀγὼ καταστὰς εἶπον ἐν μέσοις τάδε·
Σιγᾶτ᾽, Ἀχαιοί, σῖγα πᾶς ἔστω λεώς,
σῖγα σιώπα· νήνεμον δ᾽ ἔστησ᾽ ὄχλον.
ὁ δ᾽ εἶπεν· Ὦ παῖ Πηλέως, πατὴρ δ᾽ ἐμός,
535 δέξαι χοάς μοι τάσδε κηλητηρίους,
νεκρῶν ἀγωγούς· ἐλθὲ δ᾽, ὡς πίῃς μέλαν
κόρης ἀκραιφνὲς αἷμ᾽ ὅ σοι δωρούμεθα
στρατός τε κἀγώ· πρευμενὴς δ᾽ ἡμῖν γενοῦ
λῦσαί τε πρύμνας καὶ χαλινωτήρια
540 νεῶν δὸς ἡμῖν †πρευμενοῦς† τ᾽ ἀπ᾽ Ἰλίου
νόστου τυχόντας πάντας ἐς πάτραν μολεῖν.
    τοσαῦτ᾽ ἔλεξε, πᾶς δ᾽ ἐπηύξατο στρατός.
εἶτ᾽ ἀμφίχρυσον φάσγανον κώπης λαβὼν
ἐξεῖλκε κολεοῦ, λογάσι δ᾽ Ἀργείων στρατοῦ
545 νεανίαις ἔνευσε παρθένον λαβεῖν.
ἡ δ᾽, ὡς ἐφράσθη, τόνδ᾽ ἐσήμηνεν λόγον·
Ὦ τὴν ἐμὴν πέρσαντες Ἀργεῖοι πόλιν,

446

tears, even as I did at the tomb when she was being killed. The whole Achaean army stood by at the tomb for your daughter's sacrifice, and Achilles' son took Polyxena by the hand and stood her at the topmost part of the mound, and I stood near. Picked youth of the Achaean army accompanied them, ready to check with their grasp any leap your daughter might make. Achilles' son took in his hand a cup of solid gold filled to the brim and lifted it up as a libation to his dead father. He nodded to me to call for silence from the whole Achaean army. Standing before them I said, "Silence, you Achaeans; let the whole army keep silence; hold your peace, be still!" And I brought the multitude into a windless calm. Then he said, "Son of Peleus, my father, receive these libations, libations that charm the dead and summon them back up to the land of the living! Come and drink the blood of a maiden, dark and undiluted, which is the army's gift and mine! Be propitious to us, grant us your leave to cast off the mooring cables from our sterns, and allow us all, journeying home in peace, to reach our native land!"[a]

Those were his words, and the whole army joined in his prayer. Then grasping the hilt of his gold-trimmed sword and drawing it from its scabbard, he gave the sign to the picked youth of the Argive army that they should hold the girl. But she, when she saw this, said these words: "You Argives who have sacked my city, I die of my

[a] In 540 πρευμενοῦς is corrupt, but the sense must be, "Allow us to return home *in peace*, or *with no ill-will*."

540 fort. ἡσύχου vel ἀφθόνου

ἑκοῦσα θνῄσκω· μή τις ἅψηται χροὸς
τοὐμοῦ· παρέξω γὰρ δέρην εὐκαρδίως.
550 ἐλευθέραν δέ μ', ὡς ἐλευθέρα θάνω,
πρὸς θεῶν, μεθέντες κτείνατ'· ἐν νεκροῖσι γὰρ
δούλη κεκλῆσθαι βασιλὶς οὖσ' αἰσχύνομαι.
λαοὶ δ' ἐπερρόθησαν, Ἀγαμέμνων τ' ἄναξ
εἶπεν μεθεῖναι παρθένον νεανίαις.
555 [οἱ δ', ὡς τάχιστ' ἤκουσαν ὑστάτην ὄπα,
μεθῆκαν, οὗπερ καὶ μέγιστον ἦν κράτος.]
κἀπεὶ τόδ' εἰσήκουσε δεσποτῶν ἔπος,
λαβοῦσα πέπλους ἐξ ἄκρας ἐπωμίδος
ἔρρηξε λαγόνας ἐς μέσας παρ' ὀμφαλὸν
560 μαστούς τ' ἔδειξε στέρνα θ' ὡς ἀγάλματος
κάλλιστα, καὶ καθεῖσα πρὸς γαῖαν γόνυ
ἔλεξε πάντων τλημονέστατον λόγον·
Ἰδού, τόδ', εἰ μὲν στέρνον, ὦ νεανία,
παίειν προθυμῇ, παῖσον, εἰ δ' ὑπ' αὐχένα
565 χρῄζεις, πάρεστι λαιμὸς εὐτρεπὴς ὅδε.
ὁ δ' οὐ θέλων τε καὶ θέλων οἴκτῳ κόρης
τέμνει σιδήρῳ πνεύματος διαρροάς·
κρουνοὶ δ' ἐχώρουν. ἡ δὲ καὶ θνῄσκουσ' ὅμως
πολλὴν πρόνοιαν εἶχεν εὐσχήμων πεσεῖν,
570 κρύπτουσ' ἃ κρύπτειν ὄμματ' ἀρσένων χρεών.
ἐπεὶ δ' ἀφῆκε πνεῦμα θανασίμῳ σφαγῇ,
οὐδεὶς τὸν αὐτὸν εἶχεν Ἀργείων πόνον·
ἀλλ' οἱ μὲν αὐτῶν τὴν θανοῦσαν ἐκ χερῶν
φύλλοις ἔβαλλον, οἱ δὲ πληροῦσιν πυρὰν
575 κορμοὺς φέροντες πευκίνους, ὁ δ' οὐ φέρων

own accord! Let no one touch my person, for I shall offer you my neck bravely! In the gods' name, leave me free when you kill me, so that I may die a free woman! For since I am a princess, I shrink from being called a slave among the dead."

The host shouted its approval, and King Agamemnon ordered the young men to let the maiden go. [And they, as soon as they heard the last word of the man who holds the highest authority, let her go.] When she heard the command of her masters, she seized her robe and tore it from the shoulder to the middle of her waist, by the navel, and showed her breasts, lovely as a goddess' statue, then sinking to her knees she spoke words of surpassing bravery: "Here, young man, if it is my breast you are keen to strike, strike here, or if it is beneath my neck, my neck is yours to cut." And he, for pity of the girl both willing and reluctant, cut the breath's passageway with his sword, and blood gushed forth. She, though her life was ebbing out, still took great care to fall in seemly fashion to the ground, concealing from male eyes what should be concealed. When she had given up her spirit from the deadly wound, the Argives all had different tasks: some of them strewed the dead woman with leaves, while others built up a pyre by carrying great logs of pine. And anyone who failed to

---

555–6 del. Jacobs
559 μέσας Brunck: -ον C

πρὸς τοῦ φέροντος τοιάδ' ἤκουεν κακά·
Ἕστηκας, ὦ κάκιστε, τῇ νεάνιδι
οὐ πέπλον οὐδὲ κόσμον ἐν χεροῖν ἔχων;
οὐκ εἶ τι δώσων τῇ περίσσ' εὐκαρδίῳ
580 ψυχήν τ' ἀρίστῃ; τοιάδ' ἀμφὶ σῆς λέγων
παιδὸς θανούσης εὐτεκνωτάτην τέ σε
πασῶν γυναικῶν δυστυχεστάτην θ' ὁρῶ.

ΧΟΡΟΣ
δεινόν τι πῆμα Πριαμίδαις ἐπέζεσεν
πόλει τε τῇ μῇ θεῶν ἀνάγκαισιν τόδε.

ΕΚΑΒΗ
585 ὦ θύγατερ, οὐκ οἶδ' εἰς ὅ τι βλέψω κακῶν,
πολλῶν παρόντων· ἢν γὰρ ἅψωμαί τινος,
τάδ' οὐκ ἐᾷ με, παρακαλεῖ δ' ἐκεῖθεν αὖ
λύπη τις ἄλλη διάδοχος κακῶν κακοῖς.
καὶ νῦν τὸ μὲν σὸν ὥστε μὴ στένειν πάθος
590 οὐκ ἂν δυναίμην ἐξαλείψασθαι φρενός·
τὸ δ' αὖ λίαν παρεῖλες ἀγγελθεῖσά μοι
γενναῖος. οὔκουν δεινόν, εἰ γῆ μὲν κακὴ
τυχοῦσα καιροῦ θεόθεν εὖ στάχυν φέρει,
χρηστὴ δ' ἁμαρτοῦσ' ὧν χρεὼν αὐτὴν τυχεῖν
595 κακὸν δίδωσι καρπόν, ἄνθρωποι δ' ἀεὶ
ὁ μὲν πονηρὸς οὐδὲν ἄλλο πλὴν κακός,
ὁ δ' ἐσθλὸς ἐσθλός, οὐδὲ συμφορᾶς ὕπο
φύσιν διέφθειρ' ἀλλὰ χρηστός ἐστ' ἀεί;
[ἆρ' οἱ τεκόντες διαφέρουσιν ἢ τροφαί;
600 ἔχει γε μέντοι καὶ τὸ θρεφθῆναι καλῶς

carry something heard words of reproach like these from
one with a burden in his arms: "Just standing there,
churl, with no cover or adornment in your hands for the
young woman? Go and bring some tribute to the
woman's supreme bravery and surpassing nobility!" As I
say these things about your dead daughter I regard you as
of all women the most blessed in your offspring as well as
the unluckiest.

CHORUS LEADER

Terrible is the woe that has burst upon the sons of Priam
and upon my city by the fate of heaven.

HECUBA

Daughter, I do not know which of my misfortunes to look
at, so many surround me. If I put my hand to one of
them, these forbid me to do so, and some other misfor-
tune, relieving the burden of grief by other grief, calls me
away from it again. And now I could not, to be sure, wipe
from my mind what has befallen you and grieve for it no
more, but the report of your nobility has taken away the
excess of my grief. Is it not passing strange? A poor plot
of land that gets its due rain from above bears a good har-
vest and good land that does not bears a poor one, but
where mankind is concerned, the base man continues
ever base and the noble is ever noble, never changing his
nature under the blows of misfortune but always remain-
ing good. [Is it parentage or nurture that makes the

---

581 τέ Reiske· δέ C
584 ἀνάγκαισιν Herwerden: ἀναγκαῖον C
587 τάδ' Kovacs: τόδ' C
595 ἄνθρωποι Hermann: -οις C

δίδαξιν ἐσθλοῦ· τοῦτο δ' ἤν τις εὖ μάθῃ,
οἶδεν τό γ' αἰσχρὸν κανόνι τοῦ καλοῦ σταθμῶν.]
    καὶ ταῦτα μὲν δὴ νοῦς ἐτόξευσεν μάτην·
σὺ δ' ἐλθὲ καὶ σήμηνον Ἀργείοις τάδε,
605 μὴ θιγγάνειν μοι μηδέν', ἀλλ' εἴργειν ὄχλον,
τῆς παιδός. ἔν τοι μυρίῳ στρατεύματι
ἀκόλαστος ὄχλος ναυτική τ' ἀναρχία
κρείσσων πυρός, κακὸς δ' ὁ μή τι δρῶν κακόν.
    σὺ δ' αὖ λαβοῦσα τεῦχος, ἀρχαία λάτρι,
610 βάψασ' ἔνεγκε δεῦρο ποντίας ἁλός,
ὡς παῖδα λουτροῖς τοῖς πανυστάτοις ἐμήν,
νύμφην τ' ἄνυμφον παρθένον τ' ἀπάρθενον,
λούσω προθῶμαί θ'—ὡς μὲν ἀξία, πόθεν;
οὐκ ἂν δυναίμην· ὡς δ' ἔχω (τί γὰρ πάθω;)
615 κόσμον γ' ἀγείρασ' αἰχμαλωτίδων πάρα,
αἵ μοι πάρεδροι τῶνδ' ἔσω σκηνωμάτων
ναίουσιν, εἴ τις τοὺς νεωστὶ δεσπότας
λαθοῦσ' ἔχει τι κλέμμα τῶν αὑτῆς δόμων.
    ὦ σχήματ' οἴκων, ὦ ποτ' εὐτυχεῖς δόμοι,
620 ὦ πλεῖστ' ἔχων μάλιστά τ' εὐτεκνώτατε
Πρίαμε, γεραιά θ' ἥδ' ἐγὼ μήτηρ τέκνων,
ὡς ἐς τὸ μηδὲν ἥκομεν, φρονήματος
τοῦ πρὶν στερέντες. εἶτα δῆτ' ὀγκούμεθα,
ὁ μέν τις ἡμῶν πλουσίοισι δώμασιν,
625 ὁ δ' ἐν πολίταις τίμιος κεκλημένος;

599–602 del. Sakorraphos
602 σταθμῶν Wakefield: μαθών C
615 γ' Wakefield: τ' C
620 μάλιστά τ' Harry: κάλλιστά τ' fere C

difference? But good nurturing teaches noble behavior,
and if a man learns this lesson well, he knows what is
base, measuring it by the standard of the honorable.]

These are idle bolts my mind has shot. But you, sir, go
and bear this message to the Argives, that no one should
touch my daughter but that they should fence off the
multitude from her body. In a great host the mob is
unruly, and the riotous behavior of sailors is harder to
check than a fire. The man who does no base deed is
called base.

Exit TALTHYBIUS by Eisodos A.

You, old servant, take an urn, fill it with seawater and
bring it here so that I may give my daughter her last
bath[a]—bride that is no bride, virgin that is virgin no
more[b]—and lay her out for burial. I cannot give her a
funeral as she deserves but only as best I may (for what
can I do?), gathering adornment from the captive women
who share this tent with me, if by chance any has man-
aged to steal from her own home, undetected by our new
masters. O splendid palace! O home once happy! O
Priam, rich beyond all others in goods and most blessed
in children, and I myself here, aged mother of children,
how utterly we have been brought to nothing, shorn of
our former proud thoughts! After this can any of us pride
ourselves, one on the wealth of his house, another on his

---

[a] Hecuba's words perhaps allude to the bath that, in ordinary
circumstances, it would have been her duty to provide for her
daughter on the eve of her wedding. Cf. *Medea* 1026.

[b] Polyxena has become the bride of the dead Achilles.

---

[624] πλουσίοισι Bothe: -ίοις ἐν fere C

τὰ δ᾽ οὐδέν, ἄλλως φροντίδων βουλεύματα
γλώσσης τε κόμποι. κεῖνος ὀλβιώτατος
ὅτῳ κατ᾽ ἦμαρ τυγχάνει μηδὲν κακόν.

ΧΟΡΟΣ

στρ.

ἐμοὶ χρῆν συμφοράν,
630   ἐμοὶ χρῆν πημονὰν γενέσθαι,
Ἰδαίαν ὅτε πρῶτον ὕλαν
Ἀλέξανδρος εἰλατίναν
ἐτάμεθ᾽, ἅλιον ἐπ᾽ οἶδμα ναυστολήσων
635   Ἑλένας ἐπὶ λέκτρα, τὰν
καλλίσταν ὁ χρυσοφαὴς
Ἅλιος αὐγάζει.

ἀντ.

πόνοι γὰρ καὶ πόνων
640   ἀνάγκαι κρείσσονες κυκλοῦνται·
κοινὸν δ᾽ ἐξ ἰδίας ἀνοίας
κακὸν τᾷ Σιμουντίδι γᾷ
ὀλέθριον ἔμολε συμφορᾷ τ᾽ ἐπ᾽ ἄλλων.
ἐκρίθη δ᾽ ἔρις, ἂν ἐν Ἴ-
645   δᾳ κρίνει τρισσὰς μακάρων
παῖδας ἀνὴρ βούτας,

ἐπῳδ.

ἐπὶ δορὶ καὶ φόνῳ καὶ ἐμῶν μελάθρων λώβᾳ·
650   στένει δὲ καί τις ἀμφὶ τὸν εὔροον Εὐρώταν
Λάκαινα πολυδάκρυτος ἐν δόμοις κόρα,
πολιόν τ᾽ ἐπὶ κρᾶτα μά-

eminence among the citizens? These things are of no account, mere fancies of the mind and idle boasting. That man is most truly happy who from day to day escapes calamity.

Exit Hecuba's maidservant by Eisodos A, and HECUBA *into the* skene.

CHORUS

For me was fated disaster, for me was fated pain, on the day when Alexander[a] first cut down the pine tree upon Mount Ida for his sea journey to make Helen his bride, the fairest woman the sun's golden light looks upon.

Circling in their round came troubles and a fate more harsh than these. Upon the land of the Simois came a shared disaster from one man's folly, bringing ruin and involving others in calamity. The quarrel that the shepherd upon Ida judged for the three daughters of the blessed gods was decided.

Its outcome was the spear and slaughter and ruin for my house. But many a Spartan girl also sheds plentiful tears in her house beside the fair Eurotas, and the mother of young men slain in battle lays hand upon her hoary

---

[a] Paris.

643 συμφορᾷ τ' ἐπ' Stinton: -ά τ' ἀπ' C

τηρ τέκνων θανόντων
τίθεται χέρα δρύπτεταί τε
655 <δίπτυχον> παρειάν,
δίαιμον ὄνυχα τιθεμένα σπαραγμοῖς.

ΘΕΡΑΠΑΙΝΑ

γυναῖκες, Ἑκάβη ποῦ ποθ᾽ ἡ παναθλία,
ἡ πάντα νικῶσ᾽ ἄνδρα καὶ θῆλυν σποράν
660 κακοῖσιν; οὐδεὶς στέφανον ἀνθαιρήσεται.

ΧΟΡΟΣ

τί δ᾽, ὦ τάλαινα σῆς κακογλώσσου βοῆς;
ὡς οὔποθ᾽ εὕδει λυπρά μοι κηρύγματα.

ΘΕΡΑΠΑΙΝΑ

Ἑκάβῃ φέρω τόδ᾽ ἄλγος· ἐν κακοῖσι δὲ
οὐ ῥᾴδιον βροτοῖσιν εὐφημεῖν στόμα.

ΧΟΡΟΣ

665 καὶ μὴν περῶσα τυγχάνει δόμων ὕπο
ἥδ᾽, ἐς δὲ καιρὸν σοῖσι φαίνεται λόγοις.

ΘΕΡΑΠΑΙΝΑ

ὦ παντάλαινα κἄτι μᾶλλον ἢ λέγω,
δέσποιν᾽, ὄλωλας κοὐκέτ᾽ εἶ, βλέπουσα φῶς,
ἄπαις ἄνανδρος ἄπολις ἐξεφθαρμένη.

ΕΚΑΒΗ

670 οὐ καινὸν εἶπας, εἰδόσιν δ᾽ ὠνείδισας.
ἀτὰρ τί νεκρὸν τόνδε μοι Πολυξένης

---

655 lac. indic. et suppl. Diggle
662 μοι Herwerden: σου C

head and gouges <both> her cheeks, making her nails bloody with the tearing.

Enter MAIDSERVANT *by Eisodos A. She is followed by two women carrying the corpse of Polydorus wrapped in garments.*

MAIDSERVANT
Women, where is Hecuba the utterly wretched, she who outstrips every man, every woman in misfortune? No one will take this crown from her!

CHORUS LEADER
Woman made wretched with your shouts of ill-omen, what is it? How ceaselessly painful proclamations din in my ears!

MAIDSERVANT
It is to Hecuba that I bring this sorrow, and in misfortune it is not easy for mortals to shun ill-omened words.

Enter HECUBA *from the* skene.

CHORUS LEADER
But here she comes out of the tent, appearing at the right moment to hear your report.

MAIDSERVANT
Mistress, woman utterly undone beyond my power to describe, you are lost: though you see the light of day you are dead, without child, without husband, without city, utterly destroyed!

HECUBA
This is no news you bring: you say these hard words to one who knows them well. But why have you come bring-

ἥκεις κομίζουσ᾽, ἧς ἀπηγγέλθη τάφος
πάντων Ἀχαιῶν διὰ χερὸς σπουδὴν ἔχειν;

ΘΕΡΑΠΑΙΝΑ

ἥδ᾽ οὐδὲν οἶδεν, ἀλλά μοι Πολυξένην
675 θρηνεῖ, νέων δὲ πημάτων οὐχ ἅπτεται.

ΕΚΑΒΗ

οἲ ᾽γὼ τάλαινα· μῶν τὸ βακχεῖον κάρα
τῆς θεσπιῳδοῦ δεῦρο Κασσάνδρας φέρεις;

ΘΕΡΑΠΑΙΝΑ

ζῶσαν λέλακας, τὸν θανόντα δ᾽ οὐ στένεις
τόνδ᾽· ἀλλ᾽ ἄθρησον σῶμα γυμνωθὲν νεκροῦ
680 εἴ σοι φανεῖται θαῦμα καὶ παρ᾽ ἐλπίδας.

ΕΚΑΒΗ

οἴμοι, βλέπω δὴ παῖδ᾽ ἐμὸν τεθνηκότα,
Πολύδωρον, ὅν μοι Θρῂξ ἔσῳζ᾽ οἴκοις ἀνήρ.
ἀπωλόμην δύστηνος, οὐκέτ᾽ εἰμὶ δή.
ὦ τέκνον τέκνον,
685 αἰαῖ, κατάρχομαι νόμον
βακχεῖον, ἐξ ἀλάστορος ἀρτιμαθὴς κακῶν.

ΘΕΡΑΠΑΙΝΑ

ἔγνως γὰρ ἄτην παιδός, ὦ δύστηνε σύ;

ΕΚΑΒΗ

ἄπιστ᾽ ἄπιστα, καινὰ καινὰ δέρκομαι.
690 ἕτερα δ᾽ ἀφ᾽ ἑτέρων κακὰ κακῶν κυρεῖ,
οὐδέ ποτ᾽ ἀστένακτος ἀδάκρυτος ἀ-
μέρα ᾽πισχήσει.

ing the body of Polyxena when it has been reported that her burial was being eagerly carried out by all the Achaeans?

MAIDSERVANT

(to herself) She has no idea but keeps keening to me for Polyxena, not grasping her new griefs.

HECUBA

Woe is me! Surely it is not my possessed daughter, the prophetess Cassandra, you bring here?

MAIDSERVANT

She you speak of is alive: not yet do you mourn the dead before you. But see whether the uncovered corpse will seem an astonishing sight, one you had not looked for.

She uncovers the corpse.

HECUBA

Oh, oh! I see my son Polydorus slain, my son the Thracian was keeping safe for me in his house! I am utterly destroyed, my life is gone! *(sung)* Alas, my child, my child: the melody of frenzy, now I begin it, learning only now of disaster sent upon me by an avenging spirit!

MAIDSERVANT

Have you truly recognized that your son is dead, poor woman?

HECUBA

(sung) Beggaring belief are the things I see, fresh and fearful! One misfortune strikes me and then another! Never shall a day without tears and groans be mine!

---

691 ἀστ- ἀδ- Hermann: ἀδ- ἀστ- C
692 'πισχήσει Bothe: μ' ἐπ- C

ΧΟΡΟΣ

δείν', ὦ τάλαινα, δεινὰ πάσχομεν κακά.

ΕΚΑΒΗ

ὦ τέκνον τέκνον ταλαίνας ματρός,
695 τίνι μόρῳ θνήσκεις, τίνι πότμῳ κεῖσαι;
πρὸς τίνος ἀνθρώπων;

ΘΕΡΑΠΑΙΝΑ

οὐκ οἶδ'· ἐπ' ἀκταῖς νιν κυρῶ θαλασσίαις.

ΕΚΑΒΗ

ἔκβλητον ἢ πέσημα φοινι-
700 ίου δορὸς ἐν ψαμάθῳ λευρᾷ;

ΘΕΡΑΠΑΙΝΑ

πόντου νιν ἐξήνεγκε πελάγιος κλύδων.

ΕΚΑΒΗ

ὤμοι, αἰαῖ, ἔμαθον ἔνυπνον ὀμμάτων
ἐμῶν ὄψιν (οὔ με παρέβα φάμα)
705 μελανόπτερον ἂν ἐσεῖδον ἀμφὶ σ', ὦ τέκνον,
οὐκέτ' <ἄρ' οὐκέτ'> ὄντα Διὸς ἐν φάει.

ΧΟΡΟΣ

τίς γάρ νιν ἔκτειν'; οἶσθ' ὀνειρόφρων φράσαι;

ΕΚΑΒΗ

710 ἐμὸς ἐμὸς ξένος, Θρήκιος ἱππότας,
ἵν' ὁ γέρων πατὴρ ἔθετό νιν κρύψας.

ΧΟΡΟΣ

οἴμοι, τί λέξεις; χρυσὸν ὡς ἔχοι κτανών;

---

703 ἔνυπνον Hermann: ἐνύπνιον C
704 φάμα Willink cl. Hdt. 1.43: φάσμα C

CHORUS LEADER

Terrible, terrible are the woes we have suffered, unhappy woman!

HECUBA

(*sung*) O son of a mother ill-starred, what doom was yours, by what fate do you lie still in death? Who was your slayer?

MAIDSERVANT

I do not know: I found him upon the seashore.

HECUBA

(*sung*) Was he cast up, or did he fall victim of a murderous spear on the smooth sand?

MAIDSERVANT

The waves of the sea had cast him forth.

HECUBA

(*sung*) O grief! Now I understand the black-winged dream my eyes beheld (I have not missed its message), the dream that you, my child, were no longer alive in Zeus's daylight!

CHORUS LEADER

Who killed him? Can you interpret the dream and tell me?

HECUBA

(*sung*) My friend, my friend it was, the horseman of Thrace, where his aged father sent him in secret!

CHORUS LEADER

Ah, what can you mean? That he killed him to possess his gold?

---

[707] lac. indic. et suppl. Willink

ΕΚΑΒΗ

ἄρρητ' ἀνωνόμαστα, θαυμάτων πέρα,
715   οὐχ ὅσι' οὐδ' ἀνεκτά. ποῦ δίκα ξένων;
ὦ κατάρατ' ἀνδρῶν, ὡς διεμοιράσω
χρόα, σιδαρέῳ τεμὼν φασγάνῳ
720   μέλεα τοῦδε παιδὸς οὐδ' ᾤκτισας.

ΧΟΡΟΣ

ὦ τλῆμον, ὥς σε πολυπονωτάτην βροτῶν
δαίμων ἔθηκεν ὅστις ἐστί σοι βαρύς.
    ἀλλ' εἰσορῶ γὰρ τοῦδε δεσπότου δέμας
725   Ἀγαμέμνονος, τοὐνθένδε σιγῶμεν, φίλαι.

ΑΓΑΜΕΜΝΩΝ

Ἑκάβη, τί μέλλεις παῖδα σὴν κρύπτειν τάφῳ
ἐλθοῦσ' ἐφ' οἷσπερ Ταλθύβιος ἤγγειλέ μοι
μὴ θιγγάνειν σῆς μηδέν' Ἀργείων κόρης;
ἡμεῖς μὲν οὖν εἰῶμεν οὐδ' ἐψαύομεν·
730   σὺ δὲ σχολάζεις, ὥστε θαυμάζειν ἐμέ.
ἥκω δ' ἀποστελῶν σε· τἀκεῖθεν γὰρ εὖ
πεπραγμέν' ἐστίν, εἴ τι τῶνδ' ἐστὶν καλῶς.
    ἔα· τίν' ἄνδρα τόνδ' ἐπὶ σκηναῖς ὁρῶ
θανόντα Τρώων; οὐ γὰρ Ἀργεῖον πέπλοι
735   δέμας περιπτύσσοντες ἀγγέλλουσί μοι.

ΕΚΑΒΗ

δύστην'—ἐμαυτὴν γὰρ λέγω λέγουσα σέ,

---

729 εἰῶμεν Nauck: ἐῶμεν C   οὐδ' ἐψαύομεν Bothe: οὐδὲ
ψαύομεν C

HECUBA

(*sung*) A crime no word or name can describe, more than amazement can take in, impious and unendurable! Where is the justice of hosts? Cursed man, how you rent the child's flesh and cut his limbs with the iron sword, showing him no pity!

CHORUS LEADER

Luckless woman, some god, weighing hard upon you, has made you the most trouble-laden of mortals.

But since I see Agamemnon, your master, approaching, let us now hold our peace.

Enter AGAMEMNON by Eisodos A.

AGAMEMNON

Hecuba, why are you so slow to come and bury your daughter on the terms Talthybius made known to me, that none of the Argives was to touch her? We have let her be and have not touched her. But you take your time, which causes me surprise. I have come to fetch you: everything there has been well taken care of—if anything of this business can be called well done.

But what is this? Who is the dead man I see beside the tent? He is a Trojan, for the garments that clothe his body tell me that he is no Argive.

Hecuba turns her back to Agamemnon and speaks to herself.

HECUBA

Luckless one—in saying "you," Hecuba, I mean my-

Ἑκάβη—τί δράσω; πότερα προσπέσω γόνυ
Ἀγαμέμνονος τοῦδ' ἢ φέρω σιγῇ κακά;

ΑΓΑΜΕΜΝΩΝ

τί μοι προσώπῳ νῶτον ἐγκλίνασα σὸν
740 δύρῃ, τὸ πραχθὲν δ' οὐ λέγεις; τίς ἔσθ' ὅδε;

ΕΚΑΒΗ

ἀλλ' εἴ με δούλην πολεμίαν θ' ἡγούμενος
γονάτων ἀπώσαιτ', ἄλγος ἂν προσθείμεθ' ἄν.

ΑΓΑΜΕΜΝΩΝ

οὔτοι πέφυκα μάντις, ὥστε μὴ κλυὼν
ἐξιστορῆσαι σῶν ὁδὸν βουλευμάτων.

ΕΚΑΒΗ

745 ἆρ' ἐκλογίζομαί γε πρὸς τὸ δυσμενὲς
μᾶλλον φρένας τοῦδ', ὄντος οὐχὶ δυσμενοῦς;

ΑΓΑΜΕΜΝΩΝ

εἴ τοί με βούλῃ τῶνδε μηδὲν εἰδέναι,
ἐς ταὐτὸν ἥκεις· καὶ γὰρ οὐδ' ἐγὼ κλυεῖν.

ΕΚΑΒΗ

οὐκ ἂν δυναίμην τοῦδε τιμωρεῖν ἄτερ
750 τέκνοισι τοῖς ἐμοῖσι. τί στρέφω τάδε;
τολμᾶν ἀνάγκη, κἂν τύχω κἂν μὴ τύχω.
    Ἀγάμεμνον, ἱκετεύω σε τῶνδε γουνάτων
καὶ σοῦ γενείου δεξιᾶς τ' εὐδαίμονος.

ΑΓΑΜΕΜΝΩΝ

τί χρῆμα μαστεύουσα; μῶν ἐλεύθερον
755 αἰῶνα θέσθαι; ῥᾴδιον γάρ ἐστί σοι.

self—what am I to do? Shall I fall as a suppliant before the knees of Agamemnon or shall I bear my misery in silence?

AGAMEMNON

Why do you turn your back to my face and weep but do not say what has happened? Who is this man?

HECUBA

If he should thrust me away from his knees, regarding me as a slave and an enemy, I would but be adding to my pain.

AGAMEMNON

I am not, you know, a seer who without hearing could search out the path your thoughts are taking.

HECUBA

Do I regard his mind as hostile when perhaps he is not hostile at all?

AGAMEMNON

If you want me to know nothing of this business, your wish agrees with my own: for I likewise have no desire to hear.

HECUBA

I cannot have vengeance for my children without his help. Why do I keep pondering this question? I must be brave whether my request is successful or not.

(turning to face Agamemnon and falling at his knees)
Agamemnon, I supplicate you by your knees, your chin, and your prospering right hand.

AGAMEMNON

What is it you want? Perhaps to win your freedom? That would be an easy request for you to get.

ΕΚΑΒΗ

οὐ δῆτα· τοὺς κακοὺς δὲ τιμωρουμένη
αἰῶνα τὸν σύμπαντα δουλεύειν θέλω.

ΑΓΑΜΕΜΝΩΝ

καὶ δὴ τίν᾽ ἡμᾶς εἰς ἐπάρκεσιν καλεῖς;

ΕΚΑΒΗ

οὐδέν τι τούτων ὧν σὺ δοξάζεις, ἄναξ.
760   ὁρᾷς νεκρὸν τόνδ᾽ οὗ καταστάζω δάκρυ;

ΑΓΑΜΕΜΝΩΝ

ὁρῶ· τὸ μέντοι μέλλον οὐκ ἔχω μαθεῖν.

ΕΚΑΒΗ

τοῦτόν ποτ᾽ ἔτεκον κἄφερον ζώνης ὕπο.

ΑΓΑΜΕΜΝΩΝ

ἔστιν δὲ τίς σῶν οὗτος, ὦ τλῆμον, τέκνων;

ΕΚΑΒΗ

οὐ τῶν θανόντων Πριαμιδῶν ὑπ᾽ Ἰλίῳ.

ΑΓΑΜΕΜΝΩΝ

765   ἦ γάρ τιν᾽ ἄλλον ἔτεκες ἢ κείνους, γύναι;

ΕΚΑΒΗ

ἀνόνητά γ᾽, ὡς ἔοικε, τόνδ᾽ ὃν εἰσορᾷς.

ΑΓΑΜΕΜΝΩΝ

ποῦ δ᾽ ὢν ἐτύγχαν᾽, ἡνίκ᾽ ὤλλυτο πτόλις;

ΕΚΑΒΗ

πατήρ νιν ἐξέπεμψεν ὀρρωδῶν θανεῖν.

756–8 del. Kirchhoff

HECUBA

No indeed: if I punish the guilty, I am willing to be a slave
for my whole life.

AGAMEMNON

Well then, what help are you asking me to give you?

HECUBA

For none of the purposes you think, my lord. Do you see
this dead man, over whom I shed my tears?

AGAMEMNON

I see: but what will follow from this I cannot tell.

HECUBA

I once carried him in my womb and gave birth to him.

AGAMEMNON

Poor woman, which of your children is he?

HECUBA

Not one of those sons of Priam who died in Ilium.

AGAMEMNON

But did you bear another son besides those, lady?

HECUBA

Yes, and to no purpose, it seems: the man you see before
you.

AGAMEMNON

Where was he when the city was being destroyed?

HECUBA

His father had sent him away for fear he might be killed.

ΑΓΑΜΕΜΝΩΝ

ποῖ τῶν τότ' ὄντων χωρίσας τέκνων μόνον;

ΕΚΑΒΗ

770 ἐς τήνδε χώραν, οὗπερ ηὑρέθη θανών.

ΑΓΑΜΕΜΝΩΝ

πρὸς ἄνδρ' ὃς ἄρχει τῆσδε Πολυμήστωρ χθονός;

ΕΚΑΒΗ

ἐνταῦθ' ἐπέμφθη πικροτάτου χρυσοῦ φύλαξ.

ΑΓΑΜΕΜΝΩΝ

θνῄσκει δὲ πρὸς τοῦ καὶ τίνος πότμου τυχών;

ΕΚΑΒΗ

τίνος γ' ὑπ' ἄλλου; Θρῄξ νιν ὤλεσε ξένος.

ΑΓΑΜΕΜΝΩΝ

775 ὦ τλῆμον· ἦ που χρυσὸν ἠράσθη λαβεῖν;

ΕΚΑΒΗ

τοιαῦτ', ἐπειδὴ συμφορὰν ἔγνω Φρυγῶν.

ΑΓΑΜΕΜΝΩΝ

ηὗρες δὲ ποῦ νιν; ἢ τίς ἤνεγκεν νεκρόν;

ΕΚΑΒΗ

ἥδ', ἐντυχοῦσα ποντίας ἀκτῆς ἔπι.

ΑΓΑΜΕΜΝΩΝ

τοῦτον ματεύουσ' ἢ πονοῦσ' ἄλλον πόνον;

ΕΚΑΒΗ

780 λούτρ' ᾤχετ' οἴσουσ' ἐξ ἁλὸς Πολυξένη.

ΑΓΑΜΕΜΝΩΝ

κτανών νιν, ὡς ἔοικεν, ἐκβάλλει ξένος.

AGAMEMNON

And where did he send him, alone of all his sons?

HECUBA

To this country, where he was found dead.

AGAMEMNON

To Polymestor, the ruler of this land?

HECUBA

Yes, he was sent here to watch over the gold that proved
his bane.

AGAMEMNON

By whom was he killed? What was the fate he met?

HECUBA

Who else could it be? His Thracian host killed him.

AGAMEMNON

Cruel man! I suppose he longed to get his gold?

HECUBA

Exactly, as soon as he learned of the fall of Troy.

AGAMEMNON

Where did you find him? Or who brought his body here?

HECUBA

This woman brought him: she found him on the beach.

AGAMEMNON

Was she looking for him or on some other errand?

HECUBA

She had gone to fetch water from the sea to bathe Poly-
xena.

AGAMEMNON

It seems his host killed him and threw him out.

ΕΚΑΒΗ

θαλασσόπλαγκτόν γ', ὧδε διατεμὼν χρόα.

ΑΓΑΜΕΜΝΩΝ

ὦ σχετλία σὺ τῶν ἀμετρήτων πόνων.

ΕΚΑΒΗ

ὄλωλα κοὐδὲν λοιπόν, Ἀγάμεμνον, κακῶν.

ΑΓΑΜΕΜΝΩΝ

785 φεῦ φεῦ· τίς οὕτω δυστυχὴς ἔφυ γυνή;

ΕΚΑΒΗ

οὐκ ἔστιν, εἰ μὴ τὴν Τύχην αὐτὴν λέγοις.
    ἀλλ' ὧνπερ οὕνεκ' ἀμφὶ σὸν πίπτω γόνυ
ἄκουσον. εἰ μὲν ὅσιά σοι παθεῖν δοκῶ,
στέργοιμ' ἄν· εἰ δὲ τοὔμπαλιν, σύ μοι γενοῦ
790 τιμωρὸς ἀνδρός, ἀνοσιωτάτου ξένου,
ὃς οὔτε τοὺς γῆς νέρθεν οὔτε τοὺς ἄνω
δείσας δέδρακεν ἔργον ἀνοσιώτατον
[κοινῆς τραπέζης πολλάκις τυχὼν ἐμοὶ
ξενίας τ' ἀριθμῷ πρῶτα τῶν ἐμῶν φίλων·
795 τυχὼν δ' ὅσων δεῖ καὶ λαβὼν προμηθίαν
ἔκτεινε· τύμβου δ', εἰ κτανεῖν ἐβούλετο,
οὐκ ἠξίωσεν ἀλλ' ἀφῆκε πόντιον].
    ἡμεῖς μὲν οὖν δοῦλοί τε κἀσθενεῖς ἴσως·
ἀλλ' οἱ θεοὶ σθένουσι χὠ κείνων κρατῶν
800 νόμος· νόμῳ γὰρ τοὺς θεοὺς ἡγούμεθα
καὶ ζῶμεν ἄδικα καὶ δίκαι' ὡρισμένοι·

793–7 del. Nauck

HECUBA

Yes, to be tossed to and fro on the sea, after carving his body up so.

AGAMEMNON

Poor woman! Your miseries beggar all measure!

HECUBA

I am dead, Agamemnon, there is no other disaster left for me!

AGAMEMNON

Ah me! What woman ever suffered such misfortune?

HECUBA

There is none, unless you named Lady Misfortune herself.

But hear why I have fallen at your knees. If you think the treatment I have received is such as the gods approve, I will bear it. But if not, punish for my sake the man, guest-friend most impious, who has done a deed most unholy, fearing neither the gods below nor those above. [He often shared a common table with me and was numbered the most important of my friends. Though he had received all he should and been treated with consideration, he killed my son. And even granting that he wished to kill him, he did not think him worthy of a tomb but dropped his body into the sea.]

Now I may be a slave and of no account. But the gods have force and so does the law that rules over them. For it is by virtue of law that we believe in the gods and distinguish right from wrong in our lives. If this law comes

ὃς ἐς σ' ἀνελθὼν εἰ διαφθαρήσεται
καὶ μὴ δίκην δώσουσιν οἵτινες ξένους
κτείνουσιν ἢ θεῶν ἱερὰ τολμῶσιν φέρειν,
805   οὐκ ἔστιν οὐδὲν τῶν ἐν ἀνθρώποις ἴσον.
ταῦτ' οὖν ἐν αἰσχρῷ θέμενος αἰδέσθητί με·
οἴκτιρον ἡμᾶς, ὡς γραφεύς τ' ἀποσταθεὶς
ἰδοῦ με κἀνάθρησον οἷ' ἔχω κακά·
τύραννος ἦ ποτ' ἀλλὰ νῦν δούλη σέθεν,
810   εὔπαις ποτ' οὖσα, νῦν δὲ γραῦς ἄπαις θ' ἅμα,
ἄπολις ἔρημος, ἀθλιωτάτη βροτῶν.

οἴμοι τάλαινα, ποῖ μ' ὑπεξάγεις πόδα;
ἔοικα πράξειν οὐδέν· ὦ τάλαιν' ἐγώ.
τί δῆτα θνητοὶ τἄλλα μὲν μαθήματα
815   μοχθοῦμεν ὡς χρὴ πάντα καὶ ματεύομεν,
πειθὼ δὲ τὴν τύραννον ἀνθρώποις μόνην
οὐδέν τι μᾶλλον ἐς τέλος σπουδάζομεν
μισθοὺς διδόντες μανθάνειν, ἵν' ἦν ποτε
πείθειν ἅ τις βούλοιτο τυγχάνειν θ' ἅμα;
820   τί οὖν ἔτ' ἄν τις ἐλπίσαι πράξειν καλῶς;
[οἱ μὲν γὰρ ὄντες παῖδες οὐκέτ' εἰσί μοι,
αὐτὴ δ' ἐπ' αἰσχροῖς αἰχμάλωτος οἴχομαι,
καπνὸν δὲ πόλεως τόνδ' ὑπερθρῴσκονθ' ὁρῶ.]
καὶ μήν (ἴσως μὲν τοῦ λόγου κενὸν τόδε,
825   Κύπριν προβάλλειν, ἀλλ' ὅμως εἰρήσεται)
πρὸς σοῖσι πλευροῖς παῖς ἐμὴ κοιμίζεται
ἡ φοιβάς, ἣν καλοῦσι Κασσάνδραν Φρύγες.
ποῦ τὰς φίλας δῆτ' εὐφρόνας λέξεις, ἄναξ;
ἢ τῶν ἐν εὐνῇ φιλτάτων ἀσπασμάτων

before your tribunal and is set at naught, if those who murder their guests or plunder the temples of the gods are not punished, then there is no more justice among men. Therefore if you regard such conduct as shameful, respect my suppliancy. Pity me, and like a painter stand back and see what misery is mine: I was a queen but now I am your slave, I was blessed with children once, but now I am both old and childless, without city, bereft of friends, the most unfortunate of mortals.

Agamemnon turns as if trying to escape from Hecuba's grasp.

O misery! Where are you trying to escape to? It seems that I shall not succeed. O luckless me! Why is it that we mortals take pains to study all other branches of knowledge as we ought, yet we take no further pains, by paying a fee, to learn thoroughly the art of persuasive speaking, sole ruler where mortals are concerned, so that we might be able to persuade people of whatever we wish and gain our ends? Why then should anyone still expect to be successful? [The children I once had I no longer have, I myself am gone off as a slave for shameful duties, and I see the smoke of my city here leaping up.]

Well then—perhaps this part of my speech will be for naught, appealing to Aphrodite, but still I shall make the point—my prophetic daughter, whom the Phrygians call Cassandra, sleeps at your side. What weight will you give, my lord, to those nights of love? Or what return shall my

---

818 ἦν Elmsley: ἦ C
821–3 post Herwerden (820–3) del. Kovacs
828 λέξεις Diggle: δείξεις C

830 χάριν τίν' ἕξει παῖς ἐμή, κείνης δ' ἐγώ;
[ἐκ τοῦ σκότου τε τῶν τε νυκτερησίων
φίλτρων μεγίστη γίγνεται βροτοῖς χάρις.]
ἄκουε δή νυν· τὸν θανόντα τόνδ' ὁρᾷς;
τοῦτον καλῶς δρῶν ὄντα κηδεστὴν σέθεν
835 δράσεις. ἑνός μοι μῦθος ἐνδεὴς ἔτι·
εἴ μοι γένοιτο φθόγγος ἐν βραχίοσιν
καὶ χερσὶ καὶ κόμαισι καὶ ποδῶν βάσει
ἢ Δαιδάλου τέχναισιν ἢ θεῶν τινος,
ὡς πάνθ' ἁμαρτῇ σῶν ἔχοιτο γουνάτων
840 κλαίοντ', ἐπισκήπτοντα παντοίους λόγους.
ὦ δέσποτ', ὦ μέγιστον Ἕλλησιν φάος,
πιθοῦ, παράσχες χεῖρα τῇ πρεσβύτιδι
τιμωρόν, εἰ καὶ μηδέν ἐστιν ἀλλ' ὅμως.
ἐσθλοῦ γὰρ ἀνδρὸς τῇ δίκῃ θ' ὑπηρετεῖν
845 καὶ τοὺς κακοὺς δρᾶν πανταχοῦ κακῶς ἀεί.

ΧΟΡΟΣ

δεινόν γε, θνητοῖς ὡς ἅπαντα συμπίτνει,
καὶ τὰς ἀνάγκας οἱ νόμοι διώρισαν,
φίλους τιθέντες τούς γε πολεμιωτάτους
ἐχθρούς τε τοὺς πρὶν εὐμενεῖς ποιούμενοι.

ΑΓΑΜΕΜΝΩΝ

850 ἐγώ σε καὶ σὸν παῖδα καὶ τύχας σέθεν,
Ἑκάβη, δι' οἴκτου χεῖρά θ' ἱκεσίαν ἔχω,
καὶ βούλομαι θεῶν θ' οὕνεκ' ἀνόσιον ξένον
καὶ τοῦ δικαίου τήνδε σοι δοῦναι δίκην,
εἴ πως φανείη γ' ὥστε σοί τ' ἔχειν καλῶς

daughter have for her loving embraces in bed, and what
return shall I have for her? [It is from darkness and from
the delights of night that mortals receive their greatest
pleasure.] Listen, therefore: do you see the dead man
here? In benefiting him it is your kinsman by marriage
that you benefit. My speech lacks one thing still: would
that I had voice in my arms, hands, hair, and feet by the
arts of Daedalus or one of the gods, so that all these limbs
might together seize your knees and lay all manner of
pleas upon you. Master, beacon most bright for the
Greeks, be moved by me! Lend an old woman, although
she is of no account, your avenging hand! For it is the
duty of a good man always to serve justice and to punish
the guilty.

CHORUS LEADER

It is remarkable how all things come together in human
life and how law determines our closest ties, rendering
the greatest foes friends and making enemies of those
who were once well-disposed.

AGAMEMNON

Hecuba, I pity your son and your misfortunes, pity too
your suppliant hand. For the gods' sake and for the sake
of justice I desire that your impious host should pay you
this penalty for his deeds, provided there is some way that
you may get what you want and yet the army shall not

831–2 del. Matthiae

831 νυκτερησίων Nauck: νυκτέρων βροτοῖς vel sim. C

839 ἁμαρτῇ Wackernagel: ὁμ- C

855 στρατῷ τε μὴ δόξαιμι Κασσάνδρας χάριν
Θρῄκης ἄνακτι τόνδε βουλεῦσαι φόνον.
ἔστιν γὰρ ᾗ ταραγμὸς ἐμπέπτωκέ μοι·
τὸν ἄνδρα τοῦτον φίλιον ἡγεῖται στρατός,
τὸν κατθανόντα δ' ἐχθρόν· εἰ δ' ἐμοὶ φίλος
860 ὅδ' ἐστί, χωρὶς τοῦτο κοὐ κοινὸν στρατῷ.
πρὸς ταῦτα φρόντιζ'· ὡς θέλοντα μέν μ' ἔχεις
σοὶ ξυμπονῆσαι καὶ ταχὺν προσαρκέσαι,
βραδὺν δ', Ἀχαιοῖς εἰ διαβληθήσομαι.

ΕΚΑΒΗ

φεῦ.
οὐκ ἔστι θνητῶν ὅστις ἔστ' ἐλεύθερος·
865 ἢ χρημάτων γὰρ δοῦλός ἐστιν ἢ τύχης
ἢ πλῆθος αὐτὸν πόλεος ἢ νόμων γραφαὶ
εἴργουσι χρῆσθαι μὴ κατὰ γνώμην τρόποις.
ἐπεὶ δὲ ταρβεῖς τῷ τ' ὄχλῳ πλέον νέμεις,
ἐγώ σε θήσω τοῦδ' ἐλεύθερον φόβου.
870 σύνισθι μὲν γάρ, ἤν τι βουλεύσω κακὸν
τῷ τόνδ' ἀποκτείναντι, συνδράσῃς δὲ μή.
ἢν δ' ἐξ Ἀχαιῶν θόρυβος ἢ 'πικουρία
πάσχοντος ἀνδρὸς Θρῃκὸς οἷα πείσεται
φανῇ τις, εἶργε μὴ δοκῶν ἐμὴν χάριν.
875 τὰ δ' ἄλλα—θάρσει—πάντ' ἐγὼ θήσω καλῶς.

ΑΓΑΜΕΜΝΩΝ

πῶς οὖν; τί δράσεις; πότερα φάσγανον χερὶ
λαβοῦσα γραίᾳ φῶτα βάρβαρον κτενεῖς
ἢ φαρμάκοισιν ἢ 'πικουρίᾳ τίνι;

think that it was for Cassandra's sake that I laid this death
plot against the lord of Thrace. There is a point on which
I am disturbed: the army regards this man as a friend and
your dead son as an enemy; if your son is a friend of
mine, that is a private matter and not one in which the
army shares. Think about it in the light of this. For in me
you have someone ready to help in your labors and swift
to come to your defense, but slow if I am to be criticized
before the Achaeans.

HECUBA

O my! No mortal is free! Either he is the slave of money
or fate, or he is prevented by the city's multitude or its
laws from acting as he thinks best. But since you are
afraid and accord too much weight to the multitude, I
shall set you free from this fear. Share in the knowledge
of any plot I shall make against the murderer of my son
but do not share the doing of it. If a loud cry is raised by
the Achaeans or they come to the aid of the Thracian as
he suffers what he shall suffer, prevent them but pretend
it is not for my sake. All else—have no fear—I shall man-
age well.

AGAMEMNON

How shall this be? What do you intend to do? Will you
take a sword in your aged hand and kill the barbarian, or
poison him, or what help will you have? What hand will

---

859 δ' ἐμοὶ Elmsley: δὲ σοὶ C

τίς σοι ξυνέσται χείρ; πόθεν κτήσῃ φίλους;

ΕΚΑΒΗ

880 στέγαι κεκεύθασ' αἵδε Τρωάδων ὄχλον.

ΑΓΑΜΕΜΝΩΝ

τὰς αἰχμαλώτους εἶπας, Ἑλλήνων ἄγραν;

ΕΚΑΒΗ

σὺν ταῖσδε τὸν ἐμῶν φονέα τιμωρήσομαι.

ΑΓΑΜΕΜΝΩΝ

καὶ πῶς γυναιξὶν ἀρσένων ἔσται κράτος;

ΕΚΑΒΗ

δεινὸν τὸ πλῆθος σὺν δόλῳ τε δύσμαχον.

ΑΓΑΜΕΜΝΩΝ

885 δεινόν· τὸ μέντοι θῆλυ μέμφομαι σθένος.

ΕΚΑΒΗ

τί δ'; οὐ γυναῖκες εἷλον Αἰγύπτου τέκνα
καὶ Λῆμνον ἄρδην ἀρσένων ἐξῴκισαν;
ἀλλ' ὡς γενέσθω· τόνδε μὲν μέθες λόγον,
πέμψον δέ μοι τήνδ' ἀσφαλῶς διὰ στρατοῦ
890 γυναῖκα. καὶ σὺ Θρῃκὶ πλαθεῖσα ξένῳ
λέξον· Καλεῖ σ' ἄνασσα δή ποτ' Ἰλίου
Ἑκάβη, σὸν οὐκ ἔλασσον ἢ κείνης χρέος,
καὶ παῖδας, ὡς δεῖ καὶ τέκν' εἰδέναι λόγους
τοὺς ἐξ ἐκείνης. τὸν δὲ τῆς νεοσφαγοῦς

882 ἐμῶν Scaliger: ἐμὸν C
885 σθένος Jenni: γένος C

478

aid you? Where will you get allies?

HECUBA

This tent conceals a throng of Trojan women.

AGAMEMNON

You mean the captives, those the Greeks have taken?

HECUBA

With them shall I requite my family's killer.

AGAMEMNON

And how shall women overcome a man?

HECUBA

There is terror in numbers, numbers joined with guile.

AGAMEMNON

Terror, yes. But I think little of woman's strength.

HECUBA

Yet was it not women who killed Aegyptus' sons, and did women not completely rid Lemnos of men?[a]

But this is what must be done: putting an end to discussion, pray give this woman safe escort through the army. *(to the Maidservant)* You, go to my Thracian host and say, "Hecuba, she who was once queen of Ilium, bids you come for your sake no less than hers, and your sons as well since they too must hear what she has to say." As for

___

[a] When forced to marry the sons of Aegyptus, their cousins, the daughters of Danaus made an agreement to kill them on their wedding night. The women of the island of Lemnos were afflicted with a foul smell by Aphrodite after they had neglected her worship. Their husbands imported concubines from Thrace, and in retaliation they killed all the men except Thoas, who was spared by his daughter Hypsipyle.

895 Πολυξένης ἐπίσχες, Ἀγάμεμνον, τάφον,
ὡς τώδ' ἀδελφὼ πλησίον μιᾷ φλογί,
δισσὴ μέριμνα μητρί, κρυφθῆτον χθονί.

ΑΓΑΜΕΜΝΩΝ

ἔσται τάδ' οὕτω· καὶ γὰρ εἰ μὲν ἦν στρατῷ
πλοῦς, οὐκ ἂν εἶχον τήνδε σοι δοῦναι χάριν·
900 νῦν δ', οὐ γὰρ ἵησ' οὐρίους πνοὰς θεός,
μένειν ἀνάγκη πλοῦν ὁρῶντας ἡσύχους.
γένοιτο δ' εὖ πως· πᾶσι γὰρ κοινὸν τόδε,
ἰδίᾳ θ' ἑκάστῳ καὶ πόλει, τὸν μὲν κακὸν
κακόν τι πάσχειν, τὸν δὲ χρηστὸν εὐτυχεῖν.

ΧΟΡΟΣ

στρ. α
905 σὺ μέν, ὦ πατρὶς Ἰλιάς,
τῶν ἀπορθήτων πόλις οὐκέτι λέξῃ·
τοῖον Ἑλλάνων νέφος ἀμφί σε κρύπ-
τει δορὶ δὴ δορὶ πέρσαν.
910 ἀπὸ δὲ στεφάναν κέκαρ-
σαι πύργων, κατὰ δ' αἰθάλου
κηλῖδ' οἰκτροτάταν κέχρωσαι. τάλαιν',
οὐκέτι σ' ἐμβατεύσω.

ἀντ. α
μεσονύκτιος ὠλλύμαν,
915 ἦμος ἐκ δείπνων ὕπνος ἡδὺς ἐπ' ὄσσοις
σκίδναται, μολπᾶν δ' ἄπο καὶ χοροποι-
ὸν θυσίαν καταπαύσας

901 ἡσύχους Markland: ἥσυχον C
911 αἰθάλου Canter: αἰθάλῳ a: -ου καπνοῦ b

the funeral of Polyxena recently slaughtered, delay it, Agamemnon, so that brother and sister, twin care to their mother, may be consigned to burial side by side on a single pyre.

AGAMEMNON

It shall be as you ask. For in fact if the army could sail, I would not be able to grant you this favor. As it is, since the god does not grant us favoring breezes, we must wait at our ease, watching for good sailing weather.[a] May it turn out well somehow! It is the common wish of each man privately and each city that the bad should get bad treatment while the good enjoy good fortune.

Exit AGAMEMNON *and servants carrying Polydorus' body by Eisodos A, the* MAIDSERVANT *with one of Agamemnon's retinue by Eisodos B.*

CHORUS

Ilium, our fatherland, no longer will you be numbered among the cities that stand unsacked: such is the cloud of Greeks that has covered you about on every side, ravaging you with the spear. You are shorn of your crown of towers and stained most pitiably with the disfiguring mark of smoke. No more, poor city, shall I tread your streets.

At the hour of midnight I met my doom, when after dinner sweet sleep spread over my eyes. After the songs, having finished the sacrifices that bring dancing, my hus-

---

[a] This windlessness seems to be a recent development. (See above, note on line 112.) There may be a suggestion that the gods, who are responsible for the weather, are favoring Hecuba's design.

481

πόσις ἐν θαλάμοις ἔκει-
920   το, ξυστὸν δ᾽ ἐπὶ πασσάλῳ,
ναύταν οὐκέθ᾽ ὁρῶν ὅμιλον πέτραν
Ἰλιάδ᾽ ἐμβεβῶτα.

στρ. β

ἐγὼ δὲ πλόκαμον ἀναδέτοις
μίτραισιν ἐρρυθμιζόμαν
χρυσέων ἐνόπ-
925   τρων λεύσσουσ᾽ ἀτέρμονας εἰς αὐγάς,
ἐπιδέμνιος ὡς πέσοιμ᾽ ἐς εὐνάν.
ἀνὰ δὲ κέλαδος ἔμολε πόλιν·
κέλευσμα δ᾽ ἦν κατ᾽ ἄστυ Τροίας τόδ᾽· Ὦ
930   παῖδες Ἑλλάνων, πότε δὴ πότε τὰν
Ἰλιάδα σκοπιὰν
πέρσαντες ἥξετ᾽ οἴκους;

ἀντ. β

λέχη δὲ φίλια μονόπεπλος
λιποῦσα, Δωρὶς ὡς κόρα,
σεμνὰν προσί-
935   ζουσ᾽ οὐκ ἤνυσ᾽ Ἄρτεμιν ἁ τλάμων·
ἀγόμαν δὲ θανόντ᾽ ἰδοῦσ᾽ ἀκοίταν
τὸν ἐμὸν ἅλιον ἐπὶ πέλαγος·
πόλιν δ᾽ ἀποσκοποῦσ᾽, ἐπεὶ νόστιμον
940   ναῦς ἐκίνησεν πόδα καί μ᾽ ἀπὸ γᾶς
ὥρισεν Ἰλιάδος,
τάλαιν᾽, ἀπεῖπον ἄλγει,

ἐπῳδ.

τὰν τοῖν Διοσκούροιν Ἑλέναν κάσιν Ἰδαῖόν τε βούταν

band lay in the bedroom, his lance upon its peg, his eye no longer on the host from across the sea encamped on Ilion's rock.[a]

I was arranging my hair and binding it in a cap as I gazed into the bottomless depths of my golden mirror, readying myself to fall into bed. But up went a shout to the citadel: throughout the city were heard words of exhortation, "O sons of Greece, when will you sack Ilium's high pinnacle and go home?"

Clad in only a single garment, like a Spartan girl, I left my marriage bed and sat, luckless woman, as a suppliant to Artemis the revered, but to no purpose. I was carried away to the sea after seeing my husband slain. Looking back at the city once the ship had set sail for home and sundered me from Ilium, I miserably succumbed to my grief.

I cursed Helen, sister of the Dioscuri, and the Idaean

[a] The Trojans were fooled by the Greeks' ruse in sailing off to Tenedos, pretending to go home, and consequently were celebrating the departure of the enemy and completely off their guard.

---

922 πέτραν Willink: Τροίαν C
937 ἀγόμαν Willink: ἄγομαι C
939 δ' Willink: τ' C

945 αἰνόπαριν κατάρᾳ
διδοῦσ᾽, ἐπεί με γαίας
ἐκ πατρίας ἀπώλεσεν
ἐξῴκισέν τ᾽ οἴκων γάμος οὐ γάμος ἀλλ᾽
ἀλάστορός τις οἰζύς·
950 ἃν μήτε πέλαγος ἅλιον ἀπαγάγοι πάλιν
μήτε πατρῷον ἵκοιτ᾽ ἐς οἶκον.

ΠΟΛΥΜΗΣΤΩΡ

[ὦ φίλτατ᾽ ἀνδρῶν Πρίαμε, φιλτάτη δὲ σύ,]
Ἑκάβη, δακρύω σ᾽ εἰσορῶν πόλιν τε σὴν
955 τήν τ᾽ ἀρτίως θανοῦσαν ἔκγονον σέθεν.
φεῦ·
οὐκ ἔστιν οὐδὲν πιστόν, οὔτ᾽ εὐδοξία
οὔτ᾽ αὖ καλῶς πράσσοντα μὴ πράξειν κακῶς.
φύρουσι δ᾽ αὐτὰ θεοὶ πάλιν τε καὶ πρόσω
ταραγμὸν ἐντιθέντες, ὡς ἀγνωσίᾳ
960 σέβωμεν αὐτούς. ἀλλὰ ταῦτα μὲν τί δεῖ
θρηνεῖν, προκόπτοντ᾽ οὐδὲν ἐς πρόσθεν κακῶν;
σὺ δ᾽, εἴ τι μέμφῃ τῆς ἐμῆς ἀπουσίας,
σχές· τυγχάνω γὰρ ἐν μέσοις Θρῄκης ὅροις
ἀπών, ὅτ᾽ ἦλθες δεῦρ᾽· ἐπεὶ δ᾽ ἀφικόμην,
965 ἤδη πόδ᾽ ἔξω δωμάτων αἴροντί μοι
ἐς ταὐτὸν ἥδε συμπίτνει δμωῒς σέθεν
[λέγουσα μύθους, ὧν κλυὼν ἀφικόμην].

ΕΚΑΒΗ

αἰσχύνομαί σε προσβλέπειν ἐναντίον,
Πολυμῆστορ, ἐν τοιοῖσδε κειμένη κακοῖς.

herdsman Paris the Dread, for it was their marriage—no
marriage but the curse of some avenging spirit—that lost
my fatherland to me and sent me far from home. May the
briny sea not bring her back! May she never reach her
father's home!

*Enter POLYMESTOR with his two young sons and atten-
dants by Eisodos B, accompanied by the Maidservant.
Hecuba keeps her eyes fixed on the ground.*

POLYMESTOR

[Priam, dearest of men, and dearest of women,] Hecuba,
I weep as I see your city and also your daughter lately
slain. Ah me! Nothing can be relied upon, not good
repute nor yet the thought that a man in luck will never
have bad fortune. The gods stir things together in confu-
sion back and forth, adding disorder so that in our igno-
rance we might worship them. But why make these
lamentations, which get us no further on in our misfor-
tunes?

As for you, if you find fault with my absence, check the
thought. It happens that I was away in the inland regions
of Thrace when you arrived here. After I got back, your
servant here arrived just as I was on the point of coming
here myself. [She gave me the message: I heard it and
have come.]

HECUBA

Shame prevents me, Polymestor, from looking you in the
face since I have been put into such calamity. I am

---

946 γαίας Diggle: γᾶς C   947 πατρίας Dindorf: πατρῴας
fere C   953 del. Nauck   967 del. Kovacs

970 ὅτῳ γὰρ ὤφθην εὐτυχοῦσ', αἰδώς μ' ἔχει
ἐν τῷδε πότμῳ τυγχάνουσ' ἵν' εἰμὶ νῦν,
κοὐκ ἂν δυναίμην προσβλέπειν ὀρθαῖς κόραις.
[ἀλλ' αὐτὸ μὴ δύσνοιαν ἡγήσῃ σέθεν
Πολυμῆστορ· ἄλλως δ' αἴτιόν τι καὶ νόμος,
975 γυναῖκας ἀνδρῶν μὴ βλέπειν ἐναντίον.]

ΠΟΛΥΜΗΣΤΩΡ

καὶ θαυμά γ' οὐδέν. ἀλλὰ τίς χρεία σ' ἐμοῦ;
τί χρῆμ' ἐπέμψω τὸν ἐμὸν ἐκ δόμων πόδα;

ΕΚΑΒΗ

ἴδιον ἐμαυτῆς δή τι πρὸς σὲ βούλομαι
καὶ παῖδας εἰπεῖν σούς· ὀπάονας δέ μοι
980 χωρὶς κέλευσον τῶνδ' ἀποστῆναι δόμων.

ΠΟΛΥΜΗΣΤΩΡ

χωρεῖτ', ἐν ἀσφαλεῖ γὰρ ἥδ' ἐρημία·
φίλη μὲν εἶ σύ, προσφιλὲς δέ μοι τόδε
στράτευμ' Ἀχαιῶν. ἀλλὰ σημαίνειν σε χρή·
τί δεῖ τὸν εὖ πράσσοντα μὴ πράσσουσιν εὖ
985 φίλοις ἐπαρκεῖν; ὡς ἕτοιμός εἰμ' ἐγώ.

ΕΚΑΒΗ

πρῶτον μὲν εἰπὲ παῖδ' ὃν ἐξ ἐμῆς χερὸς
Πολύδωρον ἔκ τε πατρὸς ἐν δόμοις ἔχεις,
εἰ ζῇ· τὰ δ' ἄλλα δεύτερόν σ' ἐρήσομαι.

ΠΟΛΥΜΗΣΤΩΡ

μάλιστα· τοὐκείνου μὲν εὐτυχεῖς μέρος.

973–5 del. Hartung

embarrassed, before someone who has seen me in prosperity, to be in my present state of misfortune, and I cannot look at you with steady glance. [But do not think this shows ill-will toward you, Polymestor: besides in other ways custom is responsible, which ordains that women shall not look directly at men.]

POLYMESTOR

Yes, and no wonder. But what need have you of me? Why have you summoned me from my house?

HECUBA

I want to say something privately to you and your sons. Please order your servants to stand at a distance from the house.

POLYMESTOR

Leave! To be unattended is quite safe here. You are my friend and so is the Argive army here. (*The attendants leave by Eisodos B.*) But you must tell me: what help should I, a man in prosperity, render to my unfortunate friends? I am at your service.

HECUBA

First tell me whether my son Polydorus, whom you received into your house from my hand and his father's, is still alive. I shall ask you my other questions after that.

POLYMESTOR

Most assuredly he is alive! Where he is concerned, your fortune is good.

ΕΚΑΒΗ

990 ὦ φίλταθ', ὡς εὖ κἀξίως λέγεις σέθεν.

ΠΟΛΤΜΗΣΤΩΡ

τί δῆτα βούλῃ δεύτερον μαθεῖν ἐμοῦ;

ΕΚΑΒΗ

εἰ τῆς τεκούσης τῆσδε μέμνηταί τί που.

ΠΟΛΤΜΗΣΤΩΡ

καὶ δεῦρό γ' ὡς σὲ κρύφιος ἐζήτει μολεῖν.

ΕΚΑΒΗ

χρυσὸς δὲ σῶς ὃν ἦλθεν ἐκ Τροίας ἔχων;

ΠΟΛΤΜΗΣΤΩΡ

995 σῶς, ἐν δόμοις γε τοῖς ἐμοῖς φρουρούμενος.

ΕΚΑΒΗ

σῶσόν νυν αὐτὸν μηδ' ἔρα τῶν πλησίον.

ΠΟΛΤΜΗΣΤΩΡ

ἥκιστ'· ὀναίμην τοῦ παρόντος, ὦ γύναι.

ΕΚΑΒΗ

οἶσθ' οὖν ἃ λέξαι σοί τε καὶ παισὶν θέλω;

ΠΟΛΤΜΗΣΤΩΡ

οὐκ οἶδα· τῷ σῷ τοῦτο σημανεῖς λόγῳ.

ΕΚΑΒΗ

1000 ἔστ', ὦ φιληθεὶς ὡς σὺ νῦν ἐμοὶ φιλῇ . . .

ΠΟΛΤΜΗΣΤΩΡ

τί χρῆμ' ὃ κἀμὲ καὶ τέκν' εἰδέναι χρεών;

HECUBA

Dear man, what good news you tell me, news worthy of you!

POLYMESTOR

What second question, then, do you want to ask me?

HECUBA

Whether he remembers his mother at all.

POLYMESTOR

Yes, and he was seeking to come here to you in secret.

HECUBA

Is the gold safe that he brought with him from Troy?

POLYMESTOR

Quite safe: it is kept locked up in my house.

HECUBA

Keep it safe then, and do not desire what is your neighbor's.

POLYMESTOR

Indeed not! May I only get the good of what I have!

HECUBA

Do you know what I want to tell you and your sons?

POLYMESTOR

No: your account will tell me.

HECUBA

There are, friend loved as you are loved by me . . .

POLYMESTOR

What is the thing I and my sons should know?

---

^{992} $\pi ο υ$ Herwerden: $μ ο υ$ C

ΕΚΑΒΗ

. . . χρυσοῦ παλαιαὶ Πριαμιδῶν κατώρυχες.

ΠΟΛΤΜΗΣΤΩΡ

ταῦτ' ἔσθ' ἃ βούλῃ παιδὶ σημῆναι σέθεν;

ΕΚΑΒΗ

μάλιστα, διὰ σοῦ γ'· εἶ γὰρ εὐσεβὴς ἀνήρ.

ΠΟΛΤΜΗΣΤΩΡ

1005   τί δῆτα τέκνων τῶνδε δεῖ παρουσίας;

ΕΚΑΒΗ

ἄμεινον, ἢν σὺ κατθάνῃς, τούσδ' εἰδέναι.

ΠΟΛΤΜΗΣΤΩΡ

καλῶς ἔλεξας· τῇδε καὶ σοφώτερον.

ΕΚΑΒΗ

οἶσθ' οὖν Ἀθάνας Ἰλιάδος ἵνα στέγαι;

ΠΟΛΤΜΗΣΤΩΡ

ἐνταῦθ' ὁ χρυσός ἐστι; σημεῖον δὲ τί;

ΕΚΑΒΗ

1010   μέλαινα πέτρα γῆς ὑπερτέλλουσ' ἄνω.

ΠΟΛΤΜΗΣΤΩΡ

ἔτ' οὖν τι βούλῃ τῶν ἐκεῖ φράζειν ἐμοί;

ΕΚΑΒΗ

σῶσαί σε χρήμαθ' οἷς συνεξῆλθον θέλω.

ΠΟΛΤΜΗΣΤΩΡ

ποῦ δῆτα; πέπλων ἐντὸς ἢ κρύψασ' ἔχεις;

[1008] Ἰλιάδος Scaliger: Ἰλίας C

HECUBA

HECUBA
. . . ancient caves with the gold of Priam's sons.

POLYMESTOR
Is this then what you want to tell your son?

HECUBA
Yes, with you as messenger: for you are a god-fearing man.

POLYMESTOR
What need, then, for my sons to be present?

HECUBA
It is better for them to know, in case you should be killed.

POLYMESTOR
This is sound advice: this way is in fact wiser.

HECUBA
Do you know where the temple of Trojan Athena is?

POLYMESTOR
Is that where the gold is hidden? What marks the spot?

HECUBA
A black rock sticking up out of the ground.

POLYMESTOR
Is there anything further you want to tell me about what is there?

HECUBA
I want you to keep safe the money I brought with me from Troy.

POLYMESTOR
Where is it? Have you hidden it in your clothing?

EURIPIDES

ΕΚΑΒΗ

σκύλων ἐν ὄχλῳ ταῖσδε σῴζεται στέγαις.

ΠΟΛΤΜΗΣΤΩΡ

1015 ποῦ δ'; αἵδ' Ἀχαιῶν ναύλοχοι περιπτυχαί.

ΕΚΑΒΗ

ἴδιαι γυναικῶν αἰχμαλωτίδων στέγαι.

ΠΟΛΤΜΗΣΤΩΡ

τἄνδον δὲ πιστὰ κἀρσένων ἐρημία;

ΕΚΑΒΗ

οὐδεὶς Ἀχαιῶν ἔνδον ἀλλ' ἡμεῖς μόναι.
ἀλλ' ἕρπ' ἐς οἴκους· καὶ γὰρ Ἀργεῖοι νεῶν
1020 λῦσαι ποθοῦσιν οἴκαδ' ἐκ Τροίας πόδα·
ὡς πάντα πράξας ὧν σε δεῖ στείχῃς πάλιν
ξὺν παισὶν οὗπερ τὸν ἐμὸν ᾤκισας γόνον.

ΧΟΡΟΣ

οὔπω δέδωκας, ἀλλ' ἴσως δώσεις δίκην·
1025 ἀλίμενόν τις ὡς ἐς ἄντλον πεσὼν
λέχριος ἐκπεσῇ φίλας καρδίας,
ἀμέρσας βίον. τὸ γὰρ ὑπέγγυον
1030 Δίκα καὶ θεοῖσιν οὐ ξυμπίτνει,
ὀλέθριον ὀλέθριον κακόν.
ψεύσει σ' ὁδοῦ τῆσδ' ἐλπὶς ἥ σ' ἐπήγαγεν
θανάσιμον πρὸς Ἀίδαν, ὦ τάλας,
ἀπολέμῳ δὲ χειρὶ λείψεις βίον.

1028 βίον Hermann: βίοτον C

HECUBA

It is being kept safe in this tent amid the heaps of plunder.

POLYMESTOR

Where? These are the enclosures where the Achaean ships are beached.

HECUBA

The captive women have their separate quarters.

POLYMESTOR

Is it safe and clear of men within?

HECUBA

Only we women, no Achaeans, are inside.

But go into the tent—for the Argives in fact are eager to set sail and leave Troy for home—so that after getting all you must get you may return with your boys to where you have lodged my son.

HECUBA, Maidservant, POLYMESTOR, and sons go into the tent.

CHORUS

You have not yet paid the penalty, but perhaps you will: like a man falling into a flood with no harbor in sight you shall be cheated of what you set your heart on and lose your life. For where debt to Justice and debt to the gods come together, deadly, deadly is the bane. Your hopes for this journey will cheat you, for it has brought you to your death in Hades, poor wretch, and by an unwarlike hand you will lose your life.

ΠΟΛΥΜΗΣΤΩΡ

(ἔνδοθεν)

1035 ὤμοι, τυφλοῦμαι φέγγος ὀμμάτων τάλας.

ΧΟΡΟΣ

ἠκούσατ' ἀνδρὸς Θρῃκὸς οἰμωγήν, φίλαι;

ΠΟΛΥΜΗΣΤΩΡ

ὤμοι μάλ' αὖθις, τέκνα, δυστήνου σφαγῆς.

ΧΟΡΟΣ

φίλαι, πέπρακται καίν' ἔσω δόμων κακά.

ΠΟΛΥΜΗΣΤΩΡ

ἀλλ' οὔτι μὴ φύγητε λαιψηρῷ ποδί·

1040 βάλλων γὰρ οἴκων τῶνδ' ἀναρρήξω μυχούς.
ἰδού, βαρείας χειρὸς ὁρμᾶται βέλος.

ΧΟΡΟΣ

βούλεσθ' ἐπεσπέσωμεν; ὡς ἀκμὴ καλεῖ
Ἑκάβῃ παρεῖναι Τρῳάσιν τε συμμάχους.

ΕΚΑΒΗ

ἄρασσε, φείδου μηδέν, ἐκβάλλων πύλας·

1045 οὐ γάρ ποτ' ὄμμα λαμπρὸν ἐνθήσεις κόραις,
οὐ παῖδας ὄψῃ ζῶντας οὓς ἔκτειν' ἐγώ.

ΧΟΡΟΣ

ἦ γὰρ καθεῖλες Θρῇκα καὶ κρατεῖς ξένον,
δέσποινα, καὶ δέδρακας οἷάπερ λέγεις;

[1047] ξένον Hermann: -ου C

494

HECUBA

POLYMESTOR

(within) O pain! The light of my eyes' vision is being cruelly darkened!

CHORUS LEADER

My friends, did you hear the Thracian's cry of woe?

POLYMESTOR

(within) Pain yet again! Alas, my sons, for your pitiable murder!

CHORUS LEADER

Friends, yet more woes have been done in the tent!

POLYMESTOR

(within) But you won't escape me on nimble feet: I shall strike the inner wall of this tent and batter it down. There, the blow of my heavy fist has been launched!

CHORUS LEADER

Do you want us to break in? For now is the time to stand as allies beside Hecuba and the Trojan women.

HECUBA enters from the tent.

HECUBA

Smash away, spare nothing, break down the doors! You will never restore the light to your eyes or see your sons alive! I have killed them!

CHORUS LEADER

Have you really brought down your Thracian host and conquered him, my lady? Have you done what you claim?

ΕΚΑΒΗ

ὄψῃ νιν αὐτίκ' ὄντα δωμάτων πάρος
1050 τυφλὸν τυφλῷ στείχοντα παραφόρῳ ποδί,
παίδων τε δισσῶν σώμαθ', οὓς ἔκτειν' ἐγὼ
σὺν ταῖσδ' ἀρίσταις Τρῳάσιν· δίκην δέ μοι
δέδωκε. χωρεῖ δ', ὡς ὁρᾷς, ὅδ' ἐκ δόμων.
ἀλλ' ἐκποδὼν ἄπειμι κἀποστήσομαι
1055 θυμῷ ζέοντι Θρῃκὶ δυσμαχωτάτῳ.

ΠΟΛΤΜΗΣΤΩΡ

ὤμοι ἐγώ, πᾷ βῶ, πᾷ στῶ, πᾷ κέλσω,
τετράποδος βάσιν θηρὸς ὀρεστέρου
τιθέμενος ἐπὶ χεῖρα κατ' ἴχνος; ποίαν
1060 ἢ ταύταν ἢ τάνδ' ἐξαλλάξω, τὰς
ἀνδροφόνους μάρψαι χρῄζων Ἰλιάδας,
αἵ με διώλεσαν;
τάλαιναι κόραι τάλαιναι Φρυγῶν,
ὦ κατάρατοι,
1065 ποῖ καί με φυγᾷ πτώσσουσι μυχῶν;
εἴθε μοι ὀμμάτων αἱματόεν βλέφαρον
ἀκέσαι' ἀκέσαιο, τυφλόν,
Ἅλιε, φέγγος ἀπαλλάξας.
ἆ ἆ,
σίγα· κρυπτὰν βάσιν αἰσθάνομαι
1070 τάνδε γυναικῶν. πᾷ πόδ' ἐπάξας
σαρκῶν ὀστέων τ' ἐμπλησθῶ,
θοίναν ἀγρίων τιθέμενος θηρῶν,
ἀρνύμενος λώβας λύμας τ' ἀντίποιν'

496

HECUBA

You will soon see him coming out in front of the tent,
blind and with blindly reeling steps, and soon you will also
see the bodies of his two sons, whom I with the help of
the noble Trojan ladies have killed. He has paid me satis-
faction. Here he comes, as you see, out of the house. I
shall stand out of the way of his boiling Thracian wrath,
which none can fight against.

*POLYMESTOR emerges from the tent groping on all fours.
The bodies of his sons appear in the doorway on the eccy-
clema.*

POLYMESTOR

(sung) O pain! Where shall I go, where stand, where
beach my craft, moving like a four-footed wild beast on
my hands upon their track? Shall I change my course this
way or that in my longing to seize the murderous Trojan
women, my destroyers? Cruel, cruel women of Phrygia,
cursed wretches, in what hiding places are they cowering
to escape me? O Helios,[a] would that you might heal,
might heal, my bloodied lids and take away the blindness
of my eyes! Ah, ah! Soft there! I hear the stealthy foot-
steps of the women. Where can I dash, wretch that I am,
so that I may take my fill of their flesh and their bones,
making a wild beast's banquet, exacting the penalty for

---

[a] A fragment of Sophocles (fr. 582 Radt) calls Helios "the
chief object of worship for the horse-loving Thracians."

1052 ταῖσδ' Hermann: ταῖς C
1059 κατ'] καὶ Porson
1073 λώβας λύμας τ' Hadley: λώβαν λύμας C

ἐμᾶς, ὦ τάλας;

1075 ποῖ πᾷ φέρομαι τέκν' ἔρημα λιπὼν
Βάκχαις Ἅιδα διαμοιρᾶσαι
σφακτά, κυσίν τε φοινίαν δαῖτ' ἀνή-
μερόν τ' ὄρειον ἐκβολάν;
πᾷ στῶ, πᾷ κάμψω, [πᾷ βῶ,]
1080 ναῦς ὅπως ποντίοις πείσμασιν λινόκροκον
φᾶρος στέλλων, ἐπὶ τάνδε συθεὶς
τέκνων μου φύλαξ ὀλέθριον κοίταν;

ΧΟΡΟΣ

1085 ὦ τλῆμον, ὥς σοι δύσφορ' εἴργασται κακά·
δράσαντι δ' αἰσχρὰ δεινὰ τἀπιτίμια
[δαίμων ἔδωκεν ὅστις ἐστί σοι βαρύς].

ΠΟΛΤΜΗΣΤΩΡ

αἰαῖ ἰὼ Θρῄκης λογχοφόρον ἔνο-
1090 πλον εὔιππον Ἄρει κάτοχον γένος.
ἰὼ Ἀχαιοί, ἰὼ Ἀτρεῖδαι·
βοάν ἀυτῶ, βοάν.
ὦ ἴτε μόλετε πρὸς θεῶν.
κλύει τις ἢ οὐδεὶς ἀρκέσει; τί μέλλετε;
1095 γυναῖκες ὤλεσάν μ', ἃ <ἒ>,
γυναῖκες αἰχμαλωτίδες·
δεινὰ πεπόνθαμεν. ὤμοι ἐμᾶς λώβας.
ποῖ τράπωμαι, ποῖ πορευθῶ;
1100 ἀμπτάμενος οὐράνιον ὑψιπετὲς ἐς μέλαθρον,
Ὠαρίων ἢ Σείριος ἔνθα πυρὸς φλογέας ἀφίησιν
ὄσσων αὐγὰς ἢ τὸν ἐς Ἀίδαν
1105 μελάγχρωτα πορθμὸν ᾄξω τάλας;

their spite and outrage against me? Yet where am I going,
leaving behind my sons untended for these hellish bac-
chants to dismember in death, a blood-stained feast for
dogs, bodies discarded cruelly upon the mountains?
Where shall I stop, where rest, [where go,] furling my
linen robe as a ship with its sea ropes furls its sail, having
sped as guardian of my children to the fell resting place
where they lie?

CHORUS LEADER

Poor wretch, what intolerable suffering has been inflicted
on you! Yet terrible is the penalty for the man who does
shameful deeds. [Some god, weighing hard upon you, has
given it.]

POLYMESTOR

(sung) Help! Help, you Thracians with your armor,
spears, and horses, people devoted to Ares! Help, you
Argives, help, you sons of Atreus! For help I shout, for
help: come, come in the gods' name! Does anyone hear
me? Will no one come to my aid? Why are you so slow?
The women have destroyed me, the captive women!
Dreadful are my sufferings! Oh, the outrage against me!
Where shall I turn, where go? Shall I fly up to the lofty
vault of heaven, where Orion or Sirius darts forth fiery
beams from his eyes, or shall I in my suffering speed to
the black ferry that sails to Hades?

---

^{1077} σφακτά Hermann: -τὰν C $\quad$ ^{1078} τ' ὄρειον Diggle:
ὀρείαν τ' C $\quad$ ^{1079} πᾷ βῶ del. Nauck $\quad$ ^{1082} μου Hartung:
ἐμῶν C $\quad$ ^{1087} (= 723) del. Hermann $\quad$ ^{1092} βόαν (prius)
Willink: β- β- C $\quad$ ^{1095} μ' ἒ <ἒ> Willink: με C $\quad$ ^{1097} δεινὰ
Bothe: δ- δ- C $\quad$ ^{1100} ἀμπτάμενος Hermann: αἰθέρ' ἀ- C

EURIPIDES

ΧΟΡΟΣ

συγγνώσθ', ὅταν τις κρείσσον' ἢ φέρειν κακὰ
πάθῃ, ταλαίνης ἐξαπαλλάξαι ζόης.

ΑΓΑΜΕΜΝΩΝ

κραυγῆς ἀκούσας ἦλθον· οὐ γὰρ ἥσυχος
1110   πέτρας ὀρείας παῖς λέλακ' ἀνὰ στρατὸν
Ἠχὼ διδοῦσα θόρυβον· εἰ δὲ μὴ Φρυγῶν
πύργους πεσόντας ᾖσμεν Ἑλλήνων δορί,
φόβον παρέσχ' ἂν οὐ μέσως ὅδε κτύπος.

ΠΟΛΥΜΗΣΤΩΡ

ὦ φίλτατ'· ᾐσθόμην γάρ, Ἀγάμεμνον, σέθεν
1115   φωνῆς ἀκούσας· εἰσορᾷς ἃ πάσχομεν;

ΑΓΑΜΕΜΝΩΝ

ἔα·
Πολυμῆστορ ὦ δύστηνε, τίς σ' ἀπώλεσεν;
τίς ὄμμ' ἔθηκε τυφλὸν αἱμάξας κόρας,
παῖδάς τε τούσδ' ἔκτεινεν; ἦ μέγαν χόλον
σοὶ καὶ τέκνοισιν εἶχεν ὅστις ἦν ἄρα.

ΠΟΛΥΜΗΣΤΩΡ

1120   Ἑκάβη με σὺν γυναιξὶν αἰχμαλωτίσιν
ἀπώλεσ'—οὐκ ἀπώλεσ' ἀλλὰ μειζόνως.

ΑΓΑΜΕΜΝΩΝ

τί φῄς; σὺ τοὔργον εἴργασαι τόδ', ὡς λέγει;
σὺ τόλμαν, Ἑκάβη, τήνδ' ἔτλης ἀμήχανον;

ΠΟΛΥΜΗΣΤΩΡ

ὤμοι, τί λέξεις; ἦ γὰρ ἐγγύς ἐστί που;

HECUBA

CHORUS LEADER

When a man suffers calamity too great to bear, it is pardonable if he takes leave of his miserable life.

Enter AGAMEMNON *by Eisodos A.*

AGAMEMNON

I came because I heard shouts: for in no quiet tones did Echo, child of the rocky cliff, raise a cry throughout the host. If we did not know that Troy's towers had fallen to the Greek spear, this noise would have caused us alarm in no small degree!

POLYMESTOR

Dear friend—for I knew it was you, Agamemnon, when I heard your voice—do you see what has been done to me?

AGAMEMNON

What? Polymestor, poor man, who has destroyed you? Who has blinded you, made your eyes run with blood, and killed these children? Whoever it was must have nursed a great anger against you and your children.

POLYMESTOR

It was Hecuba with the help of the captive women who destroyed me—not destroyed me but more than that.

AGAMEMNON

What do you mean? You, Hecuba, have you done the deed he claims? Was it you who showed such incredible hardihood?

POLYMESTOR

Ah, what can you mean? Is she really somewhere nearby?

1125 σήμηνον, εἰπὲ ποῦ 'σθ', ἵν' ἁρπάσας χεροῖν
διασπάσωμαι καὶ καθαιμάξω χρόα.

ΑΓΑΜΕΜΝΩΝ
οὗτος, τί πάσχεις;

ΠΟΛΥΜΗΣΤΩΡ
πρὸς θεῶν σε λίσσομαι,
μέθες μ' ἐφεῖναι τῇδε μαργῶσαν χέρα.

ΑΓΑΜΕΜΝΩΝ
ἴσχ'· ἐκβαλὼν δὲ καρδίας τὸ βάρβαρον
1130 λέγ', ὡς ἀκούσας σοῦ τε τῆσδέ τ' ἐν μέρει
κρίνω δικαίως ἀνθ' ὅτου πάσχεις τάδε.

ΠΟΛΥΜΗΣΤΩΡ
λέγοιμ' ἄν. ἦν τις Πριαμιδῶν νεώτατος,
Πολύδωρος, Ἑκάβης παῖς, ὃν ἐκ Τροίας ἐμοὶ
πατὴρ δίδωσι Πρίαμος ἐν δόμοις τρέφειν,
1135 ὕποπτος ὢν δὴ Τρωικῆς ἁλώσεως.
τοῦτον κατέκτειν'· ἀνθ' ὅτου δ' ἔκτεινά νιν
ἄκουσον, ὡς εὖ καὶ σοφῇ προμηθίᾳ.
ἔδεισα μή σοι πολέμιος λειφθεὶς ὁ παῖς
Τροίαν ἀθροίσῃ καὶ ξυνοικίσῃ πάλιν,
1140 γνόντες δ' Ἀχαιοὶ ζῶντα Πριαμιδῶν τινα
Φρυγῶν ἐς αἶαν αὖθις ἄρειαν στόλον,
κἄπειτα Θρῄκης πεδία τρίβοιεν τάδε
ληλατοῦντες, γείτοσιν δ' εἴη κακὸν
Τρώων, ἐν ᾧπερ νῦν, ἄναξ, ἐκάμνομεν.
1145 Ἑκάβη δὲ παιδὸς γνοῦσα θανάσιμον μόρον
λόγῳ με τοιῷδ' ἤγαγ', ὡς κεκρυμμένας

Tell me where she is so that I may seize her with my hands, bloody her flesh, and tear her in pieces!

AGAMEMNON
You, Polymestor, what's the matter with you?

POLYMESTOR
I beg you by the gods, let me get my furious hands on her!

AGAMEMNON
Hold off: put this barbarian impulse from your heart and speak, so that hearing both you and her in turn I may judge properly why this has been done to you.

POLYMESTOR
I will speak. There was a man called Polydorus, youngest of Priam's sons, Hecuba's child, whom his father Priam gave me to bring up in my house when he feared the fall of Troy. I killed him. But hear why I killed him, how it was a good deed and prudently done. I was afraid that the boy, left behind as your enemy, might gather Troy together and found it again, and that the Achaeans, learning that one of the sons of Priam was alive, would raise another expedition to the land of the Phrygians and then ravage the plains of Thrace in search of plunder, and the Trojans' neighbors would be visited with the very bane with which we were troubled just now. But Hecuba learned of her son's death and enticed me here with the

θήκας φράσουσα Πριαμιδῶν ἐν Ἰλίῳ
χρυσοῦ· μόνον δὲ σὺν τέκνοισί μ' εἰσάγει
δόμους, ἵν' ἄλλος μή τις εἰδείη τάδε.
1150 ἵζω δὲ κλίνης ἐν μέσῳ κάμψας γόνυ·
πολλαὶ δέ, χειρὸς αἱ μὲν ἐξ ἀριστερᾶς,
αἱ δ' ἔνθεν, ὡς δὴ παρὰ φίλῳ Τρώων κόραι
θάκους ἔχουσαι κερκίδ' Ἡδωνῆς χερὸς
ᾔνουν, ὑπ' αὐγὰς τούσδε λεύσσουσαι πέπλους·
1155 ἄλλαι δὲ κάμακε Θρηκίῳ θεώμεναι
γυμνόν μ' ἔθηκαν διπτύχου στολίσματος.
ὅσαι δὲ τοκάδες ἦσαν, ἐκπαγλούμεναι
τέκν' ἐν χεροῖν ἔπαλλον, ὡς πρόσω πατρὸς
γένοιντο, διαδοχαῖσ' ἀμείβουσαι χερῶν.
1160 κᾆτ' ἐκ γαληνῶν πῶς δοκεῖς προσφθεγμάτων
εὐθὺς λαβοῦσαι φάσγαν' ἐκ πέπλων ποθὲν
κεντοῦσι παῖδας, αἱ δὲ πολεμίου δίκην
ξυναρπάσασαι τὰς ἐμὰς εἶχον χέρας
καὶ κῶλα· παισὶ δ' ἀρκέσαι χρῄζων ἐμοῖς,
1165 εἰ μὲν πρόσωπον ἐξανισταίην ἐμὸν
κόμης κατεῖχον, εἰ δὲ κινοίην χέρας
πλήθει γυναικῶν οὐδὲν ἤνυτον τάλας.
τὸ λοίσθιον δέ, πῆμα πήματος πλέον,
ἐξειργάσαντο δείν'· ἐμῶν γὰρ ὀμμάτων
1170 πόρπας λαβοῦσαι τὰς ταλαιπώρους κόρας
κεντοῦσιν αἱμάσσουσιν· εἶτ' ἀνὰ στέγας
φυγάδες ἔβησαν. ἐκ δὲ πηδήσας ἐγὼ
θὴρ ὣς διώκω τὰς μιαιφόνους κύνας,
[ἅπαντ' ἐρευνῶν τοῖχον, ὡς κυνηγέτης]

story that she would tell me of hidden chests of gold in
Ilium belonging to the sons of Priam. She brought me
alone with my sons into the tent, so that no one else
would know these things. I sat in the middle of a couch,
my legs bent in repose. Many of the daughters of Troy sat
near me as if I were their friend, some on the left, others
on the right, and praised the weaving of Edonian hands,
examining my clothing against the light. Others looked at
my two Thracian javelins and stripped me of this equip-
ment. All those who were mothers admired my children
and dandled them in their arms, passing them from one
pair of hands to another so that they would be separated
from their father. Then after such peaceful talk—you
can't imagine it—all of a sudden from somewhere in their
clothing they produced swords and stabbed the children,
while others, seizing me like a captured enemy, held my
arms and legs. I wanted to rescue my children, but if I
attempted to lift my face, they held me by the hair, and if
I tried to move my hands, unhappy man that I was, I
could do nothing because of the throng of women. Then
as their crowning blow, woe greater than woe, they did a
terrible thing: they took brooches and stabbed the pupils
of my poor eyes and made them run with blood. Then
they fled this way and that in the tent. I leapt up and like
a wild beast chased those murderous hounds, [like a
hunter, searching every wall,] beating and striking. This

[1151] χειρὸς Milton: χεῖρες C   [1153] θάκους Hermann:
θάκουν C   [1154] ἤνουν Hermann: ἤνουν θ' C
[1155] κάμακε Θρηκίω Hartung: -κα -ίαν C
[1162] πολεμίου Gronewald: -ων C
[1174] del. Prinz   στοῖχον Viljoen

1175 βάλλων ἀράσσων. τοιάδε σπεύδων χάριν
πέπονθα τὴν σήν, πολέμιόν γε σὸν κτανών,
Ἀγάμεμνον. ὡς δὲ μὴ μακροὺς τείνω λόγους,
εἴ τις γυναῖκας τῶν πρὶν εἴρηκεν κακῶς,
[ἢ νῦν λέγων ἔστιν τις ἢ μέλλει λέγειν,]
1180 ἅπαντα ταῦτα συντεμὼν ἐγὼ φράσω·
γένος γὰρ οὔτε πόντος οὔτε γῆ τρέφει
τοιόνδ'· ὁ δ' αἰεὶ ξυντυχὼν ἐπίσταται.

ΧΟΡΟΣ

μηδὲν θρασύνου μηδὲ τοῖς σαυτοῦ κακοῖς
τὸ θῆλυ συνθεὶς ὧδε πᾶν μέμψῃ γένος.
1185 [πολλαὶ γὰρ ἡμῶν· αἱ μέν εἰσ' ἐπίφθονοι,
αἱ δ' εἰς ἀριθμὸν τῶν κακῶν πεφύκαμεν.]

ΕΚΑΒΗ

Ἀγάμεμνον, ἀνθρώποισιν οὐκ ἐχρῆν ποτε
τῶν πραγμάτων τὴν γλῶσσαν ἰσχύειν πλέον·
ἀλλ' εἴτε χρήστ' ἔδρασε, χρήστ' ἔδει λέγειν,
1190 εἴτ' αὖ πονηρά, τοὺς λόγους εἶναι σαθρούς,
καὶ μὴ δύνασθαι τἄδικ' εὖ λέγειν ποτέ.
σοφοὶ μὲν οὖν εἰσ' οἱ τάδ' ἠκριβωκότες,
ἀλλ' οὐ δύνανται διὰ τέλους εἶναι σοφοί,
κακῶς δ' ἀπώλοντ'· οὔτις ἐξήλυξέ πω.
1195 καί μοι τὸ μὲν σὸν ὧδε φροιμίοις ἔχει·
πρὸς τόνδε δ' εἶμι καὶ λόγοις ἀμείψομαι·
ὃς φῂς Ἀχαιῶν πόνον ἀπαλλάσσων διπλοῦν
Ἀγαμέμνονός θ' ἕκατι παῖδ' ἐμὸν κτανεῖν.
ἀλλ', ὦ κάκιστε, πρῶτον οὔποτ' ἂν φίλον

is what I have endured, Agamemnon, for furthering your
interest and killing your enemy. To avoid making my
speech too long, if any of the ancients spoke ill of women,
[or someone is now speaking or will speak,] I shall sum up
all their words: neither sea nor land breeds any creature
like them. Anyone who has dealings with them knows
this well.

CHORUS LEADER

Stop this bold speech and do not, because of your own
troubles, lump the whole female sex together in this kind
of blame! [For there are many of us. Some are objects of
hatred, and others are born into the number of the
wicked.]

HECUBA

Agamemnon, men's tongues ought never to have more
force than their doings: if a man has done good deeds, his
speech ought to be good, if bad, then his words should
ring false, and he should never be able to give injustice a
fair name. Clever are the men who have mastered this
art, yet their cleverness cannot endure to the end. They
die a wretched death: not one has yet escaped.

That is what I have to say to you in my preamble. But
now I shall turn to this man and make my reply. You
claim that you killed my son to save the Achaeans from a
double toil and for Agamemnon's sake. Yet, vile coward,
in the first place barbarians neither would nor could be

1176 γε Diggle: τε vel τὸν C
1179 in suspicionem voc. Wecklein, del. Kovacs
1185–6 del. Dindorf

1200 τὸ βάρβαρον γένοιτ᾽ ἂν Ἕλλησιν γένος
οὐδ᾽ ἂν δύναιτο. τίνα δὲ καὶ σπεύδων χάριν
πρόθυμος ἦσθα; πότερα κηδεύσων τινὶ
ἢ συγγενὴς ὢν ἢ τίν᾽ αἰτίαν ἔχων;
ἢ σῆς ἔμελλον γῆς τεμεῖν βλαστήματα
1205 πλεύσαντες αὖθις; τίνα δοκεῖς πείσειν τάδε;
ὁ χρυσός, εἰ βούλοιο τἀληθῆ λέγειν,
ἔκτεινε τὸν ἐμὸν παῖδα καὶ κέρδη τὰ σά.

ἐπεὶ δίδαξον τοῦτο· πῶς, ὅτ᾽ εὐτύχει
Τροία, πέριξ δὲ πύργος εἶχ᾽ ἔτι πτόλιν
1210 ἔζη τε Πρίαμος Ἕκτορός τ᾽ ἤνθει δόρυ,
τί δ᾽ οὐ τότ᾽, εἴπερ τῷδ᾽ ἐβουλήθης χάριν
θέσθαι, τρέφων τὸν παῖδα κἀν δόμοις ἔχων
ἔκτεινας ἢ ζῶντ᾽ ἦλθες Ἀργείοις ἄγων;
ἀλλ᾽ ἡνίχ᾽ ἡμεῖς οὐκέτ᾽ ἦμεν ἐν φάει,
1215 καπνὸς δ᾽ ἐσήμην᾽ ἄστυ πολεμίοις ὕπο,
ξένον κατέκτας σὴν μολόντ᾽ ἐφ᾽ ἑστίαν.

πρὸς τοῖσδε νῦν ἄκουσον ὡς φαίνῃ κακός·
χρῆν σ᾽, εἴπερ ἦσθα τοῖς Ἀχαιοῖσιν φίλος,
τὸν χρυσὸν ὃν φὴς οὐ σὸν ἀλλὰ τοῦδ᾽ ἔχειν
1220 δοῦναι φέροντα πενομένοις τε καὶ χρόνον
πολὺν πατρῴας γῆς ἀπεξενωμένοις·
σὺ δ᾽ οὐδὲ νῦν πω σῆς ἀπαλλάξαι χερὸς
τολμᾷς, ἔχων δὲ καρτερεῖς ἔτ᾽ ἐν δόμοις.
καὶ μὴν τρέφων μὲν ὥς σε παῖδ᾽ ἐχρῆν τρέφειν
1225 σώσας τε τὸν ἐμόν, εἶχες ἂν καλὸν κλέος·
ἐν τοῖς κακοῖς γὰρ ἀγαθοὶ σαφέστατοι

friendly with Greeks. And what kind of favor were you so
eager to pursue? Did you have in mind to acquire some
connection by marriage? Were you his kinsman? Or
what was your reason? Were the Greeks about to ravage
the produce of your land if they sailed here again? Whom
do you think you can persuade of this? No, it was the gold
and your greed for gain that killed my son, if you were to
speak the truth.

For tell me this: how, when Troy's fortune was good
and her battlements still surrounded the city and Priam
was alive and Hector's spear was flourishing, why, I say, if
you wanted to store up credit with Agamemnon, did you
not at that time kill the boy or bring him alive to the
Argives, since you were raising him and had him in your
house? Instead when we Trojans were no more and
smoke showed that the city was in the hands of its ene-
mies, then it was that you killed a guest who had come to
your hearth.

In addition, hear now how vile you are shown to be: if
you were a friend of the Argives, you should have taken
the gold, which you admit was not yours to hold but his,
and given it to them since they were in need and had
spent a long time away from their native land; yet not
even now can you bring yourself to let it out of your hand
but still persist in keeping it in your house. What is more,
if you had reared my son and saved his life, as in duty you
were bound to, you would have won good repute: for
noble friends are most clearly seen in adversity, while

[1202] τινὶ Kovacs: τινὰ C

[1215] πολεμίοις Schenkl: -ων C

[1217] φαίνῃ Gloël: φανῇ vel φανῇς C

φίλοι· τὰ χρηστὰ δ' αὖθ' ἕκαστ' ἔχει φίλους.
εἰ δ' ἐσπάνιζες χρημάτων, ὁ δ' εὐτύχει,
θησαυρὸς ἄν σοι παῖς ὑπῆρχ' οὑμὸς μέγας·
1230 νῦν δ' οὔτ' ἐκεῖνον ἄνδρ' ἔχεις σαυτῷ φίλον
χρυσοῦ τ' ὄνησις οἴχεται παῖδές τε σοὶ
αὐτός τε πράσσεις ὧδε. σοὶ δ' ἐγὼ λέγω,
Ἀγάμεμνον, εἰ τῷδ' ἀρκέσεις, κακὸς φανῇ·
οὔτ' εὐσεβῆ γὰρ οὔτε πιστὸν οἷς ἐχρῆν,
1235 οὐχ ὅσιον, οὐ δίκαιον εὖ δράσεις ξένον·
αὐτὸν δὲ χαίρειν τοῖς κακοῖς σε φήσομεν
τοιοῦτον ὄντα. δεσπότας δ' οὐ λοιδορῶ.

φεῦ φεῦ· βροτοῖσιν ὡς τὰ χρηστὰ πράγματα
χρηστῶν ἀφορμὰς ἐνδίδωσ' ἀεὶ λόγων.

1240 ἀχθεινὰ μέν μοι τἀλλότρια κρίνειν κακά,
ὅμως δ' ἀνάγκη· καὶ γὰρ αἰσχύνην φέρει
πρᾶγμ' ἐς χέρας λαβόντ' ἀπώσασθαι τόδε.
ἐμοὶ δ', ἵν' εἰδῇς, οὔτ' ἐμὴν δοκεῖς χάριν
οὔτ' οὖν Ἀχαιῶν ἄνδρ' ἀποκτεῖναι ξένον,
1245 ἀλλ' ὡς ἔχῃς τὸν χρυσὸν ἐν δόμοισι σοῖς.
λέγεις δὲ σαυτῷ πρόσφορ' ἐν κακοῖσιν ὤν.
τάχ' οὖν παρ' ὑμῖν ῥᾴδιον ξενοκτονεῖν·
ἡμῖν δέ γ' αἰσχρὸν τοῖσιν Ἕλλησιν τόδε.
πῶς οὖν σε κρίνας μὴ ἀδικεῖν φύγω ψόγον;
1250 οὐκ ἂν δυναίμην. ἀλλ' ἐπεὶ τὰ μὴ καλὰ
πράσσειν ἐτόλμας, τλῆθι καὶ τὰ μὴ φίλα.

prosperity always makes its own friends. If you were in need of money and my son enjoyed good fortune, he would have been a great treasure to you. As things stand, you do not have him for a friend, the enjoyment of your gold is gone, your sons are dead, and your own fortunes are as they are. To you, Agamemnon, I say this: if you come to this man's aid, you will show yourself to be base: you will be benefiting a host who is impious, disloyal to those he owed loyalty, and a breaker of laws both divine and human. We shall say that you take pleasure in base men because that is your own nature too. Not that I want to revile my master!

CHORUS LEADER

Oh my! How true it is that for mortals a good cause always supplies matter for a good speech!

AGAMEMNON

Though the troubles of other men are burdensome for me to judge, yet I must do it. It would bring disgrace upon me if I were to take this matter into my hands and then refuse to deal with it. To tell you my verdict, I think that you killed your guest not for my sake or for that of the Achaeans but so that you might keep the gold in your house. Since you are now in misfortune, you say what suits your case. Perhaps in your country it is a small thing to kill guests, but to us Greeks this is an abominable deed. If I pronounced you not guilty, how could I escape blame? I could not. So since you could bear to commit disgraceful deeds, you must bear to suffer unwelcome consequences.

EURIPIDES

ΠΟΛΤΜΗΣΤΩΡ

οἴμοι, γυναικός, ὡς ἔοιχ᾽, ἡσσώμενος
δούλης ὑφέξω τοῖς κακίοσιν δίκην.

ΕΚΑΒΗ

οὔκουν δικαίως, εἴπερ εἰργάσω κακά;

ΠΟΛΤΜΗΣΤΩΡ

1255 οἴμοι τέκνων τῶνδ᾽ ὀμμάτων τ᾽ ἐμῶν τάλας.

ΕΚΑΒΗ

ἀλγεῖς; τί δ᾽; ἦ 'μὲ παιδὸς οὐκ ἀλγεῖν δοκεῖς;

ΠΟΛΤΜΗΣΤΩΡ

χαίρεις ὑβρίζουσ᾽ εἰς ἔμ᾽, ὦ πανοῦργε σύ.

ΕΚΑΒΗ

οὐ γάρ με χαίρειν χρή σε τιμωρουμένην;

ΠΟΛΤΜΗΣΤΩΡ

ἀλλ᾽ οὐ τάχ᾽, ἡνίκ᾽ ἄν σε ποντία νοτίς . . .

ΕΚΑΒΗ

1260 μῶν ναυστολήσῃ γῆς ὅρους Ἑλληνίδος;

ΠΟΛΤΜΗΣΤΩΡ

κρύψῃ μὲν οὖν πεσοῦσαν ἐκ καρχησίων.

ΕΚΑΒΗ

πρὸς τοῦ βιαίων τυγχάνουσαν ἁλμάτων;

ΠΟΛΤΜΗΣΤΩΡ

αὐτὴ πρὸς ἱστὸν ναὸς ἀμβήσῃ ποδί.

1256 δ᾽; ἦ 'μὲ Bothe: δέ με fere C

512

HECUBA

POLYMESTOR
How terrible! I have been beaten, it seems, by a slave woman and must pay the penalty to my inferiors!

HECUBA
Is this not proper since your deeds were wicked?

POLYMESTOR
Ah me, how I suffer for my children here and my eyes!

HECUBA
You feel pain? Well, do you think I feel none for my son?

POLYMESTOR
You take joy in committing outrage against me, you knavish creature!

HECUBA
What? Should I not enjoy my revenge on you?

POLYMESTOR
Soon you will not, when seawater . . .

HECUBA
Carries me by ship to the coast of Greece?

POLYMESTOR
No, rather covers you over when you have fallen from the masthead.

HECUBA
By whom will I be compelled to jump?

POLYMESTOR
You yourself will climb up toward the ship's sail.

ΕΚΑΒΗ

ὑποπτέροις νώτοισιν ἢ ποίῳ τρόπῳ;

ΠΟΛΥΜΗΣΤΩΡ

1265   κύων γενήσῃ πύρσ' ἔχουσα δέργματα.

ΕΚΑΒΗ

πῶς δ' οἶσθα μορφῆς τῆς ἐμῆς μετάστασιν;

ΠΟΛΥΜΗΣΤΩΡ

ὁ Θρῃξὶ μάντις εἶπε Διόνυσος τάδε.

ΕΚΑΒΗ

σοὶ δ' οὐκ ἔχρησεν οὐδὲν ὧν ἔχεις κακῶν;

ΠΟΛΥΜΗΣΤΩΡ

οὐ γάρ ποτ' ἂν σύ μ' εἷλες ὧδε σὺν δόλῳ.

ΕΚΑΒΗ

1270   θανοῦσα δ' ἢ ζῶσ' ἐνθάδ' ἐκπλήσω φάτιν;

ΠΟΛΥΜΗΣΤΩΡ

θανοῦσα· τύμβῳ δ' ὄνομα σῷ κεκλήσεται . . .

ΕΚΑΒΗ

μορφῆς ἐπῳδὸν μή τι τῆς ἐμῆς ἐρεῖς;

ΠΟΛΥΜΗΣΤΩΡ

. . . κυνὸς ταλαίνης σῆμα, ναυτίλοις τέκμαρ.

ΕΚΑΒΗ

οὐδὲν μέλει μοι, σοῦ γέ μοι δόντος δίκην.

ΠΟΛΥΜΗΣΤΩΡ

1275   καὶ σήν γ' ἀνάγκη παῖδα Κασσάνδραν θανεῖν.

HECUBA

With wings on my back or how?

POLYMESTOR

You will become a dog with fiery eyes.

HECUBA

But how do you know of this change my shape will undergo?

POLYMESTOR

Dionysus, the Thracians' prophet, told me this.

HECUBA

But didn't he tell you any of the trouble you now endure?

POLYMESTOR

No, for you would never have destroyed me so craftily.

HECUBA

Shall I fulfill the prophecy by dying here or living?

POLYMESTOR

By dying. And your grave will receive the name . . .

HECUBA

Perhaps some name alluding to my shape?

POLYMESTOR

. . . "Hound's Grave," a mark for sailors to steer by.

HECUBA

I do not care since you have paid me satisfaction.

POLYMESTOR

Yes, and it is fated that your daughter Cassandra must die.

1270 φάτιν Weil: βίον C

EURIPIDES

ΕΚΑΒΗ

ἀπέπτυσ᾽· αὐτῷ ταῦτα σοὶ δίδωμ᾽ ἔχειν.

ΠΟΛΤΜΗΣΤΩΡ

κτενεῖ νιν ἡ τοῦδ᾽ ἄλοχος, οἰκουρὸς πικρά.

ΕΚΑΒΗ

μήπω μανείη Τυνδαρὶς τοσόνδε παῖς.

ΠΟΛΤΜΗΣΤΩΡ

καὐτόν γε τοῦτον, πέλεκυν ἐξάρασ᾽ ἄνω.

ΑΓΑΜΕΜΝΩΝ

1280 οὗτος σύ, μαίνῃ καὶ κακῶν ἐρᾷς τυχεῖν;

ΠΟΛΤΜΗΣΤΩΡ

κτεῖν᾽, ὡς ἐν Ἄργει φόνια λουτρά σ᾽ ἀμμένει.

ΑΓΑΜΕΜΝΩΝ

οὐχ ἕλξετ᾽ αὐτόν, δμῶες, ἐκποδὼν βίᾳ;

ΠΟΛΤΜΗΣΤΩΡ

ἀλγεῖς ἀκούων;

ΑΓΑΜΕΜΝΩΝ

οὐκ ἐφέξετε στόμα;

ΠΟΛΤΜΗΣΤΩΡ

ἐγκλῄετ᾽· εἴρηται γάρ.

ΑΓΑΜΕΜΝΩΝ

οὐχ ὅσον τάχος

1285 νήσων ἐρήμων αὐτὸν ἐκβαλεῖτέ ποι,
ἐπείπερ οὕτω καὶ λίαν θρασυστομεῖ;
Ἑκάβη, σὺ δ᾽, ὦ τάλαινα, διπτύχους νεκροὺς

HECUBA

Pah! I give you back these words to apply to yourself!

POLYMESTOR

She will be killed by this man's wife, grim guardian of his house.

HECUBA

May Tyndareus' daughter never be so mad!

POLYMESTOR

And she will kill this man himself, raising an ax above her head.

AGAMEMNON

You there, are you mad? Are you asking for trouble?

POLYMESTOR

Kill me, then, for a murderous bath awaits you in Argos!

AGAMEMNON

Servants, drag him by force out of my way!

POLYMESTOR

Do my words cause you pain?

AGAMEMNON

Stop his mouth!

POLYMESTOR

Go on, stop my mouth! I have spoken.

AGAMEMNON

Cast him quickly onto some desert island since he is so bold of tongue!

POLYMESTOR is led off by Eisodos A.

Hecuba, go, poor woman, and bury your two dead

στείχουσα θάπτε. δεσποτῶν δ' ὑμᾶς χρεὼν
σκηναῖς πελάζειν, Τρῳάδες. καὶ γὰρ πνοὰς
1290   πρὸς οἶκον ἤδη τάσδε πομπίμους ὁρῶ.
εὖ δ' ἐς πάτραν πλεύσαιμεν, εὖ δὲ τἀν δόμοις
ἔχοντ' ἴδοιμεν τῶνδ' ἀφειμένοι πόνων.

ΧΟΡΟΣ
ἴτε πρὸς λιμένας σκηνάς τε, φίλαι,
τῶν δεσποσύνων πειρασόμεναι
1295   μόχθων· στερρὰ γὰρ ἀνάγκη.

children. Trojan women, you must go to the tents of your masters. For in fact I see that the breeze has now set toward home. May we have good sailing homeward and, escaping from our present troubles, find all at home in order!

Exit AGAMEMNON *with retinue and* HECUBA *by Eisodos A.*

CHORUS LEADER

Go to the harbors and the tents, my friends, to taste the misery of slavery. For fate is hard.

Exit CHORUS *by Eisodos A.*